Management Communication

Also by Thomas Klikauer

COMMUNICATION AND MANAGEMENT AT WORK

Management Communication
Communicative Ethics and Action

Thomas Klikauer

palgrave
macmillan

© Thomas Klikauer 2008

All rights reserved. No reproduction, copy or transmission of this publication may be made without written permission.

No paragraph of this publication may be reproduced, copied or transmitted save with written permission or in accordance with the provisions of the Copyright, Designs and Patents Act 1988, or under the terms of any licence permitting limited copying issued by the Copyright Licensing Agency, 90 Tottenham Court Road, London W1T 4LP.

Any person who does any unauthorized act in relation to this publication may be liable to criminal prosecution and civil claims for damages.

The author has asserted his rights to be identified as the author of this work in accordance with the Copyright, Designs and Patents Act 1988.

First published 2008 by
PALGRAVE MACMILLAN
Houndmills, Basingstoke, Hampshire RG21 6XS and
175 Fifth Avenue, New York, N.Y. 10010
Companies and representatives throughout the world

PALGRAVE MACMILLAN is the global academic imprint of the Palgrave Macmillan division of St. Martin's Press, LLC and of Palgrave Macmillan Ltd. Macmillan® is a registered trademark in the United States, United Kingdom and other countries. Palgrave is a registered trademark in the European Union and other countries.

ISBN 13: 978–0–230–51566–6   hardback
ISBN 10: 0–230–51566–5   hardback

This book is printed on paper suitable for recycling and made from fully managed and sustained forest sources. Logging, pulping and manufacturing processes are expected to conform to the environmental regulations of the country of origin.

A catalogue record for this book is available from the British Library.

Library of Congress Cataloging-in-Publication Data
Klikauer, Thomas, 1962–
    Management communication : communicative ethics and action / Thomas Klikauer.
        p. cm.
    Includes bibliographical references and index.
    ISBN 0–230–51566–5 (alk. paper)
    1. Communication in management. I. Title.
HD30.3.K574 2008
658.4′5–dc22   2008015886

10 9 8 7 6 5 4 3 2 1
17 16 15 14 13 12 11 10 09 08

Printed and bound in Great Britain by
CPI Antony Rowe, Chippenham and Eastbourne

*This book is dedicated to all those
who asked* **why**

and to those who have therefore been called a
Communist.

*"When you give food to the hungry, they call you a saint.
But when you ask why the hungry have no food,
they call you a communist".*

*By:
Roman Catholic Archbishop Helder Camera
Source: Jim Forest, Love Is The Measure:
Biography of Dorothy Day, Paulist Press, 1986 pg. 204*

Contents

Acknowledgements		ix
List of Tables and Figures		x
1	**Introduction: Communication in Management, Work and Society**	1
2	**Communication I: Basic Contexts at Work**	17
	Basic concepts of communication	23
	Communication and contextual meaning	28
3	**Communication II: Signs and Meanings**	34
	Myths and mythologies	42
	Symbols, metaphors, stories & narratives	50
4	**Distorted Communication I: Classifications**	55
	Managerial classifications as ordering instruments	63
5	**Distorted Communication II: Ideologies**	74
	The managerial creation and use of ideologies	75
6	**Distorted Communication III: Hegemonies**	91
	Neutralisation and naturalisation	96
	Routines in managerial communication and the distortion of history	101
7	**Distorted Communication IV: Culture, Rhetoric and Meetings**	108
	Managerial rhetoric and rituals	112
	Form and content of managerial meetings	118
8	**Distorted Communication V: Persuasion, Attitudes and Responses**	124
	The conditioning of workers' responses and thinking	138
9	**Communicative Action I: The Basics of Ideal Speech**	141
	Ideal speech and distorted communication	149
10	**Communicative Action II: Ethics and Communication**	160
	The universal pragmatics of ideal speech	173
11	**Communicative Action III: The Two Logics of Work Relations**	179
	Overcoming the conditioning of asymmetrical work relations	189

12	**Communicative Action IV: The Two Logics of Communication**	198
	The two logics of ideal speech and social action	210
13	**Communicative Action V: Communicative Ethics at Work**	215
	The ethics of communicative action in the labour domain	225
14	**Practical Conclusions**	231
	A universal and practical discourse forum	231
	Drafting a workable discourse forum	233

Notes	246
Bibliography	307
Index	322

Acknowledgements

As much as my first book on *Communication and Management at Work* (2007) has been written to elaborate the historical development of the link between communication and the world of work and delivered an assessment thereof from the standpoint of critical theory, this book is dedicated to a somewhat more focused issue, Management Communication. For their original and continuous support I would like to thank all those who have assisted in the conception of this book by providing constructive criticism on *Communication and Management at Work* (2007). Special thanks go to those who contributed through their highly valuable critique, their comments, and their assistance. As much as their evaluation on my 2007 book has been helpful for this book, there have been a number of people who have turned my writings and ideas into a comprehensible book.

These have been *Khalida Malik* providing her editorial assistance on the first drafts and, above all, my delightful and lovely wife *Katja* for proofreading the book three times despite being pregnant with our child. Unknowingly, I had married a former magazine and book editor. However, my foremost gratitude goes to my parents – without their support my transition from a student of very basic German schooling of the *Hauptschule* to an academic working at a university would never have been possible. I am also deeply in debt to the German trade union foundation, the *Hans-Böckler-Stiftung* who not only financed my eventual arrival at the academic level – completing studies at five universities over ten years (1986–1996) – but also supported all this through years of encouragement. The production of this book received no internal or external support or funding. Finally, I would like to thank Palgrave's editorial team, especially *Mirabelle Boateng, Virginia Thorp*, and above all *Shirley Tan*.

List of Tables and Figures

Tables

2.1	Three Forms for Rational Thinking	18
2.2	Fundamental Concepts and Perspectives on Communication	19
2.3	Three Theoretical Perspectives on Communication at Work	21
2.4	The Three Purposes of Critical-Rational Communication	22
2.5	The Conveying of Messages	24
2.6	Two Elements of Communication	26
3.1	Three Stages of Fixing Meaning	35
3.2	Intention, Literal Meaning, and Utterance	37
3.3	Strike as Signifier and Signified	38
3.4	Three Forms and Uses of Sign Interpretation	40
3.5	Four Organisational Myths	47
3.6	The *I-We-Them-It* Principle and its Use	54
4.1	Saussure's Three Elements of Language	56
4.2	Karl Bühler's Three Functions of Language	59
4.3	Re-Classified HRM Issues	65
4.4	The Six Meanings of *This is Necessary for Your Company*	66
4.5	Three Forms of Orwellian Vocabulary and Managerial Use	67
4.6	Binary Classifications used by Management	68
4.7	Types of Managerial Classifications	70
5.1	The Communicative Construction of Managerial Ideologies at Work	76
5.2	Three Uses of Ideology	84
5.3	Purposes of Ideologies	85
5.4	Modes of Operative Ideologies at Work	86
5.5	Real, Nominal and Passive Statements	89
6.1	The Nature of the World of Work	97
6.2	The Ideology of Modern Time Devices	99
7.1	Managerial Communication as Ritual	115
7.2	Structuring Levels of Rituals	116
7.3	Rehearsing Ritualistic Communication Devices	117
7.4	Communicative Distortions through Managerial Meetings	118
7.5	Stages of Meetings and their Usage	122
8.1	Four Ways of Changing Attitudes	126
8.2	The Three Cs of Persuasion	126
8.3	Persuasive Models for Conflict	129
8.4	Elements and Mechanisms that Shape Attitudes	131
8.5	Attitudes to be Shaped during Secondary Socialisation	132

8.6	Forms of Deceptive Persuasion	133
8.7	Eight Forms of Lies at Work	134
8.8	Twelve Items to Identify a Liar	135
9.1	A Threefold Nature-Transforming Relationship	143
9.2	Three Understandings of Speech Acts at Work	145
9.3	Five Types of Speech Acts	147
9.4	Three Pragmatic Relationships	147
9.5	Conditions that Establish Ideal Speech at Work	149
9.6	Forms of Non-Ideal Speech Acts	153
9.7	Three Ways to Unmask Communicative Distortions	156
9.8	Four Managerial Principles for the Use of Communication	157
9.9	Experiencing & Responding to Distorted Communication at Work	158
10.1	Gandhi's Social Sins at Work	161
10.2	Kohlberg's Stages of Moral Development	162
10.3	Bauman's Three Principles of Ethical Conduct	172
10.4	Three Conditions for Ideal Speech	174
10.5	Three Forms of Arguments	174
10.6	Sentence Formulation for Discourses	175
10.7	Four Theories of Truth	176
10.8	Four Core Elements of Ideal Speech	176
11.1	Key Forms of Structural Inequality at Work	181
11.2	Tools of Asymmetric Behaviour Modification	195
12.1	Four Elements of Colonisation	201
12.2	Three Common Core Interests of Workers	205
12.3	Four Levels of Interest Mediation inside the Labour Domain (L)	207
12.4	Action and Speech	210
12.5	Two Logics of Communicative and Strategic Action	213
13.1	System Integration and Outcomes	220
13.2	Four Elements of the Communicative Consensus Theory of Truth	222
13.3	Core Elements for an Autonomous and Communicative Domain	224
14.1	Seven Basic Principles for Ideal Speech	233
14.2	Basic Rules Assisting the Structuring of Discourse	236
14.3	Five Levels of Discursive Agreements	238
14.4	Elements Restricting Discourse	242

Figures

1.1	The Science-Practise Interface	3
1.2	The Value-Free, Objective Science, and Value-Adding Linearity	5
1.3	A Dialectical Understanding of Communication at Work	10
2.1	Communication as Speech and Action	22
2.2	A Definition of Communication	23

2.3	Communication as Communicative Action	24
2.4	The Linear Sender-Receiver-Model	25
2.5	How and What is Communicated	27
2.6	Communication with other Participants (P^n)	28
2.7	Encoding/Decoding through Interpretation	31
2.8	Contextual Domains and Contextual Understanding	32
3.1	Sign, Reference and Context	36
3.2	Three Meanings of One Sign in Two Domains	37
3.3	Four Signifiers and their Historic Signifying Mental Concepts	39
3.4	A Common Myth about Work	43
3.5	The Managerial Value-Myth	48
3.6	System Stabilising Managerialism	49
3.7	Managerial Metaphors of Corporate Communication	51
4.1	The Work–Wage Link	71
5.1	The Ideology of Exchange Justice	80
5.2	The Sign and Frame of Reference of Wages	81
5.3	The Managerial Success for All Equation	87
6.1	The Sameness of Interests	92
6.2	The Hegemonic Removal of Democracy	95
6.3	Management as Neutral Intermediary between Market and Labour	98
6.4	The Labour-Management Time Equation	100
6.5	Controlling the Past and Controlling the Future	105
7.1	Communicative Meetings as Furniture Arrangement	120
8.1	A Two-Way Model of Persuasion	125
8.2	Conditioning of Human Behaviour	138
8.3	Conditioning of Wanted Reactions to Signs and Words	139
9.1	A Textbook Case of Communicative Distortions	150
10.1	The Numeric Reality and the Illusion of Promotion	164
10.2	The Ethics of Communication	171
10.3	The Internal and External Structure of Ideal Speech	177
11.1	System Changes and Desired Outcomes	183
11.2	A Typology of Collective Action for Labour and Management	185
11.3	The Hard Work is Good Living Equation	190
11.4	The Control – Conditioning Trajectory	191
11.5	From Punishment and Disciplining to Conditioning	192
12.1	Horizontal and Vertical Communication in Two Domains	199
12.2	Three-Way Communication between Two Actors at Work	201
12.3	Contextual Domains to Establish Meaning among Actors	203
12.4	Communicative Interest Mediation among Diverging Interests	206
12.5	Two Logics of Social Action	212
13.1	The Steering Media between the Four Main Domains	217
13.2	The Central Position of Work inside the Four Main Domains	218
14.1	Perfect Information and Perfect Solutions	241
14.2	Four Inter-Related Dimensions of Ideal Speech Practice	244

1
Introduction: Communication in Management, Work and Society

Whatever was true now was true from everlasting to everlasting. It was quite simple. All that was needed was an unending series of victories over your own memory. Reality control, they called it...[1] These are the words of George Orwell in his masterpiece *Nineteen Eighty-Four*. While management might appear as everlasting – and therefore give the impression it is unending – the dominant managerially guided discourse by and about management itself is shaping not only our memories about management but also how we perceive it. Very much like any other aspect in our socially constructed and *socially communicated world* the current perception of the world of management and work has been able to establish what Orwell called *reality control*, a viewpoint that makes us see management very much from a somewhat limited range of perspectives. Similar to Orwell's *Big Brother* on the one hand and his hero *Winston Smith* on the other, these perspectives have always carried different values because they are connected to a human *subject* – a person – rather than an *object*. Ever since the philosophical *subject–object* debate had started in the ancient world of Greece two millenniums ago, the split between subject and subjectivity as well as object and objectivity has fascinated human thinking. With the rise of modernity and Enlightenment the proponents of pure scientific objectivity and *pure reason* have sought to separate human knowledge from our social existence.[2] On the very base of this idea rests the assumption that human *subjectivity* – which makes us human – can be dissected from *objectivism*. In the segregate world of clear borders between both the objective and the subjective world truth and reality almost never meet. It is assumed that any scientist walking through a laboratory or university door is no longer connected to society. The inherent dialectic between objective and subjective is hidden behind a positivist-logical separation that bears no relevance to real life but is – reformulated as an ideology – nevertheless extremely powerful.[3]

Despite significant challenges – one of the most substantial ones ever was made by philosopher Immanuel Kant in his *Critique of Pure Reason* (1781) – the illusion of purely scientific objectivity and *pure reason* is still with us today. It is widely and – to use the Hegelian term – sometimes even *unconsciously* accepted as common sense even though it may not be that common at all. It pretends to present scientific or quasi-scientific knowledge about *communication* and the world of *work* – often one-dimensionally called *management* – as purely objective.[4] This is certainly common in standard books and textbooks on management, managerial communication, business communication, and the like.[5]

All too often this sort of literature classifies the world of work into neatly organised boxes as many still believe that if we categorise things and create a simple ontology – expressed by Foucault (1994) as the *Order of Things* – we understand them. Far from it! The exact opposite might be closer to the truth because boxed up knowledge is separated knowledge that creates artificial divisions while at the same time it eclipses all connections that enable critical understanding of communication and the world of work. Most importantly, it deflects critical and, above all, dialectical thinking. The ordering of a sheer endless amount of empirical knowledge into an artificially created system is able to damage knowledge rather than deliver Enlightenment which, in fact, might be exactly the hidden task of positivistic knowledge creation. Inside the issue of human communication such ordering systems first of all separate *human* communication from *business* communication.[6] They also separate the world of work into a business and a private world as well as into the world of management and the world of labour.[7] In a final insult to dialectical knowledge, these classifications are used in a *pre*- rather than a *de*-scriptive way and in even more obscene cases they provide narrow definitions of sub-fields that *need* to be ordered. Rafts of books and textbooks that define, classify, and order socially constructed knowledge about communication and the world of work have been written in support of each of these separated sub-fields.[8] In the name of scientific endeavour and scientific objectivism, these system-supportive products of intellectual labour do no more than present what Horkheimer (1947) once termed *The Eclipse of Reason*.

In this neatly organised world the *pre*scriptive ordering boxes or categories carry labels such as management, work, labour studies, communication studies, organisational communication, and the like. These categories achieve a number of things; they secure the existence of those who live a confined life inside their equally confined field of so-called expertise, assured by gatekeepers and borderline securers that protect the comforts of knowing everything about a narrow field of nothingness. They also create the so-called experts in highly specialised fields who can rest comfortably inside a disconnected field of minuscule existence. They are important because they understand everything about a tree but have no concept of what a forest is. They can be called upon to give expert advice – as part of an ever growing class of consultants – without ever understanding what it is used for. In addition, they allow the artificial isolation of certain aspects of social life that cannot exist separately to be given the appearance that they can and are instrumental in the prevention of finding connections where connections exist. Finally, their one-dimensionality prevents any *multi-* or *supra-disciplinary* thinking which successfully thwarts the move from the one-dimensional singularity of the academic division of labour towards the often-claimed *supra-disciplinary* approach. Even the relatively simple move from a *multi-divisional* approach that keeps up artificially constructed borders between scientific communities towards a *supra-divisional*[9] approach that truly merges – all too often not so different – academic disciplines cannot take place.[10]

In addition to isolating themselves inside well-constructed scientific *disciplines* that are protected through *gatekeepers* in the form of journal editors, department heads, conference organisers and the like, these newly established disciplines – such as *management studies* or business communication including their entourage of affirmative writers – have been defined by yet an even more puzzling element.[11] In sharp contrast to traditional academic disciplines such as philosophy, psychology, sociology, physics, or mathematics, management *science*[12] claims to be strongly, overwhelmingly, actively, and primarily *practise-oriented*.[13] The true character of this particular, and at times peculiar, *scientific* enterprise was however solely designed as an auxiliary function of advanced capitalism's sub-function of management and its umbrella-like ideology of *managerialism*. Management's and managerialism's subsidiary character and support function to the prevailing system of commerce is to some extent comfortably hidden behind an oversimplified *scientific-practise* model.

Figure 1.1 shows the assumption of a trouble-free, non-contradictory interest-symbiosis between purified and *value neutral science* and a *practise* that is equally purified and *value neutral*. The uncritical assumption of this science ⇌ practise interface that was designed to eclipse what has been termed organisational goal – in fact *profits* – serves two purposes. For one, it pretends that practise inside the managerially framed world just means practise – with absolutely nothing behind it. Practise is given a clean or even cleansed white-sheet appearance that hides the all too often pathological practise of management which has been expressed as the rationality of irrationality – managerial rationale appears as means-ends or cost-benefit calculation and often results in devastating social, environmental, and human costs that can be described as pure irrationality. The ideology of cleansed practise is used as the innocent portrayal of an acceptance, if not affirmation, of the irrationalities of the present

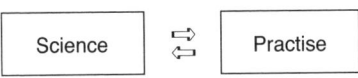

Figure 1.1   The Science-Practise Interface

system.[14] However, the real meaning of the science-practise interface is predominantly found in the idea of being a support-science, directed exclusively towards the enhancement of *organisational goals* which in turn are no more than two managerial codewords for capitalist *firms* or *corporations* while the neutral sounding *goal* – the intended connotation is *everyone has goals!* – seeks to hide the sole purpose of the whole system – profit.

Designed as an affirmative system of elements that structure meaning, management and managerialism are not only invented to hide the true character of the present production-consumption system and to deliver *value neutral*, objective, and purely scientific justification and legitimacy; because of their closeness to practise, their more directly assigned function includes the ideological expression of managerialism. As such, the practise of management and the ideology of managerialism have become part of the productive system in advanced capitalism. Unlike in the early days of liberal capitalism, advanced capitalism has incorporated science – and not only the so-called management *science* – into its very own apparatus. Because *science* has subsumed into the structure of advanced capitalism and due to its role as a vital function for system integration, it can – behind the façade of objectivism – no longer be pure, objective, and *value neutral*. It has to be an ideology precisely because of its ability to eclipse its value-*adding* character.[15]

The relationship shown in Figure 1.1 assumes an almost innocent, principally *neutral*, and at times even *natural* appearing interplay between two *horizontal* elements eclipsing the vertical arrangement of reality in which one directs the other. The idea behind the practise-science exchange is to pretend that managerial science is not *guided by*, but *close to* practise. In that way, the *educational consumer*[16] of managerial and business communication textbooks is linguistically perceived into being given access to *scientific* knowledge packaged as value free while also being promised to add real *value* to business.[17] The codeword *practise* incurs connotations to the equation *practise=value free=rational=pragmatic*. The argumentative equation of a managerial value-chain that remains *unspoken* (Poole 2006) is designed to provide an imaginary evidence for the science-practise claim.

In some cases, practise-science textbooks are written in a rather unscientific format that tends to mirror airport-lounge versions of popular literature which rather reflect the format of popular magazines such as *Cosmopolitan* than scientific publications.[18] These forms of business communication and managerialism always include versions of *handy tips* that are presented as a good managerial (=effective & efficient) communicator and convey the one-dimensional message to *buy something that 'truly adds value to your business!'* Apart from their ideological function, these texts are often no more than the sometimes unconscious, but always market-driven and uncritical expression of functionalism, pretending to be a value free and equalling *objective* science.[19] The contradiction between *adding value* to *your* business and being *value free* and therefore *real science* is conveniently glossed over. These collages of assembled texts – rather than proper books where someone expresses an idea on 200+ pages – include almost always the property-owning – and labour excluding – indicator of *'your'*.

As the link between value free and objective science is always depicted as being linear (→), these books include endless numbers of '↳' to indicate a relationship between a *cause* – management – and an *effect* – productivity – that is linguistically portrayed as linear and causal and therefore scientific. The height of *scientification* – presenting simple A→B relationships as science – is reached when the linear means-ends, cost-benefit, input-output, etc. relationships are framed inside crypto-scientific concepts such as system theory, transaction-cost theories, and the like. The ideological usefulness of such *scientification* rests on the simple assumption that the equation 1+2=3 can be presented as a contradiction-free relationship. The same, so the implicit assumption, applies to management, managerialism, and the practise-science link that is linguistically framed as $1^{(practise)}+2^{(science)}=3^{(management\text{-}science)}$ all of which equals proper science – just as input plus output equals productivity. As the mathematical equation as well as the 1+2=3 of management is commonly seen as contradiction free, management and managerialism at least linguistically assume the role of being pure, simple, easy to understand, and, above all, following a contradiction-free logic that negates the dialectic between labour and capital. These linear quasi-scientific linkages are shown as *implicit* (Poole 2006) and *explicit*. Just as the linearity of system-theory 1→2→3 – sometimes enhanced as a linear feedback cybernetic relationship 1→2→3→2→1 – lives on the non-contradictive assumption of a simple relationship between input and output seeking equilibrium, so does the science-practise link (Figure 1.1) and management itself. Crucial to understanding the linearity of management science is the exclusion of contradictions.[20] Apart from framing simple relations as science, the real task of affirmative managerial texts is to cut off all contradictions between value free and value-*adding*. How this is achieved is shown in Figure 1.2.

Rather than being a simple practise-science link as portrayed in Figure 1.1, the reality of the relationship between practise and managerialism is slightly more complex than pretended (Figure 1.2). Crucial to the science-managerialism link is that it claims to *add value* (to *your* business) while at the same time its assigned function under advanced capitalism is to be *value neutral*. The contradiction between being value free and value-adding is hidden behind the linguistic invention of a total separation of both. Managerialism has constructed two totally separated spheres to overcome this contradiction. In the first domain (1.2[i]), managerialism pretends the existence of a linear link between

managerialism[i] value-free = linearlink[iv] = objective science hidden contradictions[vi]	(iii)	managerialism[ii] value-adding = linearlink[v] = management science hidden contradictions[vii]

Figure 1.2 The Value-Free, Objective Science, and Value-Adding Linearity

pure and value free objective science while in the second domain (1.2^{ii}) it is designed to add real value to *organisational goals* (profits). The crucial task of managerialism, however, rests in the middle because it needs to construct a linguistic reality in which both are disconnected. The uncritical and unconscious consumer of management literature and business or management communication – organisational communication – is guided towards the acceptance of both domains (1.2^i + 1.2^{ii}) without ever establishing the link (1.2^{iii}) between them – even though the use of scientific knowledge in the service of management demands exactly this link (1.2^{iii}). The conversion of scientific knowledge into management's value-adding knowledge is one of the most crucial tasks of *managerialism*, providing for its existence and function in advanced capitalism.[21] Without the task to ideologically separate (1.2^{iii}) while in reality using science in the service of management, managerialism would not be required. The pretence of being value free is a necessary ideological condition (1.2^i) to hide the real task of managerialism (1.2^{ii}) and to make managerialism viable.

The links between value free and objective science (1.2^{iv}) as well as between value-adding and management science (1.2^v) are established as being linear even though both are socially constructed and dialectic rather than logically linear (→). In the second case (1.2^v), the link is essential and functional. Both domains are designed to hide the contradictions between managerialism (1.2^{i+ii}) on the one hand and the links between objective value free science (1.2^{vi}) and respectively value-adding-management science (1.2^{vii}) on the other. The common problem of all the links in Figure 1.2 is that they construct the practise-science link as linear rather than as dialectical. The overall task of managerialism is threefold as it needs to establish firstly, an *ideology-link* between objective science and managerialism (1.2^i); secondly, a functional *use-link* between science and managerialism (1.2^{ii}); and thirdly, it must keep up the appearance of a total separation of both spheres (1.2^{iii}). Based on this, managerialism can only function as an ideology as it is deemed to create several ideological links while utilising what social science has to offer ever since Taylor's *Scientific Management* (1911) introduced ideology cloaked as science to management, thus creating managerialism.

However, Figure 1.2 also shows that the presentation of the practise-science linearity (Figure 1.1) establishes only the need for ideology in its original sense – *knowledge in the service of power*.[22] To some extent the functional idea of the management-science ⇌ management-practise exchange already exposes the ideological *surface* structure of managerialism hidden inside Figure 1.1 while Figure 1.2 explains its underlying *deep structure*. Problematic however is the contradictory claim of being *scientific* while in reality managerialism is all too often not much more than practise-related *advanced newspaper reading* for present and future managers due to an almost complete exclusion of theoretical, philosophical, and ethical demands.[23] In this scenario, *science* that – at least in pre-managerialism and pre-Taylorism (1911) times – was inevitably connected to theory and philosophy can now safely exclude both. Under managerialism, the original and historical philosophy-science link has been converted into a science-practise link. The philosophy-practise or theory-practise link (Figure 1.1) no longer exists.[24]

It is not uncommon to hear the terms *theory* and *practise* in contrast to each other, as if *theory* meant something impractical or unrealistic and practise referred to the real world. Linguistically, the ideology of managerialism demands the disassociation of *philosophy* and *theory* from management and therefore in the world of management and managerial communication both have been replaced with functional, practical, and linear *science* as the task of management science and managerial communication is not directed towards human goals enshrined in Enlightenment, philosophy, and ethics but in *organisational goals*. Behind the fancy and somewhat ideological term *organisational goal* – also branded adding value – resides no more than management's task of the maximisation of profits.[25] This reduces communication to a tool, a mechanism, an input-output system, and an apparatus directed towards functionality based on instrumental rationality. To achieve this, communication in the world of work is reduced from an *abstract-philosophical-ethical science* to a *theory-free* and *practical* level.[26]

As such, managerially guided communication is not directed towards a *historical-hermeneutical* understanding that seeks to understand the *meaning* of communication and its historical development.[27] Nor is its interest geared towards a *critical-emancipatory* understanding of communication. Instead it is confined to an understanding of technical, engineering, mechanical, and empirical problems that can be reduced to the means-ends of instrumental rationality.[28] Inside the one-dimensional viewpoint of instrumental rationality that claims to be objective, neutral, and sometimes even *natural*, the humanistic-philosophical science of communication is diminished to the singularity of instrumentality. This angle is presented as scientific, objective, and *value neutral*. The vast amount of literature on communication at work is not directed towards the uncovering of the hidden structures of domination at work but rather seeks to either enhance them or to cover them up in the attempt to establish and sustain managerial domination over a process that is highly hierarchical, non-democratic, and essentially authoritarian. Almost as a routine exercise, the acceptance – if not affirmation – of authoritarianism has been shown in a recent explosion of management literature on *managerial leadership*.[29] A raft of books, seminars, MBA-courses, training manuals, degrees, courses and so on either discuss, include, or focus on the issue of leadership.[30]

Quasi-scientific argumentation has established a linear chain of value free sequences that create and sustain management as the sole operative in the world of work and beyond. This linear argumentative chain follows the assumed logic of work → objective = rational → management → leadership → value-adding → managerial communication → organisational goals.[31] Work needs to be organised in an objective and rational way (Taylor 1911). Therefore, management and managerial leadership are required because *only* this can add measurable, objective and scientific value.[32] This needs to be communicated in order to achieve organisational goals. Once the internal logic of the ideologically created chain-argument has been accepted as legitimate, all managerial actions can be built on this foundation. Like all ideologies, the managerial chain-argument is not unreal or illusory. Rather the opposite is the case. It constructs reality in a particular way by allowing only one interpretive framework that is presented as TINA – there is no alternative.[33] The managerial chain-argument is however not only supported by one-dimensional connotations to a particular selective understanding of reality but also by a raft of affirmative writers in the field of managerial quasi-science. This is evident in the establishment of so-called management studies, management degrees, management faculties, management schools, etc. Virtually all universities have established institutions in the service of managerialism. In the words of Watson (2003:166)

managerialism came to the universities as the German army came to Poland. Now they talk about achieved learning outcomes, quality assurance mechanisms, and international benchmarking. They throw triple bottom line, customer satisfaction and world class around with the best of them.[34]

The triumph of the one-dimensional managerial framework is well established, commonly accepted, and massively amplified through the quasi-scientific entourage of managerialism-supportive print publication, radio, and TV programmes. In that way, the ideology of managerialism has become an almost universally accepted theme that is portrayed to be the most important guide of present society.[35] The linearity of the commercial and managerial top-down relationship is almost unquestionably transferred to the most intimate areas of human existence and with it comes the linearity of everything. This results in the illusion that everything can be managed, everything is top-down, linear, and free of contradictions. All of this gains legitimacy through the pretence of being scientific. Mass circulated managerial press activities to gain legitimacy in the form of the linear science→practise ideology are nowhere better to be found than in the triadic relationship between (a) one of the most known universities – *Harvard University*; (b) one of the most known business schools – the *Harvard Business Schools*, and (c) one of the best-known quasi-scientific – science-practise – journals that reign unchallenged on the forefront of quasi-scientific literature on management – the American *Harvard Business Review* (HBR).

The former editor of the *Harvard Business Review*, Joan Margretta (2002:2), noted that *wherever we work or volunteer, we need management*. In the words of the HBR-editor it is not even a question of *when*-ever, just of *where*-ever we work; it is also assumed time and again that there is a '*we*' at work, cloaking Taylor's *Division of Labour* that *scientifically!* divided work into those *who manage* and those who *are managed*. So we – and yes, *we* all – need management.³⁶ There is no other way. This is TINA in its operative expression in management and its ideological expression in managerialism. Management, and with it managerialism, is portrayed as Star Trek's Borg: *accept the rule of the Borg/management! Resistance is futile – assimilate or face destruction!*³⁷ We all have to simply subsume ourselves under the – essentially non-democratic – rule of management. Consequently, one of the foremost tasks of management, including its entourage of affirmative writers, still is – even after almost 100 years of management writing since Taylor (1911) – to make us all believe that we *need* management as if it were a case of *we can't live without you!*³⁸

Why *we all need* management so bitterly has been described by the HBR-editor: *looked from a distance, it's easy to think that management is only about economics and engineering but up close it's very much about people.*³⁹ In essence, this tells us that management is not about *economics* – apart from the all too often unmentioned but ever-present and all-inclusive profit making maxim. And it is not about *engineering* either. However, it is about *people*. The very idea of *people* changes once they have been converted from individuals into organisational people. For affirmative management writers, companies are no longer companies but organisations as this term carries neutral sounding connotations such as sporting organisations and the like. In any case, once *people* have become *organisational members* – like members of a voluntary sports club or a communal organisation – they have been converted from a human *being* into a human *resource* – to avoid the word *material*. These humans are no longer people who behave like they used to behave, who communicate like they used to communicate, etc. but human resources or human material – or more correctly put workers – who are expected to behave and communicate in a pre-structured way designed by management and managerialism.

Communication is essential in an environment like the world of work where people (usually managers) manage other people (usually workers). The dominant form of communication between those *who manage* and those *who are managed* occurs at a vertical level (directing downwards and reporting upwards). Despite decades of managerial literature on *flattening hierarchies, working together, people are our most important asset, self-organising work teams will take the place of managerial hierarchies* as well as on – nowadays almost never mentioned – *industrial democracy, workplace participation*, etc., today's workplace is still authoritarian, hierarchical and divided along Taylor's lines.⁴⁰ Seen from the viewpoint of management and managerialism, the division into what Taylor invented and self-declared to be scientific in 1911 is still prevalent.⁴¹ There are still those *who manage* and those *who are managed*. Today Taylor's division can be found in almost all companies, starting with the world's oldest one, the *Weihenstephan* brewery, to the most modern corporations of *Microsoft, Google,* or *EBay*. Despite all managerial rhetoric of the famous *'we'* who are *all in one boat*, in the 21ˢᵗ century's world of work *those who perform tasks should* (still) *be separated from those who design work tasks.*⁴²

Essentially, most publications in the realm of managerialism that include the hidden contradictions as outlined in Figure 1.2 do not live from highlighting Hegelian dialectics that is directed towards truth. They do not even operate on a simple notion of dialectics: thesis (*add value* to your business), anti-thesis (*value free* science) and synthesis (the Hegelian contradiction of being *value-adding* and *value free* simultaneously demands ideology and total separation). Consequently, the objective of affirmative literature on business communication, management, and managerialism is rather linear and one-dimensional and provides functional directions fixed on organisational goals. In a somewhat plain and down-to-earth version of Hegelian dialectics that builds the underlying philosophical-critical approach towards the understanding of communication at work, the process of non-linear thinking is shown in Figure 1.3.[43]

In contrast to the simplistic practise-science linearity (Figure 1.1) that has been challenged in an analysis showing its hidden contradictions (Figure 1.2), Figure 1.3 provides a somewhat more fruitful method to examine communication in the world of work as it moves from the linear assumption of Figure 1.1 into a dialectic that can deal with the contradictions shown in Figure 1.2. The science and practise of communication inside the world of work cannot be shown as being linear as only a dialectical viewpoint can highlight and eventually overcome the hidden contradictions enshrined in the practise-science problem as well as the *value-adding* and *value free* challenge prevalent in work and work-related communication. In a second stage, any thesis about communication in the world of work is directed towards the objective affairs of both as expressed in empirical statements. This is contrasted by the *anti-thesis* based on critical reflections shown in hermeneutical counter-arguments. Both empirical statements and hermeneutical counter-arguments are expressed through their communicative components. The communicative presentation of facts moves on to an understanding of the crucial *meaning* of facts.[44] It also moves from empirical depictions towards meaning.

The outcome of a critical dialectic between *facts* and *meaning* is designed to create a critical manifestation on the state of affairs reflecting the Kantian idea of *what is*. Both – thesis and anti-thesis (Figure 1.3) – are then merged

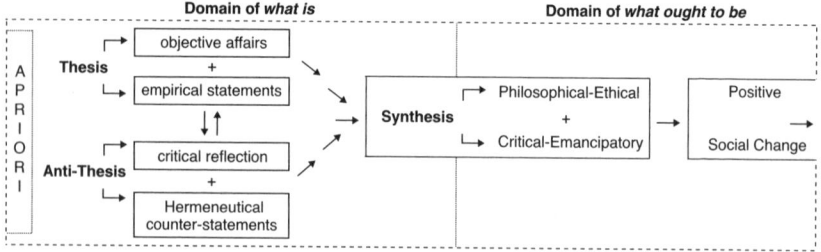

Figure 1.3 A Dialectical Understanding of Communication at Work

into a synthesis entering the Kantian world of *what ought to be*. This is an important point because the idea of dialectics does not represent a static view that simply looks at both sides of a coin. It is not like a court system that looks at both sides, considers two arguments, and makes a decision. Hegelian dialectics moves beyond this as it can only work when positioned inside the Kantian imperatives of *what is* and *what ought to be*. It therefore always has a philosophical progressive element and is forward-looking, directed towards a future state of affairs. Hence, any synthesis always needs to include considerations on *what ought to be*. The idea of a synthesis has, again, two important components. Firstly, it needs to include philosophical-ethical elements of communication and the world of work and secondly, a critical-emancipatory element.

The outcome of this synthesis is directed towards positive social change. Therefore, two important elements have to be added to the dialectical model of *thesis, anti-thesis,* and *synthesis*. Firstly, the model has to be exposed to Kant's ideas of *what is* and *what ought to be* as a dialectical model of understanding is not static but moves between both spheres of Kantian thinking. Secondly, Kant's categorical imperative that *everything in modernity has to be exposed to critique* is enshrined in the call for critique in the *thesis* and *anti-thesis* domain as well as in the *synthesis* domain. In the latter, this is further supported by a demand for philosophical-ethical and emancipatory understanding. Only when seen under the dialectical demands issued in Figure 1.3, communication and the world of work become accessible for the power of critical and dialectical understanding.

When communication and the world of work are examined under the conditions set out in Figure 1.3, four basic elements can be identified. Firstly, the idea of communication has to be introduced to set several social and communicative parameters. In Figure 1.3 this is indicated on the far left hand side as Kantian *a priori* knowledge that is prevalent in anyone entering into a dialogue about a subject matter.[45] Secondly, a critical discussion about *what is* – the thesis on communication at work – leads to thirdly, an anti-thesis to present forms of managerially guided communication at work.[46] The synthesis of both in the form of communicative action is a forward-looking conclusion that seeks to overcome the colonisation of communication – thesis – by building on the anti-thesis of communicative action. This open-ended process is directed towards practical solutions about positive social change (indicated by an opening in Figure 1.3).

Seen from Kant's *what is* and *what ought to be,* the thesis element of managerial and instrumental communication reflects on the state of current affairs in managerially guided communication as it shows *what is*. The anti-thesis moves from *what is* to *what ought to be* as it lays out a programme of communicative action that is designed to overcome managerial colonisation and also shows how communication at work can be constructed in the absence of distortions. The final synthesis is a further engagement into *what ought to be* because it constructs a programme for communicative action in a very practical sense which is achieved with the often referred idea in mind that *nothing is as practical as a good theory*.[47]

The *a priori* knowledge in Figure 1.3 not only introduces the issue of *communication at work* but also includes basic ideas and contexts of communication ranging from the simple *sender-receiver* model to *decoder-encoder* models that construct meaning between sender and receiver. Essential to an understanding of communication is not so much the knowledge about technical details of transmitting a message but how individuals create *meaning* from it. In communication theory, meaning or *semantics* is constructed via the exchange of signs – sign, signifier and the to-be-signified – between communicative subjects. Crucial for communication is not so much *syntax* but *semantics* because syntax only establishes universal grammatical rules. Syntax provides a pathway on which humans walk as they please while semantics is the core of human communication because it creates *meaning*. In other words, the human world is more a world of creating meaning than of following grammar.[48] But meaning is, and in fact has to be, contextual. When we communicate, we engage in contexts through which we construct gestures, signs, words, language, and meaning. One such context is the world of work, but inside it, even these contexts can vary, as it contains at least two domineering contexts. Forms of human communication vary from work related communication – directing downward and reporting upwards – to non-work related or social conversation inside work as well as outside of work settings.

In both spheres – the domain of work and the domain of private life – humans engage in meaning construction through a variety of communicative forms. We do so through *signs* (with words and sentences as the most complex forms), *symbols* representing certain meanings (for example, Picasso's ☮ represents peace), and *metaphors* that are used as non-literal suggestive meanings in which an expression that designates one meaning is used implicitly to mean something else (cf. *time is money*). We also communicate by using *stories* and *narratives,* especially when talking about experiences that are not necessarily objective representations or re-creations of factual experiences and identities. Based on these preliminary *a priori* considerations, the thesis part of Figure 1.3 highlights communicative distortions in the form of *classifications* where issues are classified or boxed in order to serve a specific purpose or idea. In these managerial ordering systems communication can be instrumentally directed towards a specific set of pre-designed outcomes, thus creating *knowledge in the service of power,* in this case managerial power. The creation of *knowledge in the service of power* has also been described as building ideologies. Managerialism is such an ideology because it creates knowledge that serves the specific purpose of management to achieve *organisational goals* (Orwellian *Newspeak*) or profits (*Oldspeak*).

Crucially, managerial *knowledge in the service of power* is not established under conditions of *communicative action* and *ideal speech* but is created *normatively* as a rule or during a highly guided and structured form of instrumental communication. The central idea behind this is the creation of *hegemonies*. Hegemonic meaning structures can linguistically be portrayed as universal where a particular interest is constructed in a way that it assumes universality. This is commonly achieved in a number of ways such as by making managerial knowledge appear neutral as in *getting things done through people*. Hegemonic meaning structures often carry connotations of neutralisation as they make highly value-laden issues appear value free or neutral. They also appear as being *natural*, pretending that it is natural to manage – the HBR-editor's *wherever we work or volunteer, we need management* sounds truly natural. In both cases – natural and neutral – routines are established to move from *symbolic association* through understanding to *conditioned association* through rituals and repetitions coupled with reward structures.[49] Neutralisation and naturalisation are needed because they *de-historify* managerialism so that those who are targeted – usually those who are managed – cannot make historical connections between their current situation and the history behind it. The victims of this form of distorted communication are trapped in Hegel's *Zeitgeist* – the managerial spirit (*Geist*) of the present time (*Zeit*) – without understanding its historical meanings.[50]

The establishment of hegemonic meaning structures can also be achieved by using simple rhetorical tools dating back to ancient Greece that are still highly in use today. While the original idea of rhetoric had been to develop forms of argumentation directed towards *truth*, today's use of rhetoric has become purely instrumental. It is used as a means, not as an end directed towards truth. Rhetoric has been downgraded and subsumed under instrumental rationality and instrumental communication. It has moved from being a form of argumentation about truth to an instrument of distortion. In the world of management, rhetoric and rituals that establish hegemonic meaning structure take on the communicative form of managerial meetings. In many cases, these – often managerially set up meetings that always include a chairperson – are perfect methods to establish hierarchical ordering structures that create distorted communication by assigning power to one person over others – *by virtue of the office*, as Max Weber once outlined (1924). The standard management meeting represents a form of distorted communication simply by positioning someone at the hierarchical and positional tabletop that enshrines special powers. Things as simple as seating arrangements already reflect managerial hierarchies, non- or even anti-democracy, and authoritarianism. The final version of distorted communication applies methods of persuasion that operate somewhat similar to rituals and in fact repetition is one of the vital ingredients of persuasion. Another similarity between rituals and persuasion is their base-method of relying on *conditioned* rather than on *symbolic association*.[51] Both seek to establish a frame of reference that is conditioned rather than built on symbolic or rational thinking so that the recipients of managerial terms can only understand them inside a pre-conditioned – but always managerial – context.

The anti-thesis to the thesis of distorted communication lies in communicative action.[52] In sharp contrast to the colonising powers of instrumental communication that distort communication and steer it away from truth and towards management, managerialism, and *organisational goals,* communicative action is based on a very different set of ideas. One of its core concepts is *ideal speech.* A collection of specific social parameters can be used to create the conditions for discourse under ideal speech. The idea of ideal speech is not so much found in *communication* theory but in *social* theory. It is not a communicative method like rhetoric and the like but a social idea that reflects the fact that we live in a socially constructed environment that is not a given fact but can be created, re-created, and shaped. Once the basic parameters for ideal speech – such as participants' domination-free access to communication – have been established, the power of communicative action enables participants to overcome distorted communication by critical reflections on communication as well as through critical self-reflections.

Unlike instrumental communication, ideal speech is not directed towards *organisational goals* (means) but towards finding common agreement by participating in a dialogue (ends). Once the instrumentality of means has been overcome, this domination-free form of communication can be directed towards ethical discourse. Freed from instrumental rationality, a communicative space then opens for discussion on ethical issues. The basic idea of ethical discourse – also called *discourse ethics* – relies on the possibilities outlined by Laurence Kohlberg (1971, 1981 & 1984). Kohlberg's idea is to show that the human development of morality and ethics is moving upward. According to his scale of ethical behaviour, participants in ideal speech situations can direct their engagement towards higher ethical levels which can be supported by a critical reflection on *what is* ethical in the current state of affairs and *what ought to be* ethical in an open-ended future state of affairs (Figure 1.3). Once ideal speech has moved upwards to ethical levels, the universality of Kant's *categorical imperative* forces participants to develop moral codes of behaviour that have to be applied beyond the realm of a specific ideal speech situation. In that way, ethical considerations are not only applied to participants but as a universal principle.

In sharp contrast to non-work related settings, forms of communicative action at work have to be established in an environment that is traditionally and structurally dominated by one form of power that has been assigned to management (Marglin 1974). From Adam Smith (1776) to Karl Marx (1848), Taylor (1911), and today's Margretta (2002), the world of work is still defined by the *Division of Labour* between those *who manage* and those *who are managed.* The asymmetrical relationship between both has been the subject of countless elaborations. In the field of communication these lead to two forms of internal logics – the logic of management and managerialism on the one hand and the logic of those who are managed – labour – on the other. The power-base, the position, as well as the interests of both logics – and their position in the labour

Introduction: Communication in Management, Work and Society 15

market and the world of work – are, at times, diametrically opposing. In sharp contrast to Olson's idea of a singular or one-dimensional *Logic of Collective Action* (1971), workplaces are covered by *Two Logics of Collective Action* (Offe & Wiesenthal 1980), as there is not one single actor – management – but two – labour and management.[53] The socially created fact of the *Two Logics of Collective Action* has severe implications for communication as the two actors that define the world of work not only follow two different organisational and social-action logics, but also have two different forms of communication.

Just like *Two Logics of Collective Action* there are two logics of communicative action. Inside the asymmetrical relationship between labour and management two fundamental different logics of communication collide with each other. On the one side, instrumental communication that is directed towards success and achievement and expressed as *organisational goals* relies on hierarchies and establishes communicative outcomes *normatively* – not communicatively.[54] On the other side, the quest for truth can only be realised inside a communicative forum that establishes truth communicatively rather than normatively. Only communication in the form of communicative action can establish a truthful picture of the current state of affairs in the world of work. Participants in ideal speech have to reach common understanding on what is a truthful representation of the world of work. This cannot be established normatively.[55] Truth cannot be directed, decreed, advised, or put in a managerial policy. Communicative action, unlike instrumental communication, is directed towards a fundamentally different aspect of human life. It seeks to establish *what is* and *what ought to be* in an ethical, not in a commercial way. Therefore, human communication can only be directed towards ethical, not managerial concerns.

Finally, communicative action under conditions of ideal speech elevates ethics and moral conduct to a higher level because it incorporates ethics at two levels. It firstly seeks to guide any discussion outcomes within an ethical code and secondly, the very foundation of establishing ethics is ethical as it moves all ethical philosophy and ethical considerations – in short the ethical philosophy of the past 2000 years – to a completely new foundation which consists of ethics itself in the form of ethical dialogue. No longer can ethics be created in documents, logics, argumentations, and written essays; it is only established communicatively by using ethical forms of communication to develop ethical codes of human behaviour. In this version of ethics, the ethical dialogue that creates ethics has to be ethical and in this sense has to exclude all forms of domination as they are based on power and power relations which are – by definition – unethical in the process of ethically constructed communicative action.

The domain of management is fundamentally structured against such an enterprise as its very foundation is domination in the form of hierarchies, non-democracy, and authoritarianism. Therefore conditions for communicative action and ideal speech can only be established when both domains – labour and management – are strictly separated. Only through the creation of an autonomous domain will labour ever be able to overcome the colonisation of communicative action by management's instrumental communication. This is the only way for labour to move from instrumental communication towards communicative action that is based on *ethical* rather than on *instrumental* foundations. Only this enables labour to realise Kant's *categorical imperative* to treat humans as *ends* and not as *means*. Currently however, even the mildest and most humane managerial structures – often called soft-HRM – are still far too removed from this ideal to be able to follow labour on this pathway.

Deep inside the Kantian domain of *what ought to be* and behind the synthesis idea, the concept of positive social change is to be found as an open ended process (Figure 1.3). Communicative action is a concept that not only directs our attention towards *communication* but also towards *action*. Hence, those who enter into communicative action are not only issued with the request to establish an ethical dialogue, they also need to direct their attention towards positive social change. This however can neither be achieved within the management domain nor in a joint labour-management sphere because the current realities of management's instrumental rationality and instrumental communication will render it structurally impossible. The stage of ethical communicative action can therefore only be reached once a separation between labour and management has taken place. The pragmatics of a universal discourse forum cannot be established when sectarian and particular interests – such as the managerial interest – are still at play. Kohlberg's highest stage of ethical behaviour as well as the Kantian *categorical imperative* only allow those forms of ethical discourse that are directed towards universal ethical codes of conduct. In their final version, ideal speech situations and the demands of communicative action have to adhere to a few basic parameters that make communicative action possible. These include ideas for the establishment of a possible workable discourse forum – location, duration, order of speakers, replies, forms of agreement, etc. They can never be cook-book like recipes nor can they ever be laws, rules, or regulations because the adoption of these suggestions can only ever be established inside communicative action that positions the common will of domination-free humans engaged in communicative action at the centre of all considerations.

2
Communication I: Basic Contexts at Work

Fundamentally, all forms of knowledge in academic disciplines such as traditional philosophy, social science, industrial relations, management studies, etc. are a reflection of reason embodied in cognition, communication, and action. With *Enlightenment* and modernity, rationality and reason became the core of all scientific enquiries.[56] No longer were scientific endeavours based on religious belief-systems. Modernity linked rationality and reason to the scientific endeavour of proven knowledge. Under modernity, advances in reasoning and scientific knowledge took place primarily inside a communicative framework. This new framework of communication among scientists led to tremendous developments in the understanding of the modern world. Inside this framework science has been *generally* and *universally* applied. In other words, today's understanding of the world including scientific knowledge has always been part of a *universal* form of knowledge. *Without universality, thought would be a private, non-committal affair, incapable of understanding the smallest sector of existence. Thought is always more and other than individual thinking* (Marcuse 1966:142). Such non-private and universal thought, knowledge, and reason have set universal parameters in human communication. Today universally agreed forms of human communication are conducted through universal sets of principles that guide human engagement and human conduct as set out in the *universal declaration of human rights* which is accepted worldwide and commonly agreed upon. Its universal acknowledgment has moved human relations from God and church to a universal ethical and human conduct with the declaration encompassing all humans. It links every individual to all other individuals as well as to all people. There are no exceptions and no exclusions.

Ideas that led to the *declaration of human rights* derived from the ideas of universal *Enlightenment* which replaced religious belief-systems with scientific, human, and ethical rationality. These concepts not only guide human conduct worldwide, they also set the parameters of how humans understand the world around them. The *Declaration* not only provides a universal form of human conduct but also a universally accepted common form of communication that guides humans in understanding. It is understood that communication on human conduct and human rights takes place inside a universally applied framework that explains how we understand human relations and human communication.

Out of these principle ideas modern thinking has developed three core perspectives on universal rationality. Under conditions of modernity, rationality is not seen as a one-dimensional entity but takes on different forms, each of which has a different inherent rationality, a different focus, and each form of rational thinking leads to different outcomes when brought to use in order to explain human communication. This is shown in Table 2.1.

Table 2.1 shows the difference between the three forms of rationality (a–c). This is further explained when the two concepts – power (2.2^i) and communication (2.2^{ii}) – as well as the two perspectives – strengths (2.2^{iii}) and limitations (2.2^{iv}) – are brought into the relationship of the three rationality concepts (Table 2.1). This complex idea is simplified in Table 2.2 that consists of three rows (a–c) and four columns (i–iv). An *instrumental or system-rational* (a) viewpoint examines communication from a fundamentally different standpoint when compared to an *interpretive approach* (b). A *critical-rational* understanding under conditions of communicative action (c) provides a third, radically different and fruitful way to examine communication. This is shown in Table 2.2.[57]

Table 2.2 shows the relationship between the three theoretical viewpoints (a–c) in relation to the two core concepts of power and communication. It also outlines each viewpoint's strengths (iii) and limitations (iv) and examines communication from a different conceptual and perceptive viewpoint. An instrumental or system approach (a) is largely limited to the concept of power based on scarcity of resources. Here, communication is viewed as minor or marginal. Struggles take place over control, not over communicatively established meaning structures.[58] Inside the power perspective, communication is reduced to circularity expressed as a neutral medium that moves between actors at work. At the second level (b), communication is viewed as a creator of meaning structures that are disconnected from the wider society. Concepts that could structure the use of power for an understanding of communication are largely excluded from a hermeneutical understanding of communication.

At a somewhat different level compared to a view that sees communication in system and instrumental or interpretive terms is a perspective that

Table 2.1 Three Forms for Rational Thinking

No.	Type of Rationality
a)	rational thinking directed towards instrumental rationality,
b)	rational thinking directed towards interpretive-hermeneutics, and
c)	rational thinking directed towards communicative action

Table 2.2 Fundamental Concepts and Perspectives on Communication

Theoretical Viewpoint:	(1) Concepts		(2) Perspectives	
	(i) Power	(ii) Communication	(iii) Strengths	(iv) Limitations
(a) Instrumental and System Rationality	– Decision making hierarchy – System – actor relations – Control over resources – Dependency creation	– Representational – Expresses existing power relationships – Management translates power basis into effective communication	– View of actor as bounded rationality – Legitimises dominant view of work relations – Shift from interpersonal to system view of power	– Power is limited through struggle over scarce resources – Ignores that power is exercised through consent – Communication is minor
(b) Interpretation and Hermeneutics	– Normative structures of shared meanings – Internalisation of work values	– Constructs inter-subjective systems of meaning – Focuses on relationships between sense-making symbolic forms	– Communication central – Focus on power-meaning relationship – Links culture to control – Power as socially constructed, not neutral	– Fails to situate power in large political and economical context – Excludes theory of society – Inadequate view on contradictions and power relations at work
(c) Critical-Rational and Communicative Action	– Structures of divergent group interests – Relations of hegemony – Dialectic of control – Emancipatory models	– Socio-political categories – Creates reality through analysis of ideologically structured meaning systems	– Communication & work are central categories – Links power to consent – Ideology is central to power relations at work – Work is constructed via power & communication	– Totalising view of power – Too many studies on domination and control – Insufficient studies on resistance & actors' communicative action abilities directed towards emancipation

positions communication inside (c) the critical-rational concept of communicative action.[59] This third perspective uncovers the limitations of the previous viewpoints (a+b) by critically examining their power and domination elements. While many studies on communication and work have been directed towards forms of control, authority, etc., the crucial issue of resistance and, most importantly, that of emancipation has been undervalued. This approach is no longer sufficient to explain human communication at work. While older studies on communication under perspective (a) had often been directed towards effectiveness, studies under perspective (b) tended to be limited to interpretations and meanings. In contrast, perspective (c) is directed towards the truth. Herein lies the sharp difference between a communicative understanding and analysis under (a) or (b) on the one side and (c) on the other.

Consequently, (c) does not simply view reason, rationality, and knowledge as a closed-up link between cognitive and rational validity and understanding. Understanding under (c) reaches well beyond the production and reproduction of such reason-validity links. According to Gadamer (1976:45) *understanding is not a mere reproduction of knowledge, that is, it is not a mere act of repeating the same thing.* Human understanding is a complex act conducted communicatively and directed towards the goal of truth and critical reflection. Hence, any communicative understanding should always contain at least one of these two fundamental propositions: *truth* and *critical reflection*. The truth element in any communicative understanding connects to the state of affairs in the world. Such universal worldviews are constructed inside a contextual framework in which experience is interpreted and understood.

The more instrumental or system-like concept of *critical reflection* contains elements of reflection and social action. These are seen as interventions into worldly affairs with the purpose to alter these. In this sense, they are reflections and social interventions constructed as goal-directed activities. Communicative rationality and communicative action both contain objectives directed towards *truth*. These objectives seek to establish a common understanding on the true state of affairs at work. The three core elements that guide human understanding of communication (Table 2.1 and Table 2.2) are enhanced in Table 2.3. It shows a new column depicting the theory perspective and provides an overview of these perspectives.

Table 2.3 depicts how forms of communication at work are discussed under the three well-known theoretical viewpoints of Table 2.1 and 2.2: (a) instrumental rationality, (b) interpretive-hermeneutics, and (c) communicative action. *Instrumental rationality* (a) emphasises objectivity, structure, prediction and seeks control to establish laws of communication that could guide management towards improved mechanisms for goal achieving means-ends actions.[60] The interpretive-hermeneutic approach (b) emphasises on an understanding of communication at work that sees organisations as a cultural system

Table 2.3 Three Theoretical Perspectives on Communication at Work

Perspectives/ Theory	a) Instrumental-Rationality	b) Interpretive-Hermeneutics	c) Communicative Action
Philosophical Background:	Modernity & Industrial Work	Interpretation of Work	Emancipation of Work
Sociological Background:	Work as Structure	Agency Works	Agency-Structure Dialectic
Subject versus Object:	Work as Objective Process	Subjects Conduct Work	Subject-Object Dialectic
Communicative Goals:	Prediction & Control	Understanding & Anticipation	Critical Consciousness, Ideal Speech & Emancipation
Communicative Focus:	Logical Positivism Cause and Effects	Working Reality is Socially Constructed	Material Interests Who Possesses Them
Function of Communication:	Tool Controlled by Management	Mutually Negotiated Order Communication as Circular	Communicative Action & Mutual Understanding
Knowledge Claim:	Laws of Communication	Communication as Base	Critique & Criticism
Perspective & Standpoint:	Management	Organisational Perspective	Labour
Communicated Metaphor:	Machine & Mechanics	Organism & System	Struggle over Meaning
Organisational Perspective:	Purposive Goal Achieving Means-Ends Relations	Culture, Language and Community	Instruments of Domination, Distortion & Oppression

established through the use of language in a communal effort.[61] In contrast, communicative action (c) seeks to unmask communicative distortions, emphasising that distortions and domination can be overcome by applying the concept of ideal speech directed towards *communicative action*. Whether seen from perspective (a), (b), or (c), at its most basic level, human communication and communicative action can be seen as shown in Figure 2.1.

Figure 2.1 shows that the critical rational perspective focuses on two essential aspects of communication: speech and the social relationship that is established. Both need to be addressed to understand communication and the historic development of communication at work. The critical-rational standpoint also argues that communication at work can be discussed as a

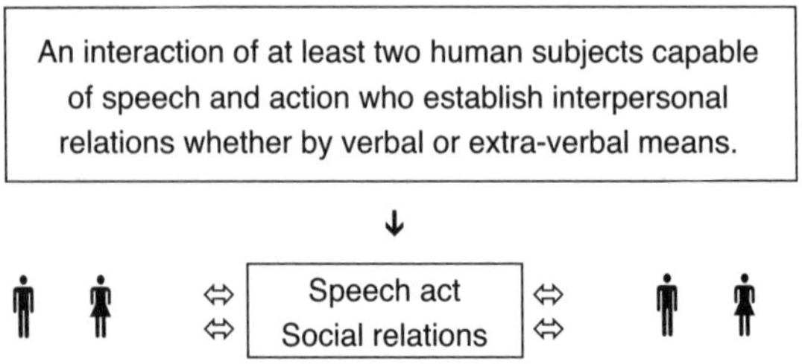

```
┌─────────────────────────────────────────────┐
│ An interaction of at least two human subjects capable │
│ of speech and action who establish interpersonal │
│ relations whether by verbal or extra-verbal means. │
└─────────────────────────────────────────────┘
                       ↓
   👤 👤    ⇔   ┌──────────────┐   ⇔   👤 👤
              ⇔   │ Speech act   │   ⇔
                  │ Social relations │
                  └──────────────┘
```

Figure 2.1 Communication as Speech and Action

historical process in order to understand current forms of workplace related communication. It follows a threefold purpose.

From Table 2.4 it is obvious that the three uses of a critical and reflective version of communicative action are diametrically opposed to the instrumental conditions of managerialism (Table 2.3[a–b]). Under managerialism, communicative relations at work are dominated by the use of communicative *devices* rather than *communicative actions*. The contrast between instrumentalism and managerialism on the one hand and the quest for *communicative action* on the other leads to new conflicts which can no longer be sufficiently expressed as a struggle over control at work. Conflict at work cannot be reduced to a *Frontier of Control* between labour and management.[62] Understanding conflict means understanding the communicative elements of conflicts.

This converts the old *Frontier of Control* into a *Frontier of Communicative Control*. There is a shift away from contradictions expressed as a struggle over control issues towards a struggle over meaning and communication. Past perspectives were able to sufficiently explain relations at work as a conflict or as contradictions between labour and management. Today, this relationship is more and more directed towards elements connected to communication. Communication has become a contentious issue at work. Control over communication is of equal importance when it comes to control over work. The process of communicative control is aided through a view of communication that restricts thinking to Instrumental Rationality and Interpretive-Hermeneutics (a & b in Tables 2.1 to 2.3). The instrumental view focuses on

Table 2.4 The Three Purposes of Critical-Rational Communication

No.	Purpose
(i)	a symbolic constitution and reproduction of knowledge, convictions, and valuations at work,
(ii)	the formation and establishment of social solidarity, and
(iii)	the cultivation of subjects capable of speech and action.

the mechanics of communication (a) or on interpretive aspects of communication (b). Only (c) provides a radically different perspective enabling a deeper and critically reflective understanding of communication. It takes the communicative action viewpoint to allow a critical examination of communication at work. Such a critical examination needs to start with the basics of communication.

Basic concepts of communication

The concept of *universal pragmatics* purports to unveil some of the most general standards that govern rational communication, communicative action, and human discourse.[63] Universal pragmatics establishes forms of social communication that we use to explicitly guide social action. In order to receive communication as meaningful it must be governed by universal norms, values and structures. Human communication is only possible when commonly agreed standards of communication become operative. A common understanding on the state of relations at work can only be established when humans communicate. In this sense, understanding means to communicate about such understandings.

This has strong connotations to the Latin word *'com'* referring to *togetherness*. Communication demands *togetherness*. If linked to togetherness, communication is a central process through which social actors and institutions develop understanding and construct meaning.

In most cases, communication as outlined in Figure 2.2 occurs between individuals such as communication between two managers, two workers, between a manager and a worker, etc. This is referred to as *inter-personal* communication because it establishes a relationship between people.

Any understanding of how people communicate also places relative high importance on the *process* of communication. Here, communication is an activity in motion or action, see Figure 2.3.

Wood (2004) has expressed the equation presented in Figure 2.3 as *we cannot 'not' communicate*. In this understanding human actions and human communicative actions (Figure 2.3) are seen as structured. Structuring elements that guide human communication can, for example, be provided through work or they can be guided by a system such as the organisational system of a workplace. But communication is not only about *action;* it is also

---

Communication becomes a systematic or structured process in which individuals or people interact through symbols to create interpretive meanings.[64]

Figure 2.2 A Definition of Communication

> human communication = communicative action

Figure 2.3 Communication as Communicative Action

about *symbols*.[65] Symbols are representatives of things. The most relevant set of symbols is *language*.[66] Communication has been seen as transferring or transmitting symbols. This is understood to occur in two main ways: Any *transmission* of messages relates to message-*senders* (i) and message-receivers (ii). As a message is sent by one and received by the other, both also engage in a process called *encoding* and *decoding*. Both focus on efficiency and accuracy as expressed in the *process or transmission model* of communication. In this model, the medium – the technical or physical means of converting a message – occurs in three ways.

While the first element (i) in Table 2.5 as outlined above is based on human interaction, the third element (iii) relates to purely technical transmission tools. The second element (ii) is concerned with production of *meaning* focusing on how messages interact with people in order to produce meaning. This is the task of *semiotics* as it is concerned with how messages are constructed in order to gain meaning through interpretation. However, most crucial is the meaning of the message, not the form in which it is conveyed (i–iii). Despite different forms of transmitting information and messages, the core issue of communication remains one of *meaning*. Communication in the human world conveys *meanings*. The world of meaning has to be socially constructed. In communication meaning does not exist by itself as it has no intrinsic value itself, nor can it be located *inside* itself or be seen as a built-in element of experiences. Instead, meaning has to be created and established between people who communicate. This is done through the communicative exchange of people's experiences. This process of establishing meaning occurs communicatively. Ultimately, we communicate to establish meaning and to understand the meaning of what managers and co-workers say etc.

This occurs at an elementary level. At the very base of all communication lies the principle concept of two or more actors communicating with each

Table 2.5 The Conveying of Messages

No.	Media	Description
(i)	*presentational*	human interactions by voice, face, body and the like
(ii)	*representational*	books, prints, paintings, organisational charts, annual reports, etc.
(iii)	*mechanical*	such as telephones, radio, videos, e-mail[67]

other. Communication is an establishment of a relationship between two actors under certain conditions. These conditions come into play (a) when there is a strong attraction between two actors, (b) when there is an object of importance to at least one actor, or (c) when an object has joint relevance to both actors. If one of these conditions is constituted, communication is established. This is shown in a basic linear *sender → receiver* model:

Figure 2.4 The Linear Sender-Receiver-Model

In Figure 2.4 communicating a message is shown to be a linear process where the message moves from (S) to (R). Receiving a message, however, is not a passive activity of the receiver who has to act in a specific way to establish communication. (R) needs to be active in order to make a message (M) one that is understood. Anything is what it is because someone engages in an act of understanding it that way. Communication cannot be established without anyone's active and cognitive participation. Receiving a message is linked to the active act of listening. This means the receiver has to make some sort of conscious effort to hear or *to attend closely*. Hence, communication always demands an activity by at least two agents. While the basic form of communication lies in the act of one actor sending a message and another one receiving it, the receiver's ability to *accept* or *reject* a message is crucial to the concept of communication. We understand a speech act when we know what makes it acceptable. Communication is established only through the double act of sending and accepting/rejecting. The willingness to accept a statement is a fundamental property of all communication.

Communication is not established by a simple S → or by an equally simple → R, but by an act that involves three core entities that have to come into play: (a) one actor (S) needs to send something; (b) the message (M) has to be transmitted; and (c) the other actor (R) has to receive the message and needs to signal whether it is accepted or rejected. As long as we acknowledge that communication between S and R on the whole is conducted with sincere intentions, i.e. people have a valid foundation for what they are saying, communicative actors are willing to present their reasons for saying something if asked to do so. This turns out to be reliable in most cases and as a consequence, communication between S and R can be established. Communication is not a one-way structure between *sender* and *receiver*. It moves between them demanding active participation in the process. Communication can only be established in a two-way process where the receiver has to signal rejection/acceptance back to the receiver. Therefore, the communication figure moves from S → M → R towards S → M ← R that *includes* returning feedback. This two-way communication that operates with feedback can be expressed as: S/R⇆R/S where the sender also becomes a receiver and the receiver becomes a sender. When this process is completed, a *two-way* communication has been established.

To understand human communication, the idea of *feedback* is absolutely crucial as it tells the sender whether a message (M) is accepted or rejected and even more so, how to adjust to the communicative needs of the receiver. But when actors communicate, they do more than simply establish feedback. Communicative action between sender (S) and receiver (R) also serves as a coordinating mechanism in which social interactions are framed. When messages are exchanged between S and R, a social relationship between them is simultaneously established. Hence, communicative action can be seen as an interaction of at least two subjects capable of speech and action who establish *interpersonal* relations. Therefore, communication always includes a *message* as well as a *social relationship* element. We use specific gestures, signs, and words to establish the relationship content of communication.[68] For instance, the simple word *'hello'* has no meaning in itself and no content but it is important for the establishment of social relations between R and S (Habermas 1995:69). Communication experts have explained non-meaning words such as 'hello' and words with meaning by categorising them into two groups:

Table 2.6 Two Elements of Communication

A) Locutionary / Performative	B) Illocutionary
How things stand, state of affairs	No prepositional content & no meaning, cf. *hello*
Assertive sentence	Performative sentence
Meaning, sense, reference, true & false	Force / felicitous, attempt to reach uptake
Prepositional Content	Inter-subjectivity & Inter-personal
Cognitive use of language	Interactive use of language
Themes as prepositional content	Assist to regulate speech acts

Table 2.6 shows these two categories as (A) locutionary or performative messages and (B) illocutionary messages. Communication through the transfer of messages (A) is designed as assertive sentences directed towards true-false responses,[69] while illocutionary communication (B) is designed to direct sentences towards the establishment of a relationship between S and R. Communication philosopher Gadamer summed this up as *speaking* does not belong into the domain of the *'I'* but in the sphere of the *'We'*. The communicative behaviours displayed in a genuine conversation are not the products of a mind working individually. *Our acts of communication are co-created by both of us acting and reacting to each other.*[70] Any communication between S and R always needs to include the relationship and the message-transferring element. Gadamer's philosophy of communication puts equal relevance to the communicative process as well as to the message-transferring element.

Communication at level A is about *what is said* (M), while communication at level B is about establishing a social relationship. Any communication between S and R always includes elements of A and B as we express our external world as a state of affairs (A) while simultaneously establishing a social relationship at an inter-personal level (B). When S and R communicate, they engage in norm-governing action as they coordinate their expectations through feedback. They also incur certain commitments from each other during the communicative action (R/SDS/R). This is what renders communication intelligible. Hence, mutual understanding between R/SDS/R entails not only a certain level of commitment between actors but also a level of accountability that is inherent in communication between R/SDS/R. At this stage, a message (M) can be distinguished by reflecting on M's two core elements: (a) *how* M is transmitted and (b) *what* M contains. This can be expressed as:

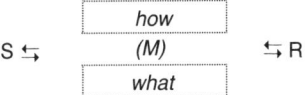

Figure 2.5　How and What is Communicated

Figure 2.5 places an emphasis on the two elements that all messages include. It shows that not only is communication a communicative act between actors that always establishes a communicative relationship but messages themselves are exposed to *how* and *what* is communicated.

The relationship between *how* (a) and *what* (b) is based on the fact that we listen with our ears but also with our eyes as we see gestures, expressions, and postures. These expressions can be equalising but they can also build or maintain hierarchies. Actors communicate symmetrically when non-hierarchical communication is established and asymmetrically in hierarchical communication. As all communication establishes a relationship that contains a *content* message (what) and a *relationship* message (how), human communication also seeks to minimise differences between communicators. A communicative process is *symmetrical* when differences are minimised and communicative relationships become *complementary*. Under symmetrical conditions, each communicative actor wants the other to say something with an intention of gaining acceptance and understanding as an exercise of difference-minimisation. In work related settings, *complementary* communication exists when management gives out orders and labour *is happy* to follow them (Watzlawick, Beavin, Jackson 1967). In Watzlawick, Beavin, and Jackson's (1967) example, forms of communication that rely on *giving out orders* maximise differences inasmuch as they clearly communicate the difference between labour (order-receiver) and management (order-giver).

In addition to communication where one person is speaking and the other is being spoken to, symmetrical or asymmetrical communicative relationships can also include persons present but uninvolved. This next stage of our understanding of communication in the S⇆R model also includes *others* that can take part in communication. The basic structure of such communication is seen in an inter-subjective relationship between S and R. In this model P represents persons and (^{n}) an unlimited number of them. Persons (P^n) are present and forced to have the intentional responsibility to participate actively or passively. In a communicative process that seeks to reach common understanding, P^n are core to the understanding of communication. Consequently, the simple S⇆R and S⇆M⇆R model is now enhanced to:

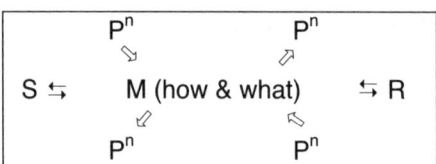

Figure 2.6 Communication with other Participants (P^n)

Figure 2.6 shows that communication in the P^n-model is primarily between S and R. P^n takes an active role and responsibility to understand. As in the S-R model, the key to the P^n-model is the establishment of meaning. Here, meaning not only depends on *what* is communicated between S⇆R and *how* this is done but also how P^n makes sense of it. In short, whether communication is conducted between S and R as a linear or feedback model or with the participation of P^n, the core element of communication lies in the way meaning is constructed. This construction of meaning does not only relate to the social and communicative relationship between S and R but also to the real or objective environment or context in which meaning is established between subjects.

Communication and contextual meaning

Philosophical thinking which originated in Greece and re-appeared with modernity's post-medieval philosopher *Rene Descartes* has been split into *subject* and *object*. Arising from *Husserl's* phenomenology and *Gadamer's* hermeneutics, meaning always takes place as an interaction between subject and object. It is not a product of an individualistic consciousness waiting to be discovered but a process in which a person – the subject – connects a sign or message – the object – to a context.[71] In organisational terms, such *contexts* are constructed from events that take place at work. The events that create the context also have a historical component that extends to workers, work, workplaces, or firms, corporations, and the like. All of them set parameters that shape interpretations and the construction of meaning. Therefore, meaning can never be simply present in a sign.[72] To understand the meaning of a sign, we must enter into a communicative relationship with the sender.[73] This is the essence of the hermeneutic approach. Meaning is not fixed somewhere but created through the interaction of people. It is not a commodity that can be possessed and traded. According to Gass and Seiter (1999:26) *meanings are in people, not in words*. Meaning is however *reproducible* and *self-identical* in all instances of repetition as communication without an identical reproduction of meaning is hardly possible.[74] Meaning without reference to something or some situation does not exist. The *situation* and *context* of a message fundamentally determine the meaning of the message. In order for a receiver to correctly understand a sender's message, both the sender's and the receiver's understanding of the situation must overlap to a sufficient extent. Communication means reaching understanding with someone about something in a *communication-in-a-situation* setup. Therefore, there is no meaning without context.

Meaning in communication is neither conveyed *through* communication, nor is it the product of individual interpretation or an objectively existing entity outside of social interaction. Communication is not simply a vehicle for information, but rather the very process that establishes meaning. For that, meaning demands context. Such contexts refer to where communication occurs and which interpretive frameworks are used to make sense of the communicative exchange. Context is vital to any understanding of communication as it shapes our interpretations. There cannot be meaning without context nor can communication be isolated from a communicative context. We create and establish context through communication and it is this context through which we communicate. We also use and rely on these contexts. Messages are interpreted through contexts and used to change them. The process of establishing sense-making or meaning depends largely on the context in which a message is received because symbols can change their meaning by moving from one context to another. In the context of labour, wages and salaries are the sole means of existence while in the context of business they are seen as a mere business expense. The same message (wages and salaries) changes its meaning by moving from one context – labour – to another – management. Possibilities of misunderstandings open up immediately depending on the context or the domain in which a message is created and to which context or domain it is transferred.

However, contextual understanding also includes another dimension. While meaning is contextual, it is also closely related to relationships as the meaning of a message is not only understood by its context but also by the relationship established between S$\leftrightarrows$R. In the case of wage and salary negotiations for example, the relationship between management and labour can define not only how a message such as a wage claim is received but also the very outcome of such communication. It can be a struggle over wages and salaries between management and labour or simply an agreement such as a commonly agreed wage. In this context *how* a receiver understands a message and *how* feedback that returns to the sender is understood is often essential for an understanding. The process of converting a message into meaning is called *coding*. A *code* is a system of meaning consisting of signs such as words that are common to members of a domain or sub-domain.[75]

The coding of word-signs inside specific domains is not a new invention. It dates back to ancient Greek mythology. The prime communicative problem in Greece was not so much related to what happens in the *mind* of a Greek God or the *minds* of Greek mortals such as peasants, labourers, slaves, masters, etc. but how to convey the wishes of the Gods to the mortals. This was the role of Hermes who was assigned the task of understanding the discourse from the God-*domain* and to articulate understanding in the very different mortals-*domain*. Hermes' domain-specific understanding and ability to transfer messages between domains was represented in the *labour* and *effort* required to understand meaning in one place and time (God-domain) and articulate it in a different place and time (mortal-domain). The domain concept is fundamental to communication – as much in ancient Greek as in modern versions of communication between any other domains.

The overwhelming amount of today's communication, including the creation of meaning, is not coming from the domain of the Gods. Today, most communication occurs inside and between human domains. As an example, communication can be an exchange among adults in the adult-to-adult domain. It can also occur in the children-domain, parents-domain, family-domain, school-domain, or the work-domain. In the same way meaning is constructed in the management or the worker domain. All construction of meaning in specific domains is socially constructed and for the most part such meaning construction has a social history. According to Thompson (1990:21):

> *the object domain of social-historical [existence] is a pre-determined domain in which processes of understanding and interpretations take place as a routine part of the everyday lives of the individual who, in part, make up this domain.*

Domain specific codes feature as an assignment of labels, jargons, terminologies, and signs with a specific meaning.[76] Usually, members of a domain identify themselves as members in symbolic terms expressed as representations of domain maintenance. These symbolic expressions can experience commonly agreed alterations and also provide linkages inside the domain as well as between different domains. Therefore, domain specific *coding* consists of rules or conventions that determine how and in what context these signs are used.[77] Schramm (1954) has expressed the process of coding as '*en'*-coding and '*de'*-coding.[78]

The model expressed in Figure 2.7 shows that a message is sent and received by a sender/receiver but does not focus on the technicality of sending/receiving or the message itself but on how messages are interpreted by sender and receiver. In Figure 2.7 both sender (S) and receiver (R) are seen as interpreters.

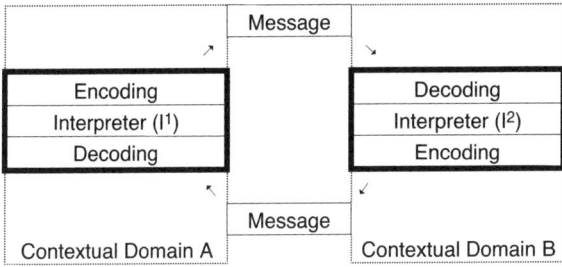

Figure 2.7 Encoding/Decoding through Interpretation

Crucially, messages have to be interpreted by both in order to establish meaning. This process occurs in two somewhat separate domains (A & B). Seen in the singular view of interpretive rationality, meaning construction becomes a process of two different interpretive rationalities that operate in two different domains.

The rather simple S⇆R-model views feedback as an add-on. This model is somewhat rudimentary because it focuses on linear back and forth communication. A more sophisticated model needs to involve *feedback*. Because of its importance to the process of communication, feedback needs to assume a central position. This feedback model also focuses strongly on the interpretive element of messages. Once a message is received in a domain, the feedback model demands that the message be *decoded*. Members (I^1 & I^2) of the domain do so by linking it to the social environment (X) of the frame of reference in which the interpreter is located. According to Newcomb (1953), the I^1-I^2-X system assumes that internal relations are interdependent. If I^1 changes I^2, then the social environment (X) will also change. If I^1 changes the relationship to X, I^2 will have to change the relationship to either I^1 or X. Crucial to the Newcomb model is that I^1 and I^2 are linked to an interpretative environment in which they interpret messages but also change the environment by doing so.

We can only understand a message or create meaning by relating it to something other than the message itself – the context (X). Communication is therefore seen as a process that establishes meaning by creating signs or words that connect to a context. Members of a communicative domain need to share a certain understanding of a code. The more members of domain A or B share this code, the more they understand each other inside their domains. Unlike the rather simplistic R⇆S model, interpretative encoding-decoding models do not operate with singular arrows (→) as they are not linear and never operate as an A-to-B one-way street. Instead they concentrate on analysing the structural set of relationships that convey meaning to a message (M). The contextual domain inside which messages, signs or words are linked to an often domain specific context in order to become meaningful can be expressed as follows:[79]

32 Management Communication

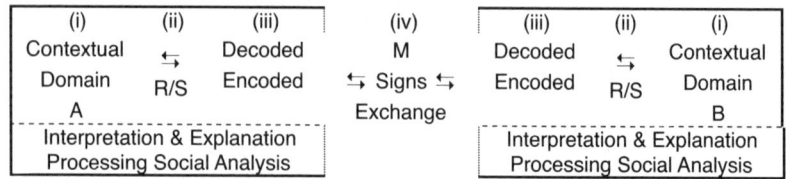

Figure 2.8 Contextual Domains and Contextual Understanding

Generally, the approach taken in Figure 2.8 sees the creation of meaning not in a word, sign or message (M) but in the people who have to construct meaning (i–iii). Meaning is not created by the simple reception of a word, sign or message (iv) but through the contextually based (i) process of de/encoding (iii). Meaning of a message (M) received from the exchange domain is constructed at the levels (i) to (iii) by en/decoding it while connecting M to *a priori* established contextual *interpretation*. Such an interpretation often takes on the form of an analysis that processes social affairs or relationships. Therefore, the process of decoding is in some ways a journey into the depths of interpretation linking the message to the *a priori* history. In sum, interpretation is seen as a process by which actors make sense of their socially constructed reality. This process is philosophically expressed as hermeneutics.

In the contextual domain of (A) *context* is seen as the entire field of experiences that is related to communication. However, complications can emerge as individuals have somewhat different experiences and may therefore establish slightly different meanings in relation to the same signs. In a rather simplistic everyday statement this is often expressed as *things can mean different things to different people*. In the reality of communication, this is impossible. However, these *different people* are in fact connected to a context that is in turn connected to society or domains. Communication among people is not possible when *different things mean different things to different people*.[80] It is only possible when there are overlapping meaning structures, overlapping domains, overlapping interpretations, and overlapping signs.

All communication among people (S/R) seeks to establish common meaning or understanding. The understanding of contents (messages) by S/R pursues connections that link *surface structures* of new sign formations to a structure of already established, i.e. *familiar,* formations in a given context.[81] It is familiarity that makes us communicate with one another, not the meaning of different things that apply to different people. Only this familiarity enables sender and receiver to communicate and understand each other.

Human communication is based on contextual understanding in such a way that different things can never mean different things to different people.[82] Sender and receiver send signals and interpret signs based on a *common* contextual understanding. Members of a society simultaneously externalise their own existence into the social world and internalise the social world as an objective reality because to be part of a society means to participate in society at a dialectic level, i.e. linguistically in the form of communication. *Linguistics* seeks to describe this by examining the actual structures of human communication.[83] *Interactive socio-linguistics* teaches us that people draw on a contextual domain that combines a multitude of variables such as age, class, gender, etc. in order to establish an interpretive framework to build an assumptive frame of reference. As an individual is not born a member of a society or domain but becomes one, a process of *socialisation* via induction and participation in societal dialectic is necessary.[84]

This process of socialisation is absolutely essential to social existence. *It would be impossible to develop a set of words or sentences whose meaning remained relatively independent from specific contexts of use* (Heath 2003:18). Hence, all signs have some common meaning as all humans also have somewhat similar experiences. The very essence of communication – reaching understanding – is an inherent *telos* of communication. Otherwise human communication would hardly be possible. Our ability to construct meaning through thought is enshrined in our ability to operate a set of signs based on a common, if not universally agreed, meaning. These signs only acquire meaning through the role they play in certain social contexts.

Contextual meaning cannot be disconnected from an understanding that is located in the historical process, as knowledge without *a priori* knowledge is almost impossible. Any knowledge we receive has a history and is placed in a historical context. Secondly, meaning is constructed linguistically in a context and thirdly, meaning is only possible in an active engaging relationship between S and R. Hence, meaning can only be established dialectically in a relationship that involves at least two active participants who are placed in a historical context using linguistic signs, i.e. language, to communicate and interpret meaning in a context. Since any understanding among communicative participants is only possible in this historical, linguistic, and dialectical context, a totally correct or absolute perfect understanding is almost impossible to find as our understanding depends on domain specific and contextual interpretation. This cannot be disconnected from linguistically transmitted messages in an historical context that is understood via an active and dialectical process. Any understanding of a sign including the construction of meaning is only possible within this framework. It is this framework that makes signs meaningful.

3
Communication II: Signs and Meanings

Signs are used to construct meaning in a contextual domain. This domain is essential for the creation of meaning. Meaning always carries *connotations*. According to philosopher *Barthes* (1967) *connotations* are essential for meaning. No connotation means that no communication takes places. Kant (1781:8) has explained this in his famous statement *there can be no doubt that all our knowledge begins with experience*. This strongly applies to Barthes' connotations. Even before we receive a sign, *a priori* knowledge has already been established. Hence all signs we receive include the process of *connotations*. The creation of meaning is essentially *posteriori*. In the words of Kant (1781:8) even *empirical knowledge is made up of what we receive through impressions*. In essence, *facts do not speak for themselves* but they meet through the process of connotation.[85] Meaning construction can only take place in a domain through *a priori* knowledge.

Signs such as IR, HRM, OB, or PRP are meaningless unless they go through the same process of de/encoding to establish meaning in contextual domains based on *a priori* knowledge. Kant (1781:13) has emphasised that receptivity or the capacity to receive (S/R) representations (signs) occurs through a specific mode which is determined by our existence as we communicate what we are. Therefore, communication is always subjective. Our individual sensory receptiveness affects the way in which we receive and understand objects. In short, we use our human senses to experience the world. Objects or signs are given to us by means of individual sensory perception. We understand the world around us literally *through our senses*. Understanding and experience go through our senses creating understanding from which more sophisticated concepts arise. It is the process of what goes through our senses linked to the conceptual understanding of objects and signs that makes what we call empirical. In contrast, the undetermined object of an empirical intuition is called appearance. The Kantian notion that the mind is a creative contributor to the construction of knowledge about the world is essential (Mumby 2000:79).

In short, signs such as *IR* or *HRM* are mere appearances of sensational objects. Understanding only takes place when empirical meaning in the form of *a priori* knowledge is attached to it. We develop conceptual understanding of the IR/HRM signs only when we add understanding to both.

Table 3.1 Three Stages of Fixing Meaning

Stages	Elements
the first stage	an actor only anticipates the behaviour of the other
the second stage	an actor begins to anticipate another actor's interpretation
the third stage	the meaning of a sign is permanently fixed in the mind of an actor

In short, a statement such as *the fact of HRM* in itself is – even if received as a sign – meaningless until we create meaning and understanding through the process of merging the sign with *a priori* knowledge through the process of contextual understanding. But meanings can also become fixed when rules for the proper use of a sign are established and an actor not only accepts it as true but also follows it. If actors not only accept HRM as true but also follow the concept and alter their behaviour, then the meaning of the sign HRM is fixed. The establishment of rules that fix meaning can occur in three stages.

Table 3.1 shows that at the first stage an actor only anticipates the behaviour of the other actor. For example, labour tries to anticipate the behaviour of management. At the second stage, the actor begins to anticipate the other's interpretation of a gesture. At this stage labour anticipates management's interpretation of, let's say, *the calling for strike action*. At the third stage, an actor can assume the role of the other actor. Through this imaginary process the actor is able to predict if an act (*strike*) may or may not succeed. This depends on whether the other actor (*management*) interprets the message (*strike*) in the way intended. In assuming management's position, labour is able to understand whether or not a sign – such as a strike or the threat of a strike – is understood by management in the way it was intended to be understood. Only when labour has established all three stages of the sign 'strike', it is able to fix *strike* in the mind of management and only then labour has fully understood how signs such as 'strike' work and consequently can make full use of them.

Overall, the science of meaning or semiotics refers to three core elements: (i) *sign*, (ii) *code*, and (iii) *domain*. Signs (i) are, for example, words like labour, strike, etc. A comprehensive *code* or system (ii) is required to understand which signs or words can be used to meet labour's communicative needs. For example, the IR code is a system of signs used to describe the relationship between labour and management while the HRM code is a system of signs used by management to integrate workers into the system of work and so on. Finally (iii) a *domain* is required inside which the codes and signs operate as a reflection on their users. In other words, the meaning of a sign can never be simply located inside a word.

A sign can only be understood as a position between speakers and listeners. Creation of meaning is an act located between two acting agencies.[86] It can only be realised in a process of active and responsive understanding

i)	sign	can be a word like *strike*
ii)	reference	such as the withdrawal of labour from the production process (meaning)
iii)	context	One actor's context (A) of a sign results in different meaning to another actor's context (B)
	↳ (A)	management: → *strike* indicates the loss of working days and interruption of production
	↳ (B)	labour: → *strike* indicates struggle for better working conditions and wages

Figure 3.1 Sign, Reference and Context

that includes (i) a sign, (ii) a code/reference, and (iii) a context or domain. As shown in the example, communication and the creation of meaning depend on three elements above.

Figure 3.1 shows that communication takes place through the relationship between sign, reference, and the external reality as a necessity for meaning. A sign such as the word '*strike*' can take on different meanings depending on different contexts/domains (A & B). For example, for a member in one domain, the word *strike* can relate to *working days lost* while the same sign might relate to *better working conditions* in another domain.[87] In each case both user and recipient of the sign need to interpret it based on the domain's context.

The mental process of encoding and decoding is conducted by an interpreter of a sign and signs like the word *strike* are never fixed or systematically defined. Hence, the meanings of a sign may vary within limits according to the experience of the user and the context in which the sign is used. In short, decoding has to be conducted actively and creatively. It largely depends on the contextual domain in which the sign is produced, understood and used. However, the interpretation of a sign is not a linear process. It is a dialectical process in which thesis, anti-thesis, and synthesis come into play. The dialectical interpretation of signs not only establishes meaning but also changes the interpretive environment of a domain.

In fact, the interpretation of a sign or word such as *strike* encounters a two-sided act. *Those who* use the word determine its meaning but meaning is also determined by *those for whom* the word is designed to be understood. In the case of the word *strike*, *those who* use the word are located in domain A while *those for whom* the word is used reside in domain B. The word *strike* is always the product of a reciprocal relationship between the speaker in domain A and the listener in domain B or addresser (A) and addressee (B). Strike, like any other word, expresses the relationship of *one* domain to the *other* in a territory that is shared by both addresser and addressee. It always reflects a social inter-relationship that constitutes an atmosphere in which the meaning of a word or sign is constructed. Only the relationships between domain A and B as well as the borders between them determine the meaning of the sign. The stronger, the more organised, and the more developed each domain is, the more vivid and coherent can the meaning of a sign be constructed and shaped. The sign *strike* can be further discussed by using three core concepts of meaning.

Table 3.2 Intention, Literal Meaning, and Utterance

No.	The Three Elements
i)	the *intention* of meaning as what is meant
ii)	*literal* meaning as from a perspective of what is said
iii)	*utterance* meaning as from the perspective of use

Table 3.2 shows three different elements of meaning. It can be intentional, literal, or linked to a perceived usage of a sign that may differ depending on the domain in which it is formulated and used. As Russian communication theorist Volosinov (1929:96) wrote, *the production processes of labour and the processes of commerce know different forms for constructing utterances*. The conditions that shape intentions, literal meaning and the usage of a sign are different depending on the conditions in the two existing domains, the managerial and commercial domain of the *production process* and the domain of the *labour process*. Under the domain specific contexts meanings can be constructed in three ways, one of which is instrumental rationality that is directed towards goal-achieving means-ends. The managerial domain predominantly targets this version. In the labour domain meaning is primarily established through communicative rationality, directed towards *reaching understanding* and truth. In this domain reaching understanding suggests a rationally motivated agreement among participants that is measured against validity claims. The rationality of an argument and its validity needs to be exposed to criticism.

In the management domain the intentional meaning of *strike* can be received (i) as a sign for a strategic threat to profit, in literal meaning (ii) as a strategy that threatens production, while the strategic use-meaning (iii) is to put pressure on management. In the labour domain, the same word takes on quite a different meaning that is communicatively established and directed towards truth. The truth direction is established by reaching mutual understanding among labour. The *intentional* meaning of a strike is to establish a common interest among labour, thus enhancing solidarity inside their domain. The *literal* meaning is to stop working as a temporary exit from exploitation to level the asymmetric power relationship between management and labour (use-meaning). This can be shown as follows:

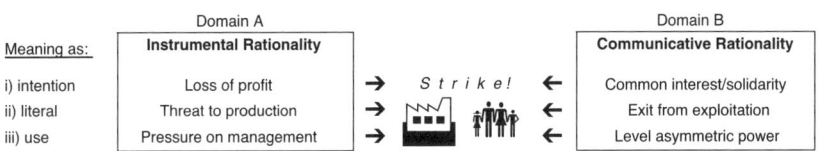

Meaning as:	Domain A Instrumental Rationality		Domain B Communicative Rationality
i) intention	Loss of profit	→ *S t r i k e!* ←	Common interest/solidarity
ii) literal	Threat to production	→ ←	Exit from exploitation
iii) use	Pressure on management	→ ←	Level asymmetric power

Figure 3.2 Three Meanings of One Sign in Two Domains

Table 3.3 Strike as Signifier and Signified

	Sign as	Form and Content
a)	Signifier	A cardboard with painted writings of *Strike*.
b)	Signified	As a mental concept of *withdrawal of work from a production process*.

Figure 3.2 depicts how the meaning of the same sign *'strike'* differs quite substantially under intentional, literal, and use meaning. While the sign may create these different meanings, it is by no means as simple as seeing the sign from three perspectives. According to *Saussure* (1906–13), a *sign* is not only a physical object – such as a worker holding up a cardboard with the words *We are on strike* written on it (Figure 3.2), but has two crucial elements attached to it: it is (a) a *signifier* and (b) *signified*. The *signifier* is the image we receive as the physical existence of the object or sign, while *signified* is the mental concept or meaning of the sign.

Key to understanding Table 3.3 is that *signifier* and the *to be signified* are not the same. The mental concept is created in our minds once we are exposed to a signifier. It is obvious that a sign like a word or the signifier changes from *language* to language but it remains a fallacy to assume that the signified or mental concept or the meaning of *strike* stays the same. For example, a strike can mean the withdrawal of labour for *economic* purposes such as to gain better wages and conditions (Great Britain), while in another language it could mean the withdrawal of labour for *social* reason to secure better pensions (Italy) or *political* reason to change a government (France). Similarly, the signifier *Works Council* could have the significance of worker-based co-determination at shop floor level, while in another language it signifies the mental concept of damaging shop floor unionism.

In other words, the meaning of a signifier relates to different mental concepts established inside a structured relationship. IR or HRM are such structured relationships. Mental concepts of the signified are developed to assist us in dividing up reality and categorise it so that we can understand it. People develop *signifiers* and mental concepts that *signify* them. They are *socially constructed* and part of the linguistic and semiotic system that members of a domain use to communicate with each other. For example, a term such as *industrial relations* has been developed as a semiotic system that allows members of a domain (managers, union members, etc.) to communicate. Later the counter-signifying concept of HRM has been developed to provide a separate mental framework that applies to the same signifier. The signifier *'strike'* can relate to different mental concepts depending on its relation to the mental concept of HRM or IR.

Since the first strikes took place during the rapid industrialisation of the 18th century, today a somewhat different semiotic system has developed. In current work regimes HRM is seeking to overlay the mental concept that

Communication II: Signs and Meanings 39

made *strike* into what it was meant to be.[88] It allows members of the work domain to communicate by using a different set of signified mental concepts. Fundamentally, the signifier has shifted from IR to HRM along with a shift of the adjacent mental concept. This has established a move away from the signified *relationship* between management and labour. The new mental concept signifies *the top-down management of labour*, now renamed *human resources*. This has not been a neutral or value free process as the mental concept of signified(s) and the physical existence of a signifier are made – or made-up – by people determined by the domain to which they belong. In this case, the mental make up of the management domain seeks to shift the mental concept of a *relationship* towards the hierarchical concept of management. A sign can only be created when the *signified* and the *signifier* are linked (Saussure 1906–13). Accordingly the signifier *HRM* and its signified mental concept of *the management of human resources* establish meaning through a relationship to other domain specific signs.

Saussure (1906–13) examined the way in which a sign creates meaning via a relation to another sign called *value*. Value primarily determines meaning. In other words, the sign *HRM* is meaningless unless it relates to other signs. As an example, HRM needs to relate to three signs – (i) *human*, (ii) *resource* and (iii) *management*. The meaning of a sign is the result of dynamic interactions between sign, interpreter, and object. Signs are always historically located. HRM as a sign was meaningless in 1920. There was no signifier and no signified. In contrast, IR had been established as a sign in the year 1920 and with it a signified mental concept. These signs have been linked to history and their meaning changed over time. This has been observed in the case of IR, HRM, management, labour, capitalism, or the market economy.

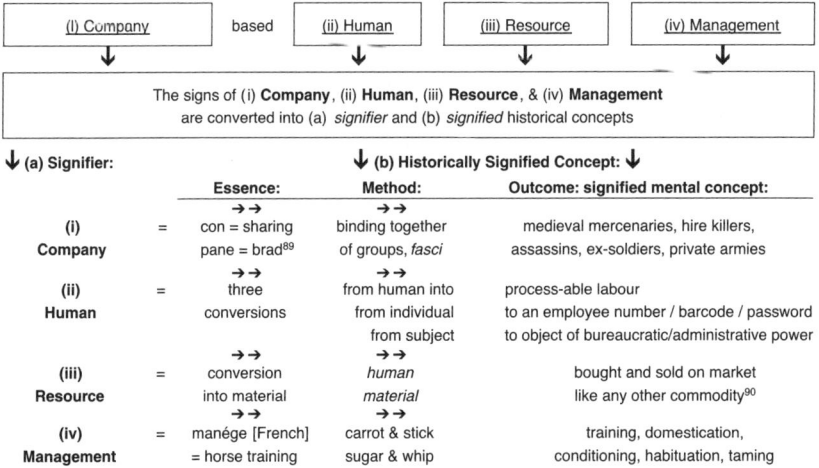

Figure 3.3 Four Signifiers and their Historic Signifying Mental Concepts

The changes of signs, signifier, and signified can be shown as a Figure (3.3) using the company term *Human Resource Management*. This statement has four elementary signs: (i) company, (ii) human, (iii) resource, and (iv) management. These four signifiers carry connotations to four relevant signifying mental concepts that have a long history.

Figure 3.3 makes visible the hidden historical concepts that signify the simple statement of *company based HRM*. The mental concept that lies deep beneath the term *company HRM* is a division of two signs – company[(i)] & HRM[(ii–iv)] – into its *signifier* and *signifying* components which reveals that *company HRM* carries strong connotations of bread-sharing mercenaries bound together in groups – the *fasci* – who are bought and sold on the market like any other commodity.

Once bought, these commodities were domesticated like horses on a training ground. The French word *manége* still carries the '*to manage*' in it. A conditioning process is applied where the commodity is conditioned like a horse, a dog, or a rat. In today's terms, modern company HRM still carries these connotations as humans are bound together in companies that carry significant militaristic structures of order giving from a military hierarchy, from the general's office to the corporate head quarter etc. Humans are still treated as numbers, having been converted into objects of power. They are still domesticated – only this is today called *to be managed*. All this occurs in a place representative of a *manége*, today called *workplace*. Finally, the stick and carrot has been replaced by money and power or in HRM terms: performance related pay (PRP), career management, management by objectives (MBO), and so on. Like horses in a *manége*, today's (iii) human material – in German Nazi-language: *Menschenmaterial* – or human resources are conditioned to properly interpret the signs – PRP & MBO, etc. – that are sent out by their HR *horse conditioning master*.

To properly interpret such signs, interpretive rules need to be established. The connection between sign, interpreter and object can be established in three ways.

Table 3.4 shows the three forms that govern interpretations of signs. In the first case of (i) *conventions* or habits it is the regular use that fixes meaning necessary to understand a sign. *Conventions* can be seen as the social affirmation of a sign. This is different to an established rule (ii) or a social agreement about the appropriate use (iii) and response to a sign. For example, the sign *HRM* has an *agreed* meaning of *managing people* while the agreed

Table 3.4 Three Forms and Uses of Sign Interpretation

No.	Forms
(i)	*conventional use,*
(ii)	*rule establishing use,* or
(iii)	*agreement* among users

meaning of the *IR* sign is that of *relationships of people at work*. Meaning, in other words, always depends on the *negotiation* of a sign between sender and receiver. Signs – like facts – do not speak for themselves. Their meaning has to be created. This applies to signs such as HRM as much as to all other signs used in the world of work.

Both facts and interpretations depend on an outside reality that is socially constructed. Searle (1969) divides (ii) rules that govern a relationship between sign and meaning as either *regulative* or *constitutive*. *Regulative rules* exist independent of their use, just like etiquette that regulates inter-personal relationships. In contrast, *constitutive rules do not merely regulate, they create or define new forms of behaviour* (Searle 1969:33). In Searle's concept of constitutive rules (ii), a sign like *HRM* links to meaning of *managing people* very much in a rule creating way. The HRM sign is not regulative as it does not exist outside of human influence but is constituted and constructed through human interaction. Its meaning is created by management hence it represents a *constitutive rule* that constitutes and by doing so also regulates an activity.

The very existence of HRM is logically dependent on a set of created rules. Without certain rules (ii) attached to the sign of *HRM* by management this sign would not exist. It depends on a (ii) *constitutive rule* that establishes a link between a socially created institution, namely management, and meaning. The creation of such (ii) *constitutive rules* enables a rule creator to establish new forms of behaviour. The social creation of the HRM sign replaced a previous behavioural code of *managing people* under the preceding concept of personnel management with a new and qualitatively different code of behaviour, the code of Human Resource Management. The old connotation of a *dirty tricks department* was substituted by new connotations of managing humans.

Academics and business writers have adopted the new sign of HRM as a kind of social agreement (iii). It was widely agreed that the new code – HRM – serves modern business needs better than the old code of personnel management. Today, the rule-establishing phase (ii) has been completed as there are virtually no business writers or academics left who have not signed up to the new agreement on how to use HRM. HRM is today the only allowable interpretive framework under which signs at work are interpreted. The agreement on how to interpret workplace affairs has been a major step towards a one-dimensional interpretive framework for work. It has established an unquestioned and unchallenged framework that links the socially created sign of HRM to a set of meanings.

The link between social constructions and meaning has been called *connotation*. The idea of connotation is most relevant to an understanding of meaning. Barthes' (1967) concept of *connotation* describes the interaction that occurs when a sign meets the feelings or emotions of the user as well as the values of a domain.[91] In the management domain, the sign HRM might meet the feeling of *managing people*. The same sign however can also create the feeling of a *dirty tricks department* in the labour domain. Connotations can be domain specific and are, in any case, closely associated with denotation. While *denotation* is the mere mechanical reproduction of a sign, *connotation* denotes the human part of the process. According to Fiske (1990:87), *the choice of words is often a choice of connotation – dispute or strike, oiling the wheels of commerce or bribery*. These examples show emotional or subjective connotations, although we have to assume that others in our society share at least part of them, that they are intersubjective. In Fiske's terms, a choice of words does not only relate to the connotations they carry but also to their common use and even to myths about certain words and concepts. In other words, the use of the term *briberies* to imply that they *oil the wheels of commerce* or terms such as *market forces* to imply they *reduce wages to create employment* may turn out to be no more than a myth.

Myths and mythologies

Myths occur when imaginary entities obscure the real relationships of human activity. They are links or associations between the imaginative and the real. Such connotations, French philosopher Barthes (1967) notes, are more socially than personally determined. Myths are social, not individual creations. They are connected to contextual understanding that is domain specific and cannot be determined individually. This has led to Barthes' concept of explaining meaning, the concept of *myth*.

A myth is a type of speech. Language needs special conditions in order to form a myth. In its original meaning a myth is a way in which a domain uses a story to explain or understand aspects of a *socially constructed* reality.[92] Myths do not just hide things; their function is to conceal, not making something disappear. A myth is a distortion of meaning achieved through stealing and restoring. It is *language-robbery* or the *colonisation* of meaning as language is both communication and an instrument of control. When myths come into play the original meaning of a word is not put back to its initial place but into another place that is motivationally defined. In the use of language *motives* and *motivations* are unavoidable. Myths are created with certain motives in mind, consequently depriving true meanings of their original intent and replacing them with mythical meanings. In communicative terms, myths are able to reach everywhere and corrupt everything.

Myths establish a relationship between *sign* and *meaning*. They obscure the sign's origins and original meaning. This process is designed to mask the political or social dimension of the original sign. Such myths are the product of a social class or a social group that has achieved dominance. Myths are always linked to domination as only certain groups, elites, or classes have the ability and the interest to create them. Myths not only hide their ideological content but also the existence of class relations itself. As Marcuse (1966:10) emphasised

> *if the worker and his boss enjoy the same television program and visit the same resort places, if the typist is as attractively made up as the daughter of her employer, if the Negro owns a Cadillac, if they all read the same news-*

paper, then this assimilation indicates not the disappearance of class, but the extent to which the needs and satisfactions that serve the preservation of the Establishment are shared by the underlying population.

In other words, the sameness of standardised consumption and the adoption of middle class behaviour serve the myth that class relations have ended while in reality there are still those who have to expose themselves to the labour market and those who live off it. But myths do not only eclipse *class*-relations, they also infiltrate *gender*-relations. An all too common myth has been that *women had to stay in the home while the men did the real work and earned the money*. Myths such as these cement gender-relations via a clear division into a male and a female reproduction realm. Even though the existence of modern labour market participation by females exposes the falseness of such myths, they are still being told and retold. These myths not only pre-design women's *natural* place of existence, they also serve as a protection against an analysis of class- or gender-relations.

Myths also act as rampant anti-intellectualism seeking to establish the myth that *there are more evil scientists than good ones, and science causes more problems than it solves*. Intellectualism and scientific discourse – and especially its critical social science version – are exposed to the myth that *refusal 'to go along' appears neurotic and impotent*.[93] How could someone not go along with HRM? Intellectualism that is critical of existing forms of domination – such as class domination, domineered gender relations, HRM, or anti-intellectualism – is hidden behind myths that seek to prevent any intellectual analysis of domination in society or workplaces. Not surprisingly, myths operate strongly against those who challenge the prevailing order. Figure 3.4 shows one of the most common myths about work.

Figure 3.4 illustrates a very common myth that is widely regarded as truthful. In reality however, there is hardly any evidence to support it. In order to portray trade unions negatively, this myth, generated by tabloid papers and corporate mass media, is designed to ideologically cover the truth. The interest of private and corporate mass media vanishes behind the veneer of unsubstantiated accusations. Such myths are proportionally related to the threat that is posed to an established order. The higher or more serious the threat is perceived to be, the more frequent or higher are the myths created about them.[94] Myths are often defined by the *bourgeoisie*, writes Barthes (1957:138–141):

The bourgeoisie is defined as the social class which does not want to be named. Bourgeois, petite-bourgeois, capitalism, proletariat, are the locus of an

---

Our dominant myth of the trade unions is that they are disruptive, hostile to the wider good of the nation, and are generally negative organisations (Fiske 1990:90–96)

Figure 3.4 A Common Myth about Work

unceasing haemorrhage: *meaning flows out of them until their very name becomes unnecessary.*

They are *partly in control of symbols and values* and can therefore communicatively protect their particular interest.[95] The control of myths as part of a controlling exercise for symbols and values is carried through a mediated reality that affects both domains. By spreading representations of myths, symbols, and values over the whole catalogue of collective images for managerial use, corporate media countenances the illusory lack of differentiation of the social classes. In a constant bombardment of false images, popular and popularised myths are beamed into every living, dining, and bedroom. The image of living conditions of the American middle class has become the guiding image for all.[96] Antiseptically, the world of work has been disconnected from the *middle-class = happiness* myth.[97]

For example, when an ordinary typist who earns a mere twenty pounds a month *recognises* or pictures herself in a lavish bourgeois-style wedding, the bourgeois myth achieves its full effect. The process through which the bourgeoisie transforms reality rests in this adoption of bourgeois *ideology* where the reality of a particular world becomes a mere image of *the* world. By creating the myth of a classless society through the separation of socio-economic reality from social existence, an image of reality is created that shifts reality to an illusion by neglecting the socio-economic reality of a socially constructed division of labour. The constructed image appears to be *natural* and in accordance with common sense.[98] The perception of being *natural* occurs in a process of struggle and gradual infiltration or *colonisation* through ideological organisations such as the mass circulated tabloids, privatised radio channels, and corporate TV, published literature and popular science (Zengotita 2005). Mediated in this way a once enlightening characteristic becomes a mere behavioural ideology.

Enlightenment ideas have become incorporated into established forms of ideological practices. In this process, the task of a myth is to create a natural justification or legitimisation of a historical intention to make the division of labour appear continuous and eternal, leading to a loss of historical meaning. The process of *de-historising* dilutes or dissolves any historical context. Humans are made to lose their memories of past experiences. The original struggles over many social achievements are shrouded in myths. The function of such a-historical myths is to disconnect reality from any historical context, manifested in the rise of the modern *depoliticised* mass media.

> *Today, the rational and realistic notion of yesterday again appears to be mythological when confronted with the actual conditions. The reality of the labouring classes in advanced industrial society makes the Marxian 'proletariat' a mythological concept.*[99]

This applies not only to Marxian notions of a proletariat but also carries over into present day realities of many social issues. For instance, the origin of the social welfare state that was founded through labour's collective action is hidden behind common myths. The collective creation of holiday benefits, labour rights, democracy, equal treatment, OHS, wages, the eight-hour working day, weekends, unemployment-, health-, and pension-funds mutually supporting workers has today been successfully hidden behind the myth that these were created by the state. The predominant myth that negates the collective origins of these achievements, funds, and social welfare programmes is constructed in two ways. They are either seen as being part of an overwhelming state bureaucracy that is misused and exploited by some sections of society or, as explained in almost all HRM textbooks,[100] as management's goodwill or corporate benefit.

Today's myths about these achievements do not focus on denying the existence of their origins. However, by simplifying and depoliticising the achievements they are made to appear innocent and natural as an eternal justification. Through the process of constantly emphasising their status as statements of facts, disconnected from labour's collective struggle over two centuries, the true origins remain hidden.

Being disconnected from labour, these myths can only exist and be effective if workers are made to believe in them. Only then are managerial myths able to reconstruct wage-labour as a *fact of life!* As such, myths still have functional and systemic qualities but they are constructed as being unrelated to politics, labour history, or economics as they are made to appear purely functional. Crucially, these myths are often converted from the factual world into the world of belief systems by presenting them as *'I believe'* rather than by saying *'in fact…'* or *'I think…'*. But what does such an apparently trivial decision accomplish? It encases a speaker in *an armour of faith*. If you *think* something you may be mistaken. The idea, for example, that a HR policy is something to be *believed in* rather than to be argued about and rationally accepted or rejected, converts labour-management relations into a communicatively established relationship of faith. People who *believe in* a HR policy might indeed be described as a *faith community* (Poole 2006:39–40). This is further supported by an organisational culture that nurtures a faith-based community.

Today's myth about the relationship between present labour and the origins of labour's achievements are not presented as a relationship based on *truth* but on *use*. Labour's achievements are depoliticised and appear a-historical,[101] reduced to no more than to serving a present need in operational terms.

> *The suppression of this dimension in the societal universe of operational rationality is a suppression of history, and this is not an academic but a political affair…the functional language is a radically anti-historical language: operational rationality has little room and little use for historical reason.*[102]

To hide labour's achievements, mediated and a-historical but operationally legitimised myths become essential.[103] One of the most important elements of the bourgeoisie, writes Barthes (1957:146), is *the fact that it is the bourgeoisie that produces myths. Left-wing myths never reach the immense field of human relationships. Everyday life is inaccessible to it: in bourgeois society, there are no left-wing myths concerning marriage, cooking, the home, the theatre, the law, morality.*[104] Myths are creations that always serve goal-oriented purposes under conditions of instrumental rationality. They are not directed towards truth but towards strategies that serve functional means-ends relations. Labour has only the language of truth and emancipation to oppose societal and managerial myths. This can assist the uncovering of many managerial myths.

Managerial myths do not portray the socially constructed location of work as capitalist enterprises for profit. The myth prefers the more neutral term of *organisation*.[105] Management's colonisation of the world of work occurs via a neutralisation of work by using an engineering ideology transformed into organisational studies, organisational theory, and organisational communication. Managerial myths seek to hide domination and power relations as much as they cloak the historical origins and political forces that underwrite the world of work. Myths are always tempting to those in power as they are in a position to manipulate their fellow human beings at work. Engineering myths seemingly link any social problem to techno-belief-systems. This is done by giving it mythical status so that engineering solutions can be linked up with socially created issues such as HR policies. The creation of this link establishes the myth and simultaneously removes the need to understand the link. The myth of the *social world = engineering world* makes the individual believe that an engineered product such as a computer is equal to a socially created HR policy. Both are made to appear sacred, like a natural process. Because myths are portrayed as sacred they are made to appear unquestionable. This is where the power of the myth takes on its real shape. Put simply, the power of the myth overrides reason and rationality and excludes rational justification for managerial acts. When using myths, management focuses predominantly on four aspects of the organisational myth.

Table 3.5 depicts how organisational myths operate in corporations that are principally seen as sites where technical issues are the main concern. The use of technical language at work masks the need for communicatively established forms of meaning. Understanding and meaning no longer appear as socially constructed but as part of a technological neutrality. Technology is made to appear neutral (a), when in fact the opposite is the case. *No mention is made of the fact that the basis on which technology acquires power over society is the power of those whose economic hold over society is greatest. A technological rationale is the rationale of domination itself* (Adorno & Horkheimer 1944:2).

These techno-rational-domination issues relate to a (b) system of efficiency, productivity, resource allocation, expertise, etc. The myth allows managers to assume a dominant position by articulating all issues with the pretence of (c) a rational framework. Managerial myths are used to reconstruct plausible

Table 3.5 Four Organisational Myths

No.	Organisational Myth
a)	**Rational and Value Neutral** The myth of an *organisation* allows a definitional view provided by management that sees organisations as objects of rationality. Organisations are purely based on instrumental rationality via a combination of managerialism and rationality. This creates a myth that gains an aura of being rational, value neutral and apolitical.
b)	**System and Science** The myth of organisational theory creates a symbiosis between system and science via an exclusion of the socially created origins of the theory. Organisational Theory links de-politicised natural science with the socially structured world of work.
c)	**Rationality and Modernity** The myth of organisational theory allows management to portray organisations as a continuation of a rational system that is consistent with other rational systems. The continued existence of organisations is a clear expression of a consistency that is created by linking organisations to modernity. Modernity, modern organisation, and organisational theory are inseparable. Modern management, modern organisations, and administrative management are a rational manifestation of *Enlightenment* and progress.
d)	**Science and Theory** The myth of organisational theory and organisational studies provides management theorists and their loyal entourage with their most relevant tasks: to design social systems that represent an engineering ideology based on instrumental rationality.[106] As a vital support function to managerialism, organisational theorists who operate within the managerial system rationale are rewarded accordingly as they provide not only a *scientific* basis for management's legitimacy but also an auxiliary occupation essential for corporations that seek to keep the myth of managerialism alive.

histories *after-the-fact* to explain and legitimise managerial power relations. Managers maintain power by framing everything within a techno-rational context, systematically excluding other organisational perspectives, such as politics, power-relationships, and, above all, the socially constructed foundations of the firm. This is supported by a significant scientific body (d) of so-called scientific literature, meetings, conferences, books, institutions, research foundations, research centres, think tanks, journals, books, and so on all of which are geared towards the sole purpose of providing scientific support for managerialism. *Scientific* management is able to find new ways of perfecting means-ends driven initiatives towards the organisational goal of profit making.

The myth of technical rationality provides a means by which structures of power and domination come into existence, are maintained, and reproduced. *Means* become *ends*. The myth offers transparency at a considerable cost and at the same time requires denial and control. Managers are not unaware that their actions are driven by values however they are continuously working towards making them appear value free. In this process, the managerial myths first of all remove all previous values from the managerial process by claiming it to be purely rational, neutral, and driven by means-ends or cost-benefit constructions. Consequently, these myths include two processes. Firstly, management is able to present itself as value free. Secondly, the managerial process of making itself value free is obscured and, somewhat mysteriously, new values as dictated by management are added. In short, the mythical chain of managerial value-myths can be shown as a threefold process:

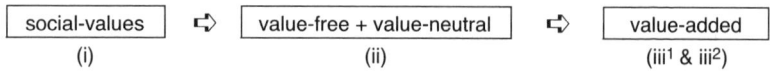

Figure 3.5 The Managerial Value-Myth

What is shown in Figure 3.5 allows managerialism, first of all, to remove all (i) *socially constructed values* – values created by labour even more than those created by society – from the business process. Once their actions have been *ethically cleared* of most societal values, managerial processes are claimed to be (ii) *value free* and *value neutral*, and in a third step they can be filled with new values. In the process of value-adding (iii) two issues come into force (iii^1 & iii^2). Firstly, (iii^1) management can literally add monetary value to the business process. This not only pushes other values aside, it also focuses the organisation on the one-dimensional goal of profit making. Secondly, (iii^2) managerialism and management add *new* values once unwanted values have been deleted. The successful completion of this process adds new managerial values to the corporation which are made to appear normal and universal.

The general and universal appearance of these new values is achieved by keeping managerial knowledge generic and abstract, away from deeper understanding. In this paradigm, any critical understanding of, for example, conflict is removed. Instead, it is portrayed as merely an issue of coordination, management, technicality, or communication, etc. Under the managerial myth, contradictions and conflicts are systemised, routinised, rationalised, and managed by the systematic suppression and distortion of the issue of conflict. The myth of *managed conflict* cloaks underlying structures such as the desire for autonomy, emancipation, humanity, and freedom and replaces them with the surface structure of a simple labour-request for money and better working conditions. While underlying desires are excluded from any contest between labour and management, surface structure expressions such as more money are managed in an engineering fashion. The myth of engineering's natural mechanics is presented as having a *natural* link to managerialism. Concurrent with the mechanics of an engineering ideology, the mechanics metaphor also plays well with the myth of the technical apparatus or machine. It negates the agency of management by dissolving its social actor status and positioning it into an engineering system.

Consequently, corporate policies are declared in a *passive* fashion, such as *it has been decided that*, or *the decision is...* etc. This is done partly to deflect from the complexities and power politics of managerial action, partly to live the myth of managerialism as a naturally given order, and partly to *enhance the mystery and power of the organisational agent*, namely management (Cheney & Carroll 1997:595). The engineering myth applied by management pretends to create a conflict-free environment that is seen as positive. Everyone seeking any disturbance is seen as a system-alien. Management's task is to portray their role as re-establishers of the good system by system-corrective measures that are communicated as *putting out the fires*. It is a remediation that defines management as the only solution to problems that were created by management in the first place but have now been shifted to others or into systems. Management appears as the only agent that can protect us from the evils that it has created and therefore becomes the medium and guarantor for system balancing correctives. *System theory* greatly assists managerial myths of a conflict-free environment by emphasising system stabilising elements geared towards balancing an asymmetrical power relationship.[107] System balancing is levelled above human action and portrayed in a circular machine-like image:

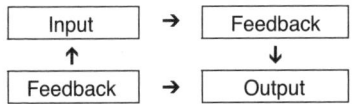

Figure 3.6 System Stabilising Managerialism

As shown in Figure 3.6, automatisms prevail in system stabilising managerialism. By pretending to be the sole agent that guarantees system equilibrium, managerialism is able to engage participants who are designed to play in a never ending vicious circle of systematic behaviour adjustments. This is powerfully supported by the idea of system theory as the medium to organise social reality in a self-controlling and self-balancing, machine-like society and work regime. Accordingly, Luhmann's *social system theory* has *no place for thought, reflective or otherwise, or for individual motivation and intention*.[108] The system approach not only ignores and excludes individual motivation, it also ignores social motivations and what could be termed the political economy of communication in a quest for total system comprehension. This is the system-theory or machine-control of human relations.

Seen as communication at work, the system approach shows a number of shortcomings. Firstly, it treats communication as a mechanical issue derived from the *Copernican* system of planetary movements. Secondly, it relates communication to mechanics. System mechanics constructs this in an unsophisticated act in which human affairs are simply related to each other without any need for reflection, motivation, and intention. This is in sharp contrast to communicating meaning that sets demands towards contextual interpretation. *System,* Roland Barthes once commented, *is the enemy of Man – meaning that the 'Man' of the humanist is all that cannot be analysed and tabulated, all that slips through the net of theoretical enquiry* (Eagleton 1994:3). Inside the system approach communication becomes boxed-in and tabulated. When constructing communication in a mechanical way, communicative subjects disconnected from political or economical issues are viewed as functions. Locating communication inside a managerial engineering ideology follows the operation pattern of a standard kitchen *fridge*. Temperatures are checked and re-checked, machines switched on and off, and cooling systems are activated. In theoretical terms, all this is no more than a rather mindless and, above all, endless circle in which system theory operates.

Inside the world of system theory communication is seen as a cybernetic issue related to information and feedback with the metaphorical image of a refrigerator (Figure 3.6) which serves as a communication balancing device in which information (such as low temperature) is measured by one system element (a pressure gauge) and transferred to another device (the engine) to be measured again and, if required, adjusted. Inside these circular, non-human, non-communicative, self-supporting, self-measuring, and self-system-balancing processes only input-output motions are at the centre of system theory. They transfer engineering notions into human interaction and eclipse asymmetrical power relations at work by viewing them as simple system adjustments or balancing problems. The engineering myth constructs communication as a system function and a system stabilising occurrence. The metaphors used are circular and communication and information flows are only deemed good and useful by management when they serve to stabilise the system. Balance is what the system demands in order to function well. A well operating refrigerator is as good as a well operating company. Each element has its prescriptive position in a world governed by the machine. This self-controlling machine is the symbol of modern management.

Symbols, metaphors, stories & narratives

Apart from myths, *symbols* are commonly used in communication and management is neither an exclusion zone for their use nor is work itself. In the productive as well as in the reproductive domain, symbols are a frequent occurrence and often linked to status, hence the idea of *status symbols*. Some objects have taken on the status of a symbol for something more abstract, such as the object of a Rolls Royce has become the symbol of wealth[109] and an expression of money. Money itself is not a symbol but is transferred to the status symbol of the Rolls Royce that can therefore be seen as a *metaphor*. Metaphors are a form of descriptive language use. They often work in two different ways: when something is either *seen as* or *articulated as* something else. Metaphors do not reveal underlying structures but obscure them by substituting reality with related terminologies.

Inside the world of work the use of metaphors is an attempt to structure labour's daily work experience. For example, the common metaphor of *let your money work* illustrates this. It is obvious that money cannot work – only labour can. The core element here is that this metaphor eclipses the true state of the labour process by pretending that an exchange medium such as money can produce commodities without adding living labour to the process. *Let your money work* hides that people have to be converted into productive labour to produce. This catchphrase portrays something that is impossible. But money is not the only metaphor that is used in the world of work.

Often metaphors derived from the areas of military, machine, family, or natural organisms are used to cover the true character of a corporation. Even communication itself when viewed from inside a business has become a metaphor:

> Its life blood, its oxygen, its brain, its central nervous system, its arteries, the blood lines along which business is transacted, the mortar/glue which binds its parts together, or the fuel which drives the engine.

Figure 3.7 Managerial Metaphors of Corporate Communication

In addition to the body-like expressions of business shown in Figure 3.7, it is, above all, the military metaphor that characterises a firm. The military is a highly structured and formal organisation with chains of command. It functions through obeying orders and following rules. It has strong hierarchies predisposing soldiers/workers as the defining characters of the organisation. In contrast to the military metaphor, the family or organism metaphor exemplifies flexibility and the perception of being a naturally given organisation. Corporations are not families. The purpose of a family is not to sell a product, nor are its internal relationships based on performance related pay systems administered by HRM. Above all, family members hardly ever get recruited or selected into a family. Family positions do, in general, not depend on annual performance reviews, and so on. Despite all this and much more, the family metaphor has been in service of managerialism ever since it needed to legitimise its existence to labour as being the truthful representative of capital.

For the work setting, Max Weber's *Protestant Work Ethic and the Spirit of Protestantism* (1904–05) showed which modern virtues support work regimes. These are dedication to hard work, duty, diligence, and time efficiency. Especially the issue of time has been important in this context. The clock has become one of the most important metaphors of time efficiency as shown in movies such as Fritz Lang's *Metropolis* of 1927 or Charlie Chaplin's *Modern Times* of 1936. In both, the clock is *the* metaphor for the conversion of time. Time becomes a commodity and can be invested in production. Under these conditions, time becomes *productive* time, something not to be wasted. Time spent doing nothing is frowned upon, hence one of the most familiar answers to almost anything has become *I am busy*. The *busy* metaphor has become a common metaphor in everyday life situations and at work. It also conveys a status function as it equates to *I am important* and *I work hard*. *I am busy* conveys a status message of *common sense* where the social status of labour is not only seen but also accepted as being lower than the status of managers.[110] Metaphors like this however are not *common sense* but socially created. They do not have to be overtly realistic but need to be imaginative. They gain meaning through the principle of *association* that involves transposing values of properties from one domain of reality or meaning to another. Such associations have to be socially constructed through language to gain meaning.

Somewhat similar to metaphors, stories and narratives appear to have also received high currency in management communication. Storytelling is one of the preferred methods of human communication that started with imaginary stories that developed into *fairytales* and later into company histories. Such stories allow management to shift definitions and by doing so, shift viewpoints and meanings. Common to all stories and narratives is the transfer of meaning derived from a poetic area into the world of management, for example when a heroic leader battles market elements to secure his company's survival.[111] Of relative importance to these stories is their ability to replace testable truth with a new line of thought. This is supported by a version of sense making that is thematically linked to language constructions imported from fictions, epic dramas, theatrical tragedies, historic novels, biographies, plots, etc. Applied by management, storytelling is no more than a rather complex managerial technique. Adequate management literature such as an article called *Strategy Retold* in the US *Academy of Management Review* shows the enlightened manager how this is done.[112] Technical rationality is applied to the art of story creation and the focus is on how the story is constructed which leads to the persuasive and convincing character of the managerial story.

Managerial stories and narratives need to achieve a range of issues highly relevant to management. Firstly, they need to shift any critical, independent, or opposing viewpoints from the realm of management, for example by converting a business plan or a managerial strategy into a story. Instead of the rationale for a business plan, images and structures of storytelling such as drama, heroes, business enemies etc. are called upon to construct the story or narrative. Such a managerial construction allows management to present its point. It comes at the cost of alternative, contradictory, or challenging viewpoints. In short, diverging or alternative viewpoints are reduced to TINA – There Is No Alternative resulting in a one-dimensional view. Storytelling assigns management with the advantage of structuring *discourse* and meaning whereby the term *discourse* is to be understood as containing words and signifiers shaped by managerial structures. The usage of words occurs inside a narrowly constructed language context that constructs meaning and allows interpretations when and where management needs or needs to avoid them. Managerially guided discourses create meaning formations that are rooted in a *bipolar* system. This linguistic system reduces communication to *either-or* options such as *be with us or against us*. It selects the presence or absence of issues, divides positives from negatives, and decides what remains hidden and what is highlighted. Access to the process of managerial storytelling is a privilege given to a few and systematically determined. The outcome is the systematic marginalisation of alternatives or challenging experiences and the manifestation of only one view.

Under managerial guidance the power that shapes discourse becomes invisible as discourse becomes highly institutionalised. Once this is achieved, a now power-free discourse is constitutive of normal and routine company practice. Pre-structured practices of discourse do not simply provide context-neutral meanings but also function as an instrumental rational form of discipline that constructs labour in a particular mode based on managerial power. In this context, power must be viewed as constructed through managerial discourse practice that structures company life and labour. Secondly, in order to receive legitimacy, stories need to convince listeners that their content is plausible. Crucial to plausible storytelling is an ability to present a story that is not too familiar to the receiver but also not too unfamiliar. A relatively familiar story or narrative to follow is to portray a corporation as having *a life* by pretending *the birth of a great company*, or *the maturity of our business*, etc. In this way, stories create overlapping areas between private and business affairs.

Thirdly, a story or narrative should have a dehumanising effect. This is achieved by applying a faceless, antiseptic, and *value neutral* language that constructs people into nameless entities, thus moving a socially constructed reality into neutral territory. For example, real existing sales managers with real names are reduced to *Sales* and real existing workers become *Production*, etc. On the other hand, managerial storytelling often includes the establishment or construction of a heroic business leader – Netscape's boss, Lee Iacocca, Bill Gates, etc. – by simultaneously negating the original source of business, i.e. labour.

Fourthly and finally, stories and narratives need to support system-integration – *we are all in the same boat* – and pretend to portray a universalistic view created through the appearance of neutrality and centrality – *central to business is, the business of business is business*, etc. Such stories are formulated in the so-called *I-We-Them-It* principle.

Table 3.6 shows how storytelling applies language as a method to remove social actors in favour of technical-rational processes and their outcomes as

Table 3.6 The *I-We-Them-It* Principle and its Use

Principle	Meaning	Strategic Usage
I	the '*I*' pretends the firm's regard and caring for the individual person	you are a very special person, just like everybody else
We	the '*we*' as system-integration	we need to improve our quality
Them	the '*them*' as external affairs to be dealt with	they are strong competition in our market
It	the '*it*' represents how a firm feels about what it does	it achieved its goal and we are proud of it

presented in business reports, fact-finding missions, the bottom-line, the market, etc. Despite the individual ideology of managerialism, the '*I*' is reduced to a manageable entity via a highly standardised treatment. The '*we*' is the most common form of system integration, as it integrates the '*I*' into a corporate '*we*', thus ending individualism effectively.[113] Of particular use is the creation of '*them*' as the external villain. The '*them=villain*' metaphor is powerfully used in real wars and business wars to rally the '*we*' (soldiers or employees) behind the usually self-appointed war or business leader. The final and even more dehumanising element is the '*it*'. It converts real existing people, humans, and individuals into functions. In sum, the *I-We-Them-It* principle is, more than any other communicative principle, able to distort reality by applying communicative techniques.

4
Distorted Communication I: Classifications

Quite often communication is not just a transfer of a message between a sender and a receiver who seek to construct meaning between them depending on their social environment or domain. In many cases, communication between people – in the non-work domain as much as in the work domain – is constructed with a specific intent in mind and is more open to the construction of these specific and often instrumental intentions at work than it is in everyday messages. At work, power inside and over communication plays a significant role. This power is somewhat asymmetrically distributed which opens up possibilities for the distortion of messages. To distort a message means to *put it out of shape*. A distortion is a sort of linguistic abnormality or anomaly that departs or deviates from the proper meaning of a sign. Intentional distortion alters the *perception* of a message, thus allowing pre-designed and purposive misrepresentations of a communicated sign.[114] Distortions impact on the language we use. They are a linguistic tool that is unequally distributed at work.

As access to language use and communication is predominantly a feature of management rather than of workers, management is more likely to construct messages with an intentional purpose. This purpose tends to be linked to the main purpose of management which is to achieve organisational goals, commonly known as profit. In the hierarchically structured work domain management is able to use its access to power in order to link its prime objective with the instruments to achieve it. Therefore, communication is increasingly seen as a domain able to serve instrumental purposes.

The language that is used reflects the superior-subordinate relationship. This applies to work based relations as well as to relations in non-work areas. Here one group of people with privileged access to media can achieve superiority over other groups. While the socially dominant class is able to construct meaning, in order for it to function this meaning has to be accepted by subordinates even if it is against their interests.

Before discussing the issue of distortions, a brief look at language itself is crucial in order to understand *how* and *in what way* language is used. Only then a deeper comprehension of *distorted* language can follow. Inevitably language and its use are linked to social existence. When we learn a language as a social human being, we also learn the socially constructed rules of the language. When we speak a language, we engage in rule-governed social behaviour.[115] The link between language and society – called socio-linguistics – can be manifested in two propositions. Firstly, language is a continuous generative process implemented in social interactions of language users, and secondly, the structure of language is generated sociologically.

In any society, *language* is the most common tool through which people communicate. Through language ideologies and myths are circulated inside and between social domains.[116] When language is used in the service of power, the conditions for ideology are set. The creation of myths resides at the level below ideology. Hence, the linguistic shape of ideology and myths is an important feature. As language is exposed to ideological content, it cannot simply be reduced to a kind of natural occurrence. Consequently, language is not a natural phenomenon but socially constructed and as such language itself is the subject of academic studies. The language used to study language is called meta-language that is the language of language. It discusses the social construction of language. As George Orwell (1946) correctly pointed out *the half-conscious belief that language is a natural growth and not an instrument for [a] purpose* is a dangerous assumption. Language is a medium to communicate and at the same time also the object and subject of philosophical discourse. Studies about language are known as the duality of language or meta-language.[117] The field of linguistic studies and the physical use of everyday language are always linked to the fabric of our social existence. Our ability to communicate derives primarily from the social relationships among humans. It does not originate in the relationships between *signs* and *facts* as the pragmatic-behaviourist perspective seeks to tell us.[118] One of the founding fathers of the pragmatic-behaviourist language study was *Saussure* (1906–13) who divided the use of language into three core aspects.

As Table 4.1 portrays, Saussure saw language always as a system of form and *parole* both of which constitute language-speech (*langage*). Language-speech or *langage* (A) is understood to be the sum of all linguistic phenomena such as physical, physiological, and psychological elements that are involved in the realisation of any speech or communicative activity. In distinguishing

Table 4.1 Saussure's Three Elements of Language

	Three Elements	Saussure's Terminology
A)	Language-Speech	*Langage*
B)	Language as System of Forms	*Langue*
C)	Individual Speech Act	*Parole*

general *language speech* (A) from *parole* (C) or the social and the individual element, Saussure was able to show that language can never be constructed purely as an act of an individual because A always depends on B and C as shown in Table 4.1. Hence: A = B + C. In sum, Saussure's *langue* (B) or language as a *system* of forms consists of phonetics, grammar, and lexicon[119] that express a certain formalism and *system* focus. This view carries the danger of seeing language as a ready-made system, able to lock language inside a narrow frame. It asphyxiates language and arrests it as a subject. Communicative humans are seen as imprisoned inside the linguistic system where system and grammar tend to subscribe to a conservative notion of system stability. They interpret living language as if it were already perfected and ready-made. Consequently, language as a system is incompatible with a view that sees language as a living, historical, and often ideological project. As language (Table 4.1[A]) is not the same as *parole* (C), an individual using language cannot be seen as being the equivalent to the social context in which individuals live and in which language is used. Both language and communicative individuals who live inside a social context depend on each other.

Language exists as a social construction into which humans are not born but learn to adapt to in the process of socialisation. Without internalisation of society's language no one would be able to interact with the environment. This interaction is not done via voluntary participation hence language is not a game we choose to play. Society-individual interaction sets the environment for the linguistic engagement between individual and society. Neither the individual nor society is free to enter into *language as a game* of voluntary choices as we are inducted into society via communication in a non-voluntary process. The philosophical invention of *language as a game* is largely attributed to Austrian linguist *Wittgenstein*.[120] Neither societies nor languages are games as games not only have voluntarism attached to it but also have *playing a game* as their subject.[121] This requires game plans, places, movements, aims, and rules that are necessarily somewhat detached from reality. Beyond this remains the fact that *all playing, in fact, can be reduced to being played*.[122] It turns a player into an object that is being played with. Unlike a game that we may or may not join, we experience language as a socially constructed arrangement (B) that is an objective fact external to and independent of our individual conscious. In sum, linguistic capabilities do not derive from games but from a structured induction into a society using a socially constructed language.

As much as language consists of words, words are always filled with content and meaning drawn from behaviour and ideology. In this way we are able to understand words to which we can respond with words that engage us behaviourally and ideologically. Concretisation of a behavioural or ideological content of a word is only possible through the inclusion of the word into the actual historical context of its original implementation. The use of words is never innocent, especially in the realm of the world of work, management and its human expression of HRM.[123] *Language is not coincident, as it were, with that which is expressed in it, with that in it that is formulated in words. Language always leads behind itself and behind the façade of overt verbal expression that it first represents* (Gadamer 1976:88). Words used in the world of work are often the words of management. For that reason, they always carry ideological connotations of the history of industrialism and capitalism as well as connotations that imply managerial rationality and control. Consequently, for a full concretisation of the ideological character of, for example, the words *Human Resource Management*, one needs to understand their historical origins such as the brutal domestication of workers into the factory system that is largely excluded from the words used in today's HRM texts.[124]

Once located inside the system imperatives of managerialism, HRM can be constructed as an a-historical project in which all words related to the brutal historical past have been removed. Workers are linguistically imprisoned into a system logic that negates Saussure's language ideas (Table 4.1^{A+B}). The language of HRM is the language of a system with abstract objectivism that traps workers inside a pre-set framework of performance management, remuneration scales, management by objective, performance related pay and so on.[125] Domination is hidden inside an administrative-technical language.[126] *Domination is transfigured into administration. The capitalist bosses and owners are losing their identity as responsible agents* [as HRM is] *assuming the functions of bureaucrats in a corporate machine* (Marcuse 1966:35). Hidden behind HRM's language use is a textbook-rehearsed language that lacks social or historical context. It appears to be domination free while having in fact a highly developed content of domination.

HRM's administrative power and domination receives meaning entirely from the communicatively established HRM system, not from any historical context. However, even in the artificial and a-historical language system of HRM, the usage of the same word can produce two mutually exclusive and even conflicting meanings. For example, workers have already renamed the Human Resource Department into a Dirty Tricks Department. They have also renamed HRM's idea of *cascading down information* into *they piss on us*. In short and despite the overwhelming linguistic ability of HRM's distortion devices, it has not completely succeeded to incorporate workers into its linguistic framework. Notwithstanding all attempts to create an encompassing language system (4.1^B) for HRM, language can never be totally reduced to a mere function that hides its ownership and power content. The example above illustrates this. Workers have found a – maybe not the most sophisticated but nevertheless an appropriate – linguistic expression of hierarchical communication, i.e. *they piss on us*.

Language is not simply a function of human ownership in a socially constructed world; words and their use still remain important. The fact that humans have a social understanding of their environment largely depends on language as any conscious engagement with the world can only occur through language. Language and human experience never arise separately; in order to work they must connect in some way or other. Language and worldly experience cannot be separated as much as we cannot separate ourselves from the world around us.

As language provides the very base of human experience, it cannot be seen as just another possession among so many things people have in a material world. Language does not arise *next* to experience nor is it simply attached to it. It cannot be seen as an autonomous element detached from human experience. Language and experience always occur together. Both have a dependent and, above all, dialectical relationship to each other. Language consists of a huge but ultimately limited number of elements. A skilful mastery of these elements leads to what Gadamer (1974) called *linguisiticality, which, rather than destroying* language purely as a vehicle for expressions that shape thoughts and identities, portrays language as something that creates self, meaning, and the world as we know it. Hence, the interaction between self, meaning, and the world is by far more complex than the view of language as a simple connection of signs and elements allows.

Inside the self-meaning-world framework, anyone who has a command of language can produce meaning, is able to understand an unlimited number of sentences and can also judge whether a certain sequence of expressions is in accordance with the rules governing the use of the language. We need to establish these links in order to understand each other. According to *Karl Bühler* (1934), language operates between speaker, listener, and the world, and serves three core functions.

Table 4.2 shows that language can never be constructed at an individual level as it is always socialised. As Barthes (1967:14) wrote *language is a social institution*. Therefore it can only be seen as a *system of values* (Saussure), the transmission of which often occurs through speaking the language. When we speak, we speak as a human being. When we speak to someone we use language. In no society does language exist without speech. Speech and language are important parts of any society. A speech-less society is impossible as language is a product and an instrument of speech at the same time.

Table 4.2 Karl Bühler's Three Functions of Language

Function	Application	Use in the World of Work
Cognitive	a symbol related to objects and matters of facts	'A strike will stop production'
Expressive	a symbol related to inner experiences	'A strike is a sign of our solidarity'
Appellative	a symbol that appeals to others, a hearer	'Let's go on strike!'

Nothing enters language without having been tried in speech. Conversely, no speech is possible as a fulfilment of communicative functions if it is not drawn from the realm of language. We are language-dependent human beings. Language is also always embedded in particular social practices that *one must accept in its entirety if one wishes to communicate* (Heath 2003:9). However, access to language and language use are not equally distributed in society or at the workplace as linguistic resources are asymmetrically distributed. Language is therefore to a large extent based on society and class.

Meaning is produced through associations and myths. This entails a dynamic act between sender and receiver (S⇆R). However, meaning creation between S⇆R through the means of language is also inextricably linked to *ideologies*. Commonly, ideologies often refer to a system of beliefs, even of illusory beliefs, but are also connected to the production of meaning and ideas thus serving as a weapon against social interests. The core aspect of ideology is its *content* as it carries ideas and values. But also the *context* of an ideology is significant. Ideologies impact on meanings through the way in which they are constructed and shared. Fundamentally, as *ideologies* are created by a group or class, they are socially, not individually determined. Inside the world of work, ideologies are prevalent in the social construction of the division of labour, the social idea of management, business and business as associations. They are also – and some might even say predominantly – found in corporate mass media. According to Berger & Luckmann (1967) and Fiske (1990:166), *ideology* has become the category of illusions and *false consciousness*. It is seen as a thought that has been alienated from the real social being of the thinker.

Ideology is an important element by which the ruling class maintains its dominance over the working class.[127] Because the ruling class controls the means by which ideology is propagated and spread throughout society, it can make the working class see its subordination as *natural*, and therefore right.[128] It can even distort the social process that establishes meaning. For example, understanding or making sense of the world of work is portrayed as something *natural*. *The Nature of Sensemaking* (Weick 1995:1) is eclipsing the socially constructed world of work into a *natural* product where work is understood as natural rather than as a social and communicative activity. This implies that nature will guide us in making sense of work and accept work and the way it is currently organised as something that one has to accept in the same way as one has to accept nature. Herein lies the falseness.

The medium that transports this kind of ideology is Weick (1995). In the non-work domain, ideology is conveyed via media set between individuals in society such as educational, political, and legal systems, mass media, publishing, and the managerial system.[129] The transmission role allows these media to fill any message transported between S and R with ideological content. Spreading into every aspect of social life, mass media turn public discourse into a spectacle, further exacerbating the process of alienation. Baudrillard (1998:50) has summed this up as:[130]

> This is the democracy of social standing, the democracy of the TV, the car and the stereo, an apparently concrete but, in fact, equally formal democracy which, beyond contradictions and social inequalities, corresponds to the formal democracy enshrined in the Constitution. Both of these, the one serving as an alibi for the other, combine in a general democratic ideology which conceals the absence of democracy and the non-existence of equality... All men are equal before the use-value of objects and goods whereas they are unequal and divided before exchange-value...thus the contemporary myths of well-being and needs have a powerful ideological function of reducing, of eliminating the objective, social and historical, determinations of inequality.

The inequality of public discourse, now largely expressed via corporate mass media, becomes formalised when the presentation of positions and counter-positions is bound to certain pre-arranged rules of the game. Such commonly and often silently agreed rules of the public discourse game shape our consensus about public matters. The rules that direct public discourse are made largely independent of most participants and are superimposed onto them. They divide public discourse and its participants into two groups – one that expresses system-conforming critique while the other provides *non*-system-conforming critique. This group however is largely excluded from the public domain. The exclusion of non-system-stabilising groups transforms the public domain into an arena of ideology reinforcement.

The conversion of the public domain into an arena for ideology reinforcement has led to a *Structural Transformation of the Public Sphere* (Habermas 1988). Once this domain had been open to society, but as the money and power code started to govern this domain, it has ceased to be an open sphere. It is now being regulated via a relationship that has increasingly replaced communicative action with the steering media of money and power. Today's public sphere is governed by mass media. Access to the public domain has been limited to particularistic considerations of system conformity. Increasingly a consensual generation of social norms such as ethics, critique, free speech, etc. is being displaced by the money and power code. The public domain itself has even ceased to be public. With relatively large corporations governing the communicative exchange domain, the public domain has been converted into a mediated domain in which corporate mass media have unlimited access while labour's access is very limited. Such one-dimensionality portrays system conformity as all encompassing while the means through which labour defines social bonds and distributes social goods such as solidarity are almost completely excluded.

As the money and power code establishes itself over humans, autonomous principles of social and working lives increasingly lose all sense of agency and participation. A truly open debate has become a mere spectre. Open debate under corporate rules of engagement with access to mass media has reduced participation to a pre-selection of system integrative actors.[131] The ideology of open participation or open public discourse eclipses the transformation of a once *public* domain into a corporate sphere that is now governed and maintained through instrumental communication.

This ideology of open discourse can only be established and maintained if it is frequently communicated. In other words, the more we are told of the importance of free speech, the more it has in fact already deteriorated. Free speech is reduced to a sign that signifies no more than corporate access to the transmission domain governed via money and power. The original idea of free speech is turned into an ideology and used against those who once fought for it. Today it is continually used to reinforce system stability. Every time a sign is used it reinforces the life of its designed meaning in a domain. It also reinforces the user who keeps its currency by using it and maintaining its connoted values. At work, signs such as HR, KPI, HRM, PRP, IR, ER, MBA, CEO, and CFO have to be constantly reinforced through their use.[132] The relationship between a sign and its myths on the one side and the user on the other is an ideological one. Using such signs repeatedly creates, reinforces, and maintains myths, values, and ideologies. It enables management to identify their membership in the management domain through the acceptance of common, shared myths and values.

Such identifications occur largely through a certain language that indicates an account of domain membership. This necessarily also involves other actors and includes a relationship between these actors that is designed to maintain various identities of a domain. To establish this, language assumes a core function as it provides the *process* as well as the *product* of domain identification. The process of identification as well as the *product* or outcome of this process is expressed through the adaptation of the language of managerialism. Domain identification through linguistically established narratives provides important clues to the way in which management manages shifting identifications inside their domain and between domains.

Under conditions of *Two Logics of Communicative Action* a duality of language identities – management versus labour – is established that allows management to establish a one-dimensional interest expression cloaked as *organisational objects*. Uncloaked, this expression stands for profit maximisation enabling management to portray their one interest as the interest of all. This creates a one-dimensional *organisational culture (!)* which bears the connotation of companies as cultural places, places for aesthetics, art, painting or classical music and the like.[133] Apart from such ideological obscenities, a company's *cultural* interest lies predominantly in profit rather than in supporting the arts or culture. Nevertheless, corporate culture needs to be portrayed as a universal culture and, most importantly, it needs to be seen as an interest to which labour can and should subscribe as well. On labour's side, however, a duality of identification takes place. Unlike management's ability to use a one-dimensional language to establish a one-dimensional interest, labour has to cope with two interests.

While on the one hand labour needs to maintain their identity to realise their objectives, their domain on the other hand demands protective measures against the distortions of *managerial talk* as expressed in instrumental communication directed towards managerial goals. This process is called *dis-identification*. It occurs through language use and is designed to prevent an overt identification with managerial goals. The process of *dis-identification* opens up potentials for communication that is free from instrumental usage. The idea of *two logics of communicative action* demands different actions from labour than it requires from management. Labour needs to establish coping mechanisms that deal with management's pretence of interest commonality between both.

While management operates with a single interest, a single identity, and with the power to colonise labour's domain communicatively, labour is forced to install preventative measures that need to deal with the dilemma of *identity-identification duality*. Labour needs to maintain its identity as labour and at the same time prevent the language of managerial goal identification from taking over their domain. Management, on the other side, seeks to prevent labour from developing sufficient linguistic measures capable of shielding against the colonisation of their domain. To do this, management relies heavily on several communicative tools one of which is to separate or classify issues and words by organising them into socially constructed boxes for *The Order of Things* to *dis*allow labour the establishment of meaningful links. Labour would need these sign-to-meaning links in order to comprehensively understand the ideology of managerialism.

Managerial classifications as ordering instruments

For linguists, classifications are at the very basis of language and thought. As social beings we are believed to learn through classifications as they categorise things while we also learn to classify things that are socially constructed. Neither these classifications nor the process of learning them is naturally given. On classifications, Searle (1996:160) emphasised that *any system of classification of objects, any set of categories for describing the world, indeed any system of representation at all is conventional, and to that extent arbitrary*. One system of arbitrary classification is the use of *tenses* to distinguish between future, present, past etc. in speaking and writing. Another one is the classification of *nouns* and *adjectives*. We are properly conditioned to use them as given. It can be 'a *weak management position*' but not '*a weak car*'.

Classifications such as these establish an order of things as a way of thinking. They can link thoughts and connections and by doing so establish control over thought and reality. Marcuse (1966:186) highlighted that *by classifying and distinguishing meanings, and keeping them apart, it purges thought and speech of contradictions, illusions, and transgressions.* Classifications are used to separate things and issues that actually belong together. They create an arbitrary barrier in an arbitrary system of classifications to make one believe that things are separated rather than linked. The main idea behind classification is to prevent issues from being linked, connections from being made and contradictions from being understood. But classifications do not only divide thought, they also divide people.

Classification systems exist for language groups or society as a whole and are also created for sub-groups or sub-domains inside society and work. At work the most common classification is the one that divides people into two domains, labour and management. But the classification game goes even further. In each domain, further sub-divisions, sub-groups, and sub-domains can be created. They are installed to differentiate between even more classifications which can be further differentiated and become a source of tensions and struggles as they have the ability to categorise people and people's thought which is always shaped and constrained by such classifications. Classifications are abstract systems introduced into an existing discourse of living processes to make these processes appear clear, classified and static. At work, they set pre-designed boundaries for discussions, communication, and discourse and classify the labour-management discourse in a pre-set way.

Any labour-management discourse is always at risk of being shaped and constrained by two sets of different classifications. Many classifications at work have been re-shaped during the last three decades. A number of linguistic terms that govern the world of work had traditionally been classified by labour. Between the 1980s and today, many issues were re-classified by moving several labour classifications into a new set of classifications. This has been one of the core achievements of *Human Resource Management*. However, before this was achieved, HRM itself underwent a significant change in its meaning. HRM had to re-classify itself towards a new meaning in order to overcome its original classification as personnel management.[134] Simultaneously, HRM's own re-classification removed many old classifications from personnel management. Under the newly constructed meaning almost all old issues have been absorbed into the new HRM framework. Today, issues that have been classified as belonging to modern HRM can be found in almost all HRM textbooks.[135]

As Table 4.3 shows, management seeks to classify work issues as HRM issues. Therefore the domain of management and HRM falsely portrays that the latter is able to classify and regulate almost all work issues *for* labour. At the same time such classification takes issues out of any discussion between labour and management. Re-classified in this way, they become non-conflicting

Table 4.3 Re-Classified HRM Issues

(i) Terms Classified as Belonging to the HRM Domain	(ii) Terms Classified as Belonging to the Labour Domain
empowerment, enlargement, enrichment, quality of work, affirmative action, equal opportunity, harassment, skill development, work climate, cross-cultural training, discrimination, employee wellness programmes, feedback, gain-sharing, glass-ceiling, group-building, job-rotation, -redesign, -satisfaction, -involvement, knowledge-creation, learning, commitment, performance related pay, performance management, profit-sharing, safety-climate, self-directed learning, co-decision making, participation, teamwork, family-work balance, and work-life balance, etc.	collective bargaining, trade unions, strike, industrial action

and non-contradictory. Linguistically, these issues are taken out of an old labour domain (ii) which is left with a few remaining old issues that are regarded as obsolete and securely placed in domain (ii). They are portrayed as old issues, irrelevant to the modern production process and forced into an outdated existence as modern HRM can now take care of them (i). Furthermore, these issues have not only been moved out of the labour domain, they have also been removed from the negotiating domain located between the labour and management domain. Above all, labour issues are made to appear negative.

In the mind of the person at work, the re-classification of many core labour issues is designed to establish a blind spot. Negative and dangerous issues (ii) are to be perceived as bad inside the mind of a person. Preferably, the classification is supposed to establish the bad connotations automatically. Without thinking about it, a person should categorise an issue as negative and anachronistic. In the words of George Orwell (1949:291), *the mind should develop a blind spot whenever a dangerous thought presents itself. The process should be automatic, instinctive. Crimestop, they called it in Newspeak* (4.3[i]). Classified in this way, dangerous and non-HRM conforming issues such as strikes, industrial action, active resistance, disobedience, work-by-rules, organisational misbehaviour, etc. are eliminated by an overlaying class of Newspeak (4.3[i]). The blind spot for them should not only automatically, but also instinctively be developed. By classifying work issues as HRM-supportive issues and locating them in the management domain – rather than in the labour or a negotiation domain – both management and HRM are able to control thought and conflict via a simple classification of issues. This eliminates conflict long before even the slightest thought of divergent interests or contradiction can arise. If – in an increasingly unlikely case – conflict should still come up, other methods of classifications are used to deal with it.[136]

A core example in the classification of conflict is the classification of problematic issues between labour and management as either *distributive* or *integrative*. Here, issues that are classified as integrative are seen as *win-win* issues between labour and management while distributive issues are considered as *win-lose* situations. Distributive classifications are seen as *sharing a pie,* integrative distribution as *expanding a pie.* In a managerial understanding, *distributive* issues are issues of conflict while *integrative* issues are defined as issues of common – i.e. managerial – interests. These common interests – as far as they exist – are highlighted through the application of a specific language, the language of *we*-issues.

In sharp contrast to the conflict-based and distributive language use of a *'them-and-us'* language, integrative language use emphasises *we*-issues, for example, *we are all in this together* or *we are all in one boat.* Hence, the managerial statement of *we have to change* can very well mean, *we* – management – have decided that *you* – the workers – have to change. A simple managerial sentence like *'this is necessary for your company'* can be constructed to carry the following six meanings:[137]

Table 4.4   The Six Meanings of *This is Necessary for Your Company*

No.	Meaning
A)	this is not *your* company but we seek to give you the illusion of it,
B)	what is necessary is decided by *us*, management,
C)	you get only told *when* we think it is necessary,
D)	you get only told *what* we think is necessary,
E)	you have no input in what is necessary as we, management, have decided this for you, and finally,
F)	we hide the socially constructed reality behind a managerial creation of necessity.

Table 4.4 shows six meanings of a simple statement made by management. This seeks to uncover the hidden meanings of a management statement. To assist in determining what is necessary and what management necessarily needs to tell workers is often done via simple classifications into what is or is not necessary for *your* company. A managerial statement like *this is necessary for your company* may not even need to be expressed as Orwellian Newspeak to take effect, however the classification of managerial language into Orwellian terms assists such a process. One of the simplest but equally effective forms of classification occurs in Orwell's *Newspeak* (1949:313). Here, all language is classified into three groups (A, B, C):

Table 4.5 Three Forms of Orwellian Vocabulary and Managerial Use

Orwell's Characterisation	Managerial Examples
A) *The A vocabulary consists of words needed for the business...it would have been quite impossible to use the A vocabulary for literary purposes or for political or philosophical discussions. It was intended only to express simple, purposive thoughts, usually involving concrete objectives or physical actions* (1949:313–314).	It is virtually impossible to construct a political or philosophical discussion by using these managerial terms: business process re-engineering, performance management, best practice, key performance indicators (KPI), systems analysis, sales requirements, total quality management, corporate asset, network company, equity-, fund-, or operations management, marketing.[138]
B) *The B vocabulary consisted of words, which had deliberately been constructed for political purposes. Countless words such as honour, justice, morality, internationalism, democracy...had simply ceased to exist* (1949:316; 318).	When opening any modern management or business book, these words hardly register in the contents or index. Terms such as *management morality* or *democratic management* simply do not exist. No word – no discourse – no thought.
C) The C vocabulary was supplementary to the others and consisted entirely of scientific and technical terms.	Today's management books are filled with technical and scientific instructions on, for example, rational decision making.

As Table 4.5 shows, some of George Orwell's ideas on how language should be used under conditions of *Newspeak* have already been implemented into the techno-scientific language of managerialism. By classifying words into three simple categories, certain words can, before being used, already be eliminated from any discourse on managerialism. In Table 4.5, any classification into *vocabulary (A)* allows an emphasis on non-political needs for business. It also allows a focus on those words that are required for the purpose of business. Words like philosophical ethics, for example, are not required in the business process.

At the second level of Table 4.5 (B), unfavourable words can be eliminated so that terms such as *democratic management* that could entice people to think: *why isn't there a democratically controlled version of management?* are erased from discourse.[139] Similarly, ethics – a subject sometimes mentioned in a back chapter of standard management textbooks under the hidden heading *'this one should be mentioned – it is fashionable to do so'* – can be re-classified as *business ethics* and removed from management.[140] After all it is not the manager – or actor – who behaves immorally; it is the business – a depersonalised structure – that behaves unethically. Such language classification removes any connotation of unethical behaviour from managers by moving it into the domain of business where it is depoliticised and depersonalised by portraying it as a function attached – or not attached – to business. Ethics is reduced to a function as it vanishes into the thin air of a *technic-ised* language. In the language of technical functionalism a non-technical issue is linguistically made to appear technical.

Finally, the C-vocabulary classification entails the largest part of language used by management, mostly in order to gain legitimacy through a number of processes. This is done by taking science into the service of management that has greatly assisted the transformation of management into managerialism. Management and managerialism have successfully adopted the language of technology and science.[141] Large sections of management and managerialism live from pretending to be technical and scientific. The C vocabulary takes away the political, social, and ethical dimension by classifying managerial actions as technical and scientific.

Such classifications determine which issues are management supportive and which are contrary to management's interests. This process is highly selective. Underneath the layer of science and technicality operates a managerially defined them-and-us ideology that classifies issues not only into labour or managerial issues but also introduces two sub-levels of classifications. The first sub-group contains issues that belong to *us*, i.e. the company. The second group contains issues that belong to *them* and are non-managerial or non-supportive of management. These issues are classified as belonging to the others, the outsiders, third parties, trade unions, ex-company, the environment, the state, competition, the market, etc.

The non-supportive vs. supportive classification is made along binary lines. They suppress dialogue and create a one-dimensional environment in which it is safe for management to operate. All alternatives are classified as non-supportive, external, and non-useful and excluded. The following are some of the binary classifications used by management:

As Table 4.6 shows, binary classifications made by management always consist of terms that are positive for management and, almost by definition, exclude terms that are negative. However, binary classifications always include negative versions but these have to be avoided in order to adapt

Table 4.6 Binary Classifications used by Management

Supportive of Managerialism	Unsupportive of Managerialism
Management and Manager	Chaos/Worker
Cooperation and Coordination	Fighting and Confusion
Facts and Truths	Fictions and Untruths
Morality and Order	Immorality and Disorder
Logic and Rationale	Illogic and Irrational[141]
Science and Technology	Myths and Anti-Modern[142]
Free Market	Over-Regulations

managerialism and management's vision of a reduced understanding of reality. These classifications operate under the force of a communicatively established one-dimensionality. Once management has successfully established supportive terms, all other terms can – almost automatically – be classified as alien and therefore must be avoided. Using such binary classification allows management to focus on the positives rather than discussing the negative and unsupportive terms. Terms that support managerialism are important as they render any debate of unsupportive terms unnecessary. Consequently, the introduction of a new managerial system, a new technology, or changes in work processes are to be connected to management supportive terms as they ensure adoption and unchallenged affirmation through workers.

Issues are often classified into a binary code that is constructed in *either/or* fashion. It seeks to classify terms into being either *supportive* or *non-supportive*. This works well when managerial language personalises issues as *you*- or *your*- issues. By categorising management-supportive issues into *your*-issues, workers are given the impression that management does something *for* them. The managerial use of integrative issues takes on the appearance of being *your* personal issue. Even work becomes *your* work and the workplace becomes *your* workplace. The medieval organisation of bread (= pane) sharing (com) mercenaries, the *company*, becomes *your* company. It is *your* individual bargaining position as much as it is *your* HRM department. *In this manner, superimposed, standardised and general things and functions are presented as especially for you* (Marcuse 1966:95). A *'you'* as an employee is turned into *you are a very special employee – just like anyone else!* Pretended individualism – with or without individual bargaining rights – is transformed into a standard element of a standard system. The individual becomes an entity of the corporation in a process that results in a corporatised individual. Engineered system integration successfully incorporates *you* into the alien structure of the modern-day *com-pane* or corporation. As Marcuse (1966:95) wrote:

> *Its success indicates that it promotes the self-identification of the individuals with the functions, which they and the others perform. In the most advanced sectors of functional and manipulated communication, language imposes in truly striking constructions the authoritarian identification of person and function.*

Once the individual and with it individuality has merged with the corporate function, HRM has succeeded. In this process *the language of corporations is like a vampire without fangs; it has no venom or bite but you don't want it hanging off your neck just the same* (Watson 2003:27).

Only those individuals who are considered susceptible to corporate language are deemed individuals who can be merged with a company. They are inclined to take on issues directed towards system integration. Issues that do

Table 4.7 Types of Managerial Classifications

No.	Types of Classifications
1)	**The Order of Things:** classifications pre-structure discussions between the two domains by providing a framework that establishes the order of things between labour and management,
2)	**Directive Communication:** classifications that are not mutually agreed upon and are not open to communication; they enforce common understanding and are established by management/HRM,
3)	**Distributive and Integrative:** HRM-classifications and distributive/integrative classifications serve to establish an *order of things*. But it also locates issues that are seen as problematic between labour and management inside the management domain,
4)	**To be Neutralised:** classifications of work issues as HRM-domain-classifications; they are neutralised as communicative issues between labour and management,
5)	**Ideological Issues:** they serve an ideological purpose in three ways: a) they exclude labour issues from the domain of labour by keeping their surface structure intact (e.g. wages) while moving their underlying meaning structure into the domain of management, b) they diminish labour's capacity for domain internal discussions, c) they establish management/HRM as the creator and administrator of classification elevating not only management's legitimacy but also its ideological domination over labour.

not serve the goal of system integration are isolated and externalised by management, removed from company life and classified as issues of external domains. Management classifies issues that are deemed relevant into several categories:

Table 4.7 shows five types of classifications. The first one shows how classifications are used to establish order in the mind of those exposed to them. The second classification divides issues into those over which management can relatively easily claim to have managerial prerogative. Once secured inside this domain, labour is more likely to accept these issues as non-negotiable even though they are. At the next level, management has to accept labour's request to see an issue as negotiable. The counter measurement is to classify the issue into an integrative or distributive one. At the fourth level, management is still able to try to neutralise issues by pushing them into the HRM domain as issues that can be solved by HRM. In the last case, issues are dealt with inside a system of ideology that can regulate issues such as, for example, wages. Management tends to present wages according

Distorted Communication I: Classifications 71

---
individual work = effort ➔ appraisal ➔ wage

Figure 4.1 The Work–Wage Link

to an internal and almost natural managerial logic. Inside this framework, wages are established through performance related pay, etc. to prove to labour that they are unrelated to the contradictory conflict between labour and capital. Labour is shown a sequence that is easy to understand and pretends that rewards for work are linked to an equation as shown in Figure 4.1.

Figure 4.1 contains two important elements. Firstly, it excludes any link to political economy. It classifies wages as a non-societal, non-economic, and non-company issue. Wages have been made an individual issue where any notions that link them to profits, to the management driven price-inflation-wages spiral, or to all other issues of wealth redistribution and societal wealth are excluded. Secondly, it establishes an unquestionable link between work and wages configured as an individual issue. Expressed in HRM's Newspeak, it is simply *performance related pay*. Finally, it also links wages to well established ideologies such as *hard work, individual effort*, or *only those who work hard achieve higher wages, get ahead, and have higher living standards*. Higher standards are not expressed in being a better person but in being a better consumer. In short, by working harder and consuming more the individual becomes more valuable to the system. While oscillating between being a good worker (in-work) and being a good customer (ex-work) – which is the only mode supportive of the system – the individual ceases to be a person.

In production as in reproduction, the core element of classification is that they are neither made by the consumer in the consumption or reproduction domain nor by the worker in the production domain. Commercial agencies as well as management have already pre-arranged these classifications beforehand but still maintain the illusion of giving workers a choice over workplace issues as much as a choice over ready-made and standardised consumer products. In reality, nothing is left to a consumer or to a worker to classify as their choices are already made under the pretence of an ideology of *free choice*.[144] In both domains, workers and consumers can only make system conforming choices between classifications presented to them. These classifications are constructed inside ideological boundaries of system demands directed towards the need of production or consumption.

While classifications link ideas in a pre-classified or pre-organised way in order to serve a specific goal, the framing of certain ideas serves a similar purpose as it shapes managerial ideas in a certain and equally pre-organised way. Inside the management domain, frames are discursively established. Once established, any idea can be placed inside such a frame so that those on the receiving end view the idea in the pre-determined manner. In that way, an idea that was originally expressed by labour can be linked to a pre-established framework. The act of framing depends on the *mental* link that assigns a person to the domain of the predisposed meanings.

Framing always encompasses a relationship that ties a managerial concept or idea to a pre-created framework that defines the parameters under which such ideas are de-coded. The asymmetrical power relations at work distribute framing abilities unevenly. Management's superior framing position, for example, allows managerial leadership inside the frame of new technology. Framed as a functional necessity, any introduction of new technologies appears inside the frame of managerial leadership. To labour as the recipient of this communicative message, the message *new technology* is supposed to create a mental link to the managerial framework of being (a) necessary for the company and (b) a sign of managerial leadership. In no way should such a message be linked to the framework of domination. Managerial framing allows management to create and communicate their ideas wrapped inside a specifically created interpretive frame that makes messages appear forward-looking, innovative, non-confronting, and legitimate and by doing so influences others in the way anticipated by the designers of the frame.[145] Language tools such as metaphors, storytelling, jargons, spin, visions, catch phrases, slogans, corporate policies, etc. can be used to establish such frames. Inside these frames specific managerial ideas are to be understood in the way management wants it to be understood. For example, once management has framed an issue as *market-driven, value adding*, or simply as *efficient*, it is shielded against any form of challenge.

Managers who are aware of the power of framing rely heavily on this communicative instrument as it increases their ability to establish an idea successfully inside *your* firm (sic). Framing also allows management to increase or lower the relevance of a managerial message. Often receivers of a managerial message are forced to judge the relative importance of the managerial idea based on the way it is framed. This occurs without noticing that the frame of reference on which they make their decision has been created by management.

The establishment of such frames is the task of management. Workers generally do not participate in the process of creating them. These frames are established so that workers do not and should not need to think and, above all, should not get involved in creating their own frame of reference.[146] They should be prevented from understanding. As a recipient, the perception of having a *free choice* over the relevance of a message would be rendered an illusion if labour had an awareness of this process. Therefore, framing is entirely pre-determined by managerial design. Management needs to establish the frames before conveying any challenging messages to labour. For example, a somewhat challenging message such as *downsizing* should not be received by labour as *we* downsize *you* or a massive dismissal or firing of workers. They should not be able to link their firing to the adding of shareholder value and to management's remuneration portfolio via increased share value bonuses. When labour receives the managerial message, they should understand *downsizing* only inside the managerial frame of reference. This is deliberately designed so that it appears disconnected to a manager, management, or managerialism. Once workers receive new and challenging messages via the mental model of framing, even such harsh measures are made to appear acceptable. To make something acceptable is also the task of what is called ideology.

5
Distorted Communication II: Ideologies

Like many other things connected with the world of work, present day ideology too is a child of *Enlightenment* and industrialism. Ideology became a powerful tool when the traditional constructors and keepers of social relations – God, Church, monasteries, clerical structures, etc. – were increasingly replaced by the rationality that governs present day societies. Literally, the term *ideology* meant the study or knowledge of ideas, combining the science or bodies of knowledge as a *-logy* of ideas, *idea-o-logy*.[147] Originally coined by French philosopher *Destutt de Tracy*,[148] ideology was the philosophical science of ideas. Its task was to uncover the nature of ideas. Ideologies have always been part of *Enlightenment*. Originally, they sought to chart the human mind with some kind of intentional precision that could map out the motions of body and mind. The *Enlightenment* version of ideology was concerned with ideas of the social world, ideas that are socially constructed.[149] Marx' *The German Ideology* of 1846 for the first time comprehensively linked modern social existence to the formation of ideas in people's minds. It stated that consciousness is never anything other than conscious existence. Humans' conscious existence represents their actual life-process. All ideologies include corresponding forms of consciousness; they are no longer to be seen as independent of social and economic existence.

Consequently, Marx viewed the dialectical function of ideology as one that supports the political, economical, or managerial process. As such it represents an existing force that shapes social relations.[150] At the same time Marx also saw ideology as an *illusionary set of ideas*.[151] These are somewhat removed from real life existence, taking on forms of an autonomous existence above reality. For Marx ideology was also involved in the creation of ideology, i.e. in the discursive activity of making ideology that constructs meaning by establishing ideas about social reality as social reality. Essentially, ideology can be seen as *meaning in the service of power* (Thompson 1990:7) as well as a set of discursive strategies to displace realities that are proven to be embarrassing to a ruling power. Consequently, ideologies carry strong connotations of self-legitimisation.[152] They serve to legitimise prevailing power structures by appearing as the rationalisation of unreasonable affairs. This hides the truth of social affairs and also creates the perception of social affairs as being natural and universal. The universal appeal is created through general characters as expressed in statements such as *that goes without saying* which generalise particular interests and, in fact, cloak the specific interest. Statements such as *the nature of things* are commonly used to give socially constructed affairs the appearance of being universal and common.

Even though these general statements appear to be of *de*scriptive rather than of *pre*scriptive[153] character, in reality ideology is commonly used to *pre*-scribe rather than to *de*scribe things. It attempts to pre-scribe *the right way of things* as the only way of life.[154] Used in this manner, ideology supports a common cultural sense of identity that does not need to be discussed or analysed beyond its existence. This is often expressed in statements such as *that's the way it is* or *these are the facts of life*. They portray a common understanding without understanding anything. Any deeper understanding ends here. Marcuse (1966:182) summed this up as *we are subjected to the rule of socially established facts*. These are total – not only linguistic – facts. When *society speaks in its language, we are told to obey*.

The managerial creation and use of ideologies

Through the process of socialisation we are conditioned to accept ideologically established facts as *facts of life* or as *the way it is*.[155] Crucial to any ideology is that it comes in *before* people think or act. Ideologies target anything *before* the thought to eliminate critical thinking that could attack the ideologies. In these cases ideologies are designed to operate *a priori* rather than *posteriori*. The ideological content of any message only becomes visible to those who are able to look beyond the message. Even though there may not be an escape from ideology or managerial ideology,[156] critical understanding enables to question the underlying and deliberately non-articulated, non-visible or concealed premises that hide behind all ideological forms of knowledge.[157] Managerial ideology restricts understanding of *what* things are and *how* and *why* they are made into what they are. Any understanding of *how* meaning has been constructed and who benefits from this is neglected.

Ideologically, any definition needs to be understood in terms of what it is, not in terms of how it was made to appear. Useful definitions of *what is* are presented as natural, inevitable, and generally as good.[158] Crucially, ideology lures people into forgetting that meaning is always socially constructed inside a social context. Managerialism and HRM are such social – or better managerial – constructions. They only occur in a specific social context called social relations at *work* and under the specific social rules of maximising profits and domination. The context as well as the rules remain unquestioned as definitions of managerialism and HRM take on the appearance of being natural: *The nature of HRM is...* – *insert anything here and it becomes*

Table 5.1 The Communicative Construction of Managerial Ideologies at Work

Communicated Ideology	Actual Meaning
Work is a rewarding activity	Work occurs in a managerially constructed but alien setting based on asymmetry between wage-earner & labour-purchaser/controller.
Managerial work effort	Managerial control over pre-determined & non-self-determined work environment removed from co-determination or democracy.
Hard work	Rewarded by management while simultaneously encouraging workers to work harder.
Performance management	Disconnection between share price and management performance and managerial tool to control workers' actions at work.
Legitimate foundation of work	Work is legitimate through managerial guidance and leadership while workers' contribution is legitimate as long as it is needed.
Authority over work	Managerial authority is self-evident as enshrined in authoritarian corporate structures while workers are given very limited authority over work restricted to immediate workplace [team] and inputs [non-democratic, no co-decision making, etc].

natural. This even hides the ideological character of work itself by constructing it as a managerial HRM theme of instrumental rationality.

Table 5.1 shows managerial ideologies at work that construct work as rewarding. They are directed towards effort, hard work, and performance. Being the sole institution to reward work, management is also in the position to exercise authority over the working order to legitimise its own existence. This allows management to portray itself and the position it has assigned to itself as self-evident. In many cases, management has established itself as the guardian of work by redefining its meaning under provisions of managerial ideology. While originally work had been seen as the strongest expression of exploitation and alienation under early capitalism, this changed with the advancement of the system. The ideology of managerialism reframed work during advanced capitalism.[159] It is no longer seen as a form of exploitation but as rewarding. The need for a reward*er* to reward a reward*ee* actively secures management's position as the guardian of work. Today, management's role in rewarding workers is almost unchallenged but this was not always the case.

Under advanced capitalism the establishment and maintenance of the ideology that hard work equals reward is one of the main tasks of managerialism. Compared to the brutal past of early capitalism, work today has increasingly become an area of sophisticated ideological framing. In this advanced form of ideology workers are incorporated into an advanced ideology system. In contrast, managerial ideology of early capitalism relied on the heroic entrepreneur, the *hero of the industrial age* who outlined *his* (mostly men!) ideas wrapped up in ideological speeches, newspaper- and journal-articles, occasional radio announcements and the like. Under the ideology of modern managerialism, this had to change significantly.

Today, the ideology of managerialism is integrated into an all-embracing system. It ranges from management education and glossy management magazines with the *Harvard Business Review* as the leading light to easy reading airport copies of self-help management books on how to manage everything.[160] The ideology of managerialism is not only integrated into technical schools, universities, colleges, and training institutions, it also determines the very existence of these institutions. In addition, the ideology of managerialism is supported and popularised through mass consumption.[161] Interestingly, it directs consumption to its own supporting ideological materials.

Managerialism is readily available in popular books and magazines and accessible via daily TV shows often labelled *Your* Business Report and the like.[162] In the world of managerialism, the daily report of the share index – FTSE 100, DAX, Nasdaq, Heng Seng, Nikkei-Index, Euro-Stoxx 50, etc. – provides an endlessly rehearsed reminder of how much we all depend on the proper mechanisms of managerialism. Under advanced capitalism, the ideology of managerialism becomes a daily occurrence that not only shapes work but also infiltrates the evening dinner. Hence, system demands for the ideology of managerialism are far greater than ever before in human history. This started with a tremendous increase in the complexities of capitalism that coincided with a corresponding increase in demand for system integration of workers and therefore an increased need for ideological support mechanisms. Unlike during the period of early capitalism, not only is there much more demand for ideology today, it also needs to infiltrate all corners of human existence. Only today's ideology of managerialism is able to reduce the complexities of modern life to make them accessible to the ordinary person.

However and in spite of all the complexities of modern life, most ideologies operate much in the same way. George Orwell (1946:7) has described this as an *invasion of one's mind by ready-made phrases*. Today, as never before, scientific knowledge supports the invasion of the mind. Even though science initially started out as a myth-destroying attack on feudal society, today many forms of science have become myths. This is particularly visible in its popularised version where the myth of science uses terms *scientifically* to negate any critical assessment. Here, the myth is directed to a one-dimensional belief into science.

Science has taken on a God-like or quasi-religious form. It is presented as the ultimate truth, a truth that is unquestioned, unchallenged, and beyond critical examination. Modern science has merged with managerialism pervading all areas of work and society. This scientific-*ation* is visible in most business reports as evidenced by scientific tables, graphs, figures, mathematical equations, scientific correlations between share price, market values, market shares, etc. where it represents a televised version of a modern textbook. Like all business and management publications, modern business news programmes have *an inbuilt bias towards the snappy phrases, the sound bytes. And so they offer phrases deliberately engineered to smuggle in their preferred point of view* (Poole 2006:8). The modern business textbook is often reduced to parrot modern business newspapers, business magazines, and business news bulletins based on sound bytes.[163] The curricular composition of the modern textbook is only inches away from advanced newspaper reading.

The whole idea behind this is not so much to understand each detail of business, managerialism, or managerial decisions about company x, y, or z, but to condition the viewer, listener, or reader in the ideology of managerialism. As summed up by Searle (1996:135), in any business report or any programme *what they get from television, movies, and reading is, of course, in part a set of beliefs and desires*. The beliefs and desires generated from '*Your Nightly Business Report brought to you by the x corporation*' are those of managerialism and the desire to be successful in it. Apart from that, any deeper or even critical analysis of the political economy is as absent as is the term *political economy* itself. The famous *Critique of the Political Economy*[164] is nowhere to be found.

Whenever modern corporate mass media are not busy propagating managerialism, they seem to spend much effort in preventing what could uncover the ideological content of the present system or the role ideology plays in supporting the *Insanity of Rationality* of the present system (Harford 2006). The non-Enlightenment part of modern mass media is best illustrated in Orwell's novel *Nineteen Eighty-Four* (1949:46). Even though somewhat futuristically it is stated bluntly as:

> *here we produce rubbishy newspapers containing almost nothing except sport, crime and astrology, sensational five-cent novelettes, films oozing with sex and sentimental songs which were composed entirely by mechanical means on a special kind of kaleidoscope known as a versificator.*

Although we still may have a way to go to Orwell's *versificator*, present-day television already represents a similar device. TVs are very much an instrument that is targeting three aspects of present society – making us consume, pacify and neutralise any possible resistance, and divert attention away from the pathologies of modern work and society.[165] With hours of daily TV watching in most advanced countries, the act of watching TV has become crucial to the communication of ideology that stabilises the current system and managerialism. The value of watching TV has not passed unnoticed even though it is a one-way form of corporate S→R communication where the message (M=ideology) becomes the focus between S (corporate mass media) and R (us), enhanced to S→M→R. The transmission of ideology (M) is of high value to the system. Thompson (1990:1–3) has summed this up as:

> *In many Western industrialised societies today, adults spend on average between 25 and 30 hours per week watching television [fostering a] mediasation of modern culture [as] the general process by which the transmission of symbolic forms becomes increasingly mediated by the technical and institutional apparatuses of the media industry.*

In sum, the transmission of modern ideology organised by corporate mass media reaches into each and every home, into each and every kitchen, and into each and every bedroom. It delivers ideological content that stabilises and supports society while hiding, eclipsing or glossing over almost all pathologies that are created along the way. This creates the perception that it is this particular ideology that makes the whole system work and provides the glue that sticks everything together while covering up the system's worst atrocities.[166]

Ideologically, these atrocities are linked to the distant past of the 19th century. While capitalism's brutal past is firmly locked in the 19th century, today's brutalities have become – at least for approximately one to two billion people in advanced industrialised countries – less of a concern. In the past social control over a rebellious working class was administered more brutally while the role of ideology had been of lesser concern. Ideology construction under early capitalism was much simpler as ideological system demands were lower. Marx thought of ideology as a rather simple and straightforward concept of accepting ideas of the ruling class as natural and normal. Ideology constructed labour's understanding of their social experiences by means and ideas that are not labour's but those of the economically, politically and socially dominant class.

One of the characteristic attributes of capitalism has been the conversion of ideologies from a mythical and religious past into modernity. Having previously been used to legitimise feudal domination and power relations, in modern times ideology is applied to legitimise a relatively new system of socially constructed labour relations. This did not mark the end but rather the beginning of ideology.[167] Marcuse (1966:13) summed this up as: *this absorption of ideology into reality does not, however, signify the end of ideology.*[168] *On the contrary, in a specific sense advanced industrial culture is more ideological than its predecessor, inasmuch as today the ideology is in the process of production itself.* The power to legitimise the capitalist system in the present world is derived from the pretended legitimacy of the market. Sometimes this is rather mindlessly expressed as *it was done because of market competition* or as *this must be done for the sake of*

> justice-in-*market*-exchanges = justice-in-*labour*-exchanges

Figure 5.1 The Ideology of Exchange Justice

competition. The managerial market ideology has achieved an unchecked and almost God-like character.[169] Under these conditions, ideologies of legitimacy and justice are converted into market-exchange-relations. The ideology of a *just* market exchange becomes the ideology of *just* labour exchanges. The ideological conversion of this process has to be established communicatively. This can be expressed as an equation.

Figure 5.1 shows the equation of justice in market relations related to the labour domain. It transfers assumptions of an existent justice in market exchanges into labour relations. This is based on the hypothesis that commodity relations in the market exchange are no different to the exchange of the commodity of labour which reduces humans to things or resources as enshrined in Human Resource Management. At its fundamental core, it is no more that a *thing=human* equation with justice attached to it. The ideological belief system of the free and just market must therefore – logically – also result in justice in labour relations. Because of the fact that this does not reflect the true state of work affairs, the link shown in Figure 5.1 has to be communicated linguistically. The ideological task of managerial language in this context is therefore to communicate this equation in order to establish linguistic control over the labour domain. The linguistically established equation between one (commodity-market) and the other (human-market) allows the conveying and distorting of the real equation that is *commodity-market≠human-market*. To cover the reality that humans *are not equal to* commodities, the language of managerialism must be deeply ideological. In another, more political sense, the commodity=human equation involves a systematic distortion in the service of class interest. The core of this ideology is the eclipse of reality as much as the ability to artificially limit critical thought via an uncritical acceptance of the human- or labour-market. Any critique that might uncover the commodity-market≠human-market equation is confined outside the prevailing paradigm of managerialism. The exclusion of critical challenges allows the communicatively established ideology to operate as a forum inside which only highly restrictive betterment can be experienced. For example, it confines the structural injustice of the labour market to the simple paradigm of the price of human labour going up or down. Any critique of the fundamentality of commodity-market≠human-market is excluded. Inside the ideologically established framework for discussions improvements are seen as being legitimate as long as they lead to minor adjustments in working conditions and wages.[170] At the same time however this closes the door to fundamental social change. While managerial ideology seeks to deny contradictions that are operative inside the established system – such as the linguistically established equality between humans and commodities – it simultaneously allows for some minor modifications channelling any conflict into system-stabilising activities.[171]

However, ideology appears to be more powerful than Marx originally acclaimed. It works from *within* rather than from *without* as it is deeply grained into the ways of thinking and living. Ideology targets the thinking below the surface and may not even change the surface form of a *sign* or message but it seeks to alter the interpretive de-coding process by linking the surface form to a newly established underlying structure.

Crucial to the understanding of ideology is that all ideologies hold some form of meaning. They always represent, depict or stand for something that often exists outside the original meaning. Without the sign to which it can be attached ideology could hardly exist and the signs that can be linked to an ideological meaning are almost endless, such as, for example, a productive good such as *hammer and sickle* representing the Soviet Union. It can be a religious sign such as *bread and wine* representing Christian communion or a consumer good. Common to such ideological signs is that they do not just reflect or mirror reality but are themselves a material reality. Crucially, these material signs always depend on an act of representation in which the sign is linked to an ideological meaning in order to be able to operate as an ideological sign.

The act of meaning creation is of absolute importance as only meaning can link an ideology to a sign and this way colonise our individuality. It forces a pre-designed meaning into our frame of reference and changes our individual consciousness. Such an ideological frame of reference replaces reality with a new socially constructed meaning of the ideological sign. Ideological signs need interpretation. This occurs via linking the sign to a pre-arranged external meaning in the form of a new frame of reference. This newly constructed frame of reference is designed and enforced to create a new ideological meaning of the sign. In short, the sign remains but the frame of reference that allows the interpretation of the sign has been altered. The real ideological advantage of this process is that the well-established sign is kept while the unsuspected viewer or user of the sign interprets it inside the new pre-determined and ideologically driven frame of reference. The way the sign is understood has been shifted to service a sign-alien purpose. This is expressed, for example, in the understanding of wages.

Figure 5.2 shows the sign (ii) – wages – remained the same while the interpretive framework moved from an old (i) to a new (iii) understanding. What

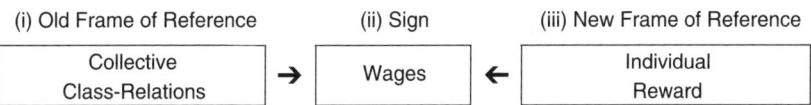

Figure 5.2 The Sign and Frame of Reference of Wages

is important is not its surface structure meaning – income, livelihood, etc. – but its interpretive meaning. Those who receive wages should still identify them as income, earnings, etc. but they should no longer understand wage-relations as a collective, societal, or economic issue. To achieve that, not the sign[(ii)] itself but the highly ideological frame of reference[(i+iii)] that makes the sign[(ii)] (wage) understandable, has to be altered in order to invade our consciousness. Once designed and successfully applied, ideological signs invade *internal* individual mental territories in a pre-constructed ideological rather than a natural sense. Ideological signs as well as their attached meaning can never arise naturally. They always need to be constructed socially with an ideologically charged motivation. In sharp contrast, non-ideological signs are constructed between social people in a process of communicatively established interactions.

All ideological signs need a person to adopt them. George Orwell (1946:7) referred to this process as *this invasion of one's mind by ready-made phrases* [signs] *lay the foundations, achieve a radical transformation* [that] *can only be prevented if one is constantly guarded against them*. An ideological sign *invades one's mind* or is adopted or internalised. Almost by definition it becomes an element of our communicatively constructed social reality. The use of ideological signs targets a consciousness that is ideologically reconstructed. This can only be defined as a social process. The creation, use, and internalisation of ideological signs are much less psychological than sociological processes. In the productive domain ideological signs can operate via managerialism while in the reproductive domain (*Überbau*) they function via mass media and a mediated reality.[172] As the domain of reproduction is the realm of ideological signs par excellence, the domain of production can never be free from ideologically charged signs. To uncover the ideological content of such signs, it is vital to determine the meaning that is attached to them in the contextual domain in which the sign is used. Ideologically constructed and domain specific meanings are never static as ideological signs move between the productive and reproductive domains and change their meanings in support of work and consumption regimes. Social relations can be influenced via ideological signs in both the world of work and the reproductive domain. Both domains operate a full range of communicatively established signs that relate to work, management, political, and economic life. These signs can be linked to ideologies and also be replaced by new, ideologically charged signs that alter the meaning of older ideological signs that have reached their use-by date.

Inside the domains managerial organisations are able to condition the use of ideological signs. These signs hide, misrepresent, and distort reality but they can never be separated from reality. If an ideological sign is to be successful in the production or reproduction domain, it has to achieve two things. Firstly, it needs to enter the domain and, secondly, create a reaction or link between sign and ideology. To some extent the sign must be associated with prerequisites that are operative in the domain and that have been experienced as reality. It must, even if only slightly, touch on domain specific realities and deny individual choice. While choice must appear to be free or individual, the only option open to an individual is the ideologically re-constructed one that has to be located inside an ideological frame of re-determined options. Individual options or free choice becomes ideological as it only opens pre-determined sets of options which are neither free nor individual but must always appear as having significance for an individual. In that way, *free choice* is pure ideology.

The usage of ideological signs depends on the establishment of their *inter-individual* significance as these signs need to be of relevance to the individual. They need to acquire social value through social internalisation. In the domain of work, a socially constructed ideological sign such as HRM needs to be adopted socially, largely without giving the individual any choice over whether or not to use it. The sign of HRM has achieved this. It has superseded *IR* that constructed social reality at work as a horizontal relationship between social actors. Instead, the ideologically constructed sign of *HRM* is directed towards a vertical hierarchical relationship shaped as top-down. Signs such as IR or HRM have become arenas for ideological struggles. They have been communicatively established and can also be re-established either socially (IR) or ideologically (HRM). Both signs shape reality inside the domain of work. Even though the sign of HRM has established its dominance, it can never totally be detached from the reality of the social domain. HRM constructs and increasingly cements the management-worker relationship as vertical. People in the world of work have accepted this and turn their world into a top-down world with a hierarchical order and command relations. This one-dimensionality of managerialism has become the accepted ideology. There has never been an individual choice over the use of the HRM sign and the sign itself has excluded any alternative view. Under HRM, social reality at work can no longer be seen as a social relationship but as top-down or *I-manage-you*.

Like any other ideological sign, the *HRM* sign has a *Janus*-face as it appears to some as representing trust and goodness while to others it depicts the greatest pack of lies seen at work.[173] Interestingly, both groups and their respective domains belong to the same language community or domain of work however this domain is being viewed in different ways. Management views the domain of work from a managerial position while workers experience it from their perspective. While such domains are socially organised along certain lines, they are also united in an immediate social situation, the situation of work. Here they have contact as real persons with one another on a specific basis that is the purpose of achieving profit, masked as *organisational goals*. The neutral sounding but ideological sign *organisational goal* is used to cloak the profit objective, not to deny it. HRM and *organisational goals* both hide their true ideologically constructed content.

The double or *Janus*-face like ideology of *HRM* or *organisational goals* suppresses distortion as well as the true underlying *meaning structure*. Ideological meaning structures rely on dogmatically shaped patterns, orders, syntaxes, and sequences of words and phrases. They are used implicitly or explicitly as rules governing an ideologically shaped discourse. The use of ideology creates a dysfunction between the surface form and implicit meanings. Ideologically constructed signs cannot be used via a direct linkage to reality as interpretations have to be diverted away from connections to an underlying meaning structure. Instead, these signs allow a linkage only to an ideologically created meaning structure. The use of ideology is always intentional as it is deliberately used by a sender. The purposive use of ideology lies in the reshaping of a once commonly perceived reality. Social reality becomes distorted as ideological reality is purposively constructed, reproduced, maintained, and communicated with intent. Ideologies only make sense when they are purposively used. This happens in three main ways (Mumby 1988:73).

Table 5.2 shows ideology in a descriptive, pejorative or positive way. The use of ideology in a strict or abstract descriptive sense is virtually impossible (5.2^i). Social groups are always connected to each other. They know their different social realities and are also always connected to other groups. Most ideologies constructed for *positive use* (5.2^{iii}) diminish, deny, or neglect the asymmetrical character of social groups in a society while a *pejorative view* (5.2^{ii}) of ideology avoids it completely. This view takes into account that

Table 5.2   Three Uses of Ideology

Ideology used in a	Explanation
Descriptive Sense (i)	Reflects the only reality that the social group knows by virtue of their positioning in a social structure.
Pejorative Sense (ii)	Maintaining a distorted and illusory relationship between social actors and the world, thereby obscuring the contradictions that *hegemonic* systems produce. Ideology articulates a view of reality that maintains and supports the interests of dominant groups and suppresses those of subordinate groups. Ideology in this sense reifies dominant meaning formations as the natural, sensible order of things so that social structures are no longer perceived as humanly constructed. It functions to secure certain hegemonic configurations by legitimising those meaning structures that favour the powerful by concealing contradictions, dominations, and power relations.[174]
Positive Sense (iii)	The driving force that motivates a particular collective to action in order to achieve a certain goal that serves the collectives best interest rather than working against it.

there is knowledge outside a social group and that asymmetrical power structures exist in society but this is seen as natural. Therefore, the pejorative use of ideology deflects from the real existing asymmetrical power relations at work and in society.

Ideological constructions also need to have an awareness of reality outside a specific social group. In short, any construction of managerialism as an ideology takes into account that ideologies from the non-work domain can be used in support of workplace ideologies. Ideology is a necessity for domination over work and society. Therefore it needs to be communicatively imposed on social practice at work. Ideologies as a hypostatising of ways in which life is conducted are pivotal for the reproduction of order and domination. For example, every worker needs to be conditioned in a highly hypostatised way that through hard work managerial positions are within reach. The ideology of HRM calls this career management. Ideologies such as these do no more than open up hypothetical options created by, opened by, and ultimately closed by management: *you can be up for promotion next year* or *in the next round I will not forget you* or *better luck next time* or *please apply next year* and so on. While such ideologies create hypothetical belief systems, ideologies in general serve different purposes.

Each purpose (a–e) listed in Table 5.3 can be achieved through applying different methods or different *modus operandi*. Firstly, an ideology can operate in the form of rationalisation of irrationality by pretending to be universal by telling a universal narrative. Secondly, an ideology can work as a displacement, as a euphemism or as a metaphor. Thirdly it can operate via standardisation but also as a symbol of unity and fourthly as differentiation or as expurgation by restricting thought. Lastly, it can proceed as naturalisation, as an eternal development or as a nominal or passive version. These five operative methods can be expressed in the following ways (see Table 5.4).

Apart from the wide range of operative modes of ideology that management can use (Table 5.4), one of the most important issues for management – perhaps the most important issue – is its own legitimacy. This is a task that has to be maintained and stabilised at all times. The ideological message is that management is not only a legitimate function and position but also worthy of support by workers and subordinates. Managerial legitimacy is such a

Table 5.3 Purposes of Ideologies

No.	Purpose of Ideologies
(a)	it can serve to legitimise management's position;
(b)	it can dissimulate as it can conceal and obscure;
(c)	it can unify positions;
(d)	it can also fragment positions; and
(e)	finally, it can serve as reification.

Table 5.4 Modes of Operative Ideologies at Work

Mode	Expressive Forms	Management Use of Ideology that is Operative at Work
1 Legitimisation	1.1 Rational	Management as rational, traditional, charismatic
	1.2 Universal	Management has universal values and is a universal institution
	1.3 Narrative	Management is embedded in times & cherished stories
2 Dissimulative	2.1 Displacing	Management uses an object to refer to another one
	2.2 Euphemisms	Management as a negative description in positive terms
	2.3 Metaphor	Management is described in figurative forms
3 Unifying	3.1 Standardisation	Management is framed as promoting shared values
	3.2 Unification	Management constructs unifying identity of individuals
4 Fragmentation	4.1 Differentiation	Management emphasises difference
	4.2 Expurgation	Management constructs enemy to increase internal expurgation
5 Reification	5.1 Naturalisation	Management constructs social issues as natural issues
	5.2 Eternality	Management constructs issues as eternal, traditional, endless
	5.3 Nominal	Management's language construction is person-free (de-human)
	5.4 Passive	Management converts actions into passive

fundamental issue that the foremost theoretician, Max Weber, expressed concern. For Weber, managerial legitimisation stems from several sources. It can be constructed by using a rational source (Table 5.4[1.1]) mirroring a technical, modern, scientific, or engineering institution. Today, managerial legitimisation can also be established on traditional management grounds as management has been governing capitalism since well over 100 years.[175] Based on its own history, the overall ideological message is *there is a traditional need to be managed!* As part of a self-invented tradition, there is also a managerial construction that favours a leader – based on the historical business leader – who is constructed as a charismatic business leader occupying a *natural* position and demanding followers to follow. Any airport lounge with a little bookshop almost anywhere in the advanced world will testify to this as it carries books *by* or *about* heroic business leaders.

Managerial ideology can also be constructed as being universal (Table 5.4[1.2]). Universalism is portrayed as serving the greater or the common good as management takes care of all interests including workers' interests and also determines *the greater good* and the interests. These are constructed *for* workers to be observed, absorbed, and adhered to via the supporting institution of management. The ideological equation reads as follows:

> managerial success = success for all

Figure 5.3 The Managerial Success for All Equation

The equation in Figure 5.3 shows that the universalism of the ideology of managerialism takes on a class-denying quality. It also denies the realities at work by paving over Taylor's division of labour, thus establishing an ideology of unitary outcomes where none exists. The communicative instrument to achieve this is the narrative. It tells a fiction, a fictional account of the realities at work. In its version of a narrative ($5.4^{1.3}$), managerial ideology relies on commonly acknowledged stories that are embedded into managerial communication. They are often a positive account of management's or corporate achievements told as fables and fairy tales and communicated as corporate legends. These forms of communication use timeless, supernatural, cherished, touching, enchanting, and even magical stories which build on stories that we have been told during childhood. In today's age of mediated realities, *Disney World* has successfully replaced fairy tale story telling.[176] Transferred into the reality of managerialism, even stories from a feudalist past become a valuable source of managerial support. These stories replace the corporate CEO with the image of the White Knight. But replacing can also become displacing.

The communicative act of displacing ($5.4^{2.1}$) uses a person that replaces another person or an act that replaces another act to construct a managerial ideology that seeks to legitimise managerial actions. Known action heroes displace CEOs by portraying them as defenders of *our* corporation against evil enemies. Often rather boring managerial actions are displaced and reframed into a setting that is non-managerial but still serves managerial interests. Similarly, managerial euphemisms ($5.4^{2.2}$) are actions, managerial institutions, or relations at work that are described or re-described as the re-establishment of order. For example, after a conflict at work or even an industrial conflict – including strikes, etc. – management seeks to re-establish its order. Managerial suppression of such conflicts puts management into a positive light as it appears as guarantor of peace and order. Conflict is portrayed as disorder or a violation of peace as industrial peace must be maintained.

The final version of operative ideologies at work is the figurative use of metaphors ($5.4^{2.3}$). As George Orwell noted in 1946, *the sole aim of a metaphor is to call up a visual image*. These visual images are very useful. Through them managerial language becomes more symbolic as metaphors seek to mobilise workers' imagination and establish imaginary connections between a managerial and an illustrative term. For example, *we are all in one boat* is a common metaphor that uses the boat analogy to depict social relations in a company. The imaginary connections work even though – and that might come to as a total shock – most companies are not boats. Suppressed, of course, is the fact that some have to pull the oars while others are steering the boat enjoying the upper deck. Obviously, the managerial boat metaphor should not reveal this fact, as its task is to distort, not to highlight the true state of social relations at work.

A second version of the metaphorical use of ideology ($5.4^{2.3}$) is called *metonymy*. This is used when attributes or adjectives are attached to a managerial action or plan without mentioning the action or the plan itself. For example, advertising often portrays a product by only highlighting its characteristics without actually showing the product.[177] This method makes representations of explicit characteristics of a managerial action without actually naming it. The characteristics can be highlighted via a link to a common standard of known descriptors. Managerial ideology can also utilise standardisation ($5.4^{3.1}$) for its action when specific actions are framed as standard actions that are widely shared and accepted by workers. Establishing managerial action in the language of corporate reality creates the perception as if special actions were standard actions. This standardisation is often part of a corporate discourse that is commonly acknowledged and accepted. Large sections of managerial and business language use standardisation much in the same way as they use unification ($5.4^{3.2}$). Here, the key issue for management is the construction of unity via an enclosing and encompassing of language which can also be achieved via corporate symbols that negate the division of labour into those who manage and those who are managed. They seek to establish common symbols of unity as expressed in corporate signs, badges, mottos, symbols, banners and the like. The ideological use of fragmentation ($5.4^{4.1}$) is quite the opposite of unity because it emphasises on distinctiveness, division, and difference as it seeks to highlight disunity rather than unity. For example, certain groups of workers who do not submit to managerialism can be constructed as alien, different, or non-fitting.[178] They are labelled as trying to destroy company unity. While they are portrayed as seeking disunity, management portrays itself as the seeker of unity. Needless to say, management is the only institution acting against disunity and those responsible for it.

A similar version of this is expurgation ($5.4^{4.2}$). It is very helpful in constructing management's enemies. Rather than just highlighting differences it goes one step further by branding as foes those who do not show an affirmative attitude to managerialism. They are shown as being evil, harmful, and threatening to the corporation. Critical questioning and dissent are quelled by constructing any disagreement or opposition as unpleasant or un-likeable.

The last section of Table 5.4 starts with the ideological construction of naturalisation. This makes managerially constructed phenomena appear natural.

Full success is achieved when management itself is seen as being natural. Consequently, all managerial actions become natural and everything that management does is just an expression of a natural occurrence. Once managerialism itself becomes a natural process rather than an ideology, the construction of the ideology that serves those in power is almost completed. Consequently, with the acceptance of management as natural comes the acceptance of HRM as natural and subsequently people accept their faith in *human resource* as natural. Hidden behind this is a reality that has been summed up in Poole's book on *Unspeak* (2006:66):

> *The template of 'natural resources' must, further, be to blame for the modern barbarism of the corporate term 'human resources'. To call human beings 'resources', firstly, is to deny their existence as individuals, since any one person will not spring up again once worn out; people are 'resources' only insofar as they are thought to as a breeding population, like rabbits or chickens. 'Human resources', first recorded in 1961, eventually succeeded the term 'manpower' in business parlance; the effect was merely to replace a crude sexism with a more generalised rhetorical violence. People considered as 'human resources' are mere instruments of a higher will. Compare the Nazi vocabulary of 'human material' (Menschenmaterial) and 'liquidation' (liquidieren, recasting murder as the realisation of profit); if 'natural resources' evinces merely as blithe disregard for the environment, 'human resources' contains an echo of totalitarian Unspeak.*

The element of nature cements the conversion of people into human resources even further as it locks people into eternity ($5.4^{5.2}$). It is designed to show that management and managerial actions are the continuation of an eternal process that is permanent, never ending, unchangeable, and unchallengeable. This ideology portrays social resistance as senseless, useless and dangerous. It is fruitless and unrewarding to challenge something that has always and will always exist. Management's decades of existence have no start and no end point. They have existed *since the beginning of time* and will be there when time ends. The nominal ($5.4^{5.3}$) and passive ($5.4^{5.4}$) use of language serves a somewhat different function. In the first instance, managerial language is constructed in a way where managerial actions become nouns. An example is shown in Table 5.5:

Table 5.5 Real, Nominal and Passive Statements

Real	Nominal and Passive
management has decided to downsize this department	a decision has been made that this department has to be downsized

In Table 5.5 a real statement such as *management has decided to downsize this department* has been transferred into *it has been decided that this department has to be downsized*. What remains unmentioned is the addendum *in order to maximise profits*. Apart from the unsaid words, the verb *decided* is converted into the noun *decision*. This gives the impression that a humanly created process is made final as the use of the noun supports finality. In a second step managerial actions are converted into passives. As the example above shows, an acting manager who is already hidden behind the wording *management has decided* has now completely disappeared behind *a decision has been made*. In this way, negative news – mostly for workers – can be cloaked in a passive language that appears as non-managerial action. Management takes a passive role and vanishes altogether to deflect any criticism on managerial decisions that are made to appear as if they were not made by management.

In sum, ideologies are proven to be a valuable source of managerial power. They greatly assist management in portraying themselves in a framework that only establishes meaning structures created by management. While originally Marx and other writers who critically discussed the political economy of 19th century capitalism saw ideology as something rather simple, this can no longer be said. With the shift towards more sophisticated forms of domination at work, system demands towards ideology have increased strongly. Today, ideology takes on many functions that were previously assigned to other forms of domination. The prime task of ideology in the domain of managerialism today is twofold. Primarily it serves to legitimise management and managerialism. In a second step, it also seeks to prevent any form of resistance by attacking it not only before it actually occurs but even before it enters the minds. It communicatively establishes an interpretational framework that only allows the one understanding that has been constructed by management. The managerial ideology has been proliferated ever since management has managed to establish itself in a hegemonic position. This deflects any challenge, even a democratic one, from management.

6
Distorted Communication III: Hegemonies

Key to a hegemonic meaning structure is to present it as universal. Sectional interests are portrayed as being universally established. Once this is achieved hegemonic meaning structures succeed in establishing a one-dimensional frame of reference.[179] Hegemony explains the ability of a social actor (such as a manager) or a group of social actors (such as management) to articulate their partial or specific interest in a way so that it appears to be the interest of all groups. Since Italian theoretician Gramsci this has been widely debated:[180]

> *Hegemony, for Gramsci, suggests the varied techniques by which ruling classes secure the consent of their subordinates to be ruled so that governing elites control the masses by creating, maintaining, and manipulating a mass consciousness suited to the perpetuation of the existing order.*[181]

Hegemonic tools are communicative tools. Without communication no hegemonic meaning structure could exist. These structures occur via the colonisation of popular consciousness through communicative activities as alternative discourses are subverted or marginalised. They seek to delete, end or negate all other forms of arguments, discussions, dialogues, and discourses.

Discourses organised through hegemonic meaning structures occur through the use of language. Individuals are *interpellated* as subjects as they become agents of specific ideologies that sustain relationships at work.[182] The secret of *interpellation* involves the recruitment and transformation of workers into believing subjects. They are made to believe that their relationship with others at work is natural (naturalisation), that it is of their own making, and that they control it. The strength of this version of ideological control lies in the fact that workers regard themselves as in control. In order to participate in their own control, they often organise employee participation, employee involvement and the like.[183] This pretends engagement and involvement inside a preset meaning framework that is organised by management. By believing in participation, employees engage in their own domination as they operate inside the hegemonic meaning structure organised by management. They believe to be the origin of meaning, not its product.

Ideologically shaped discourses do not function by simply fixing or determining labour's relationships at work but by mediating these relationships through communicatively guided practices, which correlate workers to workers and workers to society via surveillance of the discourse environment. This version of ideological discourse predisposes labour towards certain interpretive practices. It sets a one-dimensional frame around any communication among workers and encircles discourse by pretending to be an open and participative scheme. It never uses the range of interpretive possibilities that is open to management. Hegemonic meaning structures operate in several ways. Firstly, socially constructed work affairs and workplaces are removed from their historical and social origins.[184] In fact, they are ideologically reinvented as being necessary, natural, and self-evident. This establishes a hegemonic meaning structure inside which labour is allowed to communicate. Secondly, the control of hegemonic meaning structures allows management to communicate their interests in a way so that conflicting interests at work can be sufficiently suppressed. This occurs mostly by declaring the managerial interest as a universal interest.

Management is not alone in this endeavour as managerial writers, willing academics, and numerous business publications support them. *A plethora of schools of thought which attempt both consciously and unconsciously to eradicate conflict and contestability of organisational life through integrating the work-based human subject and the organisation* support these hegemonic meaning structures.[185] This is also linked to the third aspect that assists the establishment of hegemonic meaning structures. Even *Enlightenment*'s demand towards legitimacy and reasoning can be overcome through these structures. To do so, they need to be based on instrumental rationality, directed towards functional systems that rely on managerial input and labour's output. Only this is presented as being able to guarantee a stabilising system.

Fourthly and perhaps most dangerously, hegemonic meaning structures allow management to portray their interest – once accepted by workers – as evidence for a consent between both.

Figure 6.1 displays the ideological equation of the sameness of interests between management and labour. The equation of different interests combined as one universal interest renders legitimacy to management and is

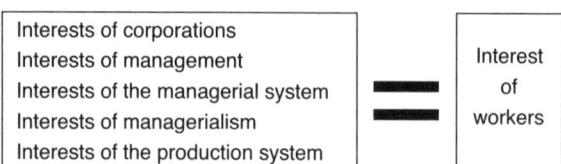

Figure 6.1 The Sameness of Interests

portrayed as the only way that leads to a positive outcome. It establishes the managerial interest as universal, as accepted by labour and, above all, as legitimate. Once workers participate in managerial schemes directed towards interests as shown in the first box of Figure 6.1, labour hands over significant legitimising powers to management. Management is deemed to present the managerial interest as a universal one because a one-sided presentation of their interest as such would create a lack of legitimacy. The pretended inclusion of workers' interests is the price management has to pay to gain labour's compliance. This is the very origin of the fact that a universal managerial interest can never be anything but ideology. Inside the managerial model of hegemonic meaning structures that combines different resources such as supplies, machinery, equipment, market access, etc., labour is just another factor that needs to be taken care of and for which management (unfortunately) has to pay – the *life cycles* of organisational *life* demand this.

Linked to an understanding of work as *life cycles,* the ideas of this cycle – or the facts of life – create yet another hegemonic meaning structure that is directed towards the assimilation of labour into the present production process. Everyday life is equated with *facts of life* and hence life in the company – ideologically termed *organisational life* – is just another practicality or *fact of life*. Hegemonic meaning structures based on *practical reasoning* convey the practicalities of working life that can easily be linked to *technical reasoning* which emphasises the technicality of the production process and reduces workers to a mere technical requirement, much like technical machines. Workers become a practicality, something practical to production. To challenge this would be to challenge the technical need of equipment. Such a hegemonic meaning structure creates legitimisation via technical systems.

Fifthly, hegemonic meaning structures limit people's ability to understand or act in their own interest. Exploitative relations at work are disguised and made to appear as legitimate. Such ideologies are often sustained by privately owned corporate mass media that create stabilising and hegemonic interests as a supplement to managerial ideology produced for the world of work. Inside the consumerist mass-culture, workers are shown as being in support of managerial interests.

Hegemonic meaning structures construct workers – if they feature at all – as willing participants in the managerial system. An open discourse about work is avoided as much as different interpretive options on work are left unmentioned. Management structures communication at work while in the private domain the mass media set strict limits.[186] In both domains the degree to which discourses can take place is severely limited. This social domination over discourse manifests definitions and, if necessary, allows for some minor deviations from common standards and norms of interaction. Under hegemonic meaning structures such interactions are shaped by the interest of the most powerful group, whether in private mass media or by management's position within a corporation.

The results of this are social and communicative inequalities. Privileged access to communicative resources reproduces social domination that leads to *Manufacturing Consent*.[187] Common consensus is reduced to an illusion in which one class establishes consensus, which is then implanted as a set of ideological or belief systems in the minds of those who are not part of a common consent forming group.[188] Social domination that creates hegemonic meaning structures therefore involves special access to various forms of discourses or communicative events. At work, management has this kind of privileged access. It also avoids equal or democratic access to communication that could create communicatively based meaning and understanding.

Finally, hegemonic meaning structures as a form of activity aimed at shaping, guiding and affecting the communicative conduct of workers allow management to manage sense making and reference framing. Management does not manage by simply ordering their activities and processing their workers; they are intimately concerned with the conversion of human subjects into objects of power. This is done through the structuring of communicative conduct via pre-arranged meaning structures that are part of what is called culture.[189] In most affirmative studies on business and management, hegemony is ideologically labelled as *enterprise culture* that pretends to be established by so-called organisational participants, thus trying to make believe that corporate culture is an open, democratic, and participative activity. By cloaking the brutality of corporate and managerial history and market forces, enterprise culture is presented as cultural, as having a soul, and as being civilised and artistic. The enterprise itself is portrayed as a *self* and as having a cultural existence that consciously constructs its culture. It seeks to convince us that corporations work on their culture in order to become a better self, a better organisation. By presenting itself as enterprise culture, this version of hegemony pretends to open up management as an opportunity for workers to participate in culture. However, behind the hegemony of corporate culture lies an ideology that pretends to establish culture by de-layering, de-bureaucratising, and de-controlling while at the same time it is being designed to re-control workers via a management guided process of controlled de-controlling.

As managerial powers via hegemonic meaning structures increase and workers are increasingly integrated into management systems, they are also given authority to control themselves. Once workers show a reasonable degree in cultural conditioning, including a sufficient degree of their acceptance of managerialism, they can be allowed to control themselves.[190] This managerially guided act of self-control is portrayed as de-layering, de-bureaucratisation and the like. It replaces one kind of hegemony (managerial control) with another (workers' self-control). In these enterprises hegemonic meaning structures have become capable of shaping workers' communicative behaviour by sublimely catering to the human need to communicate.[191] The communicative conduct that is allowed is however pre-shaped from above. Underneath the pretence of self-control rests the purely profit-driven interest. Management's task is to avoid any uncovering of this fact. The importance of incomprehension of the underlying structures testifies to the authoritarian, affirmative, and, above all, non-democratic character of managerial actions.[192]

The denial of democratic rights provides a sharp contradiction to labour's desire to have some of these rights. Under the hegemonic structures currently accepted by society, democratic rights apply to the social and political domain but not to the work domain. The workplace is governed undemocratically. The asymmetry between democratic political life and un-democratic working life is further evident in the time spent in each domain. In industrialised democratic societies, people spend approximately one-third of their adult lives in un-democratic workplaces while they exercise their democratic rights once every four years for about 20 seconds, the time it takes to give their vote.[193] Hence people unquestionably spend more time in non-democratic or authoritarian settings than with an engagement in democracy, however they are made to believe that they live in a democracy.

Unconsciously, we have handed over control to others accepting that they make us do things we otherwise would not do.[194] By allowing this we not only actively participate in, but also enhance un-democratic structures at work and elsewhere. At work the context, which would allow us to interpret democracy, has been removed. This context has successfully been shifted to the social domain. Hegemonic meaning structures have successfully disconnected democracy from the interpretive framework of work and workplace.

Figure 6.2 shows how a commonly accepted hegemony of democracy has successfully diverted attention from the non-democratic to the democratic domain. While originally workers sought to establish democracy in the work domain as well as in the social and political domain, today our understanding and with it the meaning of democracy has been – almost like a social-political version of a pathology called bipolar disorder – removed from the work domain. Today, the hegemonic meaning structure that allows us to understand and interpret democracy has been redirected from the work domain. In Figure 6.2 this redirection is shown as a weak link. Strangely,

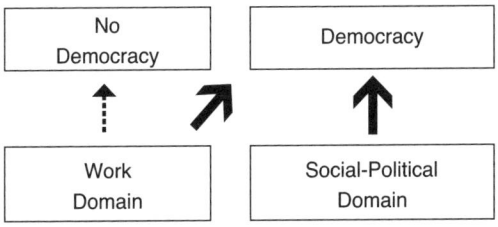

Figure 6.2   The Hegemonic Removal of Democracy

dominant hegemonic meaning structures only allow an understanding of the term democracy as linked to the social-political domain.[195] The communicatively established removal of democracy from work and workplaces has also removed democratically established rules, norms, and understanding of democracy. This has confined human freedom expressed in democracy within the political domain and away from the workplace domain. Modern mass mediated democracy is enshrined in the communicatively correct term of *giving your vote* which literally means it is given away to someone to be used at their will. Democracy has not been abolished; it is still in existence but it is constructed in a particular manner away from everyday life and everyday workplaces – a typical characteristic of ideology.

Present day conditions of non-democratic workplace relations carry connotations of authoritarianism, force, and oppression. This will continue as long as material and ideological powers operate to maintain non-democratic privileges. On top of this, we are following non-democratically established rules that govern the average 8⁺-hour-day at work in a 5⁺-day-week, and during 30⁺ years of working life. Hegemonic meaning structures have established these rules and with it those that govern them in order to be accepted more or less unconsciously. In the words of American philosopher Searle (1996:128), *indeed in many cases the rules are not even the sort of rules that we could be conscious of.* The hiding of non-democratic or even anti-democratic structures that govern our everyday lives is most successful when made to appear neutral. Management is neutral to any political interference as it is only about managing things through people. Management, so the commonly established myth, is just as neutral as technology or neutral rules that govern the workplace; even corporate governance is a neutral act.

Neutralisation and naturalisation

Neutralisation seeks to make social phenomena appear neutral by hiding their ideological content. Instead of formulating these phenomena as misleading, illusionary or alien, neutralisation seeks to misuse them by constructing them in a particular way, so that specific unwanted terms and connotations can be cloaked to hide their ideological content. One way of neutralising unwelcome contents is the naturalisation of a socially constructed reality. Naturalisation is achieved by making socially constructed issues appear natural and be seen as common sense. Common sense reflects on *the way things are,* just natural.[196] This converts a socially constructed reality into a natural reality. Through the use of naturalisation a socially organised activity such as work becomes the *nature* of work and work processes become natural processes. A few examples are shown in Table 6.1:

Table 6.1 shows that the process of naturalisation is not only applied to management, it is also applied to work. In fact almost any socially constructed process at work can be – and has been – *nature-ified*. It has intro-

Table 6.1 The Nature of the World of Work

from a socially constructed world	to	a natural world
A socially constructed reality of management	becomes	the *nature* of management
A socially constructed organisation	becomes	the *nature* of organisations
A socially constructed hierarchy	becomes	the *nature* of hierarchical top-down structures
A socially constructed decision making process	becomes	the *nature* of managerial decision making[197]

duced nature where none exists – almost nothing in today's workplace reminds one of nature: not the machinery used, not the laminated desk, not the plastic office chair, the computer, nor the air conditioning; not even the food that is consumed or the few artificially positioned token plants here and there. But the claim of being natural where no nature is found not only applies to office furniture; it is also applied to management itself. It is hardly possible to listen to any managerial talk or read any managerial magazine or textbook without being told that management is a natural process. *The nature of...* term is used over and over again. And it continues with the conversion of social phenomena into natural ones.

The distortion of socially constructed processes produces a false unity between purely formal – claimed natural – laws and the irrational and unnatural content of management. It makes it unlikely for a critical prescription – such as Kant's *ought to be* – to be able to modify existence.[198] Just as nature has no concept of *what ought to be* because *it just is,* and it is just natural, so are managerial processes. In the same way as natural reality appears to individuals as unchangeable so are managerial processes. They appear to be natural and, above all, neutral thus making the individual feel that they cannot be changed. Once the naturalisation process is completed, its ideological content sinks deep into human consciousness.

The appearance of something as natural or neutral must be established communicatively by addressing the members of a social relationship and leading them to participate in their own social and therefore ideological construction. Here, naturalisation and neutralisation are communicative and consequently social processes and as such open to ideologies. Naturalisation and neutralisation are highly valuable as both are useful to structure power relations. To cement such power relations is a constant requirement issued to management's position. Managerial ideologies are constantly facing resistance which management needs to overcome. In order to win labour's consent, management tries to neutralise their ideologies thus making them appear not only natural but also neutral. Neutralisation's task is to lock labour inside the managerially promoted top-down order in which the social construction of hierarchical orders appears as neutral as possible. However this is always a somewhat incomplete process. Neutralisation can never totally diminish labour's resistance to zero and therefore this form of linguistic distortion has to be maintained at all times.

A successful way of neutralising labour's resistance is the use of *Unspeak* (Poole 2006). *Unspeak* operates by erasing or silencing any possible opposing viewpoint. It neutralises alternative thought by claiming right from the start that only one way of looking at a problem is appropriate – the neutral way. Work or management are not spoken of as a socially constructed reality; *Unspeak* un-speaks management's power content and their constructed-ness in order not to open any avenues to *un*-construct or *re*-construct them. Neutralising versions of *Unspeak* are precision-engineered packages of language that are launched by managers and business people alike and that seek to drench workers' minds with a one-dimensional belief and make any opposing position more and more difficult to enunciate. By claiming that only management's viewpoint is a neutral viewpoint, any other standpoint is seen as unnatural, artificial, or alien. The ideological truths about management remain unmentioned as management presents itself as a neutral function between the market on the one side and labour on the other. While almost always taking side with the market and against labour, managerial ideology constructs the role of management as a technical and therefore neutral intermediary between market and labour.

Figure 6.3 shows management's most preferred version of self-portrayal. Here, it assumes the absolutely neutral role of a mere go-between, positioned between the market and labour. The issue of taking sides is hidden behind the role as a neutral mediator, which, as common sense tells us, is management's role after all. Therefore, one of the key neutralising strategies is the construction of *common sense* where the ideas of management are presented and to be accepted by labour as neutral and not even initiated by management. The idea of *common sense* uses shared meanings as an implicit acceptance of intentionally selected concepts to produce, confirm, affirm, and re-enforce specific meanings. The ideologically charged myth of common sense appears as *taken-for-granted* knowledge that is both natural and neutral. Examples are *it is common sense that management...* or *common sense tells you that management took the right decision...* etc. The idea is not to learn from these decisions or to understand them but to accept them as given. Crucial is that one cannot learn through common sense but one can learn to fit into an established order of things. Such system stabilising effects seek

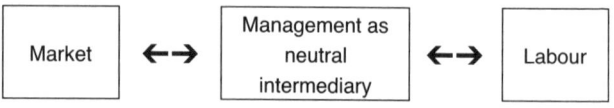

Figure 6.3 Management as Neutral Intermediary between Market and Labour

to mask the managerial formation of interest behind the myth of common sense.

While the construction of common sense supports systems of domination, it also appeals towards universality as one of its main characteristics. Common sense must play on commonly or universally established ideas to be functional. Management regimes can only maintain their dominance when their particular interests are accepted and appropriated as common. Non-democratic and authoritarian work regimes are therefore made to appear as common sense as they are best suited *to get things done through people*. Such an environment is accepted as legitimate even by subordinated labour as common sense suggests that it is ultimately in the best interests of everyone. This is so by virtue of being a system that serves the common interest.

Common sense also tells us that the time we spend working serves our personal interests. The *time clock to punch in and out* is able to deliver one of the most striking examples for the common sense neutralisation of a deeply domineering instrument of control (Mumby 1988:79). Time checking devices have been – and in many cases still are – used to control a specific element of labour, the time labour spends producing what it is told to produce. Even though the punch-in box has largely been superseded by more sophisticated 'time managing systems', they still serve the same purpose of controlling time which – today as in 1806 or 1906 – has been a prime demand issued to management. Whether through swipe cards, computer log-ins, or other methods, the use of time clocks to *punch in and out* remains a material reality for many workers in many organisations today. It achieves several things.

As Table 6.2 shows, a relatively simple instrument of managerial control can achieve a number of ideological elements. Firstly, it locks into labour's minds that time and reward are firmly linked as they appear natural and not as a managerial construction. Secondly, it greatly supports the ideology of *a fair day's work for a fair day's pay,* thus making the link between fair work and fair time appear natural. Thirdly, it maintains a two-tiered structure of labour and management as shown in Figure 6.4.

Figure 6.4 shows that the managerially constructed time control via punch-in or other devices serves several purposes. Firstly, it somewhat disconnects the domain of management from the labour domain as it applies

Table 6.2 The Ideology of Modern Time Devices

No.	Ideological achievements of time controlling devices
i)	it links time with reward in the mind of workers
ii)	it allows the idea of *a fair day's work for a fair day's pay* to appear natural
iii)	it maintains a two-tiered pay structure
iv)	it cements that workers get wages and management receive salaries

Domain:		Level of Flexibility:	Ideological Achievement:
Management	=	High time flexibility	Disconnected from time constraints
↕	↕	↕	↕
Labour	=	Low time flexibility	Time link appears as natural

Figure 6.4 The Labour-Management Time Equation

two different time controlling logics. Secondly, the equation sign '=' is only shown *inside* each domain but not *between* domains. Thirdly, it differentiates the two domains into a *high* and a *low* time flexibility domain. Fourthly and most importantly, it links time constraints and time freedom to different ideologies. While almost totally disconnecting management from any time constraints, for labour time control makes the link between time and work appear natural.

In sum, the time equation (Figure 6.4) takes management out of the labour-management equation by linking time to domain specific ideologies. While management enjoys time flexibility for business lunches, business meetings etc., labour is offered only low time flexibility. This links labour ideologically to time while simultaneously allowing management to escape this link. Timing devices such as swipe cards and clocks ideologically structure differences within the two different organisational realities. They create one reality for workers and another for management. This is also one of the clearest expressions of the existence of an organisational class system. But the simple act of timing goes even further. Time clocks also differentiate between two kinds of labour inside the labour domain. There is labour that is paid by the hour and is usually manual and labour that is compensated by salary. The second class classifies labour as somewhat less exposed to tight time control regimes. Usually the second class is considered cerebral and is not constrained by strict managerial monitoring. It is allowed a limited amount of freedom over the use of time. Most importantly, the ideological distinction between workers and management is reproduced through an actual material sanction for labour (rule receiver) while the same does not apply to management (rule creator). Management constructs absenteeism as a violation of workers' organisational responsibilities. Any form of absenteeism for labour is disallowed or strongly discouraged while this is not the case for management. It all depends on the position inside a managerially constructed hierarchy.

Lastly, time clocks bracket the working day for workers, signalling its beginning and its end. But this does not start with the arrival at work. Already when a little plastic strip on a cheap alarm clock jumps to a pre-set time, like pre-set versions of Pavlov's dog we are conditioned to jump up, have breakfast and go to work (Pavlov 1928). Furthermore, we are made to believe that this is a natural process.[199] Hence our behaviour has been structured well before we arrive at work. Punching time cards only indicate the point at which behaviour becomes even more pre-structured. While prior to the arrival at the workplace our behaviour is organised by pre-organisational needs, at work the organisational needs of the company structure our behaviour. At the end of the working day, *punching out* indicates the end of one's *organisational responsibilities* and the start of an equally pre-structured journey home to take on another pre-structured existence: A consumer walking through supermarket aisles behaving in accordance with the pre-structured lay-out of a supermarket that hides the goods needed (milk is always at the back) and presents the goods we do not need right in front of us.

Time, whether spent in a supermarket or at work, is not spent naturally. It is pre-organised and pre-structured with particular ideological intentions.[200] *Ideology* does not therefore merely reflect the material conditions of existence; it acts back upon them to fulfil its function of framing what is common sense, what is true, good, and possible within the context of these material social practices. Time clocks are not merely a reflection of a particular socio-economic structure. They are, in addition, one of the means by which the structure of relations between different interest groups is reproduced ideologically. The relationship between the ideology of time keeping and its managerial expression as an infrastructure of timing clocks, punch-in cards, swipe cards, log-in codes, etc. is therefore dialectical. Once time is ideologically cloaked as normal, just, rational, neutral, and even natural, thus disguising its ideological character at work, it accomplishes management's ideological objectives. Disguising the true meanings of time has a socio-political as well as a contextual dimension. The ideological construction of working time is rarely understood outside the management-labour domain. Managerial systems are organised in the interest of cloaking ideologies. They try to promote, naturalise, and disguise processes by making them appear as mere routine activities that just have to be done.

Routines in managerial communication and the distortion of history

Managerial ideology seeks to present interests as common by enshrining them in communicatively established *routines* of everyday practise expressed as *the way things are done around here, get on with the job*, etc. Routines are designed to become highly standardised speech acts that structure communication. Managerially structured communication uses *the blind and rapidly spreading repetition of words with special designations* to establish workers' obedience.[201] Such routine or standardised speech acts are taken for granted to such a degree that social actors are embedded and arrested in communicative power structures.

These power structures are not only established, they are routinely sustained via rehearsal and recurrence, reiteration, and constant reappearances to create consent that is established not communicatively via agreement but through an element of system integration. Routines are forced into a social relationship from the outside. This occurs in the domain of production as well as in the domain of reproduction. A routine-*isation* of communication – which intentionally makes communication a routine – is one of the main characteristics of a communicative process leading to *Manufacturing Consent*. Inside this process workers of all levels are enticed – willingly or unwillingly – to adopt, enforce, and reinforce the legitimate power. The power of management, of a company, or a society is rehearsed over and over again. This, of course, also characterises the prevailing system of production.

Practically from birth, humans are immersed in routine-*ised* versions of communication, trained and re-trained to be consumers first, and citizens second, if at all.[202] Most of our time is constructed as an oscillation between the roles of consumer and worker. Any free time between both is to be utilised and allocated to either one. Most of our off-work activities today are structured around consumption. Present-day humans are designed to either consume or find ways to add value via commodities.[203] This is routinely communicated through an unimaginable amount of advertising which manufactures consent via directing human activities and communication towards standardised products. At work, the ideology of *Manufacturing Consent* is most evident when employees announce: *I am just doing my job* or *that's the way it has always been*. These are two of the most routinely expressed examples of acceptance of asymmetrical power relations. They satisfy someone else's decisions or actions. The ideology of *Manufacturing Consent* serves as one of management's organisational principles that routinely demand reproduction and system-maintenance to preserve the interest of management over and above labour's interest. Ideologies that manufacture consent have been routinely communicated since the rise of the factory system.

In the history of management, routine-*ised* historical representations are found in rehearsed words, images, and symbols, in forms of corporate movies, company films, managerial or legal records, oral history, personal records, state and private documents, even advertisements. Every company's anniversary testifies to this with – largely similar – company books describing the company's history in routine words and phrases. As writers of affirmative company history are not free to invent historical events, they interpret and shape these via an ideologically determined choice between *facts* that they use and those that they ignore. Company histories are highlighted via so-called *important events* that are chosen – or rejected – according to certain criteria. For example, depending on whether the historical relationship between *capital* and labour or between *management* and labour should be shown, different *facts* are selected.[204] Once the *important events* have been chosen, they are routinely presented and interpreted to show what they are designed to show. This is neither a neutral nor a natural process, but an ideological one, which occurs not only in management driven company histories but also in labour history.

For example, in Kaufman *et al.*'s (2003) *Industrial Relations to Human Resources and Beyond*[205] dissatisfaction and revolt against horrific working conditions, horrendous industrial accidents, unbearable living standards, poverty, and life in ghettos are romanticised while labour is viewed as a *problem*.[206] The *epic struggle* of labour has a *natural* outcome in gain-sharing forms of compensation, the articulation of formal labour policies, and provisions for employee benefits, ending in *today's concept of high-performance organisations*.[207] Here, as in company books, an ideological paradigm is constructed that promotes a particular version of a historical past and also represents a vision not only of a socially constructed past but also of the present and the future (Nealon & Giroux 2003:97). In short, what appears is a *construction* rather than a *reconstruction* of history. This version of ideology hides the social construction of history. It often relies on naturalisation and neutralisation presented as *just reporting historical facts*.

In addition to ideologically reconstructing a factual version of the past, many historical studies of companies, management or its people-managing sub-division of HRM carry strong connotations to a study of literature as the mastery of narratives and stories moves to the centre.[208] Even though studies on history are inextricably linked to the politics of the day, they all too often reflect certain deeply held ideological presuppositions. Even in those books specifically written *for* companies, the historical politics-economy-company link is hidden behind voluminously large collections of never ending historical facts that are presented as a sequence, allowing the author to mask their apparent ideological character.[209] Such historical depictions of the past cloak the fact that they have been purposively and actively produced. Their social construction is deeply covered up in an ideologically shaped presentation of artefacts, portrayed as a mere uncovering of historical facts.

In some extreme cases the account of a company's history takes on storytelling or narrative elements that carry connotations to the world of *literature* rather than to the world of business, management, or workplace relations.[210] The narrative way of telling company history or the history of management itself can take on several forms. In most cases hegemonic meaning structures are brought to bear by a heroic company leader who battles the elements to get *his* (usually a male CEO) company through rough and stormy seas, i.e. the image of competition that brings the best to the forefront is evoked. In other forms of narratives, fictional causalities are established to support the ideology of managerialism. Here, credit or blaming occurs in order to shift managerially created problems to other spheres thus freeing the hero from any blame. In such narratives class relations are absent almost by definition as all (groups of) people are treated as indistinguishable. The core ideological element in these narratives is to portray today's standing of the heroic leader or company X as a result of individual effort in a market system. In short, success legitimises the methods used to get there. This sort of success is often attributed to special qualities of a charismatic, clever, smart, etc. corporate leader – and which workers are lacking. The issue of the charismatic leader can especially be created when company size allows for the distancing of the leader from the followers, i.e. workers. Only when social distance has been established, a normal person can be portrayed as charismatic. Charisma is socially constructed but in order to be an effective tool in narratives it has to appear natural. Emotional strength is another characteristic of a charismatic leader because such leaders naturally have some sort of emotional potency that can be called upon to ensure corporate survival. All this serves the illusion that the individual is the sole agency that has achieved success and which is totally independent from market forces and economic, political, regulative, etc. circumstances. Lastly, the narrative can rely on the illusive idea of fate and destiny because both serve well in the hands of the powerful to construct a hegemonic narrative that is above economic and social relations.

Once these core narrative elements are set, the construction of the narrative can take place by firstly deciding in which way the narrative is to be *framed*. This is crucial because it already decides which part of the real history is to be left out and which one is included. In this way the narrative can be *focused* on some simple messages that the story is set to portray. Clusters of events are brought forward while others are moved into the background. *Filtering* is a second tool that is used to negate or delete certain unfavourable events. Here, managerially unwanted and unwarranted events that are not conducive to the creation of the story are filtered out. Once this is done, some characters in the narrative can be subjected to *fading,* for example when unwanted founding members of a company fade into the background while others collapse temporarily so that certain events in the narrative can be constructed in a different light. Events in the company's history can also be combined or *fused* framing the truth in a particular and highly affirmative way. Other events can be fused with side issues to pretend their relative unimportance. The final tool in the armoury of the narrative is the idea of *fitting*. This is the simple re-interpretation or re-presentation of sections of the narrative to make it appear in an intended way. Using narrative storytelling techniques allows management to create hegemonic meaning structures not only over corporate histories but also over certain events that took place.

Historical studies, however, are not the result of a dispassionate uncovering of facts. They are meaning constructions that communicate a message to the present. They are often constructed in a way so that historical learning depends on one specific way in which history is to be understood and interpreted. Even claims such as *those who do not learn from history are doomed to repeat it* have to be exposed to possible hidden ideologies. Hence, affirmative historians – labour, and management historians as much as writers of the history of HRM – not only construct an ideological view of the past, they also shape our understanding of the present and the future. To uncover any ideological content in a construction of history and the interests that are served by the construction of a particular historical past, one needs to question any claim of *value neutral*ity of history. As Orwell (1949:260) once said:

> Who controls the past controls the future:
> Who controls the present controls the past

Figure 6.5 Controlling the Past and Controlling the Future

Orwell's statement (Figure 6.5) links any historical understanding of the past to the historical understanding of the present. Those who seek to make us understand the past in a particular way do so because of an interest that is linked to the present. Nowhere is this more evident than in standard books on the history of managerialism, capitalism, etc. Today's standard school, college, or university textbooks on history largely control present day understanding of the past. The only accepted version of the past is a mediated past. Inside its ideological one-dimensional framework, diverging or even critical views of any possible alternative interpretation of the past are made unacceptable. Today's history is still full of presenting good kings, kind queens, heroic battles, decent prime ministers, good entrepreneurs, evil dictators, trouble-making trade unions, welfare oriented industrialists and the like.[211] But they often have one thing in common as they tend to hide the everyday lives and the suffering of peasants under feudalism and workers under capitalism.[212]

As much as those *who are managed* are largely absent from present day textbooks on management and HRM, they are also missing in standard historical texts. Equally, as standard historical texts concentrate on the *kind king*, this ideological image returns in the version of the *kind boss*.[213] If *those who are managed or ruled over* are not negated altogether in the historical context of work, they are consciously or unconsciously constructed as subjects to the good ruler. The loyal subject image cements the view that rulers are necessary and that they are good. In modern times HRM shows the modern manager how to be good. Expressed in anecdotes and invented case studies, the good ruler or good manager is happily invented or exploited in most textbooks even when they are largely exceptional in reality. Any kind employer is used to the utmost extent in an effort to find supportive evidence of a glossy past of managing people at work that supports the present day ideology of ever lasting kindness of HRM.

The ideological content of historical studies is even more evident in the classical top-down approach to history in which a role reversal is applied. Labour force that initiated the transition from feudalism to capitalism and created wealth and industrialism is reversed and degraded to the *labour problem* (Kaufman *et al.* 2003). The history of capitalism and managerialism is viewed from the privileged position. Today, the unconscious, semi-conscious or conscious promotion of the managerial ideology seeks to influence predominantly those who are in an unprivileged position.[214]

This serves an ideology that deflects from labour as an active agent in history to those who are in power as the shapers of history. It strongly reinforces an ideology in which ordinary workers take no part in history as the history of industrialism, managerialism, and HRM-ism is created via a never to be replaced top-down view of the world in which *those who manage* and *those who are managed* have their historically natural place. Any historical abuse of power by capital or management vanishes into the background and – if it is shown at all – is made to appear as being part of a history that took place in the past. This past is constructed as having a starting and, what is more important, an ending point. In that way managerial cruelty and capitalist nastiness and mercilessness can be assigned to a past that is over. It can be safely locked in a box called history thus removing it successfully from the present. The present is shaped as disconnected from the past. We live in different times now!

Constructed in this way, the heroic entrepreneur defends *his* achievements against all the evils of the market and competition. He – usually a man – achieves this without having to be reminded of all the cruelties of the past as they are kept safely in a box with the label *history* on it. This distorts our understanding of the human cost of managerialism, the damage it creates for society and the environment. As Zinn (1973:54) wrote:

> History can blind us or free us. It can destroy compassion by showing us the world through the eyes of the comfortable. It can oppress any resolve to act by mountains of trivia, by diverting us into intellectual games, by pretending 'interpretations' which spur contemplations rather than action, by limiting our vision to an endless story of disaster and thus promoting cynical withdrawal, by befogging us with the encyclopaedic eclecticism of the standard textbook.

More than in political history, the history of industrialism and managerialism, including the history of large corporations or business leaders, is full of examples that construct history inside an ideological context that views the world of work through the *eyes of the comfortable*. The ideological project of these texts is directed more towards *blinding us than freeing us*. They *oppress us with mountains of trivial* issues about the brave founding fathers of company X or Y. They *spur contemplation rather than action* via the construction of an ideological company history that tells us *that's the way it was* and most importantly: *that's the way it is*. Industrial actions that achieved social, material or community benefits are excluded from company history as much as they are excluded from standard HRM textbooks.[215] In the tailored world of easy-to-use textbooks, the world of work is reduced to short sound bytes. This is a clear reflection of today's TV-engineered marketing processes conveniently *used* by today's business and management students. These textbooks suffer from reductionism that forces every form of knowledge into one-dimensional understanding using questionable and invented anecdotes, misleading case studies, inadequate examples, and silly management statements. This version of knowledge is checked at the end of each chapter to ensure that the learner has been sufficiently conditioned. A learner's adoption of pre-constructed knowledge is affirmed through the positioning of sometimes ridiculously silly questions.

It all serves one purpose: to show that there is a good-hearted – HRM or otherwise – manager who just wants to get things done through people with a little bit of value being added. Goodness can only come from a kind-hearted company boss or from the equally kind-hearted HR manager. The ideological goal of all of this is to limit our vision by overwhelming us with an intentionally constructed endlessness of historical facts, designed to prevent critical social understanding and, most importantly, social action. Hence, standard textbooks on company X or Y, on management or on HRM tend to be rhetorical rather than enlightening, persuasive rather than critical and instrumental rather than substantial.

7
Distorted Communication IV: Culture, Rhetoric and Meetings

As we have seen, a representation of sectional interests is portrayed as a universally established hegemonic meaning structure.[216] Under self-serving, self-persuasive, and self-diluting statements such as *yes, I know it could be called immoral, but that is not an element I can take into account professionally*,[217] managers of all types are only too willing to pursue the establishment and maintenance of hegemonic meaning structures as long as these deliver knowledge into the hands of power. It appears as if too many of them have moved on from the old management ideology of *they do not know what they do* to the new ideology of advanced managerialism: *they know what they do but they do it anyway*.[218] The creation of hegemonic meaning structures essentially fosters the ability of one social group to articulate their partial or specific interest in such a way that it appears to be the interest of all groups.

Ideologically shaped discourses do not function by simply fixing or determining labour's relationships at work but rather by mediating these relationships through communicatively guided practices. Workers are correlated to workers, to management, and to society via system surveillance of the different communicative spheres. The communicative concept of discourse is reduced to a pure ideology that predisposes labour towards certain interpretive practices; it never completely utilises the vast range of interpretive possibilities that is open to management and which is used to construct a communicative environment that guides labour's discussions into a direction pre-designed by management.[219] This occurs in different ways: firstly, socially constructed work affairs and workplaces are removed from their historical and social origins and treated – or in fact ideologically reinvented – as necessary, natural, and self-evident. Any discourse among workers is disconnected from the historical frame of reference. Workers' debates are created to be non-historical as they should not be able to uncover the history behind their actions at work. Secondly, *Enlightenment*'s demand towards legitimacy and critical reasoning are overcome through hegemonic meaning structures. These are based on instrumental rationality directed towards functional systems.

Managerial discussions are constructed so that they rely on management's input and labour's output. Any communicative exchanges constructed as input-output-systems are highly stabilising and almost always directed towards the maintenance of the managerial system.

Thirdly, the control of hegemonic meaning structures allows management to communicate their interests in a way so that conflicting interests at work can be sufficiently suppressed via the pretence of the universalistic managerial interest. Work and production need to appear conflict-free. No discourse under these guidelines should lead to the discovery of the underlying contradictions. Discussions should be logical, as they should follow a logical sequence and should not be *dialectical*. Any thinking in contradictory terms that positions an issue as *thesis* (workers' interest) and *anti-thesis* (managerial interest) is avoided as it could uncover inherent contradictions leading to *synthesis*. The result of such a process of critical thinking might not be in management's interest. The anti-critical and anti-contradictory thinking inside linear logics is supported by a *plethora of schools of thoughts. They attempt – consciously and unconsciously – to eradicate conflict. They also seek to end any contestability of organisational life through integrating the work-based human subject* and support such hegemonic meaning structures.[220]

Fourthly and most dangerously, the pre-construction of discourses allows management to portray their interest, once accepted by workers, as evidence for consent between both. Interests of corporations, of management, of the managerial system or managerialism, the interest of the present production system, and the interest of workers are presented as one and the same and even though they are different, are expressed as universal and legitimate. Although labour is seen as just another cost factor in combination with costs for supplies, machinery, equipment, and market access, management has an additional cost, the cost of the ideological inclusion of workers in the company. According to this ideology, labour is seen as a fact of life for which the company has to pay for while never allowing any discussion on who created this fact of life and what are the factors behind it. Together with *life cycle theories*, the facts-of-life ideology provides another example for managerial domination of meaning. Both *life cycle* and *facts-of-life* ideologies are directed towards legitimacy and the assimilation of labour into the present production process. Such *practical reasoning* is provided to everyone as a fact of the world of work. It offers, of course, practical understanding of everyday life and is not to be found in theoretical discussions about work.

Any hegemony over meaning based on *practical reasoning* is a manifestation of the practicalities of managerial working life. Furthermore, hegemonic domination over meaning based on *technical reasoning* emphasises the technicality of the production process thus reducing workers to a mere technical need much like technical devices and machines. To challenge this would be to challenge the technical need of equipment. This ideological techno-worker link secures management's position. The domination over meaning not only incorporates labour into the managerial system, it also creates legitimisation via technical systems.

In addition, hegemonic domination over meaning also limits people's ability to understand or act in their own interest because exploitative relations at work are disguised and made to appear as legitimate.[221] Often ideologies produced by corporate mass media also represent stabilising interests.[222] This is a vital supplement to managerial ideology produced for the world of work. Inside the consumerist mass-culture, workers are reduced to stakeholders in a system that appears to be in support of their interests.[223] This system is designed not to open up any discourse that allows different interpretive options, either at work or in the public media. Communication at work structured by management mirrors communication in the public-private domain.[224] At work, the managerially structured communication sets strict limits to the degrees in which discourses can be opened up. The same applies to the public domain. In both domains discourse is strictly defined by managerialism or by corporate media.

The use of social domination over discourse at work and external to work requires narrow *definitions* of terms. If necessary, it also allows for minor deviations from the standards and norms of interaction.[225] These interactions are always shaped by the interest of the most powerful group, be it private mass media or management's position in a corporation. Social domination by one group results in social and communicative inequalities at work and outside of it. This is reproduced by the enforcement of privileged access to both domains. Such asymmetrical access to communicative resources allows some to communicate while others are prevented from doing so. This results in *Manufacturing Consent* and the creation of an artificial consensus which is achieved in a process by which one actor produces and then implants a set of ideological or even misleading belief systems into the minds of other members over whom the actor rules. All forms of social domination involve special access to various forms of discourse or communicative events. At work, management has this kind of privileged access to communication and discourse. This position of communicative domination makes it easy to restrict equal or democratic access to communication that could create communicatively based meaning and understanding.

Communicative domination allows management to shape sense making and reference framing as two possible fields of action for workers. It is a form of activity that is aimed at the shaping, guiding, and affecting of workers' communicative conduct. It does not simply determine their activities or process workers; it is intimately concerned with converting human subjects into objects of power through communicative conduct pre-arranged on the foundations of hegemonic meaning.

In most affirmative managerial studies communicative domination has been labelled *enterprise culture*. By using the neutral and almost natural sounding term *culture*, management and their willing writers are able to hide communicative asymmetries and the communicative domination. While cloaking the brutality of market forces and managerial domination, *enterprise culture* presents managerial hegemony as *cultural*, as having a soul, and as being civilised and artistic. The enterprise itself is portrayed as a *self* and is constructed as having a *cultural existence*. Woven into the ideology of *corporate culture* is a consciously constructed body of ideas that extracts cultural elements from societal culture so that corporate culture appears as civilised and cultured.[226] Work and all profit driven activities are ideologically reformulated and presented as *culture*. Managerial processes are therefore turned into cultural processes that were put in place for the company to become a better self. When workers participate in corporate culture, they are made to forget that they participate in a profit making activity. In order to be a better organisation any company is seen as in need of some form of *organisational culture*.[227] The existence of culture in an organisation enables management to pretend that companies have some artistic value or aesthetics.

Of course, this is true *Unspeak*.[228] It brands anything that is directed against the specific form of *managerial culture* as *uncultured* or *culturally dysfunctional*. Managerial, organisational, and corporate culture are no more than elements of a one-dimensional culture of managerialism in which management's action is considered as contributing to the *organisational culture* while any form of workers' dissent is seen as *uncultured* or *culturally dysfunctional*. Culture that is constructed in this way becomes pure ideology designed to smother any unwarranted interest or protest. All of this lies beneath the blanket of managerial monoculture that has strong system integrative imperatives as it defines any *resistance* as uncultured.[229] The establishment of corporate culture is a superb instrument that is highly valuable for the hegemony of management. However the ideology of organisational culture does more than that; it is able to even hide the existence of managerial hegemony by presenting it as organisational or enterprise culture itself. In this way, management is able to pretend to be open to culture and offer workers an opportunity to participate in the creation of the organisational monoculture. Workers are made to believe that they can participate in de-layering, de-bureaucratising, and de-controlling while in reality their participation acts as a tool for the re-controlling of workers through the managerial process of controlled de-controlling. The more management establishes organisational culture via communicative domination, the more it can pretend that workers are able to participate in removing layers of managerial control. The managerial power of hegemonic communication is increasingly able to integrate workers into a control system that is guided by ideologies. It sells to workers an organisational culture that gives them increased authority to control themselves.[230] This is no more than a communicatively established cultural control system. By subliminally catering to crucial human needs enterprises are capable of shaping workers' communicative behaviour. The underlying ideology of organisational culture impedes any comprehension of the managerial process that is, in fact, purely profit-driven and cloaks the process that is guided and directed towards a totality of authoritarian, cultural affirmative and, above all, non-democratic managerial actions.

The denial of democratic rights cloaked as organisational culture in the workplace provides a sharp contradiction to democratic rights in a political context. Despite all claims, or better, precisely because of the ideological construction of companies as cultured organisations, they can continue to be governed undemocratically.[231] Unconsciously and under the blanket of an *organisational monoculture,* workers have been handed over more controlling instruments that allow them to control themselves. Even this has been accepted as cultural. The fact that undemocratically governed companies can never be cultural companies remains unspoken. By accepting the ideology of organisational culture we are further enhancing un-democratic structures.[232]

The context in which we interpret democracy has been successfully replaced by the interpretive context of organisational culture. The ideology of organisational monoculture has been able to shift an external and pleasurable or aesthetic activity into the world of work. This has been achieved without any contribution to real culture. The managerial achievement is twofold; firstly, it cloaks the fact that organisations operate largely without culture, beauty and aesthetics; secondly, it hides the non-democratic character of work even though democracy is part of our culture. The communicatively established removal of democracy away from work and workplaces has also removed rules, norms, and expected understandings of democracy and culture of work.[233] There are no organisational discourses on organisational music or organisational paintings, whether modern, Cubism, or abstract paintings, on modern literature, etc. In short, organisational culture is a culture without any content other than cloaking the domination of non-democratic managerial decision making. In these uncultured and un-democratic workplaces cultural relations among cultural participants are based on the culture of force and oppression. This will be the case as long as material and ideological powers smother participative democracy with a managerial monoculture based on the ideology of managerialism. To achieve non-democratic workplace relations management negates participation and replaces it with organisational culture. In this process, management makes heavy use of rhetorical and ritualistic tools.[234]

Managerial rhetoric and rituals

The art of convincing people has been seen as rhetoric since the Roman statesman *Cicero* (106–43BC) developed his five functions of rhetoric. These are *inventio, dispositio, elocutio, memoria,* and *pronuciatio.* The first, *inventio* is about the arrangement of arguments. *Dispositio* means to emphasise and to express while *elocutio* stands for the presentation of an argument. But at the core rhetorical action (*actio*) is not so much the art of acting but to speak, which derives from the Greek *rhetor*.[235] Combined with the Latin word *eloquent* today's meaning of the term rhetoric was created. Even though this term is strongly connected to a means-ends idea, the threefold goals of rhetoric – to instruct, to move, and to please – are rather mechanical. More generally rhetoric can be narrowed down to two essential components: a) its persuasive function as the art of constructing or finding an argument and b) its ornamental or figurative character as a style of language used in a decorative or pleasing fashion.[236]

One, quite often applied, rhetorical tool is to suppress alternatives.[237] Rhetorically these alternatives are called *extremes*. The rhetorical attack on alternatives can also be directed against a person. This occurs when someone who expresses alternatives is labelled an *extremist*. To label something as *extreme* or call someone an *extremist* is to denounce him merely for his position. In this way non-managerial or non-profit-supportive ideas or persons who have such ideas are often censured. The tool operates on a managerially invented and always imaginary spectrum of managerial ideas in which any truthful engagement with *what* is actually said is avoided. An extreme position is managerially defined and located outside of the accepted managerially constructed discourse. Consequently, it can be neglected or denied which relieves management from the need to have to listen to arguments or persons. Once this process is accomplished management has created a highly valuable protective tool that excludes standpoints which are made to appear unreasonable and, above all, *essentially extreme*, a label applied to those who should not even enter managerially structured discourses.

At the opposite end of the scale of this management tool the moderates who hold *moderate* views, i.e. views concurrent with management, are to be found. Similarly, concurrent views are also labelled as *balanced* which carries connotations of neutrality because they can be presented as good or bad, positive or negative. Balanced views are highly welcomed in managerial discourse as they balance out one managerial or non-extreme idea against another, thus confining ideas inside the managerial framework. Rhetorical tools are able to hide the asymmetric power of managerialism by presenting it as being balanced. Once a management-compliant view has been labelled as *balanced* or *neutral*, it is effectively shielded against critique. By using rhetorical tools to label a view as balanced, moderate or extreme, management is able to shape discourses. After all, it is management who defines what is extreme, balanced, or moderate. To operate in the false *extreme* versus *moderate (= balanced)* dichotomy is a distorted way of communication.[238] It only serves to deny alternatives and contradictory viewpoints in an effort to construct a one-dimensional dialogue between labour and management. When management speaks of balance, extreme or moderation, it *unspeaks* critique.[239] Such labels are rhetoric versions of *Unspeak* as they exclude, leave unmentioned or simply *un-speak* critical or unwanted issues.[240]

Rhetorical rules are used to rule out alternatives. In many cases, communication uses rules according to the intentions of what is communicated. These rules are constructed in different contexts and the communication or speech acts are characterised by the use of pre-determined forms of expressions supported by a pre-established sequence of patterns that avoid differentiations issuing general restrictions to communicative freedom.[241] Such speech acts or forms of communication are called *ritualistic communication*. It describes any non-verbal or verbal action that is no longer, or only to a limited extent, individually understood. The ritual takes over individual intentions to communicate. Ritualistic communication appropriates specific necessities of certain communicative situations and is often highly standardised. It follows pre-patterned behaviour inside schematised forms of communication. *It is designed not to extend but to diminish the range of thoughts, and this purpose was indirectly assisted by cutting choice of words to a minimum* (Orwell 1949:313). Such ritualistic and choice-limiting communication exposes a relatively high degree of conventional and servicing speech regulation. It *serves* rather than *enables*. It services the managerial intent while lowering any alternative interpretations or restricting these to a bare minimum.

Participants in ritualistic forms of communication are commonly reduced to act within pre-organised and pre-defined roles. Ritualistic communication coerces labour into a ritualistic execution of pre-assigned communicative sequences. These ritualised forms of communication serve to ensure support, enforce, and reinforce specific managerially institutionalised ends. Ritualistic communication strongly supports ritualistic behaviour directed towards managerial or corporate goals. The role of the participating workers who have been locked inside these ritualistic processes is reduced to a mere acceptance of the ritualistic communication devices used by management and directed towards recognition and subsequent approval of pre-arranged communicative hegemony. The ritualistic form of communication is somewhat *parrot-like* as the potential of language use approximates the language usage of a parrot. It repeats the same things over and over again, is cliché ridden and lacks meaning and energy, but is full of rhythm and always performed as a ritual.

Ritualisation – the turning of communication into a ritual – strongly contributes to a managerially guided form of communication. It is designed to uphold managerially issued systems of hierarchies and rules. Ritualistic communication enshrines management value systems that, over time, become inseparable from managerial ends. Such forms of communication are always linked to reality. They enter human understanding through the back door. Therefore, ritualistic communication always relies on conventional expectations such as an obligation to be loyal or faithful to corporate goals. Ritualistic communication not only seeks to influence communication and individual decision making but also aims to exclude forms of communication that offer alternatives. This shapes communication in a preset and intentional way.

Ritualistic communication is an extension of pre-regulated forms of managerial communication. It comes into play when non-ritualistic forms of communication conducted by management lack superior codification, i.e. when management experiences insufficient prescriptive determinants to shape communication or when normal communication is unable to fully operate as hegemonic communication. Once ritualistic communication comes into force, management speakers are able to use the whole repertoire of pre-determined expressions. The goal of ritualistic communication is to situate dialogue inside a pragmatically defined communication exchange

Table 7.1 Managerial Communication as Ritual

Forms	Managerial Use of Ritualistic Communication	Illustrations
a) Restriction	– Exactly defined managerial situation for use of ritual – Wording and sequence pre-established – Avoiding alternative interpretations or competing meanings – Prescription sanctions directed towards non-compliance	Institutionalised and corporatised acts of communication directed towards highly structured procedural forms of workplace interactions.
b) Extension	– Highly standardised situations for communication – Use of the full repertoire of ritualised communication – Communicative formula linked to situational circumstances	Structured application through pre-arranged settings emphasising ritualistic procedures at work.
c) Ritual-Making	– Use of pre-determined schemata of expression & speech acts – Use of communication disconnected from actual situation – Reliance on abstract rather than concrete communication – Avoidance of awareness of hierarchy & superiority – Evading & hiding of any reference to individuals	Strong use of commonplaces, maxims, proverbs, slogans, stereotypes, persuasions, empty formula that avoid factual situations but support corporate goals.
d) Routine-Making	– Non-ritualistic communication based on automatism – Instrumental rationality of Management is supported	Standardised communication allowing workers' input, but not decision making.

directed towards corporate goals. It is one-dimensional as it reduces complexities by ritualising them.

All forms of ritualistic communication seek to reduce the complexities of social interaction at work. They are used to distort communicative exchanges that are strongly linked to work as well as relationships at work. By pretending that they are unalterable, ritualistic communication fulfils a system maintenance function. It guarantees an unambiguous interpretation of corporate goals and seeks to establish a ritualistic identification with the issues talked about. Essentially, ritualistic communication carries four elements. Firstly, rituals are used as devices to restrict communicative engagement. Secondly, they provide a valuable extension of non-ritualistic managerial communication. Thirdly, communication is vital in establishing ritualistic action at work and finally, the process of establishing routines can be guided. Table 7.1 shows some of these elements.

Table 7.1 shows that management can utilise rituals to either restrict communication (a) or use them as an extension of communication (b). It also illustrates the process of creating *rituals* (c) and *routines* (d). The actual ritual – as a restriction or an extension of communication (a & b) – should be seen as separate from the making or creation of rituals or routines (c & d).

Table 7.1[d] states that a certain automatism can be used to create a routine that is supportive of the instrumental goals of management. Predominantly, this can be achieved by moving un-structured communication into the realm of structured communication. In the process of *routine-making*, management can allow workers to have a supportive input in management's plan; however, such inputs are always limited via highly structured communication devices. Labour's participation in the creation or making of routines always occurs by stealth and is an unconscious and hidden process. It always avoids real decision making by concealing management's power and intentions to make and later use routine forms of communication against labour.

Restricting communication is also at the heart of another form of ritualistic communication as shown in Table 7.2 below.[242] Here, management seeks to limit workers' communicative choices through the structuring of

Table 7.2 Structuring Levels of Rituals

Levels	Form of Rituals Used
(i) Sequencing	ritualistic communication is established through a sequencing of managerial communication segments;
(ii) Re-Occurring	the use of particular and re-occurring speech acts such as clichés, phraseologies, or empty formulas, via suggestive speech acts; repetition;
(iii) Pre-Planning	the pre-planned wording of certain managerial expressions that can entail sanctions.

communication where communicative situations are planned to achieve considerable reductions of workers' linguistic choices. To achieve this, three core elements of structuring are used: the sequencing of communication as ritualistic communication; re-occurring and reappearing communication; and managerial pre-planning of the ritual. These become operational (see Table 7.2).

Table 7.2 shows how in the first form of communication rituals are created by following a managerial set of sequences. This is done via the compartmentalisation of communication into tidily constructed boxes that are rehearsed again and again until they achieve a securely established form of communicative conduct. The ritualised language is not communicatively established via common understanding, but its

> *meaning is fixed, doctored, loaded. Once it has become an official vocal, constantly repeated in general usage, 'sanctioned' by intellectuals, it has lost all cognitive value and serves merely for recognition of an unquestionable fact* (Marcuse 1966:98).

The sanctioning by intellectuals occurs in the realm of HRM through the textbook writers who classify, if not invent, a whole set of terminologies that construct labour's communication.[243] Once established as a *quasi-academic* discipline and taught in today's management and business schools, these ritualistically rehearsed classifications become part of the managerial folklore of today's HR-managers.[244] Knowledge is classified, served in sequences, and rehearsed over and over again until it reaches the ritualistic status of an *unquestionable fact*.[245] Relatively important to sequencing[(i)] is that these forms of communication are made to re-occur[(ii)]. Without the re-occurring element pre-planned[(iii)] forms of communication cannot be established as routines. In many cases of ritualistic communication these levels include the rehearsing of communication devices.

Table 7.3 shows some of the managerially used stereotypes usually designed as a system integrative device. These common stereotypes are used as communicative expressions of knowledge that has ceased to be reflective. The managerial language used in such stereotypes has closed down any link to living context. The formulation of ritualised communication tends to

Table 7.3   Rehearsing Ritualistic Communication Devices

Types	Examples
Common maxims	we are all in one boat
Proverbs	in a company of the blind, the one-eyed man is king
Common places	the business of business is business
Managerial slogans	that play on celebrated books, plays or films

produce new forms of content. Previously meaningful formulas have been emptied and re-filled with ritualistic meanings. It is a classical example for a case when *form* supersedes *substance* and *content* of communication. Communication is reduced to a mere *form* or *shell* that has deliberately been emptied of almost all meaning and content. Here communication is driven into an extreme form of automatism, made to appear automatic and also turned into a routine. This automati*sation* and routini*sation* occurs in everyday communication between management and labour. It is designed to attack or destroy all the prerequisites of communicative understanding that could come out of *communicative action* and is the opposite of communicatively reached understanding. Created inside the asymmetrically structured communicative hierarchy at work, these forms of communication are used as persuasive instruments directed towards the shaping of workers' attitudes.[246]

Form and content of managerial meetings

The distortion of communication is not only achieved via conditioning and managerial speech construction but also by arranging or setting up the forms in which labour-management communication takes place. While standard textbooks see such managerial meetings as *a necessary evil in any organisation*, in reality they are constructed as one of the most powerful institutionalised forms of managerial communication (Blundel 2004:303). Before any communication can take place in such meetings, management pre-decides the meetings' character by setting the communicative scene through classification.

Table 7.4 shows the variety of managerially classified forms of meetings. Irrespective of such meetings being constructed as managers-to-managers or as managers-to-workers meetings, they are all specific forms of communication. When constructed as management-to-workers communication, such meetings are an extremely useful tool for managers. In the case of a pure (i) *briefing meeting*, management has the option to simply deliver information or certain forms of knowledge they deem necessary for workers. This is knowledge that management views as *workers need to know* rather than *workers should*

Table 7.4   Communicative Distortions through Managerial Meetings

Type of Meeting	Description	Purpose
i) Briefing	delivers information	purely top-down, managerial forum
ii) Investigative	gathers information	allows using workers' ideas
iii) Advisory	gives information	management tells, workers receive
iv) Consultative	voice option	gives workers illusion of being consulted
v) Executive	makes decisions	involves managers, directors, trustees, etc.

know. Instead of being informed comprehensively over organisational directions, etc. workers are given selected information that provides them with just enough knowledge to operate and be efficient.

This managerial ideology is not based on comprehensiveness but on efficiency expressed as *communications are tools to assist in getting work done. The only justifiable reason for communicating is to accomplish the objectives established for the organisation* (Himstreet & Baty 1961:17). Of course, such partial and non-comprehensive knowledge has been designed specifically in order not to allow workers to understand or even analyse the purpose of certain organisational activities or specific work tasks. Above all, the link between workers' activities and the all-powerful profit motive is cloaked (Marris 1966:18). Rather than giving selected information in a hierarchical and managerial top-down version, *investigative meetings* (ii) are managerial constructions that allow management to collect information from workers for a pre-defined subject. The idea is not to gain workers' critique on management or managerialism but to accumulate information with a specific purpose in mind that is often hidden from workers. This form of meeting allows management to pretend that they listen to workers, as they allow restrictive and instrumentally guided information sourcing, thus giving workers the feeling of being able to provide something useful to management.[247]

The *advisory meeting* (iii) is a step further where management advises workers in specific work tasks or hands out specific information to them. Often such advisory meetings are labelled *staff meetings* or *employee meetings*. Almost *naturally* they are never announced as *workers' meetings* as the organiser of such *non*-workers' meetings is management, but they are designed to take on the appearance of being *natural*.[248] In natural *advisory meetings*, managers or *human resource managers* advise their *human resources* of things they deem to be relevant for them. After all, the phrase *human resource implies that people are undifferentiatable assets that can be used up and replaced* (Poole 2006:206). In the functional world of HRM, humans are reduced to objects of power that can be used, used up, replaced, be told or not be told what HRM or management has in store for them.

One step below the advisory meeting resides the *consultative meeting* (iv). It allows workers the option of *voice* (Hirschman 1970) and is also designed to show loyalty. These meetings are definitely not open to Hirschman's *exit* option in the form of boycotts, strikes, rejecting management's requests and the like. They only allow the involvement of workers to create a facade of their participation in managerial decision making processes. This is achieved without challenges to management's prerogative of a managerial *right to manage*. Generally, managerial processes of decision making are not part of these consultative meetings. Workers are only to be consulted while decisions are made elsewhere and properly removed from workers' input. Consultative meetings are also not co-decision making meetings.

Decision making is transferred into *executive meetings* (v) separating workers' diminished role as shown in Table 7.4[i-iv] from any determination of decision making. Unlike briefing-, advisory-, investigative-, or consultative-meetings that can be conducted as manager-worker meetings, meetings that include serious decision making are constructed, and often announced, as *executive meetings*. This separates communication with labour from making decisions about labour. In most cases access to such meetings is provided to the selected few and is exclusively located in the management domain.[249] The hierarchical character of all five forms of meetings is deeply inscribed in their pre-constructed purposes. Sometimes hierarchies are reproduced by simply arranging something as banal as office furniture (Figure 7.1). Most managerial or management-workers meetings are held in traditional seating arrangement. The idea is to present management in a powerful communication position while workers take a minor position. Communicative structures are often manifested in these seating arrangements. For example, most meetings are arranged in the following way (see Figure 7.7).[250]

Figure 7.1 contrasts the arrangement for a typical management meeting (A) with its hierarchical functions to a non-typical meeting (B) with non-hierarchical forms of communication. In type A, communication is guided by the unique position of the chair that controls and guides such meetings. In the non-hierarchical version of a meeting (B), communication is directed to the fulfilment of non-distorted ideal speech concepts (Habermas 1997 & 1997a).

Unlike the often ideologically labelled *round table*, most managerial meetings are neither held on round tables nor do they fulfil a round '**O**' of equal participants. They are '**▲**' hierarchically organised. Type A meetings hardly ever fulfil the communicative idea of a round table (B) as they are rarely constructed as a discourse among equals. While in some cases they may reflect round table discussions purely by their office furniture arrangement, all too often they are not conducted as such. On the other hand, type B arrangements can be done on square tables, yet they are truly round table discussions as they provide undistorted access. Almost by their very definition, hierarchical managerial meetings (A) are one of the clearest expressions of

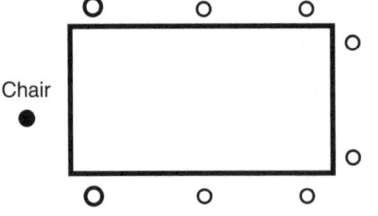
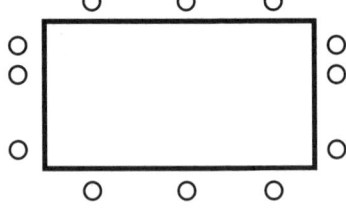

Figure A: standard management meeting   Figure B: non-hierarchical meeting

Figure 7.1 Communicative Meetings as Furniture Arrangement

hierarchical communicative structures prevalent among management. Often communication in these hierarchical meetings is directed *from* and *to* a chair who oversees them.[251] Most meetings shown in Table 7.4[i–v] are held in seating arrangements that are a reflection of A rather than B.

Apart from seating arrangements, managerial chairs of such meetings possess additional tools that enable them to distort communication. The simplest level starts with the drafting of an agenda or the setting of tasks for the meeting. This allows management, even before the meeting starts, to pre-design not only how the meeting is conducted but also its content and, more importantly, it defines which issues are *not* part of the meeting. It also allows management to define and agree on certain strategies – the original meaning of which is to deceive the enemy – and tactics used during the meeting.

If managerial meetings do depart from management's pre-designed purpose, one of the first tools that can be used is an adjournment. Rather than being a true adjournment, it allows the management chair to end the meeting. A second tool is the transfer of unwanted issues into a box labelled AOB or *Any Other Business*. In later meetings these can conveniently be forgotten. Issues that are inconvenient for management can also be postponed through a series of adjournments until management is sure these issues are forgotten. Thirdly, challenging issues can be shelved into another box called *matters arising* as a point transferred to the end, the next or any other meeting. This is usually done when issues warrant no further discussions or are of no further help to management. Similarly, such unwanted issues are sometimes successfully *shelved* in two ways. Firstly, management transfers them by setting up or creating separate meetings; secondly, they are transferred into already existing meetings which are usually minor meetings with diminished responsibilities. Management often uses these simple methods to kill off any unwanted motions, discussion, issues, etc.

To make sure an unwanted issue 'dies' somewhere on the way, meetings are often set up as *ex officio* where they are stacked with members by virtue of their position. This provides yet another way of management shelving unwanted issues. Similarly, meetings can also be stacked with *proxies*. These are used when management has identified an unwanted person. The proxies are put in place so that critical participants can be excluded. In addition, a simple scheduling or, if needed, re-scheduling can set up a meeting with wanted participants while excluding unwanted ones. Similar effects can be achieved via pre-designed meeting locations allowing participation to vary in the way management seeks it. Even when meetings are held on a regular basis, chairs can re-schedule and re-locate them depending on managerial intentions. This is often used to allow the participation of proxy members that are deemed to be beneficial.

As a further option, management combines or separates issues into motions that are predicted to be defeated or to pass. *Points of order* also allow a skilful chair to construct a meeting and its outcome in a way that is beneficial to management. If such a chair suspects a possible and unwanted outcome, a reference to a needed *quorum* can undermine the meeting's outcome as much as a reference to the transferral to an executive meeting for decision making. This relates to the so-called *ultra vires* powers of a chair as chairs are often given the powers to declare a motion to be *outside their powers* rendering it to transferral to a hierarchically higher meeting. Finally, a call *through the chair* can be issued as a normal practice. Here, all comments and contributions have to go through a chair who channels and controls any unwanted notions and comments.

As much as a skilful managerial chair can use all options as outlined above, he/she might also design a meeting simply through the ability to logically sequence the meeting's flow. Terms such as logical, productive, natural and so on are often used to hide the true intentions of the meeting's designers. The sequencing places simple items first in order to gain workers' approval on easy and non-challenging issues. Once this has been achieved the meeting moves on to more contentious issues. This tactic can be used in conjunction with a *consensus items first* method that is designed to achieve similar goals. Other instruments to be used by a chair are the move to discuss agenda items before *late arrivals* appear or after *early departures* have left the meeting.

The final way for chairs to influence meetings is the scheduling of issues as either *less important* or *more urgent* to management. This method can be used for instant alterations of agendas at the start or during a meeting. The timekeeping ability of the chair is as much useful a tool in the structuring of a meeting as is his ability to keep to a set agenda and the adequate coverage of certain items that are deemed to be relevant. In some cases, a chair can exercise *crowd control* to end any discussion that is not wanted. Skilful chairpersons are aware of the different stages in the dynamics of a meeting. These stages are general in character and can be applied to almost all communicative groups of people that assemble for meetings. Like any other group, people who meet for communicative purposes in long-term meetings tend to go through these development stages that have been identified as follows:[252]

Table 7.5 Stages of Meetings and their Usage

Stage	Communicative Activity	Usage by Management
i) Forming	People meet & establish group	to shape initial composition
ii) Storming	Disagreement, conflict, hostility	to identify trusted leaders[253] & issues
iii) Norming	Agree on standards, purpose, process	to define operative engagements
iv) Performing	Achieve purpose & maintain process	to efficiently perform a task
v) Adjourning	Complete task & dissolution of meeting	to reach goal, assess & disassemble

Table 7.5 outlines the stages that can apply to individual meetings as well as to a range of meetings set up by management. In the (i) initial phase of such meetings, people or members of a meeting establish themselves as participants of a group or specific working group. This stage allows management to pre-compose a group for a meeting. It also allows changes or alterations of the meeting's composition if management identifies members that are deemed not suitable. In the second phase (ii), management receives additional insights into the members' behaviour. When participants develop agreements and disagreements, management can assess whether this leads to conflict or even hostility towards management and use their options to intervene when such conflicts are in opposition with their goals and plans. Management can also intervene when meetings do not achieve the goals that have been designed for them.

Once such stormy periods have passed, management is able to adjust and influence the process of *norm-setting* (stage (iii))[254] as it more or less defines the operative engagements and standards of conduct. As such, procedural arrangements are able to maintain the meetings while directing them towards their managerially desired goals. Management will – often as a pre-planned strategy – predetermine working arrangements. By doing so, it can significantly influence the internal affairs of meetings. Having set the meeting norms, the next stage locates performance (iv) as its central activity. This only occurs after the forming, storming, and *norm setting* processes have been accomplished. At this stage, management focuses on working towards the purpose of the meeting in an effort to guide the meeting towards its pre-set goals and objectives. In the final meeting stage (v), management directs the meeting towards the completion of their work task and also starts to prepare the participants for the dissolving of the meeting once the members of the team have completed their pre-set tasks. Management, then, is free to assess the workings of the meetings and compare its achievements with the goals they set out and can also assess individual members in order to select *useful* candidates for future meetings.

8
Distorted Communication V: Persuasion, Attitudes and Responses

At the most basic level, persuasion is a form of influencing people in a process of guiding them toward the adoption of one's views without coercion.[255] It is also seen as a form of communication in which influencing is taking place *without* conscious awareness. One of the early and most famous successes of persuasion in commerce took place in 1957 when *during the showing of the film Picnic, James Vicary, a marketing researcher, flashed on the screen for 1/3000 of a second the message, 'Drink Coca-Cola' or 'Hungry? Eat Popcorn'. He repeated the message every five seconds throughout the film. The time exposure was so brief the messages were not detectable by the human eye; they were subliminal, below the level of conscious perception. After continuing his research for six weeks, Vicary reported that Coca-Cola sales in the theatre lobby increased by 57.7% and popcorn sales rose by 18.1%.*[256] While this version of persuasion is a rather specialised form of *subliminal persuasion*, most persuasion today takes place somewhat less hideous and less repulsive even though the core of operating behind the backs of the target – to use persuasion language – remains the same. So does the fact that persuasion occurs without the consciousness of the target but with the full consciousness of the persuader. It always involves a *conscious* effort directed towards influencing thoughts, *attitudes*, or actions of a receiver.[257] Much of what we say and do is *reflexive* (conditioned association), as opposed to being *reflective* (symbolic association). Persuasion operates much more on the *reflexive* than on the *reflective* level. While targeting *reflexes* it simultaneously seeks to suppress *reflections*. Persuasive actions demand that we are not aware of the persuasive intentions.[258]

Persuasion seeks to ensure that issue-relevant thinking is as much diminished as thinking about the content of a message. Reflection on ideas and information, including their underlying concepts and meanings, is pressed deep into the subconscious of people. Neither should the quality of arguments be scrutinised. Persuasion is a form of identity and attitude management.[259] It is viewed as an object that can be engineered.[260] It is influential precisely because it predisposes but does not do so through impositions. The

Figure 8.1 A Two-Way Model of Persuasion

process of persuasion is not a one-way street.[261] It does not simply operate as persuader → receiver or as persuader → target audience. Like communication in general, persuasion is a two-way process (↔).

The two-way model ↔ of persuasion resides in its cooperative process. Persuasion is always an involving process. In fact, it relies on the *active* cooperation of a receiver or audience.[262] This is its strength but also its weakness as refusing to be engaged ends all persuasive processes. However, as persuasions are – and by definition they have to be – conducted in secrecy, active cooperation is difficult to achieve. Since a*ctive* engagement is important for persuasion as target audiences or receivers are asked to alter their perceptions, beliefs, or attitudes,[263] persuasion can only operate when the receiver establishes a certain meaning based on the message received from the persuader.

Figure 8.1 shows that the defining element of the cooperative model of persuasion is an unconscious perception of having no alternatives. The target audience must be convinced to accept the shaping of their attitudes without being able to contemplate it.[264] *To achieve persuasion, one can be trained in becoming a persuader but training in persuasion ran both ways: you tried to persuade and you knew persuasion when it was aimed at you* (Lanham 2006:27). Because of this, scientific or psychological ideas and mechanisms behind persuasion are kept away from workers and the general public as far as possible.[265] Critical knowledge about its mechanisms destroys the very idea of persuasion in the consumption as well as in the work domain. Nevertheless, persuasion uses four key techniques to change the attitudes of a target-audience.

As Table 8.1 demonstrates, persuasion is an attitude creating process directed towards the shaping of new attitudes (a) by creating new beliefs and attitudes where none existed before.[266] Table 8.1 also shows that persuasion can be directed towards the shaping of already existing attitudes (b). Thirdly, persuasion involves the reinforcing, strengthening or solidifying of already existing attitudes that are held by workers.[267] These are attitude-enforcing processes (c). Finally, persuasions can be used to eliminate already existing attitudes in an extinguishing process (d). Whatever the targeted attitudes of persuasions are, they all have one issue in common; they all seek compliance with a pre-arranged, pre-selected, constructed, and enforced target goal.

Consequently, persuasion carries compelling connotations of *compliance-gathering* strategies. These are directed towards an instrumental aggression dimension via compliance, identification, and internalisation. Instrumental

Table 8.1 Four Ways of Changing Attitudes

No.	Attitudes	Goals
a)	attitude-creating processes,	to establish a completely new attitude about an existing work process,
b)	attitude-shaping processes,	to shape an anti-management into a management affirmative attitude,
c)	attitude-reinforcing processes,	to support system stabilising attitudes among workers,
d)	attitude-extinguishing processes	to delete managerially unwanted attitudes such as solidarity among workers

goals of *compliance gathering* are to be found in a tendency that focuses on *short-term* changes or immediate actions and strategies. *Long-term* persuasion, instead, is primarily concerned with an internalisation of belief-systems or *opinion altering actions*. These are intended to have a much greater longevity.[268] The key targets of persuasion are our attitudes and opinions. Those who seek to persuade us seek to create or change our attitudes, beliefs, and values in a pre-designed direction via an application of strategies and tactics. One such strategy is the so-called 3-Cs.

Table 8.2 shows that persuasion can be achieved in a three-way process. When one person persuades another, such attempts are measured as success, hence the idea of persuasion is linked to the concept of success. Persuasion is a form of distorted communication. It does not seek to establish communicative understanding but the opposite. Success in persuasion goes hand in hand with the limitation of freedom. It restricts an individual's ability to think independently or hold an independent attitude and influences, alters or colonises someone's mental state through communication.

The limitations of freedom to think independently are measured, commonly via the application of *before* and *after* surveys.[269] At work, as in other situations, they are called attitude surveys. Management relies rather frequently on them as a valuable instrument that is able to measure workers' attitudes *before* the exposure of a managerial message and *afterwards*. This enables management to evaluate changes in their workers' attitudes. Put bluntly, they assess the changes in workers' freedom to think independently. In some cases, the collection of such attitude data is applied to specific

Table 8.2 The Three Cs of Persuasion

(i)	Challenge existing attitudes
(ii)	Change these attitudes
(iii)	Commit workers to attitudes a persuader seeks to establish

sets or sub-sets of workers that have not been exposed to the messages. In a next step, these results are then compared to the group that has been exposed to certain messages to measure the *success* (!) of invading workers' minds. No lesser than George Orwell has noted the invasion of the mind.[270] However, while Orwellian mind-control operates largely with brain-washing, modern persuasive techniques are more heinous and more sophisticated. Terms such as *brain-washing* and *mind-control* have been applied to psychological and communicative influencing strategies but *persuasion* operates on a different level as a non-coercive form of influence. In contrast to *brain-washing* and *mind-control* methods where people feel they have no choice, persuasion seeks the opposite; it offers people the illusion of choice while secretly directing their intentions towards pre-organised recommendations that are packaged for private *acceptance* and *internalisation*.[271] When people act under mind-controlling forces such as duress and coercion they often depict behaviour showing *public* compliance and affirmation without *private* acceptance. In contrast, persuasion targets private acceptance and affirmation depicted in a public showing. It aligns both to establish a truly system-integrative individual. Once this has been achieved, forms of public control – as present in Orwell's *Nineteen Eighty-Four* – can be avoided because control has been diminished and affirmation established.[272]

However, persuasions still operate with some Orwellian techniques. As George Orwell (1946:7) said the goal is the *invasion of one's mind by ready-made phrases* to alter our attitudes. At their core attitudes are psychological mechanisms that underlie and explain individual variations in social conduct. Individuals rely on attitudes as a general system for evaluating social and working reality. Attitudes help to assess workplace events such as relationships to co-workers or managers, actions at the workplace, social institutions and the like. They are indicators of mental states relevant to persuasion because of their relationship to actions.

Predominantly, attitude surveys and instruments of persuasion are not solely applied to investigate and assess workers' attitudes; the prime motivation behind them is to shape their attitudes. Above all, the goal is to translate attitudes into managerially useful action that supports pre-designed planning. This can be achieved in a number of ways. In some cases, managerial designers of attitude surveys on workers only target certain attitudes that are to be altered in either a positive or a negative way. In other cases, some attitudes are assessed in order to evaluate if they are *silent* and non-threatening. Alternatively they may be found to be *active* attitudes that can constitute a threat to the managerial planning of the attitude-change processes.

Successful attitude changes that translate into managerially useful actions of workers are classified as *induced compliance*. Here, individuals are *induced* to act in a way that is contradictory to their beliefs and attitudes. Their willingness to act or to take on new ideas has been established even though these new ideas are dissonant to their beliefs. Such induced-compliance actions have the potential to result in conflict because workers are made to act in a way they otherwise would not. Often induced compliance is accompanied by a significant amount of *incentives* offered by management to engage workers in actions they would not perform otherwise. The task of persuasion, however, is to either weaken workers' attitudes or nullify them altogether. Attitude surveys are handy tools in this process. They also deliver helpful insights into which underlying information can be used to assist attitude changes and which hinder such changes. Occasionally workers might already have a *positive* attitude towards managerial statements or actions. In this case managerial planners of attitude changes can *positively* enhance these *positive* attitudes. This allows management to achieve their goal by *fostering* actions that are supportive of management while at the same time it can prevent workers from pursuing undesired actions.

Sometimes the task of a managerial persuader is not so much to encourage people to have attitudes supportive of management but to encourage them to act on existing attitudes as long as these are in the interests of management. For example, workers' intention to perform or not perform certain work tasks is a function related to two essential factors: Firstly, workers' attitude towards a task and secondly their subjective norms. They represent the general perception of whether management desires the performance or non-performance of the task. Hence, intentions to act or not to act are influenced by (i) *personal attitudinal judgements* as a personal evaluation of one's action as well as by (ii) *social-normative considerations*. These are linked to (a) whether management thinks a worker should or should not act and also (b) what co-workers think and whether one should or should not act.

In order to encourage workers' action or non-action, management is able to manipulate both the personal attitudinal consideration as well as the social-normative consideration. Both can be shaped if, for example, management has found that workers generally have a positive attitude. While these positive attitudes may be directed towards the company and management, workers can still appear to be willing to strike against the company. In this case management calls to attention the inconsistency of workers' attitudes and actions, a process that is called *hypocrisy induction*. It seeks to induce conformist actions via an exploitation of an attitude-action contradiction portrayed as *hypocrisy*. Often management fosters this beforehand by portraying the company as positive to enhance positive attitudes towards it. This is also done to induce positive attitudes towards a product. Both product and company are utilised by management for *hypocrisy induction*.[273]

In addition, both are used as a behavioural control mechanism as workers' might have personal attitude judgements towards the company but also strong *social-normative considerations* towards their co-workers' intentions and their readiness to strike. Commonly, management seeks to deal with this conflict as summed up in Table 8.3.

Table 8.3   Persuasive Models for Conflict

No.	Methods of dealing with conflict
a)	managerial persuaders might create opportunities for successfully performed actions seen as non-action in a strike via an encouragement of personal attitude judgement (i) linked to a positive attitude towards the company,
b)	persuasive management can also encourage positive attitudes towards the product of the company by enhancing personal attitude judgements (i),
c)	management might persuade workers directly by weakening social-normative considerations (ii),
d)	persuaders can use positive examples of non-action by some (strike breakers, managers, etc.) as an attack on social-normative considerations (ii), and
e)	by simply encouraging workers to make a difference in supporting *your company* or *you can do it* as an attack on social-normative considerations (i)!

Table 8.3 lists a range of behavioural control mechanisms for management. To achieve their goal of persuading workers to be compliant and to adopt managerial attitudes (a-e), management relies on four essential types of techniques. These are: (i) avoidance, (ii) suppression, (iii) adjustment, and (iv) capitulation. Avoidance (i) uses *counter-persuasion* and seeks to counter social-normative consideration by trying to show that workers are wrong in their attempt to strike.[274] Usually, counter-persuasive messages are conflicting messages because they are designed to conflict with workers' positive attitudes towards solidaristic issues. These messages run counter to workers' long-held attitudes. Quite often counter-persuasive messages are packaged inside a well-targeted campaign by management or an organised employer interest to dismantle deeply held values and alter enduring cognitive schemata held by workers. For example, workers should avoid establishing any historical connection of an industrial conflict so that this can be – non-historically – reduced to a pure and simple cost-benefit exercise where costs (temporary loss of income) are portrayed as high while benefits (minor wage increase, etc.) are portrayed as low. In the interplay between the work and non-work domain, corporate mass media avoid the presentation of any positive outcome of such social action so that workers can no longer make historical connections between collective social action and benefits or the advancement of human society.[275]

Counter- or avoidance-persuasion uses techniques such as sidestepping and challenging social-normative attitudes through layers of preventative measures such as communication of routines, myths, ideology, etc. Avoidance strategies also include the elimination of any alternative source that fosters social-normative attitudes such as barring trade unions from access to meetings, exclusion of workers, etc. or through the tailoring of meetings. In this way, unwanted groups of workers can be denied access by using the scheduling technique. The conscious exclusion of certain workers or their representatives is cloaked inside a method that appears technical and therefore rational and legitimate. The same can be achieved by setting up artificial divisions along so-called business units, departments, and other divisions.

The suppression (ii) of social-normative attitudes operates in a similar way. It seeks to suppress, harass, and intimidate workers' spokespersons, especially those who carry attitudes that management regards as unwanted. The suppression of social-normative attitudes is almost exclusively designed to weaken attitudes of solidarity among workers.

In its third form (iii) management encourages the adjustment of workers to managerial views by diverting or re-shaping workers' attention. In cases where workers do not positively adjust to management's demands, so it is rhetorically portrayed, the future for these workers is bleak. Capitulation (iv) seeks to make clear to workers that management has won and there are no alternatives to managerialism thus forcing workers into capitulation. Management seeks to shape workers' attitudes in such a way that they are left with no other choice than to accept managerialism. This is the height of the one-dimensional structuring of attitudes. Workers are persuaded to accept management, fully including all management practices from HRM to downsizing, business process re-engineering, performance related pay, restructuring, and so on.[276] To achieve this, management tends to prepare the ground through the use of the aforementioned attitude surveys.

In almost all processes of organisational change, workplace reorganisation and restructuring management relies on *attitude surveys*. They are used to measure what workers think about the working situation and to assess managerial measures required to change workers' attitudes so that they can accept managerial plans for workplace changes.[277] This is often done through surveys that rank workers' attitudes on a scale from one to five. They also ask workers to indicate their attitudes on a scale from good to bad, undesirable to desirable, positive to negative, harmful to beneficial, etc. Above all, the most common measurement is the so-called *Likert Attitude Scale* (1961 & 1967) that measures attitudes on the range of 1 to 5. It often asks workers if they agree with a presented statement by indicating whether they (1) strongly disagree, (2) mildly disagree, (3) disagree (4) mildly agree, or (5) strongly agree.

Such techniques are simple to use and easy to operate as they deliver management with important tools for the development of persuasive strategies. The first advantage of these techniques is their directness. The knowledge gained from workers is fed directly into the design of managerial plans to alter workers' attitudes and make them accept change processes. The second benefit for management lies in the ability to shape the statements presented to workers. Unlike political surveys in the public or mass media domain that seek to deliver favourable results via suggestive questioning, at work management's goal is usually another one. Here, surveys are often used to shape

Table 8.4 Elements and Mechanisms that Shape Attitudes

No.	Element	Mechanism
a)	Promises	if you comply with our new work arrangements, we will reward you
b)	Liking	when managers are as friendly as they can be to achieve compliance
c)	Pre-giving	when management gives out a reward before a managerial request is made
d)	Positive-reinforcement	if you become a successful leader for restructuring, good things will come to you again
e)	Negative-reinforcement	if you reject our offer to be active in restructuring, your future here might not look good
f)	Punishing threats	if you do not become a change-agent, you will lose your position
g)	Aversive-stimulation	is used when management pushes workers until s/he complies

workers' attitudes by pushing certain statements while holding back on others. A careful reading of such surveys reveals how management is seeking to frame one issue and un-frame other, usually alternative and critical, issues that are contradictory to management's interest.

The third advantage of such attitude surveys is their ability to deliver information about workers' minds which relates to what and how certain attitudes are shaped and what influences them. These are investigations into the deeper spheres of workers' attitudes. In a further step, they can become useful when shaping workers' attitudes via the maximisation of rewards and the minimisation of punishment which serve as a social adjustment function at work. Such social adjustments are created via compliance gained through several rewarding mechanisms.

As Table 8.4 shows, the goal of attitude structuring lies in promises (a) – even in empty ones – the pretence of liking (b), pre-giving (c), positive and negative reinforcement (d & e) but much less so in punishing threats (f) and aversive stimulation (g). The goal of persuasion is not punishment as a coercive strategy. Persuasion prefers rewards, incentives, inducements, flattery, ingratiation, and even bribery to make workers' attitudes useful to management.

The mechanisms are, for example, used by management in the process of secondary socialisation as newly recruited workers are made to adjust to the work regime and interact with superiors and co-workers. At least six attitudes that are used by management to enhance the process of secondary socialisation can be identified.[278]

Table 8.5 Attitudes to be Shaped during Secondary Socialisation

No.	Attitudes
a)	personal attitudes towards work and work regimes,
b)	social attitudes towards the structural imperatives of an enterprise,
c)	value attitudes towards paid employment,
d)	social adjustment attitudes towards social interaction at work
e)	social identity attitudes towards a re-shaping of one's identity while being at work, and
f)	self-esteem attitudes towards the maintenance of sense of self-worthiness at work.

Table 8.5 shows a number of workers' attitudes that are to be shaped and re-shaped by management. If workers fail to show positive attitudes towards work, these can be adjusted during the process of secondary socialisation. To highlight the value of paid employment, the adjustment process is directed towards general social attitudes (a–c). In the latter three examples (d,e,f), human or social attitudes are converted into managerial ones as they are useful for the achievement of organisational goals. All of these changes are achieved communicatively. The very last element (f) of *self-esteem* and *self-worthiness* can be powerfully supported when compliance with work regimes becomes self-persuasive. Here, self-schemata – the abstract essence of a worker's perception of him- or herself – become self-creating and self-sustaining. In this case, managerial communication creates pre-engineered workers who themselves generate their very own self-persuasion through the creation of system conforming messages that are no longer a replay of managerial messages but original and self-created. They contain enough ideology for workers to either change their attitudes or alter their beliefs or redirect their behaviours into a direction sought by management.

The communicative shaping of these attitudes occurs via the use of what is called *language intensity*. As the use of language differs between labour and management, it strongly reflects the intensity in which it is used. *Language intensity* is the extent to which a speaker's attitude deviates from neutrality. A more neutral use of language tends to result in deficiencies in persuasive intentions. Management is able to overcome this and achieve their goals by turning to a more *intensive* use of language. For example the use of the word *enemy* in relation to *competition* reflects a diversion from neutral language use. In the managerial world of communication language intensity is often achieved through the construction of particular narratives that mirror the language of the military – *one has to win a battle for market shares, advertising-blitz*, etc.[279] Here, managerial language portrays itself and the company in emotionally favourable terms. The use of emotionally intensive language is also negatively directed towards undesirable attitudes and to attack undesirable actions by workers. Here workers who deviate or challenge managerially defined goals may be labelled the *enemy within* to isolate, diminish, or decimate them.[280]

One instrument that can be used to persuade workers to refrain from undesirable actions is reinforcement. *Attitude reinforcement* is applied on the assumption that workers are more motivated to avoid pain and seek pleasure. Hence, HRM uses concepts of rewards and monetary remuneration to shape attitudes. These concepts provide a highly successful instrument of persuasion. A second persuasive tool is *language expectancy* as workers hold certain expectations about what kind of language is used by management. By serving this expectation management gains another tool for persuasion. In everyday life as much as in work situations, people adjust their style of communication and language to the appropriate locale. This is mainly done in order to gain approval and increase their communicative effectiveness (Himstreet & Baty 1961). Management adjusts their use of language depending on whether they are talking to workers or inside the management domain. Managers are often trained to service specific domain expectations of language use and ensure that the language is comprehensive and persuasive. When such expectations are violated, persuasion becomes more difficult to achieve.

Another form of persuasion that goes well beyond any form of language intensity lies in attempts to operate in a deceptive way. *Deceptive persuasion* is used when management alters the character of information given to workers.

Table 8.6 shows five deceptive methods that are used in strategies to seek workers' compliance during the process of persuasion. Deceptive communication is always designed for instrumental ends with specific means attached to it. Deceptions can be part of a persuasion strategy that is directed towards workers' beliefs, attitudes, behaviours and actions at work and rely heavily on deliberate information distortions (8.6^{i-v}). In short, deceptive *communication is more often used to influence than to inform.*[281] Overall, deception is the strategic use of persuasive language that moves well beyond the replacement of neutral language. It is not confined inside the borders of commonly accepted language use but rather uses and abuses language with unethical

Table 8.6   Forms of Deceptive Persuasion

No.	Form
(i)	amount or extent of information given
(ii)	correctness of information altered
(iii)	quality of information
(iv)	relevance of information given to workers, and
(v)	simply modifying the clarity of information provided

Table 8.7 Eight Forms of Lies at Work

Type of Lies	Description
To benefit others	In this case, management assumes that it knows best what is good for workers and to achieve this, it removes ethical considerations in order to lie.
To use affiliates	Management lies to workers about a task that can be done by management in order to have it done in association with affiliates (workers).
To avoid invasion	This occurs when managers lie to workers about their work in order to prevent workers from invading their area of work and responsibilities.
To avoid conflict	A manager tells a worker that her/his complaint will be dealt with and discussed but not right now as s/he has to do something else right now.
To appear better	To sustain the social creation of the division of labour, management needs to maintain a superior position tending to pretend that they are better than they are.
To protect self	When blunted mismanagement results in a downturn, management tends to protect itself by lying to workers accusing them to be the cause of the problem.
To benefit self	A manager tells a worker to work harder and to stay longer (unpaid overtime) so that s/he can reap the benefit of an annual bonus for increased productivity.
To harm others	Given their self-assigned position of superiority management can use the giving of wrong or insufficient directions about work tasks to workers to harm them.

intentions that reach beyond commonly established language norms. However, this is exactly what lies at the heart of attempts to achieve the goal of persuasion. *We all know that in the case of the lie, language, precisely in being spoken, can in fact conceal.*[282] To conceal something is to lie. It is not just to assert something false that is known to be false. It is intentional concealment. Gass and Seiter (1999:244–245) have identified eight forms of lies that are used in attempts to persuade.

As Table 8.7 shows, managers who operate strongly with the methods outlined above are in danger of developing a *Machiavellian* personality. They tend to avoid inter-personal relationships at work, manipulate co-managers and workers for selfish goals and display a general lack of ethical and social considerations. Apart from such extreme cases, usually a number of deception strategies are used in persuasion. These are distortion or equivocation, omissions or concealment, falsification and information manipulation. When applying deceptive, deceitful, lying or two-faced, etc. techniques, people often feel physically different; they feel more aroused when telling lies than when telling the truth. Hence – apart from polygraphs operating on this premise – lying is linked to behavioural acts that make it possible to

Table 8.8   Twelve Items to Identify a Liar

a) blink	b) move their hands	c) make speech errors
d) speak briefly	e) include irrelevant information	f) make negative statements
g) shrug	h) a person not really involved	i) pitch their voice
j) hesitate more	k) use levelling terms	l) use more discrepancies

detect liars. Zuckermann and Drivers (1985) have developed twelve indicators that detect liars.

While lying (Table 8.8) might be an extreme form of persuasion and used sparsely – or not so sparsely at all – other methods of persuasions are more common for management. One of these persuasive methods is the construction of symbols. These are used to communicate certain persuasive messages in order to shape workers' attitudes. One way of operating persuasively is the use of *deliberate* persuasions. This is done when HR statements or policies are used to determine future attitudes of workers. Persuasive strategies used by management can also be of *forensic* character. This is applied when reports and analyses of past occurrences – company history, etc. – are used to prove past actions by management. Sometimes they simply portray managerial actions of the past in a positive light. This often means the application of *euphemisms* when names for something unpleasant are avoided.[283] Managerial reports are no longer manufactured; they are *crafted* reflecting on *good old fashion* and *hand made*. For example the manufacturing of strategy is now called crafting strategy.[284] In the same way *firing* or *sacking* workers is now termed *we will have to set you free, we will let you go*, we *downsize*, etc. The *average* business practice has become a *standard* business practice, implying common use and occurrence, common sense, and, above all, unquestionable acceptance.[285] The HR department no longer has *informers* (moles, spies or grasses), only *informants* to convey information. Finally, corporations and companies have associates while trade unions and workers have bedfellows and henchmen and – unlike managers – their leaders are always self-styled troublemakers. *In capitalist society, trouble is caused by radicals and outside agitators* (Bolinger 1980:120). In that way the representatives of capitalism – management – are free to blame others.

Management also resorts to the use of *blaming* or *praising* certain workers or managers or certain events to achieve persuasive goals. This is often used in eulogy speeches. Similarly, such speeches and similar forms of communication can be used to enhance a persuader's credibility as managers claim *I have the experience necessary to be in charge of this department*. Such communication can also appeal to workers' emotions when the *pathos* of working towards *organisational goals* is highlighted or when the *Hierarchy of Needs*[286] – a standard management textbook fair – is called upon. A convincing persuader can pretend to service a managerially constructed hierarchy of human needs while at the same time narrow workers' access to so-called basic – i.e. managerially allowed – needs: a) physiological needs, b) safety needs, c) belonging needs, d) esteem needs, and e) self-actualisation needs. Finally, in order to persuade, management can also utilise simple logical reasoning by establishing certain links between two facts constructed by management. This is done in the following way: *because of your dedication[i] our[ii] company has met its annual objectives[iii]* where (i) often means no more than work intensification, short lunches, overtime, etc., (ii) does not mean *your* as the company is not owned by *you*!, and finally, (iii) means well done for you and bonuses for managers. In sum, a persuader speaks of production figures and annual targets, budgets, productiveness, etc. but never of managerial rewards.

To make such forms of persuasion successful, managerial announcements first of all rely on inventions to create an idea or concept around which announcements are made. This deliberately excludes undesired issues. Secondly, persuasive announcements demand the ordering of these ideas that are constructed in a way to give them the appearance of an internal logic. Following this logic, announcements are made so that those who receive them are induced into following their internal order. This closes all possibilities that could offer an option to question the '*Order of Things*'. At the same time it also removes all options to challenge what has been said. Thirdly, the persuader will use a certain style and language in order to impress workers. Impressive speeches are rarely questioned and after all the goal of persuasion is the presentation of a winning argument. It does not have to be a good or correct one; it just needs to win. Fourthly, the mode of delivery is adjusted in manner, voice, and gesture to present an announcement in an optimal persuasive way. Lastly, this process includes the maximum use of eye contact and other techniques to increase credibility. All this leads to the memorisation of those parts of an announcement that the managerial persuader deems to be relevant. At the same time, sections of the announcement that workers might deem relevant move into the background where they remain securely locked until workers have conveniently forgotten about them.

Virtually, all announcements and speeches made by management have only one target, to change or alter one's ideas, attitudes, behaviours, or actions. To achieve this, management constantly rehearses the demands of the market for the company's future to make workers change or alter their ideas about working. This is required as working has moved from a fulfilling activity towards a market driven mindless act performed during eight (or up to ten) hours per day, five (or six) days a week for about 40 years of life.

In a second form of managerial persuasion announcements are designed to decrease workers' demand for more information. Once workers request more information, they receive more *managerial* information. The provision of managerial information is strongly encouraged. Highly pre-structured questions are explicitly allowed and even wanted as they, again, shape workers' mindsets into the direction of management who are only too happy to provide that information. At a third level, persuasion seeks to de-emphasise contradictory information that could hinder the flow of believable statements. Contradictions of the market or inside management are avoided. Much in the same way, one of the core contradictions of capitalism itself is excluded. Workers are made to believe that the contradiction between low wages leading to economic growth on the one hand and consumers' need to purchase the products on the other hand simply does not exist.[287] Workers' curiosity to understand these contradictions is cut off.

A fourth element is the utilisation of workers' curiosity to learn more about work and their company. Management directs this curiosity into areas where they can benefit from it. On other occasions, diversions are used to escape the more unfavourable realities of the managerial process. This is often done by a comparison of managers with fictional people from well-known movies, theatrical plays, popular literature, etc. It is conducted with specific correlations in mind. Fictional people and events are made to support workers' positive perceptions of management and the company much in the same way as cultural perceptions are used to spread the message of *work hard and earn your money*. All of these persuasive techniques are strategically and instrumentally used in managerial speeches, in company announcements, reports and the like, as well as in more direct forms of managerial communication. Management uses questions to connect to their audience or individual workers. Highly suggestive questions – such as *'right?'* or *'wouldn't you agree?'* etc. – are designed to rhetorically seek compliance with the managerial statement. This form of questioning can even provoke pre-calculated reactions by workers to emphasise certain points and highlight pre-set issues. These types of questions are not authentic questions; they are used instrumentally, very much in the same way as polite forms of communication such as *thank you* or *please*. They create some sort of intimacy between persuader and the targeted person and establish a false closeness that is able to increase the credibility of the persuader. Addressing workers by their names enhances familiarity and intimacy. On the other hand, an over-emphasis on familiarity or closeness through the use of empty adjectives is generally avoided, as this could sound hollow or lead to a weakening of hierarchies. Managers tend to avoid any weakening of hierarchies because their very existence depends on their maintenance. However, persuaders do not avoid the use of comparisons. Comparing their ideas with other testimonies and general facts of workers' real life experiences increases managerial credibility. At the same time it reduces challenging questions. In their grammatical constructions, management uses familiar words, well known concepts and recognisable sentences.

Skilful persuaders will analyse unacceptable or unfavourable sentences or contents as well as any other unacceptable form of communication. This is done in an attempt to refine communication between management and labour so that persuasive messages achieve what they are designed to achieve. To be successful, a persuader would also use easy recognisable slogans – corporate mission statements, value statements, etc. – as linguistic statements designed to create an emotional connection between managerial messages and workers.[288] This includes a certain amount of repetition to rehearse core persuasive mission statements. Management has also been using rhythms and alliterations when each sentence or section starts with the same or similar sounding words to enhance one-dimensional thinking. These structures are able to reduce discourse of scholastic inquiry. They foster a singularity of sequence a→a→a while negating an examination of both sides of the coin in a plus/minus or +/– version. The linearity of a→a→a is specifically created so that any critical thinking that could examine managerial issues in a dialectic framework is avoided. It is designed to disallow the thesis (workers), anti-thesis (management), and synthesis (solution) model of thinking. Workers' thinking should not be allowed to take place in a forward moving fashion that highlights the inherent conflict of interest between workers and management. Thinking should be reduced to up and down, pros and cons.

The conditioning of workers' responses and thinking

The +/– construction is only used in a pre-designed black-and-white fashion where good management always wins. It shows that bad things are bad (–) and good things are good (+) and constructs a *black & white* view of the world in a way that hides the fact that it is management who defines what is good or bad and pretends that there are happy endings when the good (i.e. management) wins. All one has to do is to believe in what is being told. This form of communicative reality distortion is at the very heart of almost any popular fiction, movie or TV show. The goal of such *belief in the good* and *happy ending* stories is not *Enlightenment*. They present an authoritarian fashion that is enshrined into *I know what is good for you*.[289] The authoritarianism resides in management's claim to have superior knowledge and the natural right to tell *you*. This is usually constructed via so-called conditioning divided into classical (Pavlov 1928) and instrumental conditioning (Skinner).[290] The basic premise is that human behaviour can be conditioned by linking it to an external factor. For example, the sound of a door does not cause any reaction in a dog but once the opening of the door is linked to the dog's breakfast, over time it will react positively to the sound of the door. Skinner transferred this to human behaviour.[291] The behavioural link can be shown as follows:

	Action:	Link:	External Factor:	Link:	Reaction:
(i)	Door opens	→	None	→	No specific reaction
(ii)	Door opens	→	Linked to food	→	Reaction: dog releases saliva
(iii)	Door opens	→	Not needed	→	Reaction: dog releases saliva

Figure 8.2 Conditioning of Human Behaviour

Figure 8.2 shows what Pavlov discovered and Skinner applied to human behaviour. Core to this is that an unlinked behaviour can – over time – be transferred to a pre-set (externally designed) behaviour. Once a specific action is associated with an *external factor* (ii), dogs – as well as humans (Skinner) – take on new behaviours (iii). This new form of behaviour remains in operation even when the factors that alter the behaviour (ii) are removed. In short, the opening of the door becomes synonymous with food. The dog or human is conditioned. Pavlov's (1928) original *dog* experiments have been applied to *human* life. For example, a signal by itself may not mean anything but linked to danger it can mean 'run away'. In Skinner's instrumental conditioning, the Pavlovian link either supported or sanctioned action. This can be done via (i) positive reinforcement, (ii) negative reinforcement, or (iii) punishment. HR managers usually use all of them. Under positive reinforcement (i), workers' actions are supported via the provision of something good (money, rewards, and promotions). Under negative reinforcement (ii), workers' actions are associated with the withdrawal of something positive (no more overtime, no more meal breaks, etc.). Under punishment (iii), workers are actively punished as HR managers have the authority to sanction and discipline them.

In both cases – Pavlov's dog and Skinner's conditioning of human behaviour – persuasion and conditioning occur behind the backs of those who are influenced.[292] *External factors* however have to be successfully communicated. This link as much as Skinner's instrumental conditioning (i, ii, or iii) are established communicatively. Communication takes on a vital role in both models. To a somewhat limited extent conditioning can be used to create certain reactions to specific signs or words that management seeks to either enhance or degenerate.[293] The conditioning of words can be shown as follows:

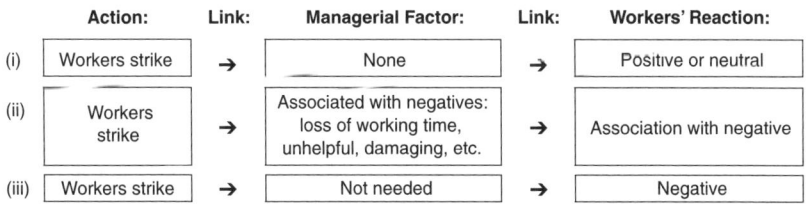

Figure 8.3 Conditioning of Wanted Reactions to Signs and Words

Similar to Figure 8.2, Figure 8.3 shows how management or managerialism via corporate mass media seeks to persuade workers to associate originally positive or neutral signs (i) such as *strike* with negatively loaded terms (ii) so that – over time – workers associate the sign negatively (iii). This is repeated time and time again. *Behaviourism* calls this process *pairing*. It establishes a mental link between an originally positive sign (*strike*) and a negative image so that the meaning of a sign is converted now carrying negative connotations. Over time, workers are conditioned to believe that certain signs (*strike, trade unions* etc.) are negative.

According to Skinner's ideas on conditioning, signs need to be associated with positive and negative enhancers and punishment. Management has been seeking to link signs such as *strike* to positive reinforcement via promises, monetary inducements, etc. to link non-strikers who go to work to positives thus creating a positive association with the sign *work*. Negative enhancers operate by linking the withdrawal of positives. In the last case, strike is associated with loss of employment, demotions, etc. and in that way the term becomes associated with punishment.

In reality however, classical and instrumental conditioning is not as easy as Pavlov and Skinner seek to tell us. Persuasion through these methods not only seeks to reduce humans or workers to white lab rats; it has also not shown to be overtly successful.[294] However, managerial persuaders who rely on conditioning as a supplementary method have not completely withdrawn from it. After all, this form of conditioning provides very useful tools to structure or distort communication by seeking to change the meaning of specific signs used and abused at work. In sum, this method seeks to alter workers' perception of certain signs *before* they meet with management to discuss certain issues such as strikes, etc. During the meeting itself other methods of communicative distortion are applied.

Having comprehensively discussed the several versions of distortions that are being used in the area of communication, the conclusion can be drawn that the world of work is not totally governed by those distortions. Despite all attempts to distort communication via classification, ordering systems, ideology, hegemony, neutralisation, routines, rhetoric, rituals, persuasion, structuring of attitudes and management meetings, the *Kafkaesque* or *Orwellian* nightmare of a *Marcusean totally administered* workplace is far from being a reality. Today's work regimes might use all the techniques and communicative tools intended to distort communication but total system integration into the administrative, and increasingly one-dimensional, world of management has still not been fully achieved. In Hegelian terms, the world of work is still seen as a place where thesis (workers) meets anti-thesis (management) creating a synthesis (outcomes). Expressed somewhat less philosophically, the world of work is still governed by two main actors – labour and management – and neither one has achieved total power over the other. The current world of work in not a world where *the struggle was finished. He had won the victory over himself. He loved Big Brother* as the final words in Orwell's *Nineteen Eighty-Four* predicted so long ago.[295] Today's world of work is still a place where workers resist the presence of communicative distortions. But how they can move towards *communicative action* and *ideal speech* is discussed in the following chapters.[296]

9
Communicative Action I: The Basics of Ideal Speech

The relationship between management and workers is not only a communicative one but is also exposed to communicative distortions. To overcome such distortions, *communicative action* can provide a solution. Many of the previous elaborations on communicative distortions and the techniques used to create communication that is instrumentally guided – rather than directed towards truth – carry connotations of a grim future for communication at work. This future appears to be moving in the direction of a Kafkaesque, or even Orwellian nightmare of corporate communication use. However, the future of communication at work might not be as grim as previously depicted. There are possible remedies that can link communication at work with an interest directed towards undistorted communication. Historically, work has always provided a forum for communication. As human history is also the history of work and tool making, the relations at work have always been communicative relations. Tool making was the definitive moment for humans to leave the realm of animals.[297] This meant they had to conduct work together in small groups. In order to operate in small working groups they needed to communicate with each other.[298] This placed the element of communication at the centre of human activity.

Historically, work has always been an activity that transforms nature by using tools. Tool making and work are at the core of human existence bound together in early groups, tribes, and collectives, and eventually creating human *Gemeinschaft* and *Gesellschaft*, i.e. society. The collective work directed towards the transformation of nature, collective tool making, and socially structured work are activities that are almost impossible to conduct other than in a coordinated and collective fashion that relies on communication. The process of the collective cannot be isolated from collective work efforts. The collective effort towards a common goal has for most times defined animal existence and early human life. For hundreds of thousands of years cooperation, not competition has been the sole organisational form of human survival.[299] It has never been an event conducted by a single human but always by a collective.³⁰⁰ The origin of human existence is intimately and inextricably linked to collaborative, cooperative, and collective efforts. In these efforts the human ability to communicate inside these collectives was essential. Collective work and communication have transformed humans into societies, thus creating a fundamentally different kind of 'animal', the modern human. Humans share three features that are distinctively different from animals. Firstly, the human skeleton adapted to striding locomotion; secondly, humans have modified teeth and jaws allowing for speech acts,³⁰¹ and finally, they have brains large enough to create and comprehend complex signs in the form of communication and language.³⁰² The ability to use language as a system of symbolic referencing is the most fundamental feature of human's ability to communicate. Crucial to human existence has been the construction of a relationship between the three core aspects of communication – (a) a word (sign), (b) its meaning, and (c) its reference that determines its meaning in relation to other words. Essentially, this requires humans to relate words to other words in order to interpret meanings and references correctly. This is the essence of syntax. Crucial, however, is that humans have developed language and sophisticated forms of communication out of a need to collectively organise work rather than for art, culture, and enjoyment.³⁰³

The transformation of nature through work – as much as the distribution of work's results – has been a social and, above all, communicative activity among humans. Work is essentially socially organised labour. Therefore, the development of work is closely linked to the development of humans and human society. Not surprisingly, work has always remained a core category of human existence or, as Marx (1890:193) once put it,

> *a spider conducts operations that resemble those of a weaver, and a bee puts to shame an architect in construction of her cells. But what distinguishes the worst architect from the best of bees is this, that the architect raises his structure in imagination before he erects it in reality. At the end of every labour process, we get a result that already existed in the imagination of the labourer. He not only effects a change of form in the material on which he works, but he also realises a purpose of his own that gives the law to his modus operandi, and to which he must subordinate his will.*³⁰⁴

The Marxian concept sees work as a purposive activity, imagined beforehand, and realised after it was pre-constructed as an image. A century after Marx, Habermas has viewed this process as instrumental action.³⁰⁵ He saw work related communication as strategic communication, always directed towards achieving a goal or success. Traditionally, work creates a nature-transforming relationship as well as a social-communicative one.³⁰⁶ The latter can be divided into two independent parts – one that defines the social, and one that defines the communicative relationship.

Table 9.1 A Threefold Nature-Transforming Relationship

Item	Process
(i) Instrumental	A purposively guided process of making tools and weapons by established technology directed towards work tasks;
(ii) Social Cooperative	Cooperative relationships through a division of labour establishing cooperating organisational forms, and
(iii) Communicative	The production and distribution of goods demand a high level of coordination that can only be established communicatively.

When we work together with others we also communicate with them. This not only establishes an instrumental relationship (Table 9.1^i) directed towards achievement of a work task, it also creates a social (9.1^{ii}) and, above all, a communicative relationship (9.1^{iii}). Therefore, work is always a three-fold activity. This triple relationship of work is manifested in three key work related processes.

Table 9.1 shows the link between three work processes that have to be established communicatively. Consequently, from the origins of work to its present forms, work has always had three dimensions, an instrumental-technical$^{(i)}$, a social-cooperative$^{(ii)}$, and a communicative dimension$^{(iii)}$. Only this threefold relationship establishes a socially constructed collective system that allows the production and distribution of products in a socially and communicatively established form. These social and communicative processes are what we call *the economy*. Therefore the terms work, labour, social, collective, coordination, society, and communication are inextricably linked. In sum, work always represents a tri-dimensional process.

Over time these core attributes of work have resulted in evolutionary learning processes. Conducted over the last two-plus million years, human work has led to the development of cognitive and technical processes which form the base for today's instrumental rationality and also structure our moral, societal, and meaning-constructing processes. What we do today is largely the result of a communicative rationality that started long ago.[307] In today's world of work, it is exactly this communicative rationality that is utilised by management as a concept supportive of goal oriented instrumental rationality. The understanding of modern work processes without an understanding of *communicative rationality* is therefore largely impossible.[308]

The modern use of the terms rationality and communication dates back to the *Enlightenment*. During this period, philosophy and social science sought to understand the world through rational means rather than through religion (Held 1997:154). Within this understanding, modernity always meant *instrumental rationality* as well as *critical rationality*. More recently, Habermas (1997) has added a third dimension to the two rationalities of *Enlightenment*;

he inserted *communicative rationality* to highlight the communicative dimension in the establishment of modern society and work relations. To discuss work and society through these three forms of rationality has not only had implications for the productive and the reproductive domain but also for the way in which we speak or communicate. Today these three forms of rationality can be found in any *speech act* we undertake.[309] They determine the meaning of speech acts during the process of one person speaking and another person's reception. On this Gadamer (1976:65) has emphasised that

> *whoever speaks a language that no one else understands does not speak. To speak means to speak 'to' someone. Speaking does not belong in the sphere of 'I' but in the sphere of 'we'.*

What becomes clear from Gadamer's (1976) quote is that speaking is not only a communicative but also a social act. At work such speech acts take on two forms. *Instrumental speech* (Table 9.2ª) is used when purposive speech is directed towards goal achieving tasks. However we also communicate issues that are not directly – or not at all – related to work tasks. Such speech acts have a different purpose. They are not task-driven or directed towards achieving a specific work task but directed towards understanding and *critical-interpretive* goals (Table 9.2ᵇ). In sum, instrumental speech (a) and critical-interpretive speech (b) contain very different types of speech acts. Critical-interpretive speech however is closely linked to speech acts that are directed towards communicative action. Once instrumental speech is separated from critical-interpretive speech, the latter is likely to result in communicative action (c). Only critical-interpretive speech acts (b) can lead to *communicative action*. These speech acts are shown in Table 9.2.[310]

Table 9.2 shows how speech at work can be structured to achieve certain goals. The separation between speech acts of type (a) and type (b) is clearly marked through a line 'I' while the link between (b) and (c) is marked as '→' to indicate the likelihood of movement from (b) to (c). Under this model, every speech act at work can be viewed as either related to (a) or to (b). Instrumental speech acts (a) are directed towards instrumental goals such as functional support for existing structural asymmetries. But speech acts can also be directed towards the creation of a workplace culture that is critical or non-supportive of prevailing structures (b). Here, speech acts are directed towards the unmasking of domination, asymmetrical structures, and authoritarian characters.

Speech acts that operate at an instrumental level (a) tend to use technical, scientific, or engineering language directed towards system integration.[311] In contrast, speech acts at the critical-interpretive level (b) rely on workers' values, a critical counter-culture, and solidaristic ethics. They are directed towards the creation of a workplace that enables labour to socially integrate

Table 9.2 Three Understandings of Speech Acts at Work

Concepts of	Three Understandings of Speech Acts at Work		
	a) Instrumental Speech	b) Critical-Interpretive Speech	c) Communicative Action
Objective/Purpose	Functional speech relations	Integrated cultural foundation	⇧ Reveal domination & aid emancipation
Method	Empirical evaluation, system imperatives & functionalism	Ethnographical understanding and interpretation of rules & procedures	⇧ Critique of ideology, asymmetric structures, & hegemony
Future Metaphors	Progressive liberation	Strengthening of integrative values	⇧ Changes in social structures
Company metaphor	Economic work-relationship	Work as social organisation	⇧ Political unevenness of power
Core problems	Firm is market place of ideas	Communicative community	⇧ Firm is a location for exchange
Communication	Effectiveness and efficiency	Misunderstanding and illegitimacy	⇧ Domination, distortion, colonisation
Narrative style	Information needs, transfers	Affirmation of social groups at work	⇧ Communicative action & ideal speech
Chronological order	Scientific, technical, engineering	Aesthetic and story-telling	⇧ Critical dialogue and ethical discourses
Work/Management	Modernity, rise of capitalism	Pre-modern value systems	⇧ Communicative modernity
Atmosphere and Culture	Control and surveillance	Commitment and work ethics	⇧ Communicative & social action/change
Core Concerns	Positive and optimistic	Kinship and communal	⇧ Solidarity among workers and suspicious towards management
	Social disorder, revolt, etc.	End of individual and freedom	⇧ Authoritarian structures, domination

themselves inside the labour domain. This domain needs to be constructed in a way so that it is resistant to the managerial system of domination.[312] Once this is achieved, possibilities for communicative action (c) are opened up. In (b), and even more so in (c), contradictions are made visible through the promotion of communicative action under conditions of ideal speech.[313] This seeks social integration based on communicative solidarity among labour and provides a discursive forum for critical discussion on asymmetric forms of domination at work. The construction of a critical-interpretive domain directed towards *communicative action* at the workplace can have a profound impact. The nucleus of communication inside the critical-interpretive domain and the sphere of communicative action (b+c) is no longer purposive-rational strategic action directed towards success (a) but communicative action (c) directed towards understanding.[314] This can be seen as an interaction of at least two actors capable of speech and action, who have established an interpersonal relationship with each other which reaches far beyond the communicative part of the theory. It suggests that guides for action can be established among participants by reaching agreement or understanding on a plan for coordinated action based on a shared definition of the situation. It is vital for *communicative action* that participants or social actors conduct their plans for action cooperatively. Only a collectively defined social action is able to bring out the results that have been set forth.

Social actors communicating towards ideal speech need to avoid a fundamental risk. The failure to reach understanding on a commonly agreed course of action prevents such action. The risk of failure on a plan for social action that is not based on common understanding increases with the level of disagreement. At the opposite level, avoiding or minimising the risk of failure goes hand in hand with an increased level of social agreement. Hence, reaching common or collective understanding can be seen as a precondition to social action. Most behaviour takes place either consciously or intentionally and most social action involves social actors. Non-solitary collectively engaged social action takes into consideration the behaviour of others. Since the orientation towards social action is communicatively established and directed towards human behaviour, the collaborative and social act of ideal speech must reflect this directionality.

Fundamentally, *speech acts* always reflect on two issues. Firstly, that a speaker is *saying* something and secondly, by speaking s/he also *does* something. Speech therefore is speaking and action at the same time. Conscious speaking acts result from perception and reflective thinking.[315] They emerge from behaviour that exhibits a fundamental feature of humanity – the social fact that human acts are essentially social. The human individual has a mind that acts in as far as it symbolically internalises these social acts. *Speech* acts and *social* acts are of equal currency. Abandoning speech acts means firstly to abandon speech and acting in society and secondly abandoning

Table 9.3 Five Types of Speech Acts

Types	Explanation	Examples
a) Assertive	Related to true and false claims.	The company has made 10% profit last year.
b) Directive	Obliges a listener to act.	We need to strike now!
c) Committing	Which commits a speaker.	Together we bargain, divided we beg.
d) Expressive	Revelatory of a speaker's psychological state.	I will be with you all the way!
e) Declarative	Which causes something to happen.	A strike will be called tomorrow.

society itself. At work this abandonment equals the negation of workers as they are reduced to speechless entities. It takes away a vital element of any human being and results in the relinquishment of any possibility to move from critical-interpretive speech (b) to communicative action (c). Every type of speech can be seen as a social and human act and take on different forms. Such *speech acts* can be divided into five categories.[316]

According to Table 9.3, *assertive* speech acts[a] are to be judged via their truth content or via a false or disproving claim.[317] *Directive* speech acts[b] are directed towards conveying requests, invitations, instructions or orders and commands that oblige some sort of action. *Committing speech acts*[c] encourage a recipient to commit to something while the *expressive speech act*[d] is of an informative character that expresses, justifies, and accounts for certain actions. Lastly, *declarative speech acts*[e] are directed towards *cause-and-effect* relationships. These five standard *speech acts* – seen as activities of participants as well as interpretive activities directed towards sense making – take on three core elements as an attempt to develop views on social affairs directed towards mutual understanding.[318] They can be understood in three pragmatic ways (Habermas 1997a:120).

Table 9.4 shows that speech is directed towards the issue of *truth* where actors seek to reach common understanding about the true state of affairs[i].

Table 9.4 Three Pragmatic Relationships

Level	Relationship
Objective[i]	something in the *objective* world, i.e. the totality of entities about which true statements are possible, or
Social[ii]	something in the *social* world, i.e. the totality of legitimately regulated interpersonal relations, or
Subjective[iii]	something in the *subjective* world, i.e. the totality of experiences to which a speaker has privileged access and which can be expressed before a public.

This includes an examination of issues from a variety of viewpoints.[319] According to Gadamer,

> *nothing that is said has its truth simply in itself, but refers instead backward and forward to what is unsaid. Every assertion is motivated that is, one can sensibly ask of everything that is said, why did you say that?*[320]

The essential questions are: why and what? In speech acts within the social sphere participants' communicative action is directed towards social issues[(ii)] and how interpersonal relations are established and conducted. The essential question here is: *how*? Somewhat conceptually different to (i) and (ii) is the subjective sphere (iii) because in this sphere speech acts are reduced to the provision of information. The essential questions of an information provider are firstly: am I sufficiently informed about the issue at hand and, secondly: how can I transfer the previously gained knowledge to a specific audience. In conclusion, almost all forms of speech acts take place in either of the three spheres or as a combination of some or all of them (Table 9.4). Speech acts that are designed to encourage *communicative action* as outlined in Table 9.2[c] (above) set forth specific demands towards all participants in this form of communication. Above all, social actors at work need to ensure that colonising attempts from 9.2[a] (above) are reduced to a minimum or excluded altogether as these distortions hinder or prevent any movement towards *communicative action* (9.2[c]) or ideal speech.

One way for workers to avoid the colonisation of ideal speech situations by management, managerialism, and managerial communication is to adhere to the conditions that establish ideal speech.

Table 9.5[i-vii] shows the seven conditions that *all* have to be established if workers seek to employ a form of communicative action that guides communication towards Kant's *what is* – the truthful state of affairs – and toward Kant's *what ought to be* which is directed towards emancipation that ends all forms of social domination. In this process participants of speech acts have to fulfil a number of conditions that are – exclusively – directed towards the self-guidance of discussions. They do not seek to regulate *what is said* as long as this does not present an unconscious and uncritical mirroring of domineering speech and power structures that seek to infiltrate ideal speech from the managerial domain, also transmitted through the socially dominant ideology of managerialism. In achieving this, participants of ideal speech have to keep in mind that this is a form of social communication with two or more participants. Ideal speech cannot be established singularly; it has to be social (2–2⁺). The second and maybe even one of the hardest parts to establish is the exclusion of all forms of communicative distortions. Similar to this, the demand for equality and symmetric speech acts relies on symmetric access, symmetric power relations, etc. There cannot be a primus, a leader, or a chair*man* (!). Finally, ideal speech can only be established when

Table 9.5 Conditions that Establish Ideal Speech at Work

No.	Conditions for ideal speech that have to be met
i)	any process directed towards ideal speech implies that at least two workers [no longer objects of managerial power] come together to communicate towards reaching agreement about the truthful state of affairs;
ii)	in order to reach common agreement on the truthful state of affairs it is absolutely vital that communication between two or more participants is genuine, earnest, non-strategic, non-distorted, and non-deceptive and that the agreement is able to reflect this;
iii)	a genuine and truthful agreement that is communicatively established has to be reached by the force of the better argument alone;
iv)	the force of commonly agreed better arguments can only prevail if communication is not hindered and is domination-free; the absence of all external (managerial) and internal (unconscious mirroring of power relations) constrains is vital;
v)	ideal speech is not hindered when symmetric relationships are established between all participants so that chances to employ speech-acts are equally distributed and contributions are made and assessed on an equal basis;
vi)	ideal speech situations are reached when speech acts are based on constructive, comprehensible, truthful, sincere, legitimate, and ethical contributions that are directed towards all others and have established common agreement;
vii)	crucially, ideal speech is a process that sets parameters only on the form but not on the content of what is communicated insofar as what is said does not violate the conditions laid out above[i-vi]

all (seven) conditions are fulfilled. Participants need to critically reflect and reassess these conditions; otherwise distortions that are often hidden and extremely destructive to ideal speech can either end it or lead to false outcomes and faked consensuses.

Ideal speech and distorted communication

The concept of ideal speech is the core property of any communication and speech theory directed towards assisting workers to uncover hidden distortions and move towards *communicative action*. It can only be established when an *ideal speech situation* is created. Unconstrained communication, the opposite of distorted communication, is at its base (Habermas 1997). *Systematically distorted communication* that institutionalises meaning structures is not established through a rationally derived consensus that seeks common understanding but through the *imposition* of claims to truth, rightness, etc. which are managerially imposed rather than discursively redeemed.[321] Distorted communication can be seen as a product of the dialectical relationship between ideology – managerialism – and a material interest, the drive towards organisational goals, i.e. profits.[322] It is an ideological tool that systematically creates, maintains, and reinforces managerialism. Systematically distorted communication is not just achieved through known communicative control mechanisms such as formal and informal control through reporting systems, levels of order-giving, procedures, the shaping of a certain communication culture, the pre-designing of personal relationships at work, and communicative networks, etc. It is a much more sophisticated system that prevents the movement of communication into the direction of ideal speech. Virtually almost all textbooks and books on organisational communication, effective business communication and the like offer endless examples of how this is done.[323] They reduce organisational communication to a simple and pure device to transfer knowledge.

Figure 9.1 depicts a textbook case that can be found in many texts on business or managerial communication.[324] In which way this approach creates distortions at several levels is highlighted below:

i) Information transfer

Communication is reduced to information, indicating a non-discursive approach. It allows managerial messages to be formulated and transmitted without being challenged. In this concept '*what*' has been communicated is reduced to a mere piece of information. *Information* is what appears to be important, not questions about how and why. Communication is reduced to a *thing* that is passed on from one person to another. This implies that communication is some sort of channel for a commodity possessed by 'A' to be passed on to 'B'. It also implies that one side – management – knows while the other side – workers – simply receive information inside the hierarchical relationship.

ii) Transfer

Communication has been further reduced to a simple transfer indicating linear thinking. It is not based on a model that includes two-way communication with feedback. The receiver (R) is not given an option to accept or reject the message. Unlike in real communication that always operates in two ways ↔ and never in one →, R is seen as a passive, not an active part. The receiver is constructed as a passive reception box ☐ and this box metaphor completes the one-dimensionality of communication.

> *Information[i]-transfer[ii] views communication as a metaphoric pipeline[iii] through which information is transferred from one person to another[iv]. Managers thus communicate well when they transfer their knowledge[v] to subordinates[vi] and others with minimal spillage[vii].*

Figure 9.1 A Textbook Case of Communicative Distortions

iii) The pipeline metaphor

Communication is further reduced to the metaphor of a pipeline where human communication is constructed as a technical instrument that carries immaterial goods from one end to the other. This engineering ideology sees communication as a technical object (a pipeline). The *line*-arity is already part of the very word pipe-*line*. As in a real pipeline that transports something from one location to another, the communicative metaphor does not allow any feedback.

In addition, any external influences, such as challenging views to management's linear form of communication, are seen as disturbances to communication and are shielded by the pipeline's metal frame. This supports the idea that if management adopts this sort of linear communication, it is safe from unwarranted influences. A metal frame has encapsulated managerial communication.

iv) One person to another

By using the faked view of a personalised company where the term 'person' is used as a euphemism for companies, corporations or firms, communication in managerial work settings is portrayed as just another form of communication from *one person to another*. In reality however, humans who are forced into a managerial setting where specific hierarchies are assembled to prohibit alternative motivations occupy such places. Inside these socially constructed settings, people either become managers or workers, today called *human resources*. They are assembled in highly structured and hierarchical relationships and forced to communicate inside these structures.

The use of the term person-to-person communication falsely suggests a non-existing symmetry and equality that may be part of a liberal society in general, but certainly does not exist within the non-democratic, control based structures of a company where the ideology of '*one person to another*' faces the reality of hierarchy that is specifically created to convert the liberal idea of an individual into an organisational tool exposed to *the will of management*.[325] In this environment it is much more likely that communication takes place between a manager and a worker, ideologically relabelled *human resource*.

v) Knowledge

Communication is further distorted by the idea that only managers hold the *knowledge* and workers are lacking it and therefore need to be provided with it. This may be appropriate in certain instances but not so much in others. In the non-discursive, top-down form of communication, management is the sole producer of knowledge while workers are exclusively the receivers. Here, knowledge is not a product of a communicative relationship created communicatively among workers or between workers and managers; it is exclusively assigned to the domain of management.

vi) Subordinates

Upon managerial decision knowledge can be transferred to *subordinates*. Inside the managerial framework of distorted communication workers are framed as secondary entities. They are no longer considered humans but reduced to ordinates, sub-ordinates or sub-humans. Their mere productive function turns them into minors, inferiors, lowers, or second-rates. This cements a hierarchy in which workers are made knowledge- and clueless. Management on the other side is portrayed as the exact opposite. Their position is seen as major, first rate and of foremost importance.

vii) Minimum spillage

Finally, inside the engineering ideology of the pipeline model, communication is further narrowed and directed towards one-dimensionality by securing the exclusion – minimum spillage – of all non-linear forms of communication that are depicted as *spillage* and include any form of communication that is not in the managerial interest and does not follow their model of communication. To complete the distorted model of *organisational communication*, any communication that is non-hierarchical is seen as spillage or harmful, even if it follows the pipeline model A → B.[326] Management seeks to avoid spillage by sticking to a prescript model of distorted communication.

The previous example is just one of many held in the average textbook on organisational communication. Some further examples that reduce labour and labour's dependence on management for information are shown in Table 9.6. All of them are designed to systematically distort communication. Management often chooses to deliberately control access to important information that would otherwise assist labour. Managerial distortion reaches not only into the control of messages – *what* is communicated – but also into *how* these messages are communicated. Rather than being open forums, distortions are one-dimensional message transferrals from management to labour. In this process management dominates communication and has the powers to either exclude or construct labour as a passive receiver. *Ideal speech* cannot be developed under distorted forms of communication. It needs a situation where communication is free from domination. Management therefore has a serious interest in distorting communication. To achieve a situation of *ideal speech* the following constraints need to be eliminated (see Table 9.6).

Table 9.6 shows that business corporations face a structural dilemma when dealing with distorted communication. On the one side, they are required to use instrumental communication as they are forced to comply with a market that determines profits as the sole reason of existence. On the other side, there is a constant demand to hide instrumental communication. The imperatives of communication also demand the pretence of human, non-instrumental forms of communication. Both the eclipse of instrumental communication and the simulated human communication are

Table 9.6 Forms of Non-Ideal Speech Acts

- pre-set agendas,
- power relations or games,[327]
- gender divisions,
- hierarchies and elitism,
- narrowly defined issues,
- compliance gaining strategies,
- superior-subordinate interaction,
- power-as-dominance structures,
- myths of realities,
- rhetorical tools[328] & deception,
- structural limitations & constraints,
- highly structured discourses,
- lies, manipulation, distortion, etc.,
- complete silence during work,
- concealment, bluffing,
- ideologies (Barthes 1957 & 1967),
- standardised speech acts,
- intellectual self-limitation,
- manipulate contexts of meaning,
- tell decisions in passive form,
- worker-management demarcations,
- pre-structured decision making processes,
- pre-decided avenues for sense-making,
- pre-compartmentalisation of issues as political,
- applying socio-technical control systems,
- content loss across institutional boundaries,
- inner self-withdrawal as absenteeism,
- meeting-leaders & discussion organisers
- subordination to privileged interests,
- technical and nature-like language,
- communicative division of labour,
- monopolisation of communicative discourses,
- fear of authoritarian oppressors,
- self-protecting etiquettes of interaction,
- marshalling respected people to gain trust,
- misrepresent cost-benefit risks,
- focusing on task only by ignoring process,
- the prohibition of images (socialism, etc.),
- manipulatively obtained support,
- people-less talk of management,
- hidden agendas,
- interpersonal deception,
- information inequalities,
- unresponsiveness,
- obfuscation,
- shaping artificially created needs,
- problem framing,
- overwhelming data delivery,
- hiding omissions,
- an authoritarian workplace,
- asymmetrical power relationships,
- meetings as rituals and routines,[329]
- monopolistic distortion of exchange,
- domineering management culture,
- pre-defined discussion issues,
- non-participation and passivity,
- renunciation as self-censorship[330]
- pressure to reach a decision,
- dictation of system imperatives.

required to eclipse the structural logic of managerial interests versus labour's interests.

On the other hand the profit maxim requires compliance and a cooperative or harmonious relationship between labour and management in order to make the system work. Hence, an often rather fictitious and pretended empathy for employees is created – often on the premise of divergent interests but always covered up by communicative forms that create harmony such as the all-inclusive *'we'* portraying the one-dimensional rationale of the one best way behind management's reasoning. Such instrumental approach towards a one-dimensional goal relies on the strategic use of communication to promote a unified interest. The faked *'we'* seeks to cloak the dominance of the managerial interest that is the organisational goal of profit preserved in the privileged position of management. The divergence of interests can only be uncovered if the *'we'* is split into labour's and management's interests. The unifying *'we'* seeks to mix managerial instrumental communication with labour's interest in ideal speech and by doing so hinders or ends ideal speech rather than enabling it. Ideal speech is further stalled through the ideology of managerial*ism* that replaces horizontal forms of communication with vertically structured communication that is made to appear neutral or technical. In accordance with non-communicative technical or natural laws, these versions of communication operate strongly against any form of ideal speech that is neither governed by technical nor by natural law or by managerial systems and rejects all top-down or hierarchical ordering systems.

In almost all company structures vertical communication is enshrined as a hierarchical system of communicative channels. By pre-formatting communicative structures inside organisations, communication between management and labour is pre-conceptually distorted even before it takes place. Disregarding any form and content, the already distorted horizontal and hierarchical communication cannot lead to ideal speech. The order of the communicative infrastructure within the managerially created company culture is deliberately designed to subordinate labour, to avoid ideal speech, and to move labour towards *Manufacturing Consent* that is *normatively* rather than *communicatively* secured. Fundamental to any communicative infrastructure expressed as company culture is its undemocratic character. This hierarchical version of corporate culture reduces labour's communicative involvement and participation to a mere chimera of communication. Unlike anything remotely representing ideal speech, it excludes labour from the power of decision making. Ideal speech on the other hand is always communicatively secured. It is not normatively established via rules, force, orders, hierarchies, etc.

Managerial systems operate in order to integrate workers into a wide range of initiatives such as quality circles, improvement schemes, teamwork, joint production committees, welfare committees, etc. They are designed to provide management with access to workers in the form of communicative forums and also incorporate workers into a pre-defined power structure that presents itself as democratic and participative and that involves employees. Held under managerial guidance, these committees can hardly offer conditions under which ideal speech could be conducted. These set-ups always operate inside a pre-set power field that prevents ideal speech and finally leads to both total managerial administration and workers' total dependency on management settings.

Managerial avoidance strategies that seek to preclude ideal speech communication are often announced as being democratic.[331] They are however managerial announcements and if successfully implemented they are no more than tools for false democratisation processes. The managerial language applied to these announcements uses terms such as *have your say!, be part of it!*, or *we are listening to you!* etc. and by pretending to empathise with workers, management is able to strengthen the pre-established managerial harmony. In reality managerial claims of *working together* or *listen to your concerns* always occur under the agenda of a profit driven corporation that directs communicative exchange towards instrumental communication rather than towards *ideal speech*.

(Such) *extended participation of labour in management and profit wouldn't by themselves alter this system of domination – as long as labour itself remains a prop and affirmative force* (Marcuse 1966:38).[332]

In Marcuse's above outlined normative argument resides the fact that by participating in the system of company-directed communication, workers can never overcome it. As long as the communicative system is based on the managerial *system of domination* to which workers have to subscribe, forms of communication directed towards ideal speech cannot be established. As managerial domination infiltrates all forms of communication at work, the ups and downs of the *Cycles of Communicative Control* or *Iron Cages of Communication* will prevent ideal speech.[333] Forms of managerial domination may vary and occur on either higher or lower pre-structured and pre-arranged conditions but the essential forms of domination and hierarchies remain established and, in order to cover these, communicative distortions come into play.

Communicative distortions are directed towards two issues. Firstly, they are designed to allow system integration by masking demands for democratic and communicatively grounded consensus to avoid communication that could move towards the realm of ideal speech. Secondly, communicative distortions allow management to receive worker's affirmation in a pre-constructed framework in order to gain legitimacy from workers whenever deemed necessary.[334] Relevant for both these issues is the masking of domination and hierarchies which blocks an essential entry point for a critique based on communicative action and ideal speech. To allow critique and unmask communicative distortions, the following three gateways need to be utilised:

Table 9.7   Three Ways to Unmask Communicative Distortions

Forms		Description
(i)	Empirical	An *empirical* investigation into forms of communication, organisational and political-economic structures that underlie management's actions;
(ii)	Interpretive	An *interpretive* investigation into the meaning and experience of management's communicative performance as well as labour's ability to counter managerial communicative structures; and
(iii)	Normative	A *normative* investigation into management's respect or violation of fundamental social norms of language use as such norms enable the socially constructed environment to be intelligible.

Table 9.7 shows options to test managerial communication based on empirical, interpretive, and normative investigation. In this way systematically distorted communication can be exposed and corrected. Once workers become aware of managerial forms of domination and hierarchies, these can be analysed by examining their empirical content[i] and, even more importantly, a detailed interpretation can be carried out on *what* has been said and *which* interpretive structures provide a framework to establish meaning[ii]. Finally, forms of managerial communication can be normatively analysed by comparing them to the demands of *communicative action* and ideal speech[iii]. These investigative tools enable workers to not only understand *how* management communicates but also *why* they communicate in their specific ways. This understanding prevents workers from being trapped in the Orwellian (1949:83) dictum of *I understand HOW; I do not understand WHY*. Apart from realising why managerial communication is distorted, the distorted content can be further unmasked. Four key principles allow a further examination of hidden agendas that underlie managerial communication (Forester 1985:210–214).

In conjunction with Table 9.7, Table 9.8 shows how managerially distorted communication can be analysed by comparing it to issues that establish ideal speech. Under conditions of ideal speech, communication has to include the four principles of comprehensibility[i], sincerity[ii], legitimacy[iii], and truthfulness[iv]. Testing managerial communication on these four principles can already highlight severe deficiencies. However, communicative distortions can also be corrected. Table 9.9 transfers comprehensibility[i], sincerity[ii], legitimacy[iii], and truthfulness[vi] into a more comprehensive matrix that allows an accomplished reflection of organisational levels of

Table 9.8 Four Managerial Principles for the Use of Communication

Principle	Description
(i) Comprehensibility	Does management communicate work related issues *comprehensively*, so that one can understand what in fact is happening at the business level and beyond the borders of an enterprise? Is managerial communication precise, inclusive, intelligible, complete, broad enough to form a view thorough and ample enough?
(ii) Sincerity	Does management's communication offer *sincerity*? Is communication done in good faith? Is there no scope for manipulation left? Has management avoided misleading people? Does communication lead to guided decisions as opened up under conditions of rational choice that offer choices within management organised confinements?
(iii) Legitimacy	Is management's communication *legitimate*? Does one's acceptance lead to a legitimisation of managerialism? Is management's claim a hidden legitimacy of a corporate judgement covered in professionalism?
(iv) Truthfulness	Is management's communication based on *truth*? Can one believe and trust in what has been said? Is there any evidence supporting their claim? Is the evidence good enough? Is the offered information upon which one acts or reaches a decision truthful or untruthful, even unintentionally?

communication and managerial tools used to communicate. Table 9.8[a] shows how distorted communication can be experienced at the workplace level in a management–labour (L→M) relationship. More importantly, Table 9.8 also offers some responses to overcome these distortions. These distortions and responses are outlined more detailed in Table 9.9.

Table 9.9 shows how labour can experience distorted communication (a) but also how distorted forms of communication can be detected and corrected (b). This can be achieved under the four principles of ideal speech[i–iv]. Distorted communication is highly unlikely to be comprehensive, sincere, legitimate, or truthful. As a key condition, it always needs to be authoritarian, hierarchical, and instrumental. The core method of correction lies in the exposure of distorted communication through open, critical, and democratic means.[335]

While the detection of distorted forms of communication leads to the removal of obstructive language and the unmasking of hidden interests, its correction is occupied with the presentation of positive communicative forms such as democratic communication processes. Rather than being one-dimensional, this method allows divergent viewpoints that are geared

Table 9.9 Experiencing & Responding to Distorted Communication at Work

a) Four Principles to Detect Distorted Communication

Practical level	(i) Comprehensibility	(ii) Sincerity	(iii) Legitimacy	(iv) Truthfulness
M→L Communication	Ambiguity & Confusion	Deceit & Insecurity	Out of Context Meaning	Misinformation
Critical Questions	What?	Can I trust management?	Is this right/correct?	Is this true?
Organisational Level	Exclusion through Jargon	Rhetorical reassurance	Unresponsiveness	Information Withholding
Critical Questions	What does this mean?	Can we trust?	Is this justified?	Is this truthful?
Communicative Tools	Mystification	Misrepresentation	Un-Accountability	Truth Obscured
Critical Questions	Is the meaning understood?	That is their line?	Who are they to say?	What don't they tell us?

b) Responses to Correct Distorted Communication based on Four Principles

Practical level	(i) Comprehensibility	(ii) Sincerity	(iii) Legitimacy	(iv) Truthfulness
M→L Communication	Revealing M's Meaning	Checking M's Intentions	M's Roles & Contexts	Checking M's Evidence
Critical Questions	What does that mean?	Does M mean this?	Do I need to accept…?	Is M's claim true?
Organisational Level	Minimising Jargon	Get Counter Advocates	Co-Decision Making	3rd Party Expertise
Critical Tasks	Clean up Language	Check whether to trust M	Involve Others	Check data, calculations
Communicative Tools	Demystification	Expose hidden interests	Democracy of Process	Debate, Polit. Criticism
Critical Questions	All this really means is…	If no one speaks, they win.	Legitimate Pressure	Democratise Truth

towards the remedy of distorted communication. Crucial to the comprehension of distorted communication is the fact that it never seeks to reach mutual understanding. Instead of understanding being established communicatively inside the framework of ideal speech, it is reached normatively. A non-communicatively established agreement is a faked agreement. It is not reached democratically inside open conditions but via the two core managerial elements that guide distorted communication: domination and hierarchies. However, systematically distorted communication can be overcome through self-reflection generated in ideal speech situations in which emancipation reflects a universal interest that exists despite the occurrence of distorted communication.[336] According to McCarthy (1978) ideal speech only occurs in *a situation of symmetrical free speech in which all participants have an equal chance to employ constructive, regulative, and representative speech acts*. This translates into truthful, unhindered, and un-distorted *discourse* that needs to be symmetrical rather than asymmetrical, free from domination, and free from hierarchies.

Unfortunately, current managerial forms of communication can hardly meet these conditions as they need to occur inside a set-up that is directed towards the social practice of equal participants. This set-up however demands that all participants have an effective equality of chances to take part in a dialogue. The conditions for ideal speech situations are not *linguistic* in character but rather *social*.[337] These can be summed up as human are humans because of relationships with others. Therefore the Kantian *means* and *ends* existence of being humans depends on a *social* rather than a *linguistic* world. This applies to form and content of communication inside which individuals reach common understanding and judgments. Such *universal ethical judgements* (Mead 1964) are found in *ideal speech* and not in definitional or linguistic terms. In Habermas' understanding of *ideal speech* the universal expression of *all voices* through participation on communicative action represents common and universal ethical judgments. Universal ethical judgments based on communicative action and ideal speech are foundations of a common understanding that goes well beyond simple statements such as *the voice of all is the universal voice*. It demands a conscious act of rational communication among actors directed towards understanding. Speech acts directed towards communicative understanding and conducted under conditions of ideal speech have reached a somewhat higher ethical standing than ordinary management talk.

10
Communicative Action II: Ethics and Communication

Whenever labour unmasks distorted communication, it seeks to connect the world of work to *communicative action* and ideal speech which always means to also connect it to ethical and moral standards. Communication tends to be constructed as a technical tool such as a tube or a *pipeline through which information is transferred* until it enters the realm of ethics, morality and communicative ethics.[338] Social and communicative relationships have strong *moral* and *ethical* connotations.[339] The link between ethics and communication is nothing new. When human society moved out of the feudalist past, God and the Church were no longer able to define, create, use, and abuse moral standards.[340] Once relieved from the metaphysics and mysticism of religion and church, modern societies had to find new modes of moral conduct.[341] Humans could no longer rely on the pre-constructed – and in fact *invented* – and as somewhat *higher* portrayed authority. They had to set up their own moral and ethical standards.

The issue of communicative ethics has been discussed ever since *Jean Jacques Rousseau's* Dijon lecture on *Discourse on the Moral Effects of the Arts and Science* in the year 1750. Ethical communication has been linked to moral behaviour connecting modernity and enlightenment to the world of work.[342] *Adam Smith* (1723–1790) took this up by demanding ethics and morals in the human conduct of society. For him, this translated into the moral conduct of economic affairs. Before his work on *The Wealth of Nations* (1776), Smith's first book on *Moral Sentiment* (1759) formulated moral requirements. He saw the economic and political system as ultimately based on moral foundations in order to prevent the creation of an amoral, if not immoral, society and business.

In the 20th century *Mahatma Gandhi* (1925) took up the issue of morality and society. He quoted that the world provided enough to every man's need but never enough for every man's greed.[343] Searching for a moral code of human conduct Gandhi found that modern societies behave relatively unethically. To change this, he identified the *Seven Deadly Sins of Society*. Among those Gandhi saw *four* sins that are crucial to the world of work:[344]

Table 10.1 Gandhi's Social Sins at Work

Social Sins	Description
a) wealth without work	*getting something for nothing*, manipulate people and things, get-rich-quick schemes, pyramidal organisations, etc.
b) knowledge without character	disconnecting knowledge from moral development, creating specialised knowledge without linking it to overall understanding, and not developing universal morals such as kindness, fairness, dignity, and integrity
c) commerce & business without morality & ethics	How we treat each other in the sprit of benevolence, of service, and of contribution. An economic system has to be based on moral foundations. Not conducting business as covert operations, with hidden agendas, or in secrecy. Business has to be conducted in the light of morality and agents need to be able to justify their actions.
d) science without humanity	If science is reduced to a technique and technology, it quickly becomes denigrated into *human against humanity*. Technology should not become the domineering paradigm of science. The science-humanity link is to be emphasised as an inextricable link between both. Universal ethical standards have to be applied to all scientific endeavours.

Table 10.1 shows Gandhi's four work-related sins. The world of work has the ability – at least for some – to create wealth without work (a). As management is able to apply knowledge without character (b), this often leads to business and commerce without morality and ethics (c). Finally, the managerial process often applies science without humanity treating humans and the environment as a *means* rather than an *end*. These four sins have created severe pathologies in our society.[345] In the tradition of *Jean Jacques Rousseau's* demand for moral human conduct, *Adam Smith's* demand for moral conduct in economic affairs, and *Mahatma Gandhi's* (Table 10.1) demand for moral conduct in society, Mead (1964) developed the philosophical concept of *universal ethical judgement*. Laurence Kohlberg, a psychologist, has developed Mead's idea even further.[346] Thinking inside the tradition of his philosophical predecessors, Kohlberg developed seven stages of moral development. These stages provide a universalistic foundation as well as a moral structure under which human communication at work can be discussed. In order to understand the moral development of humans, Kohlberg also developed a *scale* of moral development.[347]

Table 10.2 shows an overview of Kohlberg's seven levels of moral development. In fact, it lists eight stages, however, Kohlberg regarded the first stage (0) as somewhat irrelevant to moral development. He argued that newborns

Table 10.2 Kohlberg's Stages of Moral Development

Stage	Orientation	Moral Motives
0	Impulsive and amoral	None
1	Obedient and Avoidance of punishment[348]	Irrational dread of punishment Fear of those in authority
2	Personal benefits & rewards Getting a good deal for oneself	How to get most pleasure and gain for oneself Calculating the personal risk and payoffs of an action
3	Conforming to social expectations Gaining approval	Avoiding disapproval by associates and close ones Wanting to be praised, liked & admired, rather than shamed
4	Protecting law and order Maintaining the existing system of official social arrangements	Performing formal duties and responsibilities Meeting official standards Working for the best interest of an institution
5	Promoting justice and welfare within a wider community, as defined in open and reasonable debate	Following principles that serve the best interest of the great majority Striving to be reasonable, just and purposeful in one's action
6	Defending everyone's right to justice and welfare, universally applied	Applying well-thought principles Being ready to share and debate these openly and non-defensively with others
7	Respecting the cosmos as an integral whole An openness extending well beyond humanity	Respecting the intrinsic value of the cosmos with its wider harmonies and paradoxes

cannot develop moral understanding. He defined this early stage as zero or '0' because moral development is hardly possible at this stage.

0. At stage zero: impulsive

Whatever I want at any time is seen as right, regardless of the consequences and without any form of social concern. This stage does hardly exist in management-labour relations because both are dealing with fully developed human beings matured beyond the stage of non-existing moral values, even though at the height of management's conception – the early years of Taylor's *Scientific Management* – management expected from their workforce what resembled child-like, impulsive, reflexive, and stimulus-response like behaviour. However, even today the exploitation of children is still nothing new in the current system even though it has been largely outsourced to non-advanced countries. Before child labour was outsourced and with it the attempt of managerialism to push highly unethical forms of work out of the spotlight of corporate mass media, child exploitation was more directly welcomed as it is today. During the years of Taylor, *widely adopted systems were totally dehumanising, reducing skilled work to tedium, and a recent report in the American Machinist suggested the ideal workers for them would be the mentally retarded. The author advocated a mental age of 12* (Roper 1983:73). Under managerialism – combined with affirmative corporate mass media – work forms that exploit child labour under the maxim of *out of sight is out of mind* have largely ended in advanced countries as modern post-industrial work regimes demand a different kind of worker.[349]

Today, both actors in the world of work – management and labour – have developed some form of mature and moral understanding when entering into work arrangements – even though child labour should not be totally left out as is not exclusively an issue of the developing world.[350] Nevertheless, even morally conscious behaviour can be targeted by what has been called *scripted behaviours* when a worker's actions are carried out with little or no conscious awareness. Essentially, they follow a pre-organised script – almost like a movie script – without much critical reflection. Trivial or highly routinised activities conducted in extremely familiar settings that provide clear schemata for well-developed work patterns – just as prescribed by Taylor – are sometimes carried out in an absent-minded or mindless fashion. The reason for conducting such actions is often deeply embedded in the scripts – at least that is what individuals are made to believe. Rational reasoning is seen as being enshrined in the managerial process only so that those on the operative side – those who are managed – are made to feel that they do not need to monitor the morality of an action that is carried out as *scripted behaviour*.

1. At stage one: obedience and punishment

Obedience and punishment play a powerful role in human lives.[351] Many behavioural scientists such as Skinner and linguists such as Chomsky have noted this. Punishment – along with positive and negative reinforcement – has been one of the core elements of Skinner's theory on conditioning.[352] Linguist Chomsky however has been critical of Skinner's behavioural theories on conditioning.[353] In his critique, Chomsky writes (1971:33) except when physically restraining, a person is the least free or dignified when he is under threat of punishment. *While management hardly ever restrains workers physically at today's workplaces, the threat of punishment has not ceased. In Skinner's model of obedience for punishment avoidance management-labour relations would be seen as highly dictatorial if they allowed people in authority to use punishment.*[354] *In this model, the rules are set in a non-democratic, dictatorial way and must be precisely obeyed. Disobedience will lead to punishment such as fines, loss of employment, etc. and is to be avoided. Furthermore, Skinner assumes that* punishable behaviour can be minimised by creating circumstances in which it is not likely to occur.[355] *Self-preservation therefore becomes an all-important concept. In this scenario, the individual is solely preoccupied with the demands of those in power and how to avoid causing them anger.*[356] Some forms of managerial communication convey exactly that. Monk (1997:57) has called this *Management by Fear*. In this model the giving and receiving of orders defines the communication between management and labour. Adorno (1944:22) has summed this up as *the ones who help because they know better turn into the ones who humiliate others through bossy privilege*. Social relations that are constructed in this way define communicative relations as highly authoritarian, governed by domination and top-down hierarchies.[357]

At this stage authority – the power associated with a position in an organisation – is enshrined in what constitutes the hierarchical relationship. Without hierarchy authoritarian relationships at work are hardly possible. Each actor in this structure has a clearly defined position and even those at the bottom are still made to believe that they have subordinates – even though these might be externalised (wives, husbands, children, pets, etc.). The core pattern of this cemented hierarchy defines the authoritarian, asymmetrical, aggressive, violent, unequal, and domineering relationships. In hierarchies that produce authoritarian relationships each level has authority over the immediate below as well as over all echelons below that. The structure is clearly pyramidal. In the world of work, such pyramidal structures are not only designed to generate authority but – through Human Resource Management's idea of promotions – to create a pathway to the top even though numerically this remains an illusion for the vast majority of workers. The following example of a relatively simple company structure consisting of roughly 5,500 workers and five hierarchical levels demonstrates this:[358]

Figure 10.1 shows that on the promotional level in an ordinary hierarchical company, the hierarchy and with it the authority are set against those at the bottom – those who are managed – rather than those who manage. The lower the position the more illusionary the chances become to be promoted to the top. In a company with one CEO and ten managers, nine will lose out while one – if no one is hired from the outside – may be promoted to be CEO.[359] If one assumed the chance of promotion to CEO level, the numerical improbability becomes staggering. While there might be a 10:1 or 5:1 possibility to be promoted to the next level, in reality those who will never be promoted are in the vast majority and this becomes more evident the greater the

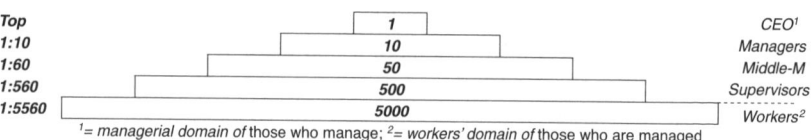

Figure 10.1 The Numeric Reality and the Illusion of Promotion

distance is between top and bottom. In fact, those in authority are numerically shielded against those in the lower ranks. While hierarchies are not unique to authoritarian structures – they exist in all companies – under authoritarian rule they are of particular significance as each promotional level (Figure 10.1) provides additional barriers against promotion and communication by asphyxiating individuals inside rigid and sharply divided hard borders that are numerically set against organisational mobility. A typical company hierarchy in fact resembles more the shape of a flat cake than that of a pyramid. Equally, the communicative structures reflect the authoritarian hierarchy of the companies so that individuals communicate inside their respective domains with the sole exception of reporting up to the next level and directing downwards to the level below. Apart from this, no other level of communication is stipulated. Inside the hierarchy of authoritarianism, not only communication but also conformity is directed towards the stability and sustainability of authority and this is not based on pay, praise or promotion but on obedience and the avoidance of punishment.[360]

2. At stage two: benefits and rewards

At stage two, management acts essentially in their own interest.[361] It acknowledges that making deals with labour may be necessary in certain situations; however, such deals are purely governed by management's self-interest.[362] If management deems a working relationship with labour as absolutely necessary, this is conducted through *'give and take'* bargaining. Communication with labour only takes place when it serves the interest of management and, if at all necessary, is reduced to *win-lose* strategies. Any information provided to workers is viewed as a loss to management. Communication is reduced to a *means* or an instrumental tool without having any intrinsic *ends*. Consequently, management ignores labour and refuses to communicate whenever communication with labour is deemed unnecessary. Labour as well as anyone at lower levels is treated and made to feel as cogs in a machine. Management also frames lower cogs as objects of managerial power and forces them into a framework in which they are reduced to aspiring to be a bigger cog. HRM calls this career and performance management.

This is the stage of Machiavellianism where the key to success is the desire to manipulate others for one's own benefit, the *'me, myself, and I'* view of the world and the world of work respectively. In the world of all against all the use of strategy [deception of the enemy] is the order of the day and forms of deviousness and deception may be applied whenever these are required to get ahead. Machiavellian personalities can be found working successfully in professional occupations, particularly in those that deal with people such as HRM as they excel in bargaining – and even more so – in bargaining a better deal for themselves.

3. At stage three: conforming to expectations

Management positions labour in a way that forces them to be supportive to management. This is done to prevent labour from taking on any critical or contradictory positions. It also avoids management's interests in sustaining itself. Labour shows loyalty and lives up to managerial expectations. Communication at this stage is based on obedience that seeks approval and endorsement by management.[363] It is highly distorted under management's communicative monopoly. Stage three is also the stage where management no longer directly attacks workers. According to Adorno and Horkheimer (1944:12), a managerial ruler no longer attacks a worker's life, body, or property. All of this remains intact. In fact, management does not operate using phrases like *you must think as I say or die* – their motto is *you are free not to think as I do*. Non-compliance however is punished through exclusion – *from this day on, you are a stranger among us*. Compliance on the other hand is supported inside a managerial frame of reference, constructed around the managerial use of the language of *trust* and a one-dimensional shared interest.[364] To convey this image, management strongly communicates the ideology of *we are all in one boat*.[365]

At this stage management uses an inclusive language to support compliance and the language of social exclusion when workers are non-compliant. Labour is forced to value management for its own sake. Management and managerialism become, in effect, a self-image of labour who adopt management's claim of believing in a shared interest. By identifying themselves with an ideology that defines interest as managerial interest, labour becomes part of managerialism. However, this identification only serves management who has achieved what it had set out to achieve – the conforming worker. Research has shown that individuals who have been socialised towards a work regime *carry institutional roles as conforming workers to transient settings that simulate the authority setting for more permanent organisations* (Katz & Kahn 1966:304). In other words, if workers move from primary socialisation during the pre-work period to the work domain, they *carry* authority conforming elements and will continue to do so even when they move between the work and the non-work or consumptive domain.[366] Once workers reach the work domain, they have already undergone years of conditioning to system compliance. At work, system conformity is further fostered through authoritarian ideologies that are communicated in the off-work domain.[367] After years of primary socialisation, workers recognise the symbols of authority that demand conformity in work settings. The school principle's office becomes the work supervisor's office.[368] Conforming to the authority is also established through clear work rules and work related requirements that carry forward the rules and requirements internalised at earlier stages. Conformity is policed through a system of hierarchical structures that mirror the structures previously adopted at home or at school. In both the primary and secondary socialisation processes expulsion or the threat of expulsion to nonconformers has been part of the system. In sum, when individuals are converted from humans to human resources they carry over a tremendous amount of conformity-enhancing attitudes. As long as workers behave inside the conforming boundaries set by management and accept these boundaries as legitimate, the structure of authoritarian conformity lives on.

4. At stage four: rules, laws, and order

At stage four, labour is seen as fulfilling its role by performing its duty.[369] Management invents and enforces role and duty and also upholds policies, formal regulations, rules, laws, and procedures.[370] These are means-ends generalisations as they tell workers what to do and how to behave in a general sense using a technical and bureaucratic language that enforces rule compliance. Inevitably however, rules must be linked to those who are supposed to follow them in order to be *follow-able* so that workers are complied to follow rather than break them. The task is therefore to close Hirschman's (1970) exit-option, lower the voice-option, and increase the loyalty-option. Secondly, rules are *prescriptive* as they direct workers' action towards what managerially *ought to be* and away from what *ought not to be*. Thirdly, rule-governed behaviour must be *adjustable* so that those workers who do not conform can be exposed to managerial rule-adjustment initiatives. In general, workers' rule-deviance is evaluated negatively while conformity and compliance are evaluated positively. Finally, managerial rules are impersonal and as such decrease the visibility of managerial power relations. Rule-based patterns of behaviour that guide the relationship between management and labour can be portrayed as free of power and conflict, simply because they are based on rules. They even take on a neutral or natural appearance.[371] Labour only needs to adapt to the natural force of the managerial rule. Labour's role is seen as being a compliant contributor to the good of the business and to make special efforts to act consistent with managerially defined *official* roles, duties, and standards. Labour strongly subscribes to properly formulated rules and procedures which often appear more natural and serious to those '*to be ruled over*' than to those who make the rules. Labour is captured in the ideology of rule-obedience. The height of managerial rule that can be achieved at stage four has been summed up by Adorno & Horkheimer (1944:12) as *immovably, they insist on the very ideology that enslaves them*.

The managerial ideology workers are made to subscribe to is strongly communicated to labour who is supposed to service managerial business needs and goals as a whole. Communication at this stage moves between distortion and instrumental strategic communication and is driven by a means targeting a managerial goal. It cannot follow the principles of ideal speech as it is seen and constructed as an instrument only. Consequently, instrumental communication takes place inside instrumental rationality and both are directed towards the system integration of labour. Most communication between management and labour that takes place at this stage serves the managerial imperative of formal rules that support the need of the business.

5. At stage five: justice and welfare

At this stage management shows some sort of interest in the betterment of social affairs, human, civil, political, and economic justice, and human welfare.[372] Usually this is more evident for those *outside* the company than for those *inside*. Ethics is largely externalised so that outsiders see the company as being an ethical customer or understanding *corporate social responsibilities*.[373] Internally, ethics is reduced to having in place an ethics policy or an ethical code of conduct and ethical issues are communicated as an add-on as long as they are in support of management.

Ethics or moralities are often reduced to being a surplus, a kindly afforded substitute to the managerial process that adds value to the operation.[374] It is not seen as an inherent part of its activity and can – or cannot – simply be added to the company if management wishes to do so. Watson (2003:48) has summed this up in the following way: when those who speak the managerial language

> wish to demonstrate their concern for the less fortunate or the less profitable, or the community at large, they speak of addressing the triple bottom line through corporate social responsibility known as CSR...Principally...their language has been stripped of meaning. They don't have words like generous, charitable, kind, and share...welfare, wealth transfer, social service, social benefit, social policy, and social contract.

In short, Watson's look at the starved language of management makes visible that their focus is neither on *social* issues nor on *morality* and, above all, not on *social morality*. On the labour side, things are somewhat different. At stage five, labour is able to start acting for a better society as a whole and moving beyond the confines of the business. Early forms of communication that are directed towards *communicative action* and ideal speech are opened up, enabling labour to remove some forms of distorted communication and challenge, or even end domination and hierarchies altogether. This lays the foundations for communicative relationships at work that are governed by the basics of *participatory democracy*.[375]

At stage five, two different concepts of communication between management and labour are starting to collide. This becomes prevalent when the two diverging logics of communicative and collective action face each other. On the one hand, non-democratic but highly instrumental forms of action, enshrined in instrumental communication, are upheld on the side of management. On the other side management also supports forms of communication that allow *participatory or deliberative democracy* under conditions of ideal speech and *communicative action*.[376] These forms of communication are non-strategic and non-instrumental. They are not confined to efficiency and means-ends ideologies. Instead, this version of communication allows labour to find common agreement directed towards the upholding of human ethics and rights and to communicate inside the labour domain where forms of participatory democracy can flourish. Democratic versions of communication are seen as ethical even if existing institutions such as business and management do not support them.

Over and above business, organisational, and institutional needs, concern for a greater good is developed. A wider public interest is served when universal principles of basic justice and human rights are followed. The influence reaches far beyond present forms of system stabilising rules, conventions, and laws. Communication between labour and management starts to shift between instrumental communication serving the instrumental purpose of management and communicative action directed towards truth, mutual understanding, and democracy.

6. At stage six: universally applied justice and welfare

Stage six starts with the application of well thought out principles. Both sides – labour and management – are ready to share and debate these openly and non-defensively with each other. Communication becomes less distorted and moves away from self-serving managerial goals. It is no longer confined to instrumentalism but instead established in a trustful way on principles concerning respect for the other side as an end in itself. Respectful, non-distorted, and open discussions are not seen as a mere instrument to meet the other side's purposes but enable management as well as labour to adopt a reflexive and self-critical approach in ethical decision making. As the discourse participants are constantly reviewing the discourse, consistency in the decision making process is being established. Distorted and instrumental communication is rejected once both sides start to move towards communicative action under symmetric conditions of ideal speech. This may result in an overcoming of the asymmetrically distributed ability to achieve ideal speech. While under previous forms of managerially directed communication, management's aim was to make other modes of thoughts impossible, stage six is much more directed towards an enabling rather than restricting form of communication.[377]

7. At stage seven: universal humanity and the integration of a holistic perspective

At stage seven, ethical rights are extended beyond issues that are immediately useful to management. They are communicatively established and directed towards humanity as such. The concept of *human rights* is applied to a wider context rather than being restricted to human beings alone and ethical awareness also goes beyond fellow humans. It also embraces other forms of life such as animal species and ecological systems regardless of their social utility.[378] At stage seven the relationship between management and labour includes communication directed towards the inclusion of issues related to nature, environment, plant life, and animals. Labour and management need to develop an awareness of the integrity of the environment and other systems as ethical communication at stage seven always links them to human society outside the confines of the company as well as to the universe. These links have to gain in importance if ethical communication is to be achieved irrespective of their immediate importance for homo sapiens.

In sum, Kohlberg's moral scale shows how communication between labour and management and inside their respective domains can move upwards. It can occur between a highly authoritarian communicative relationship and one that is confined to rules and laws (Table 10.2$^{1-4}$). At the next level (10:2^5), communication starts to shift between instrumental and distorted communication on the one hand and communicative action based on democratic principles on the other. Here, two strongly opposing concepts of communication face each other, one based on instrumental communication and the other on communicative action and ideal speech. These differences are increasingly solved when communication moves into stages six and seven where labour and management are governed by open, non-instrumental, non-distorted, and highly ethical communication. Symmetrical relationships free of domination are established between labour and management based on the four principles of ideal speech: openness, truthfulness, sincerity, and rightness. However, Marcuse (1966:143) saw truth inside an existing order as problematic because *when truth cannot be realised within the established social order, it always appears to the latter as mere utopia.* Therefore – at the highest stages of Kohlberg's scale – ethical communication always entails some form of utopia that often represents what *ought to be* rather than *what is*.

It appears as if true forms of ideal speech or *communicative action* are somewhat difficult to establish given the current relations at work. Hence, under present conditions of labour-management relations, truthful communication may not be possible to establish. It can, however, develop when the asymmetrical context of the present world of work is either removed or diminished. Then the domination free conditions for ideal speech can be established in order to enable *communicative action* as an ethical exercise. The relationship between communication and Kohlberg's seven stages of moral development can be seen as an ethical and communicative practise.

The strong connection between ethical development and communication shows how labour and management can adjust their communicative behaviour. Seen as an overall relationship between both, Figure 10.2 (below) links Kohlberg's seven stages of moral development at the *vertical* level to communication at the *horizontal* level where communication moves between instrumental or strategic communication (i) and *communicative action* (ii). At the horizontal level forms of communication range from instrumental/strategic communication that services self-interests and institutional interests (i) to communication seen as communicative action directed towards mutual understanding and truth (ii).

Forms of ethical communication that seek to go beyond self-interest and institutional gains are likely to occur at stages 5 to 7. The developments are shown on a sliding scale on which communication moves from instrumental/strategic communication to communicative action. When both are combined, communicative ethics based on Kohlberg's seven stages can be shown as follows:

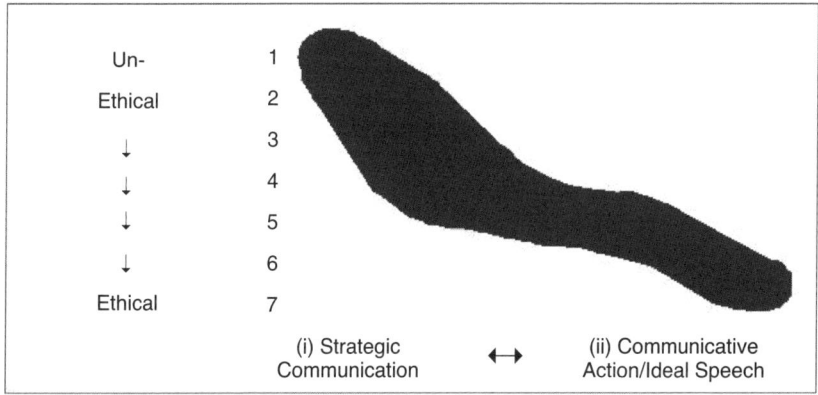

Figure 10.2   The Ethics of Communication

Figure 10.2 shows that the ethics of communication is not a simple correlation between two factors nor is it simply a matter of linearity. Communication moves towards higher ethical levels when it leaves the strategic, instrumental, asymmetrical, and hierarchical stage of self or institutional interests and managerial or organisational goals. In short, the more principles of ideal speech are established in communication, the higher the ethical stage. As interests move beyond instrumental/strategic goals ethical forms of communication increase. In many cases however, management finds it difficult to move communication beyond the confines of strategic and instrumental communication. Therefore relatively large areas of managerial communication remain at the lower end of the ethical scale.

At the lowest moral level, communication is highly authoritarian and directed towards the avoidance of punishment (Table 10.2^1). Here, communication is structured in a way that conforms to the three principles of ethical conduct as identified by Bauman.[379]

Table 10.3 shows that the lowest levels of ethical communication (Table 10.2^{1-4}) offer nothing but highly limited options for labour. Communication is simply used by management to transform persons into *object*s of

Table 10.3   Bauman's Three Principles of Ethical Conduct

No.	Principle
1)	Communication transforms human subjects into objects of power and knowledge transcribing labour into a set of quantities.
2)	Communication is also governed by routine bureaucratic means-ends calculations.
3)	A communicative distance between *causes* and *effects* is created intentionally and consequences are separated. Finally, *the 'to be ruled'* (labour) are placed in a false position of choice that is manipulated and pre-set by the ruler (management), so that labour's choice appears as real but is in fact highly limited to the confines set by management. Rationality and choice become weapons of management leaving labour with a faked prisoner dilemma. They are forced to choose between one interest (cf. job security) at the expense of other interests (cf. higher wages and better working conditions).

power by applying the organisational language of bureaucracy and efficiency. This represents the extreme opposite of Kant's dictum never to treat people as a *means* but rather as *ends*.

As ethical levels increase, communication offered by management becomes more viable to labour (Figure 10.2). At the middle level (Table 10.2^{3-5}), it constantly oscillates between two opposing ends, from the lowest to the highest ethical levels. At its highest level, communication has moved into completely non-authoritarian communicative action under symmetrical conditions of ideal speech, directed towards mutual understanding and truth (see Table 10.2 & Figure 10.2^7). The interest of speech participants has moved well beyond strategic and instrumental aspects.

The project of establishing a symmetrical speech *community* directed towards understanding and meaning demands the establishment of discourse under conditions of ideal speech. According to Habermas (1990:196), four core aspects need to be established in order to guide universally accepted, ethically grounded discourse. Discourse needs to be deontological (i), cognitive (ii), formal and methodological (iii), and universal (iv). The first principle relates to Kant's practical reasoning and categorical imperative. It originates in *deon*, the Greek word for *duty* and establishes a binding norm inasmuch as participants feel morally encouraged to engage in truthful communication. Kant's categorical imperative and the Greek idea of *deon* are universally understood as providing an agreement on ideal speech that should be followed. The second aspect views moral actions as grounded in moral-rational insights and rightness (ii). It has strong qualities of truth. Ideal speech needs to be established formally and methodologically (iii). It can also be reached under principles and procedures that have been established and applied in order to reach morally sustainable outcomes. Finally, universal principles (iv) are not bound to time and location. They need to be applied so that ethical discourse can be conducted at any time and any place. Conditions that establish ideal speech are seen as a duty. They are part of an agreed form of discourse (i) that emphasises a communicative-rational grounding in truth (ii). Such duties are established under agreed principles and discourse procedures (iii) and, in order to be fully installed, they must be universal in character (iv) and also have to be established as an ethical discourse (Figure 10.2$^{5-7}$).

The universal pragmatics of ideal speech

The establishment of a universally grounded and ethical discourse is supported via the theory of ideal speech. This theory sets up additional parameters that assist the formation of ethical discourse for communicative action. In order to give participants the ability of mutual understanding, ideal speech demands *communicative competence* in all speech-acts. Communicative competence reflects on the relationship between the actors in a social situation. It consists of the ability to follow social rules – not those governing sentences and syntax but rules that govern speech in a social setting. Communicative competence is related to communicative rationality as expressed in human speech.

Of prime relevance is the fact that ideal speech also demands the ability to construct well-formed sentences that relate to reality. This is expressed as the creation of a prepositional sentence directed towards truth (a) as well as the ability to express intentions as a linguistic expression of what is intended (b).[380] Finally, it also needs to include communicative performances (c) that conform to recognised ethics, norms, and values as accepted by society (10.2$^{5-7}$). To achieve these provisions for *ideal speech*, Habermas (1997:25) emphasises three conditions that have to be met (see Table 10.4).

In Table 10.4 competent, thematic, and cogent arguments are seen as the core conditions of communicative action and the systematic way of reasoning. They form the basis for statements that are connected to validity claims. Put simply, one cannot argue unless one is willing to argue sincerely. Willingness to be sincere and truthful as well as the pursuit of truth support each other. If such forms of arguments are put forward in an argumentation, this discourse strives towards a universalistic and ethical ideal. In this context, discourse can be seen as an ideal version of communication. Discourses are events under which rationally motivated arguments, targeted at reaching agreement and common understanding, are exchanged. Discourse takes on three forms of argumentation. In the first version – constructed as *theoretical discourse* (i) – problematic arguments on controversial truth claims are thematised. In the second version – constructed as *practical discourse* (ii) – the issue of normative rightness is the basis for argumentation. In the third version – constructed as *explicative discourse* (iii) – forms of comprehensibility, well-formed-ness, or rule-correctness of symbolic expressions

174 Management Communication

Table 10.4 Three Conditions for Ideal Speech

Conditions	Description
(i) Competency	general symmetric conditions have to be established so that every *competent speaker* can enter into argumentation. Participants in argumentation have to presuppose in general that the structure of their communication, by virtue of features described in purely formal terms, excludes all forces – whether they arise from within the process of reaching understanding or influences it from the outside – except for the force of the better argument (and that it also excludes, on their part, all motives except that of a cooperative search for the *truth*);
(ii) Thematise	participants are free to thematise a problematic validity claim and are relieved of the pressure of action and experience in a hypothetical attitude and only with reasons – whether the claim defended by the proponents rightfully stands or not;
(iii) Cogency	participants have to produce cogent arguments that are convincing in virtue of their intrinsic properties and with which validity claims can be redeemed or rejected.

are thematised. As all arguments can either be *accepted* or *rejected*, according to Heath (2003:54) the issuing (sending) and receiving (positive/negative) of these arguments lead to the following:

Acceptance or agreement on the part of the hearer is equivalent to recognition of a validity claim raised by the speaker.

In sum, any argument issued by a participant in ideal speech takes on at least one of the three forms for argumentation shown below.

Table 10.5 shows the theoretical, practical, and aesthetic discourse relating to problematic expressions. These are *cognitive-instrumental* forms of com-

Table 10.5 Three Forms of Arguments

Form of Argument	Description	Test/Target
theoretical	if they are asserted and justified solely with a view to whether they are *true*;	truth
practical	If they are asserted and justified with a view to granting what is said; validity as reason for *action*, the practical justification is the justification of a reason;	action and reason
aesthetic	if they are asserted and justified with an aim to lending the object of these statements validity as a reason for adopting *world-shaping views*.	world shaping view

Table 10.6 Sentence Formulation for Discourses

Sentences	Forms
(i) Descriptive	*descriptive* sentences, which serve to ascertain facts in the broadest sense, can be accepted or rejected from the standpoint of the truth of a proposition;
(ii) Normative	*normative* sentences (or ought-sentences), which serve to regulate actions, can be accepted or rejected from the standpoint of the rightness (or justice) of a way of acting;
(iii) Evaluating	*evaluating* sentences (or value judgements), which serve to appraise something, can be accepted or rejected from the standpoint of the appropriateness or adequacy of value standards (or the "good"); and
(iv) Explication	*explications*, which serve to explain operations like speaking, classifying, calculating, deducing, judging, and so on, can be accepted or rejected from the standpoint of the comprehensibility of well-formedness of symbolic expressions.

munication that relate to learning from mistakes and failure of interventions as well as *moral-practical* forms of communication that deal with normative conflicts and issues being disputed from a moral point. Finally, *explicative discourses* relate to understanding, linguistic rules, the meaning of expressions, the interpretation of language, and the practice of translation. In such forms of discourse language, as *the art of communicating our thoughts* (Rousseau 1755:15), takes a central role. Language – or the way in which we communicate – becomes the central medium through which actors communicate. These forms of argumentation are mostly expressed through speaking and therefore through sentences. According to Habermas (1997:39) there are four forms of sentences that are related to *discourse*.

The four forms of sentences in Table 10.6 are linked to Habermas' (1979:3) four validity claims that are required in order to establish communicative action.[381] These validity claims are essential for communication under conditions of *ideal speech*. Communicative action based on validity claims can only be established when both the speaker and the listener accept the *truth* of an assertion without doubting each other's sincerity. Once these conditions are established, meaning can be ascribed on the basis that the sentence is considered as true. Heath (2003:21) sees this as *positioning something like a desire to tell the truth* governing all speech acts. Therefore telling the truth becomes constitutive for linguistic meaning.[382] Truth is of vital importance to ideal speech. Anyone who is fully capable of communicating in a language has at least some implicit grasp of the concept of truth. Theories on truth have been categorised into four levels – (i) correspondence theory, (ii) coherence theory, (iii) pragmatic-consensus theory, and (iv) semantic theory:[383]

Table 10.7 shows that ideal speech can only be established when a speaker accepts the normative validity of a statement. It cannot develop when the

Table 10.7 Four Theories of Truth

Theory	Description
Correspondence Theory (i)	True sentences are those that correspond to or are true in virtue of some actual states of affairs in the world.
Coherence Theory (ii)	Those sentences are true that cohere with or entail, are entailed by or are consistent with our beliefs.
Pragmatic-Consensus Theory (iii)	Habermas pragmatic-consensus theory of truth asserts that the meaning of truth must be established in terms of value claims about the truth of statements. Truth is established through the application of communicative action under conditions of ideal speech, tested under Habermas' four value claims. Ultimately, truth can only be established socially.
Semantic Theory (iv)	Truth is a semantic device for staging a sentence as a material equivalence between the original and other sentences in the meta-language.

listener doubts the seriousness of the other agent's intention. Essential to the communicative relationship directed towards ideal speech is the acceptance of *truthfulness*. Once the above outlined conditions are established, the concept of ideal speech contains four key elements.

Table 10.8 shows basic conditions for the establishment of an ideal speech situation. These conditions can be divided into *external* conditions that have to be met from the outside of a speech situation as well as *internal* conditions

Table 10.8 Four Core Elements of Ideal Speech

a) Comprehensibility	b) Truth	c) Truthfulness	d) Rightness
linguistically intelligible	of propositional content or existential presuppositions	honest or sincere	appropriate in light of existing norms and values
Language	'The' world as external character	'My' world as internal character	'Our' world of society
------	Representation of 'reality'	Disclosure of speaker's subjectivity	Establishment of legitimate interpersonal relations
------	Cognitive: objective attitudes	Expressive: expressive attitudes	Interactive: conformative attitude

that guide communication once the frame of ideal speech is established (Figure 10.3 below). In the outer area social, not linguistic conditions for ideal speech have to be met. In the inner area, validity claims are based on four elements that guide the dialogue. Each actor participating in ideal speech discussions has to meet all four conditions that can be shown in a simple figure:

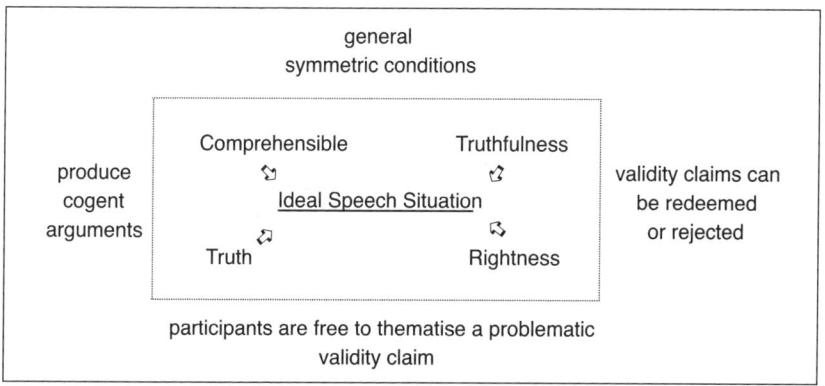

Figure 10.3 The Internal and External Structure of Ideal Speech

Habermas' conditions for ideal speech and communicative action display a clear picture of communication that can be summed up as follows:

The concept of communicative action refers to the interaction of at least two subjects capable of speech and action who establish interpersonal relations (whether by verbal or by extra-verbal means). The actors seek to reach an understanding about the action situation and their plans of action in order to coordinate their actions by way of agreement. The central concept of interpretation refers in the first instance to negotiating definitions of the situation which admit of consensus (Habermas 1997:86).

The complete framework of communicative action and ideal speech must be established in full and without any damage. Communication will be seen as disturbed when at least some of the conditions for ideal speech are missing. Furthermore, when communication among participants is not directed towards reaching understanding, a vital condition is not satisfied and communication becomes an instrument of system integration that structures communicative exchanges under conditions of deception and distortion. This leads to an objectively false consciousness that gives rise to *structural* violence.[384] These violations of important structural elements that have to be met in ideal speech situations create systematic restrictions on communication. Once the stage of violations has been reached, distortions become established in formal conditions of speech acts and deeply enshrined in the communicative practises where they distort and prejudge communicative objectives and distort the social and subjective assertions of communicative participants.

In such cases the domain in which ideal speech was supposed to take place has degenerated into a communicative forum open to manipulative elements.[385] The mere perception of communication enables those in charge of an organisation to manipulate other organisational members against their own interest. Managerial validity claims are turned into pure illusions of truthful validity claims while objective forces under conditions of instrumental action only satisfy systematic restrictions. Ideal speech and *communicative action* cannot be established and maintained. Overall, according to Heath (2003:4) *the key idea in Habermas' theory of communicative action is that speech acts cannot be planned or executed with entirely strategic intent.*

In other words, ideal speech acts and *communicative action* cannot be instrumentally guided towards strategic goals. They need to fulfil conditions that free communication from system interferences. Only an unhindered environment free of domination allows the flourishing of ideal speech and *communicative action* directed towards positive social change. Once applied to the workplace, this version of speech act faces two dramatic challenges as in the world of work two fundamentally different logics are in operation – one is directed towards critical rationality while the other focuses on instrumental rationality. This poses one of the most serious challenges to ideal speech and *communicative action.*

11
Communicative Action III: The Two Logics of Work Relations

There are various forms of communication that have implications for labour and management and all of them have the potential to influence the outcome of communication. Concepts such as communicative rationality, ideal speech, and, most of all, *communicative action* also have major implications for the formulation of interests by management and workers. Management's demand for instrumental action exists under conditions of instrumental rationality based on market demands. These demands are largely external to management's realm of influence but can be successfully harvested for goals such as system integration. Any managerial communication inside the specifications of system integration results in limitations as it is constrained within *means-ends* confinements. It is for this reason that as long as management operates under severe system constraints, demands towards communicative action face acute challenges.

Claus Offe and Simon Wiesenthal have discussed the structural challenges to management and managerialism. In their seminal work on the *Two Logics of Collective Action* they have put forward two different logics under which labour and management operate.[386] Their work has been in response to earlier and equally influential contribution by Olson (1971). Unlike Offe and Wiesenthal's *two* logics, Olson's one-dimensional viewpoint indicates the singularity of *"The" Logic of Collective Action* (1971). While Olson offers a one-dimensional logic of behaviour and social action, Offe and Wiesenthal (1980) reject such a way of thinking.[387] In the tradition of the Hegelian-Marxian concept of dialectics – thesis, anti-thesis, and synthesis – they argue that two different rationalities are present at work, the rationality of labour and the rationality of management. Offe and Wiesenthal's work reflects on both sides while Olson does not make this distinction.

Olson's argument is closely linked to rational cost-benefit or means-end analysis as a deciding factor that directs collective action. In sharp contrast to Olson, Offe and Wiesenthal emphasise that workers also make additional decisions that are not based on a simple cost-benefit or means-ends rationality. For example, the structural force of the labour market has already made the decision for labour on whether to join the market or not.[388] For labour this choice is non-existent or no more than a highly hypothetical, fictional possibility. On the other hand, workers are able to decide on whether or not to join, participate in, or commit to various organisations that represent their interests beyond the boundaries of the company.

Predominantly such decisions are not taken on the basis of Olson's rational calculations but in terms of how labour perceives themselves and their relationship to others. While a few may join an organisation purely on the grounds of Olson's simple rational-calculative model, most do not. They join movements and organisations for reasons other than cost-benefit returns or the goal of an organisation. One of their motives lies in their potential to communicate about interests which gives labour the option to have an input in interest formulating discourses. At the same time these discourses assist in the shaping process of individual interests.[389] Any forum that provides for such discourses has inherent potentials towards a transformation of individual interests and may eventually lead to the conversion from individual interests into collective interests as the construction of meaning is collectively and communicatively achieved. This has also implications for social action as conducted in models of participative or deliberative democracy. However, this form of decision making process is not found at today's workplaces.

Offe and Wiesenthal initiated their discussions about labour-management relations at work by looking at the fundamental structural inequality that is inherent in both. This inequality is hidden behind the ideology of a formal and equal contractual relationship between employer and employee. At surface level it emerges as *formal* employment. The fundamental contribution of Offe and Wiesenthal's theory, however, is that it looks beyond these superficial perceptions. It provides a more comprehensive perspective on how workers and capitalists deal with the two different forms of logics – the logic of structural inequality surfacing in the pretended contractual form of equal partners as well as the logic of unequal labour market positions and the resulting inequalities at work.[390]

From the start, these two logics lead to two different logics of employment as well as to two different logics of the position that an individual occupies at work. Consequently, these two forms of two different logics are resulting in two different logics of communication and social action. This serves to correct liberal assumptions about a free labour market where two actors engage in an equal exchange. According to Offe and Wiesenthal (1980), this ideological assumption negates the historical and structural asymmetry that defines employment, but it is precisely this form of inequality that is the key aspect of the relationship between management and labour. It takes on three forms.

Table 11.1 shows the organisational forms that labour and capital can engage in given their differing positions and different logics. As capitalists are able

Table 11.1 Key Forms of Structural Inequality at Work

Two Actors	Organisational Forms under the Two Logics of Collective Action
1. Capital:	Capital has at least three organisational forms at its disposal:
(i) Company	the company, firm, or corporation as their standard forms of business organisation under which dead and living labour is combined in productive and profit making ways;
(iii) Informal	informal cooperation via collusion, breakfast cartels and the like, and
(iii) Formal	business organisations such as employer associations and industry groups.
2. Workers:	Workers form organisations *after* they entered into work/companies. This means that workers can establish two organisational forms:
(i) Internal	Organisation *in* a capitalist company and
(ii) External	Workers can form representative association external to companies

to separate their capital from themselves by investing it in an organisation, they can also separate these organisations which is expressed in three forms (1^{i-iii}). Workers on the other hand cannot as easily separate their economical life from their total self. Labour is not able to separate their *ability* to work from the actual process of working in the same way as capital can separate capital from companies and insert management to represent them in a company. Labour's position in the production process demands *physical* and *intellectual* presences at one location – the company. In sharp contrast to capital where the owner can be separated from the use of capital, workers cannot split their physical ability to work from their body. Their bodily existence and their ability to work are restricted to the organisational form of the company.

Workers can only join or form an association *after* they have gained employment by a management or a company (11.1:1). Consequently, their associations, usually expressed in workplace representatives linked to trade unions, can only be *secondary* organisations ($11.1:2^{i+ii}$). This is in sharp contrast to employers' *primary* organisational forms, i.e. the company ($11.1:1^i$). While capitalists operate in a singular organisational form, workers face two contradictory organisational forms as they are organised by two different entities – the capitalist company ($11.1:1^{i-iii}$) on the one hand as well as their representative associations ($11.1:2^{i-ii}$) on the other. Workers have always seen a need to create their own associations against the organisational power of management even though these are far less flexible when compared to companies' ability to organise capital.[391] Management as the representative of capital are not faced with diverging organisational realities. They are free to conduct their affairs inside the one-dimensional organisational framework.

The fact that workers – unlike management – have to deal with two opposing organisational realities creates an organisational dilemma for them. While management can create various forms of company-to-company links such as trusts, joint ventures, mergers, acquisitions, cartels, strategic or functional alliances, etc., workers' choices are limited.[392] They cannot create mergers and acquisitions in the same way as companies. They can only establish organisational forms via associations. This creates severe organisational asymmetries between those *who manage* and those *who are managed*. These asymmetries go even further.

In sharp contrast to other commodities such as capital or machinery that function inside the productive relationship, labour's position is unique. While capital and machinery can be detached from the owner when traded on the financial market or the market for machinery and equipment, the commodity traded at labour markets – labour power – is not *detachable* from the seller.[393] It cannot be separated from labour as work cannot be separated from workers. Wage labour therefore inevitably gives rise to a relationship of social control over the labour process. The *non-separable* character of human labour from labour power demands social control of the purchased labour at the point of work. The asymmetric relationship between the owners of machinery – *dead labour* – and labour power – *living labour* – inevitably leads to control and domination. Because humans cannot be separated from human work, management needs to control them in the same way as they control work.

To achieve this, the asymmetrical relationship between labour and capital has taken on specific forms. Edwards (1979) has outlined widely acknowledged forms of control ranging from direct, technical to eventually bureaucratic control that reflect the different stages in the development of capitalism. The issue of control can be exemplified by using the example of workers' *discipline*. While disciplining workers – ranging from physical punishment and beatings (disciplining and reprimanding) to direct, technological and bureaucratic control (overseer, time-&-motion, policies) – has been crucial to workers' domestication and the success of early capitalism, the coercive methods that create obedience had to be altered under conditions of advanced capitalism. Workers' communicative action can no longer be directed to elements that have been dominant in the past when seeking to reflect modern workplace relations. However, such a discourse also demands that the dialectics between elements of early and advanced capitalism are not communicatively eliminated.

Under early capitalism a harsh, almost militaristic, education system prepared future workers for discipline and obedience in industrial work regimes. As capitalism advanced and with the rise of corporate mass media, the educational domain had to adopt changes to reflect the development.

Individuals started to be conditioned into accepting the virtues of private capital and no longer needed to be punished and disciplined into work. In other words, any form of communicative action directed towards work needs to enshrine the dialectics of the educational and work interface. Under the regime of advanced capitalism, ideological hegemony is established through a congruent arrangement of two domains: managerial work regimes and corporate mass media.[394] Forms of worker-centred communicative action have to take this into account. The desired outcome of the advanced base-superstructure interplay – directed towards white rather than blue-collar and towards service rather than manufacturing – is no longer the simple creation of obedient workers as system survival can no longer rely on masses of domesticated and coerced workers who are punished and disciplined into obedience.

System advancements demand an entire new form of system integration, as it can no longer be sustained through the creation of obedience and punishment. Consequently, communicative action must be directed towards the emancipation of workers from structural domination rather than from previous forms of obedience and punishment regimes. System demands of advanced capitalism are directed towards workers who are self-motivated, self-driven, and creative but locked firmly inside the framework of system affirmation and system integration. Communicative action therefore needs to target those processes that establish and maintain system integrative forces in workplaces under the regime of managerialism. However, communicative action based on dialectical understanding in the Hegelian sense cannot totally negate earlier forms of system imperatives. On the other hand, it focuses the critical-emancipatory powers of communicative action on today's manifestations of system integration. The development *from* early capitalism *to* advanced capitalism is shown below.

In Figure 11.1, the change of the base-form (11.1^i) from early to advanced capitalism resulted in the fundamental restructuring of the base-superstructure arrangements (11.1^{ii}) as the new system of advanced capitalism demanded new desired outcomes (11.1^{iii}). As much as early capitalism failed to create workers' affirmation to the system, it had to coerce them into compliance via the, at least partially, very brutal process of disciplining them.[395] This has been one of the clearest expressions of the two logics of work because under managerial

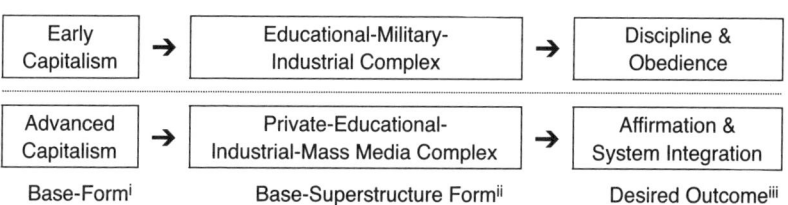

Figure 11.1 System Changes and Desired Outcomes

logic workers had to be disciplined while under workers' logic resistance or *organisational misbehaviour*[396] has been one of the most viable responses to capital's demand for system integration. During the early days of capitalism the issue of discipline took on four forms – *punitive-authoritarian discipline* (a), *corrective-representative discipline* (b), *accommodative-participative discipline* (c), and *celebrative-collective discipline* (d) with *rules (being) informal and unwritten and control* (being) *exerted in the name of the collective rather than some authoritative part.*[397] Crucial however is that *discipline is finally turned inside out: from being entirely external it becomes entirely internal by a series of developments toward self-control.*[398] The crucial issue in the one-dimensional society is no longer control or self-control but the overcoming of its theoretical framework (Marcuse 1966). Instead, the modern workplace is guided by *positive* and *negative reinforcement* as well as *extinction* and *feedback* thus applying all elements of *behaviourism.*[399] In the asymmetrically structured workplace, the logic of system integration demands from modern management the application of more sophisticated psychological techniques – not to strengthen control but to create affirmative workers who themselves support system integration.

More than all other forms of management such as supply-chain management, operations management, financial management, or marketing, the issue of the continuously required and always unstable commodity of labour demands ever more sophisticated integrative techniques to assure labour's compliance with the process. As long as the *commodity* of labour is different from any other commodity and as long as labour maintains its rather unusual character, it occupies a unique role. This role is always defined by the impossibility to separate work from workers. Machinery, computers, or production equipment are radically different. Owners of machinery (dead labour) who have also purchased labour power (living labour) can combine both to enable production which occurs in an organisational form called company. While such companies – once the organisational form of bread (*pane*) breaking and *com*munal sharing (*com-pany*) free-lance mercenaries of the Medieval Age – confine workers to the workplace, their ideological task is powerfully supported by mass media's communicative power. Under conditions of advanced capitalism the oscillation between being a worker and being a consumer not only dilutes the idea of workers as citizens in the public domain, it has also ended the idea of workers as organisational citizens. The modern logic of system integration demands that workers subscribe to a system that is just as alien to their lives within the system of consumption. The pathologies of both the work and private domain are off-loaded to society and increasingly have to be covered by the class of those who are employed.[400]

Management has to organise, manage, and dominate labour in order to maintain the productive combination of both domains. This occurs communicatively. In order to organise the labour process, a small group of owners and managers have to combine their machinery, computers, desks, assembly lines, etc. with *living labour* that comes in relatively large numbers. In order to participate in this process, humans have to be transformed into labour, are made to sell their labour power at the labour market, and become part of an unequal and non-voluntary commercial exchange.[401] Most of these transitional arrangements are established communicatively and enable the asymmetric character of the relationship between capital and labour to become operational. This not only dictates labour's acceptance of their position in the relationship of authority, it also makes this relationship appear normal. Most communicative structures in our present society are established in order to make current work arrangements and their transitional demands appear as being normal thus rendering humans adaptive to the managerial process without ever realising what is happening. This process creates affirmative humans who approve and conform to managerialism. They are able to exist inside the confinements of the asymmetrical system created by management and live in asymmetrical relationships that can be expressed as follows:

Figure 11.2 illustrates the substantial differences between the two logics of collective action for management (a) and labour (b). For one, the differences in the structural conditions (i) – small group size versus large group size – define management and labour. The small group size of the management domain

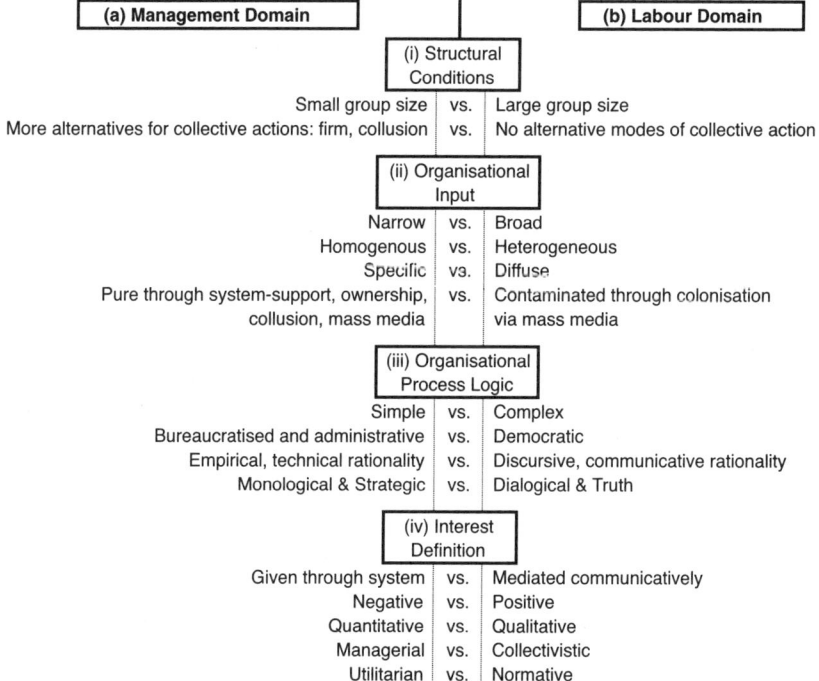

Figure 11.2   A Typology of Collective Action for Labour and Management

entails low transaction costs and less divergent interests that require internal recognition.[402] This enables companies and management to operate highly functional and specific interest associations. The absence of any colonisation of the one-dimensional managerial interest relieves management from many communicative needs such as the establishment of internal processes that seek to compensate interest infiltration by opposing interests. This is supported via strong and powerful corporate mass media that help to portray managerialism as TINA, There Is No Alternative.[403] By *in*corporating society into the ideological mindset of managerialism, corporate mass media have effectively closed all visions of life styles that offer alternatives to the existing forms of societal organisations which only seek the maximisation of profit.[404] Only a few variations of managerialism – as found in managerial networks, companies and corporations, holdings, joint ventures and franchising – are left to choose from. Inside these minor forms, organisational input (ii) for management is narrow as their group size is limited. Labour, on the other hand, faces the opposite problem. As their group size increases, their input becomes broader and their homogeneity decreases. This leads to increasing demands for communicative action.

The significant difference in demand for communication is most prevalent when the two logics of organisational processes (iii) come into play. While management is able to construct their organisations simply as bureaucratic and administrative based on instrumental and technical rationality, workers have to take different aspects into account. Their organisations are more complex as they must be democratic and cannot just follow bureaucracy. They have to establish solutions communicatively via open discourse arrangements directed towards truth rather than through technical rational processes. Managerial processes, in comparison, allow one-dimensional logics directed towards *means-ends* ideas and cost-benefit analyses, not truth.[405]

While management operates with a specific, clear and present interest (iv), labour's interest appears by far more diffuse. One might emphasise that *capitalists can easily separate themselves from their capital, there are fewer confronting identities like race, ethnicity, or nationality to deflect collective action on behalf of class interests*.[406] Any structural problems of the one-dimensional, *monological* or instrumental forms of communication in the management domain are further simplified through this separation. Interest formulation on labour's side is by far more exposed to colonising effects via corporate mass media whose communicative efforts are – along with management, corporations, companies, and managerialism – directed towards the system integration of labour. This leads to a high degree of opposing interests infiltrating the labour domain. An increasingly mediated reality (Zengotita 2005) causes interest problems even for labour's organisational form itself as Brimeyer *et al.* (2004:49) note that

> much of the media's coverage of labour unions has often centred on negative aspects such as strikes, corruption, and greed. The negative depiction of unions

is not restricted to the evening news or the business section of the daily paper but also appears in comics, movies, and television shows [with a] *consistent bias against unions.*

This makes interest definition an inherently difficult process for labour as not only their interests but also their organisational forms are attacked. While interest definitions for management are to a large extent provided by system supportive elements, labour faces a higher degree of interest divergence, expressed in three substantial interests – an interest in high wages (i), an interest in the continuation of wages (employment security) (ii), and an interest in working conditions (iii). Labour's interests need to be established communicatively and interest mediation between these interests also needs to take place. According to Gay (1996:52),

> *as wages are costs to the firm, and the deprivation inherent in effort means cost to the employee, the interests of management and wage-earner are diametrically opposed. At one pole there stand the workers. With nothing to sell but their labour power, their interests can easily be delineated. At the opposing extreme are the employers and their 'servants of power', management and the like – who service them. Their 'objective' interests are linked to the perpetual expansion of profit through increasing productivity…keeping wages low, weakening the collective power, and reducing their capacity to disrupt the process of accumulation, while simultaneously casting a cloak of 'ideological legitimacy' over the essentially exploitative nature of employment relations.*

Managerial interest domination provides a clear view of what they want to defend due to their hegemonic position in society – managerialism – and their one-dimensional interest in profit maximisation. Therefore domineering interests can largely be defended *negatively*. Rather than positively defining interests through supportive arguments, management's position of domination allows the defending of interest negatively through communicative links to their social and economical position and their power. Defending managerially defined interests is presented as defending an all-inclusive and commonly accepted *status quo*. Management is able to *negatively* defend their interests by gearing these towards the *status quo* without the need to deliver supportive arguments. They can exclude or negate all other interests behind the overall profit maxim. Labour is not able to do this because it does not have a one-dimensional interest. It depends on interest mediation through dialogue that focuses on *qualitative* interests and cannot simply enhance their interest *quantitatively*. Labour has to find a democratic approach in which it can communicatively mediate their three highly heterogeneous interests. At the same time they need to defend this process against interest colonisation. Unlike labour, management can easily increase its interest numerically. In fact, any quantitative increase in shareholder values, and therefore in profits, is most welcome.

As George Orwell (1946:7) emphasised *this invasion of one's mind by ready-made phrases...can only be prevented if one is constantly on guard against them*.[407] Because of their structural dependency on open forms of discourse, labour is much more likely to perceive their own interests in a distorted way. Managerial ideologies such as *we are all in one boat!* have a strong impact on the labour domain and labour's ability to communicatively establish their interests. These distortions have to be rationalised and unmasked in communicative processes to compensate for the structural disadvantage of labour's asymmetrical position in the world of work.

Management seeks to position workers inside the confines of system integration in order to prevent ideal speech and validity claims directed towards truth. However, their own entrapment inside the hierarchies also *dis*-enables management themselves from utilising *communicative action* or ideal speech. Having structured the world of work in a *top-down* manager-worker dichotomy, management would be hard pressed to alter existing arrangements. However, in order to move towards domination free speech conditions management needs to achieve exactly this – which poses a serious challenge to them. After all, hierarchies, control and domination define their existence.[408] Hierarchical structures define and simultaneously control labour-management relations as expressed in the dichotomy of blue- versus white-collar workers. Both are often presented as separate but equal entities when in fact they are organised hierarchically. To cover this, managerial ideology seeks to construct both as horizontal rather than vertical thus denying the *status quo* of domination.

Problems may arise when the differences that stem from the diverging responses to a specific work situation are not acknowledged. When wage-labour is compared to management, these differences become visible. Secondly, there is also the fact that blue- as well as white-collar workers are increasingly faced with identical situations caused by job insecurity, downsizing, relocation, etc. even though this does not necessarily also imply an identical situation for capital. The asymmetrical power relationship between management on the one side and blue/white collar workers on the other is still in existence.

Labour's structural disadvantage originated in the division of blue and white labour versus capital. Once humans enter the pre-structured world of work, they are transformed into labour through capital and management who need to combine *dead* labour (machine, tools, etc.) with *living* labour (workers) and control this process continuously by controlling labour. Capital's interest is unified into one interest that is directed towards profit expressed in instrumental action while labour is faced with a multitude of interests due to the multitude of their needs to which there is no common denominator.

Management is able to revert to numerous options to increase the efficiency in production and thus maximise profit. Labour's options to provide for efficiencies in reproduction outside the production process and by the use of communicative action are however limited. The limitations are manifested in three ways. There is a legal prohibition for labour as well as legal regulations that restrict activities outside the labour market (a). Labour is also largely concentrated in large urban agglomerations (b). Such living conditions are designed to make it virtually impossible for property-less workers to subsist in ways other than those offered by the labour market. Finally strong system integrative elements (c) are forcing labour into a *One-Dimensional Existence* governed by the logic of consumption and mass media communication (Marcuse 1966). This leads to labour experiencing a one-dimensional existence as worker in the productive domain as well as a one-dimensional existence as consumer in the reproductive domain and provides a framework that labour cannot escape.

Overcoming the conditioning of asymmetrical work relations

The costs of living outside the currently established system – i.e. being unemployed or unwilling to participate in the system processes – are asymmetrically distributed against labour. In a system that allocates power to capital or the managers thereof rather than to those who have to sell their only property – the ability to work – to those who purchase it, power relations as well as cost-benefits are shaped in a way that disadvantages those on the labour market who have less property to offer. Even though some of the labour market's agencies have been renamed – from workers to employees or production associates, etc. – the fundamentals of their market relations have not fundamentally changed since Adam Smith (1776). Inside the system that has prevailed ever since, labour's relatively powerless position has been compensated by the, at least partly fulfilled, promise of material interest and manifested in the substantial rise of living standards since the days of Adam Smith. The most dramatic change in the history of capitalism took place roughly 130 to 160 years later, when the development of mass-production led to mass-consumption. This also changed capitalism's function and the role of labour. In the Fordist world of advanced capitalism, labour could no longer simply be reduced to the system of work but also needed to be integrated in the off-work sphere.[409] The asymmetrical relationship between capital/management and labour had to be extended into the private sphere where workers had been converted into consumers while capital retained its position as mass-commodity supplier. In short, labour experienced *double system integration* – it is integrated into the production process at work as well as into the consumer process off work. Two hundred years after Adam Smith, in advanced capitalist societies this double integration has been completed. Labour's original hope for a better and more human life as well as a better and more human society has successfully been reduced to the hope of more material wealth.[410] The original idea of changing asymmetric power relations in order to end all forms of domination has been converted into the acceptance and affirmation of power relations, compensated by consumerism.

The process of affirmation and acceptance not only cements asymmetrical power relations at work, the link between consumption and work also creates a strong system affirmation that reaches far beyond the workplace. Therefore, communicative action has to be directed towards the uncovering of this ideologically cloaked link. The traditional idea that work has to be accepted in order to achieve modest material wealth and decent living standards is no longer fundamental to present work-societies. Having been successfully conditioned and experienced since generations, today's ideology also includes the factor of consumption:

hard work = consumption = good living standards

Figure 11.3 The Hard Work is Good Living Equation

Ever since Fordism, when *advanced* capitalism overcame *liberal* capitalism as outlined by Adam Smith, the original ideology of *hard work=good living* has been extended by the insertion of *consumption* (Figure 11.3) and is powerfully supported by the off-work domain of consumption. Communicative action needs to make this link visible and also provide a critique of the link. The ideological content is not self-evident but had to be conditioned from the moment Fordist mass-consumption integrated or manipulated workers into the system of consumption.[411] This has been the task of the privately owned and profit-driven mass media who achieved labour's double integration through mass-marketing and mass-advertising.[412] It has also led to fundamental changes at work as well as in the off-work domain. Under the asymmetrical system of *double integration*, work relations and consumptive relations moved from *control* to *incentives*. While the old system relied on control at work and in the private sphere – Henry Ford's network of spies, etc. – the system of double integration is based on incentives and ideological system affirmation. Fundamentally, the link shown in Figure 11.3 has rendered *control* largely obsolete while cementing asymmetrical power relations at work and in the private domain.[413] Therefore, it is no longer sufficient to focus the analysis of work relations under conditions of communicative action on control. As system integration and affirmation in both the managerial and the consumption domain have largely superseded the issue of control, communicative action needs to redirect its analytical force towards the mechanisms of *double integration*.

In the *model of double integration*, labour is not forced into working and consuming by control but conditioned and manipulated by a gigantic apparatus that covers two domains. In the work domain, the apparatus that assures system integration and affirmation is called Human Resource Management. In the consumption domain, the same task falls onto corporate mass media. Combined they have successfully achieved system integration in both domains. Work and social life no longer function as domains of resistance but as spheres of affirmation. While Hegel's contradictions (1807 & 1821) and the Marxian dictum of *das Sein bestimmt das Bewustsein*[414] have not been overcome, both are powerfully eclipsed by a gigantic ideological apparatus (Althusser 1965) that is communicated through the *Restructured Public Sphere* and supported by the rise of workers living in an *Affluent Society*.[415] The resulting *double integration* works in two ways. Much in the same way as ever more sophisticated advertising techniques are used to achieve system affirmation, increasingly state-of-the-art HRM techniques are applied to achieve the same in the work domain. While the consumption domain relies completely on mass media, the work domain also gains from manipulative ideologies – such as hard work – portrayed via mass media in the off-work domain. Corporate mass media provide a powerful umbrella that supports system affirmation through consumption and at work. In both domains, this is achieved through conditioning. The most powerful element against the conditioned acceptance of the oscillation between work and consumption lies in the central weakness of this *behaviourist* conditioning model that works behind the backs of those who are to be manipulated. Being based on *conditioned association,* it is highly vulnerable against challenges by *symbolic association* which is a major characteristic of communicative action and finally leads to the uncovering of the hidden mechanisms of *conditioned association*.[416] The fact that present society is highly asymmetrically structured provides communicative action with a platform from which a critical analysis of the underlying structures can be highlighted and turned into emancipatory powers.

The asymmetry of power at work and in the private domain is reflected in the asymmetrical power relations that have been outlined in behaviourism's core idea of top-down management in the form of *controller* and *controlled*.[417] In Skinner's *behaviourist* model, the division of labour into labour and management or the managerial top-down split into *those who manage* and *those who are managed* is mirrored in *controller* and *controlled*. At its most fundamental level consumption and hard work are no more than the behaviourist

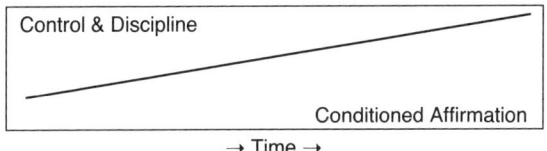

Figure 11.4 The Control – Conditioning Trajectory

version of *conditioned* responses to the system. In essence however, mechanisms of system integration have moved from control to conditioning.[418] Today this process is in many ways completed or close to completion. Control diminishes as mechanisms of conditioning improve. This is not an either/or process but a process in which one declines while the other increases.

The theory of *behaviourism* and its inner workings can be expressed conceptually. The assumed nature=human link of positivism – from Comte to Popper – expressed in the theory of *behaviourism* equates animals to humans. In the hands of *behaviourism* pigeons, rats, dogs, etc. are reduced to *objects of power* in laboratory testing. This is applied to humans where human individuals are reduced and manipulated in a *positivist-psychologist* and *human-object* top-down relationship. In both the animal and the human sphere *behaviourism* operates with one crucial idea that seeks to create a manipulated control-discipline environment in which both –animal and human – can be conditioned so that control and discipline can be removed and the animal/human becomes a conditioned entity that operates in accordance with the ideas of *behaviourism*.[419] Put brutally, one does not need to control a pigeon to push a red button in order to receive food once the button-food link is sufficiently conditioned. Similarly, one does not need to control people to attend Christmas-Sales when they are advertised once the link between consumption and a good life is sufficiently conditioned. And lastly, labour does not need to be controlled and discipline and punishment can be removed once the link outlined in Figure 11.3 above – *hard work= consumption=good living standards* – is sufficiently conditioned.[420] In the development of managing people at work, this is what has taken place during the last decades. Using Ackroyd & Thompson's (1999:148–149) concept of punishment and discipline, the move from traditional approaches to domestication that relied on punishment and discipline towards more sophisticated conditioning techniques can be shown as follows.

Figure 11.5 shows the historical development of punishment and discipline – that relied on control of workers – towards the conditioning of workers that eliminates the need for control. For decades, traditional approaches followed

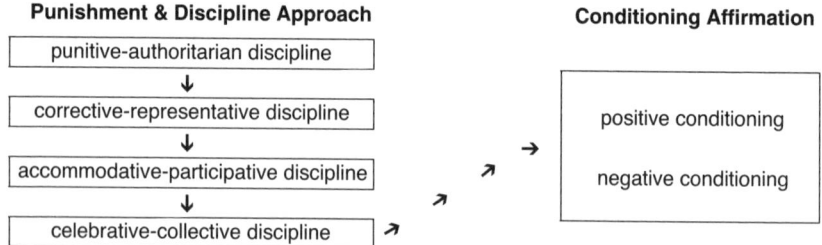

Figure 11.5 From Punishment and Disciplining to Conditioning

the well-known model of a four-step approach: step 1: oral warning; step 2: written warning; step 3: suspension of pay/final warning/probation; and step 4: termination. While these procedures may still be found in many policy manuals of today's HR officers, their application is much less needed once the new forms of conditioning have been introduced (Redeker 1983 & Grote 2006). In essence, the introduction of *behaviourism* into the workplace seeks to condition workers long before the need for the traditional disciplinary procedure surfaces. In short, it eliminates discipline and punishment before it needs to be applied by focusing on the creation of system affirmative workers. In this process, the interplay between the consumption and the work domains is crucial in order to make *behaviourism* fully work towards the system integration of workers/consumers.

In the work domain, certain, what behaviourist theoreticians call *stimuli* [good life] have been conditioned so that the *response* [work] becomes a *conditioned response* [hard work and affirmative attitude to work]. For a behaviourist the asymmetrical relationship that renders the work=consumption=good life equation possible (Figure 11.3) cannot be established through *symbolic association* because *symbolic association* operates via a cognitive process while *conditioned association* establishes the associative or mental link between *work* and *reward* through conditioning. The link between work and reward in the mind of labour as the *object of power*[421] is conditioned via a raft of Human Resource Management techniques that are also supported by corporate mass media. First and foremost it is crucial that the *object of power* is not aware of the conditioning process. Rational analysis or critiques (*symbolic association*) of the link (Figure 11.3) have to be excluded in order for the asymmetrical relationship to work. In the words of *behaviourist theoreticians* Gallistel & Gibbon (2002:2), *in associative models of the conditioning process, symbolic knowledge of the world is not required*. For example, when serious attempts are made to exclude any critical scrutiny of *wage-fixing* methods i.e. the asymmetrical definition of wages by management – as it is common practise in HRM – the work-wage link has to be conditioned because *symbolic knowledge* or *critical understanding* of the world of wages is *not required* and, even more importantly, has to be avoided. This provides a clear possibility of access for any communicative action directed towards the unlocking of the hidden processes of HRM's *conditioned associations*. Since the work-wages link is ideologically based, it has to be supported through constant reproduction and reinforcement of the *conditioned associations*. This makes sophisticated HRM techniques and work or organisational psychology underlined by an ideological apparatus through corporate mass media necessary.

Once established, the link between work=consumption=good life (Figure 11.3) cannot be assumed as being continuously functional as *the strengthening of an associative bond through repetitive experience is the basic idea in the associative conceptual framework* (Gallistel & Gibbon 2002:5). As an example, for them repetitiveness and the *time sequence* that establishes and maintains a link between conditioned response [hard work] and reward [wage] is absolutely crucial and must initially occur within a narrow time frequency. Once the adoption period has firmly established the work-wage link over time, the time frequency can be widened. Historically, this is most visible in the world of work when looking at the time between *work* done and *wages* paid. During the link's adoption period the time corridor was roughly one day as expressed in day-labour. Once the link was successfully established, the time corridor between work and wage was widened to one week and eventually to one month. Ultimately annual wage figures were adopted but still broken down into weekly or monthly wage payments. This shows the successful completion of the conditioning process to establish and maintain the link shown in Figure 11.3 and, above all, its deep manifestation. Communication in the work as well as in the consumption domain has become the key ingredient for the *double integration* and the sustainability of asymmetrical relations at work and elsewhere. This need for communication provides an ideal entry point for communicative action as it can highlight the cognitive weakness of a link that has to be conditioned and constantly reinforced to maintain the asymmetrical relationship between management and workers.

The asymmetry of the relationship between those *who manage* and those *who are managed* is powerfully mirrored when modern HR-managers as those who manage – assisted by work or organisational psychologists – design system integrative models for the conditioning of those who are managed.[422] Arnold (2005:291) has developed a detailed method outlining *possible rewards for organisational behaviour modification*. Comprehensive *behaviour modification* has been a core concept of *behaviourism* ever since its conception. In this model, the link between *sign* (*wage*) and *meaning* (*work hard*) is not created via *symbolic association* or the cognitive understanding of a social process but as *conditioned association* where a communicative link is established through the instruments of *behaviourism*. In the above example this is achieved through a *conditioned response-reward* link.[423] In the *behaviourist* model workers are exposed to two forms of rewards – *contrived on-the-job rewards* (a) and *natural rewards* (b).[424] The asymmetry of these rewards lies in their design and application by those *who manage* and the often unconscious acceptance of the reward system by those *who are managed*. The sophistication of the asymmetrical model divides the contrived on-the-job rewards (a) into four further sub-classes: a^i) *consumable rewards,* a^{ii}) *manipulatables,* a^{iii}) *visual and auditory rewards,* and a^{iv}) *tokens*. The so-called *natural rewards* (b) are, of course, all but natural since they are socially created in the highly structured setting of the workplace. Despite their cloaked appearance as natural rewards (b) they are further classified into two sub-classes: b^i) *social* and b^{ii}) so-called *Premack rewards*.[425]

Needless to say, in order to achieve an efficient result with the tools shown above in Table 11.2, *behaviourist* ideas demand that the managerially desired

Table 11.2 Tools of Asymmetric Behaviour Modification

a^i	a^{ii}	a^{iii}	a^{iv}	b^i	b^{ii}
Coffee breaks	Desk accessories	Office with window	Money	Friendly greetings	More job responsibilities with job rotation and job enrichment[426]
Treats	Wall plaques	Piped-in music	Stocks/Shares	Informal recognition	Early time off with pay
Fee lunches	Company car	Workplace	Stock options	Formal acknowledgment of achievement	Extended breaks
Food baskets	Watches	Redecoration	Passes for films	Invitation of coffee/lunch	Extended lunch periods
Easter hams	Trophies	Company literature	Trading stamps	Solicitation of suggestions	Personal time off with pay
Christmas turkey	Commendations	Private office	Paid insurance	Compliments on work progress	Work on personal projects during company time
Dinner invitation	Rings/ties/pins	Popular speakers	Dinner tickets	Recognition	
Company picnics	Home appliances	Book club discussions	Theatre tickets	In-house journals	Use of company machinery or facilities for personal projects
After-work drinks	Home shop tools	Performance feedback	Holiday trips	Pat on the back	
Cheese parties	Garden tools		Coupons for stores	Smile	Use of company recreation facilities
Beer parties	Clothing		Profit – sharing	Verbal or non-verbal recognition or praise	
	Club privileges				
	Special assignments				

Source: Arnold 2005:291

behaviour that is to be *manipulated* (!) and the consequent reward occur within a narrow time frame. Another important condition is that any reward that those *who manage* have designed for those *who are managed* is being offered only when the *desired* behaviour is shown by a worker who has now been turned into an object of the power of *behaviourism*. The key in this model is that the definition of *desired* behaviour is asymmetrically distributed to those who manage, leaving the sole power to define behaviour to management. In a final step, what is even more important than the *desired* behaviour is the *outcome of behaviour, not the behaviour itself* (Arnold 2005:288). In the mind of the sophisticated manager, the behaviour of the employee is divided into two categories: a) behaviour that is deemed to contribute to profit and b) behaviour that is deemed not to. Once this categorisation has been adopted, management's pre-designed conditioning plan (Table 11.2:a^i–b^{ii}) is applied to *manipulate behaviour*. Not only the openness of *behaviourism* and with it organisational psychology but also its high levels of sophistication allow communicative action to apply its critical powers to work.

In sum, the application of behaviourism to the world of work has been termed *organisational behaviour modification* (OBM) – not to use the value-laden and negatively connoted word manipulation – with the crucial feature that power is allocated to *the personnel within the organisation that are influencing organisational performance*.[427] This is the identifier for those *who manage* and who are able to direct workers' behaviour towards profit maximisation. OBM is by no means a passive system that is assigned to individually identifiable forms of behaviour. It is rather the opposite. OBM encompasses a raft of operational and interventionist strategies and tactics that are geared towards the manipulation of workers' behaviour. While it increases the frequency of desirable behaviours, it weakens undesirable forms of behaviour by applying *positive* reinforcement as shown in Table 11.2 – when managers support profit enhancing behaviour of workers through positive elements – and also through *negative* reinforcement – when positive aspects of work are withdrawn or threatened to be withdrawn – as well as *extinction*.

Negative reinforcement, however, is not to be mistaken with punishment, i.e. the application of something negative. Modern managers who run a highly *behaviourist* workplace rely heavily on positive and negative reinforcement while at the same time seeking to reduce or diminish all forms of punishment or disciplining (Figure 11.4). Another element in the repertoire of OBM is the use of extinctions that are applied when workers' behaviour can neither be altered by positive nor by negative reinforcement. According to *behaviourism*, any behaviour that shows neither positive nor negative responses is extinct. In sum, OBM is more than a reactionary development of the stick-and-carrot approach of previous generations as the stick-side of the equation is more or less diminished in favour of more sophisticated techniques that that seek to lock workers inside a mental framework that is highly conditioned. Techniques such as OBM rely on external assistance in the form of responses that have a long history of conditioning, starting with a chocolate bar for good behaviour in infancy, continued through years of schooling with good marks for compliant behaviour, until the work-money conditioning takes over that continues the conditioned reward structure at the work and consumption level. This process of conditioning is tightly linked to the history of capitalism. Unlike the historically outdated *stick-and-carrot* approach, modern OBM not only relies heavily on communication but also seeks to create a one-dimensional mindset in which workers are made to feel TINA – There Is No Alternative.

As much as present societies seek to reinforce conditioned behaviour directed towards work and consumerism, management always needs to communicate to workers that managerialism linked to consumerism is the only alternative as there are always other forms of communicatively established realities. Mass media and management are continuously on the watch to extinguish any form of alternative discourse that could, even remotely, rely on communicative action. Once workers overcome these managerial intentions and identify TINA for what it is – the mere mirage of an ideology – communicative action can further exercise its analytical, critical, and, above all, emancipatory power and the expression of socially positive interests can be established communicatively under conditions of ideal speech. This is designed to lead to communicative action based on understanding that is reached in a non-hierarchical way and grounded on critical reflections. At work the communicatively established application of social action depends on labour's ability to reach shared agreements about the *objective* world of work that is still recognisable.[428] In order to establish social action, three issues need to be achieved simultaneously. Firstly, *communicative action* under conditions of ideal speech must be directed towards the objective or material affairs of workers. Secondly, such communication has to take place within communicatively established social norms that create moral consciousness. Finally, the subjective or inter-personal facets of any communicative situation have to be taken into account. In conclusion, the logic of two collective actions demands the logic of two forms of *communicative actions* – one that critically analyses the world of work in all its objectivity and one that overcomes current structures of domination through the application of communicative action.

12
Communicative Action IV: The Two Logics of Communication

Argumentation as an attempt to transform something collectively *problematic* into something collectively *valid* is at the core of all forms of discourse. *Communicative action* and ideal speech are forms of communication that establish validity. Because labour and management operate under the condition of the *Two Logics of Communicative and Collective Action*, the problem of validity varies between them.[429] For labour, validity is established as co-ordinated communicative action while management relies on instrumental communication to establish it. In the communicative or exchange domain (C) that links the labour (A) and the management domain (B), two fundamentally different modes of communication meet. Generally, collective action in each domain begins with a group of social actors whose subjective beliefs and/or objective social relations position them in an environment of common circumstances that generates a shared interest located inside their domain. Labour can communicate about their interests in the labour domain, while management does the same in their domain.

As the modern organisation is based on instrumental rationality, hierarchy, domination, and a division between management and labour, the two domains are not of equal value. The structural determinant of today's company life assigns different properties to each domain. In other words, communicative options are asymmetrically distributed between the two domains while communication plays a central role in both. Habermas (1997a:310–312) has expressed this as follows:

> *Members of organisations act communicatively only with reservations. They know they can have recourses to formal regulations, not only in exceptional but in routine cases; there is no necessity for achieving consensus by communicative means. The scopes for decision making can, if necessary, be utilised in a strategic manner. Inner-organisational relations constituted via membership do not replace communicative action, but they do disempower its validity basis so as to provide the legitimate possibility of redefining at will domains of action oriented to mutual understanding into action situations stripped of liveworld*

contexts and no longer directed to achieving consensus. The liveworlds of members, never completely husked away, penetrate here into the reality of organisations. There is no doubt that the coordinating mechanism of mutual understanding is put partially out of play within formally organised domains.

Habermas' *members of organisations* are not a singular entity but a pool of members that is divided into two groups – management and workers – who have different *reservations* and different access to formal regulations. They also establish routines in different ways. While decision making for management is achieved through instrumental communication, labour establishes it through a form of *communicative action* called ideal speech that is directed towards common understanding.[430] This is achieved through the demands set forth by ideal speech – symmetrical speech relations, and empowering, domination-free, and horizontal forms communication that seek to avoid hierarchies, authoritarian positions, instrumentalism, and, above all, instrumental communication.

Management's *dis*-empowering and vertical forms of consent manufacturing are largely based on managerially defined hierarchies with clear functional assignments and establish consent through power-relationships. While for the group that uses horizontal, hierarchy-free, and domination-free communication, consent finding involves a high degree of empowering discourse, in the vertically structured group that applies hierarchical communication, domination is associated with disempowerment. The horizontal and empowering versus the vertical and *dis-empowering* communication is depicted in the following figure:

Figure 12.1 shows how vertical and horizontal communication occurs inside their group or domain. In the labour domain, communication is much likely to be structured in a non-hierarchical way as labour does not require hierarchy as a core organising principle.[431] Domain (B), in contrast, operates with a vertically structured level of hierarchy as the core organising

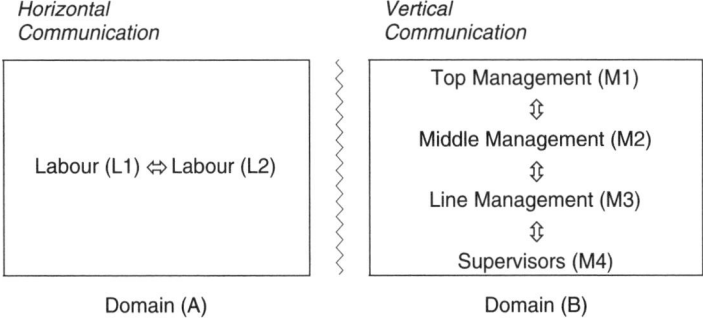

Figure 12.1 Horizontal and Vertical Communication in Two Domains

principle. The vertical structure of the management domain is mirrored in respective communication structures that are designed as order-structures in a top-down (M1–M4) or upward (M4–M1) fashion. Communication is either organised as a command structure – M1→M2→M3→M4 or as reporting structure – M4→M3→M3→M1. Common to all *top-down/down-top* or order giving versus reporting structures is their reliance on hierarchy that turns most day-to-day communication into vertical communication. Even when managers meet in their functional capacity as finance, marketing, operations, HRM, etc., these domain specific meetings are intended to represent vertical forms of communication. All too often this *hierarchisation* of communication replaces the need for horizontal communicative structures and only allows the operation of non-democratic instrumental communication.

In contrast to domain (B), members of domain (A) tend not to experience such hierarchisation of communication as workers in non-managerial positions operate less in vertical but more in collective work arrangements. Even though there are strong managerial attempts to introduce some sort of hierarchy to the non-managerial workforce, much of their work occurs without hierarchical structures and allows horizontal communication. However, through occupational segregation (Marsden 1999) – the separation of non-managerial staff into white- and blue-collar workers – they are to some extent exposed to management's functional hierarchies.

Such communicative system integration through management can, to some degree, act as an effective measure against horizontal forms of communication as it reduces solidarity while it increases top-down structures.[432] Overall, occupational structures are directed towards segregation and are more prevalent in managerial than in non-managerial staff.[433] The conditions of domain (A) with functionalities of work tasks do not lead to vertical structures of communication while the managerial functionality in domain (B) does so. The reason for this may be that workers have to complete specific work tasks while management's only task is that of managing where it requires crucial elements such as hierarchies, domination, order, and instrumental communication. However, both labour and management not only communicate inside their respective domains, but also with each other.

Communication at company level between L1 and M1 can never be strictly separated into two clearly defined boxes. It occurs within the dialectical relationship between communicative action and instrumental communication. The asymmetry of the two logics of collective action becomes visible in the relationship between L1 and M1 as members of each domain communicate differently with each other and linear communicative configurations (L1→M1 and equally M1→L1) are fundamentally different. Whereas in the first case, *an employee must consider whether or not they will be perceived as constructive or adversarial, as well as the risk of retaliation associated with dissenting* (Kassing 2002:189), management, in the second case, faces almost no *risk of retaliation*. The communicative domain between L1 and M1 can be shown as a third domain, the communication domain (C), located between the two domains. Here, the fundamental communicative contradictions between wage-labour and capital-management come to light. The exchange domain in which L1 and M1 meet can be shown as follows:

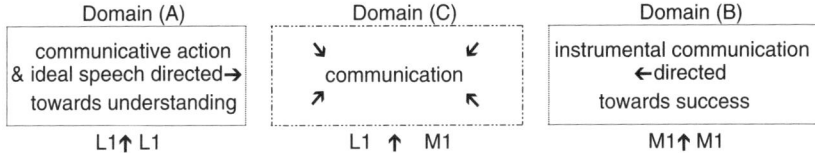

Figure 12.2 Three-Way Communication between Two Actors at Work

As Figure 12.2 shows, communication can be seen as communicative action and ideal speech (A) versus instrumental communication (B). Under conditions of the two logics of collective action, workplace communication among the two actors, labour and management, takes place at three levels – as communication among labour (L), communication among management (M), and between both. To show the different ways in which communication takes place in each domain and between domains, these domains need to be constructed separately. To enable communicative action for actor L1 inside domain (A), a contextual division of domains is required. This disallows management to utilise a separate entry for infiltration or *colonisation* to allow distortions of value systems in this domain. According to Habermas (1997a:356) such colonisation can be characterised in four ways.

Table 12.1 shows that *colonisation* of communicative patterns in the world of work occurs in various ways. It arises when social forms of communication are converted into structured forms that convert social life into purposive driven life that is steered through external forces (i). Colonisation also occurs when social relations are distorted via the conversion of humans into labour (ii). Here, the structural determinants of the organisation replace

Table 12.1 Four Elements of Colonisation

No.	Character
i)	when traditional forms of social existence and communication are dismantled,
ii)	when social relations become exchange relations as in the case of employment where pre-organised workplaces regulate social relations and communication,
iii)	the labour power of the employed is mobilised for voting procedures that are a tolerated process based on trade-offs against social rewards,[434]
iv)	when withdrawn from the world of work and the public domain privatised hopes of self-actualisation and self-determination are transferred into a consumer/client model.[435]

the organic structures of society. When social relations are formally organised, communication experiences a changeover that demands that forms of social life are altered by system integration. This inevitably creates not only social but also communicative pathologies.

System integration encroaches upon domains of action that previously fulfilled their functions under conditions of social life. More than structured existence steered by external forces, social life is able to escape the colonisation of communication. Therefore, a work domain that functions as a forum for discourse directed towards mutual understanding, communicative action, and ideal speech is able to transfer these elements and defend itself against system imperatives that seek colonisation. This is only possible when open forms of communication are separated from domains directed towards system integration. Any domain that seeks to enable communication in an uncolonised way needs to be constructed as a domain that is able to resist intrusive elements.[436]

A communicative domain that seeks to operate under conditions of ideal speech needs to protect itself from colonising effects and system imperatives that stem from instrumental communication and managerialism. It needs to resist all alien items and invasive concepts such as instant or immediate success, cost-benefit analysis, means-end concepts, etc. This process also has to be reflected in the separation of communicative integration – which is achieved through the medium of solidarity – from system or hierarchical integration – which is achieved through the two steering media, money and power. A communicative domain that allows ideal speech needs to be protected from these two fundamental steering media of all modern corporations. Once this is achieved, ideal speech can flourish as the domain is protected against the colonising effects of system imperatives enshrined in instrumental rationality.

Such a domain allows for specific and contextual discourse that is directed towards understanding and the establishment of meaning or sense making.[437] *Meaning* becomes a systematic property that is established in special environments which are not at the disposition of a single or individual actor. Nevertheless it is constitutive for a group of individuals. *Membership in the ideal communication community is, in Hegelian terms, constitutive of both the 'I' as universal and the 'I' as individual.*[438] While meaning is constitutive for the 'I' and composed by a group of individuals, it can only be established by virtue of reaching understanding which is accomplished through language exchanges.[439] This establishes the goal of assimilating or internalising *meaning* that is reached through common understanding.

But meaning is not only established through the exchange of arguments constructed inside the framework of ideal speech. It is also created through self-conscious reflections.[440] Such reflection towards a common understanding of meaning also constitutes identity as the goal of such an exercise is to alter a previously held position. In this process, a person becomes a personality by virtue of participating in a community that seeks to establish meaning by reaching understanding. Such a communicative community uses language towards coordination with the goal to *bind the will of responding actors*.[441]

Once labour has fulfilled the demands issued by ideal speech and has reached common and, above all, communicative understanding, it can meet in the communicative domain (Figure 12.3). In this domain both sides tend to establish meaning from information gained in their respective domains (L1 and M1) as well as in the exchange domain (L1↔M1). No longer can meaning simply be seen as a *set of shared meanings among organisational members* (Grant et al. 2004:15). Social actors at work are not just *organisational members* but operate in three core domains. They do not even primarily establish meaning in the exchange domain (C) where the actors L1 and M1 meet. Predominantly meaning is established in their respective domains (A and B). Communication in domain (C) sometimes appears incompatible, incomprehensible, asymmetrical, conflict-oriented, or even adversarial using hidden agendas and distorted forms of communication. But in the safety of their respective environments or domains, it can be freed up from system disturbing elements. This allows a relatively unhindered form of meaning establishment.

The ability to control communication and therefore the shaping of meaning construction is however asymmetrically distributed. Managerial control of production, labour, and investment always includes the simultaneous control of organisational communication and discourses. The control of discursive practices is also mirrored in the control over communicative alternatives that allows the pushing of colonising elements such as TINA: There Is No Alternative.[442] The asymmetrically distributed power allows the creation of organisational meaning and organisational sense-making. This can be expressed as follows:

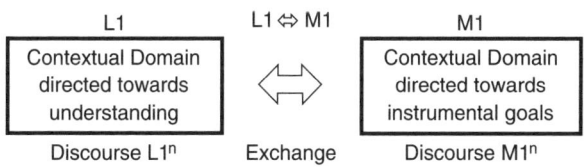

Figure 12.3 Contextual Domains to Establish Meaning among Actors

Figure 12.3 shows that there are differences in the way meaning is achieved. The process of reaching understanding in domains L1 and M1 is dependent on the interpretive accomplishments of each domain. Both contextual domains gain in importance for commonly reached understanding (L1) and the agreement on instrumental goals (M1). While meaning in domain M1 is created under conditions of instrumental action, in domain L1 it is established through the application of ideal speech and communicative action.

In the managerial domain actors are unable to create a collective identity as a necessary condition for truthful and authentic collective action (Offe & Wiesenthal 1980). Members of the M1 domain achieve collective action without comprehensively creating a Weberian (1922 & 1924) *ideal type* of understanding that would necessarily be located inside the realm of critical, truthful and authentic understanding and always entails an element of Kant's what *ought to be* – without which Weber's ideal type of understanding is unthinkable. Contextually established meaning cannot be seen as reflecting the general interest. It is always more than just a compromise between actors. It needs to contain an element of *what ought to be*. However, the general interest contains a moral strength that resides in a collective and common understanding beyond a single actor. It is commonly established through communicative methods which are found in the communicative idea of ideal speech.

By reaching understanding in each contextual domain (L1+M1), both actors can come to an agreement about validity claims. This manifests their understanding on regulated norms that are specific to their domain and at the same time reinforced and altered by the process of finding understanding and commonly achieved interpretation. Actions in domain L1 and M1 are coordinated on the basis of two different traditions. In domain L1, action is based on communicatively established meanings while in domain M1 it derives from instrumental communication that leads to instrumental action. This can be also expressed in *social* versus *system* integrative terms.

Social integrative and communicatively established actors (L1) operate in an open *environment* and gain from the mutual understanding of normative contexts. Domain L1 depends on social integrative forms for communication directed towards reaching communicative understanding. M1 on the other side is less dependent on social and communicatively established integration because of their ability to utilise elements of system integration through authoritarian steering methods. Most decisions made in domain M1 do not require communicative coordination as they are founded in other methods.[443]

According to Weber (1924:18–19) M1 depends on eight elements: rule-bound, power of the administrative organ, hierarchy, technical rules and norms, separation of ownership and management, the office position, written rules and officialdom/bureaucracy. None of these are related to social-communicative integration but many relate to system integrative elements. As system integrative elements dominate M1, this domain is governed by the mechanics of a hierarchical self-regulating system that maintains its boundaries. Its system demands are directed towards stabilising elements and also institutionalise mechanisms directed towards a hierarchy of actions nested inside one another. Such systems appear to be stable and functional but there is a continuous need to preserve stability that exists only under conditions of an external environment. They constantly have to adjust to this environment. Internally, system domestic disequilibria are the norm for self-regulating M1 systems. They also provide for the demanding task of risk-avoidance.

Reaching common understanding in each domain is not only a communicative process but also contains sociological elements. Such a process develops, confirms, renews and stabilises social membership of a group or societal community.[444] The group or work community provides a structural component that determines the status (rights and duties) of a group member. It also legitimately establishes an order that defines the relationships among members. More so in domain L1 than in M1, any coordinated action based on common understanding has a stabilising influence on members of the domain. Consequently, *group identity can be measured by the solidarity among members* (Habermas 1997a:140). In both domains commonly reached understanding contains integrative elements that are directed towards the strengthening of interpersonal relationships among members in each domain through the participation in the process of *sense-making*. In both domains, social reality is not a given fact but established through *the social construction of reality* (Berger & Luckmann 1967). Nevertheless the social realities of the domains are quite different. The labour domain is experiencing more difficulties than the management domain because the latter is more capable to construct social reality. Simultaneously, the communicative abilities between both domains are distributed asymmetrically, which is a result of the way each domain has been socially constructed.

The social construction of labour means that labour's use-value is a necessary condition for the labour process while its exchange-value is the ability to gain wages. Asymmetric relationships result from an unequal distribution of the cost for not working. An exit strategy from the labour process is far more costly for labour than it is for capital. Asymmetrical relationships between management and labour have led to two logics of *interests*. This is reflected in what people gain or lose from an interaction, event, or relationship. While capital's main interest is profit, labour has to come to terms with three core interests.

Table 12.2 shows labour's three core interests. Interest mediation between these three interests demands that group members in the labour domain (A) are forced to mediate their divergent interests communicatively. Therefore members of domain (A) need to have access to an interest mediation

Table 12.2 Three Common Core Interests of Workers

No.	Interests	Issues
1)	an interest in	wages,
2)	an interest in	continuation of wages/employment security,
3)	an interest in	working conditions

process. Under conditions of interest mediation, members of domain (A) have to establish a commonly accepted interest. This ensures that most members of the group are included in the mediation process.

Most importantly, it also ensures that no one is excluded from sharing any benefit achieved by the group. This distributive process has to be symmetric. The group also needs to find a solution for the input and output sides of any balance or preference given to one of the three core interests (Table 12.2). This has to occur despite management's creation of vertical stratification and a false hierarchy of interests. Members of the labour domain (A) need to create some form of protection against system colonising attempts as successful colonisation can lead to divergence among the three core interests and to a false positioning of members alongside vertical stratification. Overall, however, the common interest in sharing a gain that cannot be achieved individually leads to a strengthening of the collective interest among members of domain A.

The next level of communicatively established interest mediation however can be even more problematic. Here, the two logics of interests between management and labour incur the Kantian problem of *what is* versus *what ought to be*. Capital does not need to define its profit interest as it is provided by the system in which management operates. Labour, on the other hand, cannot create a common interest among workers by simply stating *what is*. It always needs to mediate between at least three interests (Table 12.2). Conditions of interest mediation demands can be established by a reference point on the question of *what ought to be*. Hence interest creation in the labour domain always includes a reference to future developments. It is always speculative, utopian, and geared towards what ought to be. As such, the complexities of the two communicative logics (L1+M1) of interest creation or mediation can be shown as follows:

Figure 12.4 seeks to reduce the complexities of interest mediation that occurs predominantly inside the two domains (M1 and L1). These are governed by two different logics of collective and communicative action. Interest mediation in the capital/management domain (M1) is governed by the logic of a singularity of interest, i.e. profit. According to Bowman (1982:572) *capitalists try to cooperate because their mutual contradictory individual interests can be achieved only through the collective action of their competitors*. While

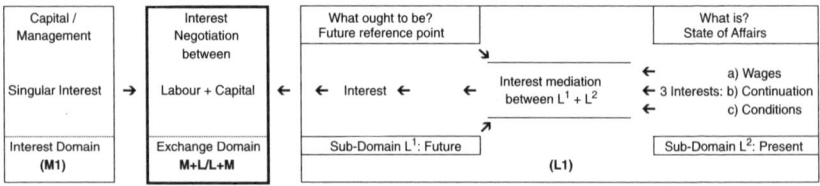

Figure 12.4 Communicative Interest Mediation among Diverging Interests

capitalism sets one capitalist against another, system survival depends on capital's commonality of interests. While this creates the problem of the individual capitalist (firm, company, etc.) versus the system, in this case, system-survival is levelled above individual capitalists.[445] The system is more important than the individual firm. The continuation of capitalist reproduction ensures capital's survival even though it does not guarantee the survival of a particular capitalist. System survival demands are strong among capitalist enterprises. This supports domain specific interests between one company (M1) and others (M^n). The system imperative is a defining element of the relations between M1 and M^n. But perhaps it is even more defining in the M1–L1 relationship.

Even though we are told *we are all classless nowadays* (Hoggart 2003:100), classes have been with us ever since capitalism divided human society into those *who manage* and own productive property, who invest, and have one specific interest and those *who are managed* and who have no productive property, largely do not invest, and have a number of different specific interests.[446] Marx (1846b) assigned these interests to class relations similarly expressed in the domain of interest negotiation (M+L).[447] Following Marx, one can argue that members of the modern bourgeoisies/management (M1) have one-dimensional interests inasmuch as they form one class (M1). This is set against the labour class (L1) that has opposite, antagonistic interests as they stand face to face with management (L+M). Actors inside the management domain (M1) operate under the concept of profit as a defining element. This shapes their interest in a one-dimensional way and provides for the logic of collective action inside domain (M1). On the opposing side, however, things are very different. Interest mediation in the labour domain is by far more complicated and complex. Several interests have to be mediated in domain (L1).

Table 12.3 summarises the levels of interest mediation that form the labour domain. As previously outlined in Figure 12.4, two sub-domains exist in this domain (L^1 and L^2). Labour has to mediate interests that are related

Table 12.3 Four Levels of Interest Mediation inside the Labour Domain (L)

No.	Interest Mediation
1)	Above all, interest formulation can only occur under a specific process that is based on a communicative relationship among actors in domain (L).
2)	Interest mediation has to occur between two sub-domains (L^1+L^2).
3)	Interest mediation inside each sub-domain has to be established. Inside sub-domain L^2 unity/dominance between three interests (a–c) has to be established. Inside sub-domain L^1 future interests have to be established.
4)	Lastly, the free-raider problem must be addressed in the labour domain (L) so that workers are willing to participate and contribute to the relatively high costs of collective action.

to *future* achievements (L^1) as well as to the *current* state of affairs (L^2). L^1 seeks to analyse future interests under Kant's *what ought to be* and therefore carries constructive elements into the future. The domain L^2 analyses the current state of affairs. The logic of collective action demands that interest mediation between L^1 and L^2 is never disconnected but progresses within the dialectical relationship of both sub-domains. The communicatively established mediation (Table 12.2 and Figure 12.4^{L2a-c}) can never only be a reflection of the current state of affairs but must also be directed into the future as it impacts on both L^1 and L^2. This model is further complicated by possibilities of contradictions between labour's three interests.

Once labour has established a collective interest in domain L^2 and linked this to domain L^1, a common interest can enter the exchange domain (L+M). Only then can it be negotiated with management. Such negotiations shape the relationship between L1 and M1 and also affect domain-internal relationships inside domain L1 as the sub-domains L^1+L^2 are shaped by the impact on the current state of affairs and the future.

In the exchange domain (L+M), labour faces complications that may result from *de-linguisitified* exchange processes. In these processes issues that had been agreed upon linguistically become subject to a version of non-language as they are removed and regulated through power interests. These forms of meaning establishment are guided by hierarchies rather than by communicative understanding and are able to colonise the exchange domain. Managerial instrumental action and communication does not need to follow values, socially established norms, or ethics as management is able to establish instrumental action and interest formulation *non-linguistically*. There is a strong asymmetry of communicative needs between L1 and M1. The non-discursive form of communication in domain M1 can be carried over into the exchange domain (L+M). As one of managerialism's foundations lies in instrumental action, it can also enforce this instrumentality in other domains by using instrumentalism to convert the exchange domain (L+M) as well as the labour domain into non-communicative and non-linguistic domains. Managerial exchange patterns as much as management's very existence are based on instrumental rationality and expressed in instrumental communication.

Overall, the logic of communicative interest mediation in domain L1 demands high levels of communicative action that exceed by far the levels of interest formation in domain M1. At this point, the two logics of *collective* action move well beyond their status and enter deeply into the two logics of *communicative* action.[448] Communicative demands in both domains are asymmetrically structured against the labour domain and distributed in a way that creates high levels of complexities within the labour domain where demands for communication are exponentially higher. Labour's interest mediation demands a communicatively established understanding in both L^1 and L^2. It also needs to ensure that the outcome of this mediation is linked to the three key interests (Figure 12.4^{L2a-c}). All demands directed towards communicative action have to be based on ideal speech. This is highly challenging for the M1 domain as it operates on instrumentality. In conclusion, actors in domain M1 experience a lower level of communicative needs compared to actors in domain L1 where system imperatives support interest formulation.

The communicative process further demands from labour that it reaches understanding on interests that secure labour's *willingness to understand* as well as its *willingness to act* in order to establish communicative action. This is fundamentally different from communication in the M1 domain in which management can be reduced to *speaking to itself*. Communication among labour must entail *speaking for labour*. Herein lies one of the key access options for management in order to colonise the labour domain and distort communication in this domain. Management can override communicative demands towards the establishment of mutual understanding. It can convert communicative processes in the labour domain by constructing communication as a simple S⇌R-model. This is done through the reliance on the power asymmetry that gives management the upper hand. Hierarchical communication under conditions of power directed towards instrumental rationality denies truthful communication directed towards reaching understanding as power replaces understanding.

Finally, actors in domain L1 face additional structural asymmetries. As labour has to sell their labour power in order to participate on an asymmetrically structured labour market, they also participate in managerial structures.[449] In doing so, labour is not only forced to participate in managerial regimes but also actively takes part in communicative system integration that generates managerially guided and self-supporting belief systems about work processes. Through their active participation in the managerial regimes, workers are made to invent arguments about alien work regimes and solidarity among workers that are directed against their own beliefs so that the fiction of work-related care arrangements perpetrated by Human Resource Management leads to the refutation of these values in order to establish affirmation towards managerial work regimes.[450] As such, labour becomes alienated not only from the production process but even more so from itself. Estranged in an alien form of work existence, labour finds it hard to assess their position. The understanding of their own interests and position is severely hindered through alien forms of existence and instrumental communication. A barrage of dividing factors including the raft of images portrayed by mass media complicates the communicative process of interest mediation even further.

Non-class identities such as gender and ethnicity are powerful factors that can interfere with communication that is directed towards interest formulation. Furthermore, managerial wedge-politics via *divide-and-conquer* strategies can be applied communicatively in order to hinder any communicative process that seeks to establish communicative understanding under conditions of ideal speech. Together with an inherently alienated process of employment, such strategies provide an effective tool that obstructs interest mediation in the labour domain. In sharp contrast, the identity of an actor in domain M1 is much less affected by alienation and *divide-and-conquer* strategies. Their identities are based on the imperatives of system integration. Ultimately, the instrumental use of language in domain M1 tends to be parasitic. Its function is directed in a way so that only one side (management) is able to pretend to have an orientation towards goals.[451] Instead of language being portrayed as the very instrument of domination as such, it is portrayed as a communicative medium or a tool that achieves goals.[4521]

The two logics of ideal speech and social action

In the hierarchical top-down order of management–labour relations any rationality of action relates to the two logics of communicative action. Discussion and communication should ideally result in social action that is characterised by four basic modes of action: a) teleological action as instrumental action; b) social action through speech acts in conversation and discourse; c) normatively regulated action; and d) dramaturgical action. While teleological action (a) sees technically and instrumentally useful knowledge as its core, speech acts (b) rely on empirical-theoretical knowledge.[453] Normatively regulated action (c) focuses on moral-practical knowledge while dramaturgical action (d) embodies aesthetic-practical knowledge. The last two forms have only limited existence in the world of work as forms of moral and ethical consideration are largely excluded. Similarly, drama, plays and similar forms of aesthetic action rarely find expression inside the workplace. The first two modes of action (a & b) are exemplified in the following table as *action* versus *speech*.

Table 12.4 shows the difference between purposive or instrumental action (A^{i-iii}) on the one side and communicative action or speech action on the other (B^{i-iii}). The latter has to communicatively establish agreement under

Table 12.4 Action and Speech

	(A) Purposive Action	(B) Speech & understanding → social action
(i)	Determination of the goal of an action independent of means of an intervention	Determination of a goal of an action dependent on means of an intervention
(ii)	Goal = causally-achieved state	Goal (= understanding) = non-causally achieved state
(iii)	Goal in narrowly defined objective world	Goal in the extra-defined objective world

conditions of ideal speech while purposive action is geared towards means-ends reasoning and relies on linear causality rather than on communicatively established agreement and mutual understanding. Social relations in A structure actors, individuals, and collectives deliberately towards goals (A^{ii}). There is a very limited evaluation of alternatives that guide a select course of action.

Under ideal speech on the contrary, social action can only result from non-linear and communicatively established understanding (B). Here, goals are developed discursively and non-causally (B^{ii}) and are directed beyond immediate goals. They are not narrowly defined along technical and instrumental means (A^{iii}) but extend well beyond the boundaries of current work regimes (B^{iii}). Social action can only develop on the basis of a communicatively established rationality for a communicative agreement of social action. This, however, occurs on various levels.

The levels of social action are shown in Figure 12.5 below. Management's choices are located at the second level, i.e. one level below *social action* as management tends to opt for instrumental rather than communicative action due to its traditional orientation towards goal-achieving and means-ends reasoning based on instrumental rationality. Instrumental action is disengaged from demands to reach understanding while goal-achieving efficiency becomes ever more important. This promotes a model for instrumental choice. Technical ways are seen as solutions to solve problems as technology pretends to be scientific, value neutral, non-personal, non-subjective, non-human and, in its final consequence, dehumanising and inhuman (Bauman 1989).

Labour on the other side needs to opt for communicative action in an effort to reach common understanding for social or industrial action. In this context, the two versions of social action can be seen as system-integration of goal-directed actors on the management side and the communicative socialising of subjects capable of ideal speech on labour's side. At the next level (Figure 12.5), management's instrumental option can be further divided into *concealed* or *latently-strategic* instrumental action and *open* instrumental action. Labour, on the other hand, sees action towards reaching understanding or consensual action as essential. At the final level, management can only opt for open manipulative action or systematically distorted communication while labour can direct its attention towards action or discourse.

The combination of action and discourse is essential for labour to merge discourse and ideal speech into communicatively directed action. In this process to reach *understanding* means to reach *agreement* between *speaking* and *acting* subjects. Action is represented through communicative establishment and subsequently the achievement of goals. In this process, communicatively established and commonly agreed upon standards must always be reflected upon.

Figure 12.5 shows the relationship between communication and social action. In a sense, labour is more likely than management to adopt a

212 Management Communication

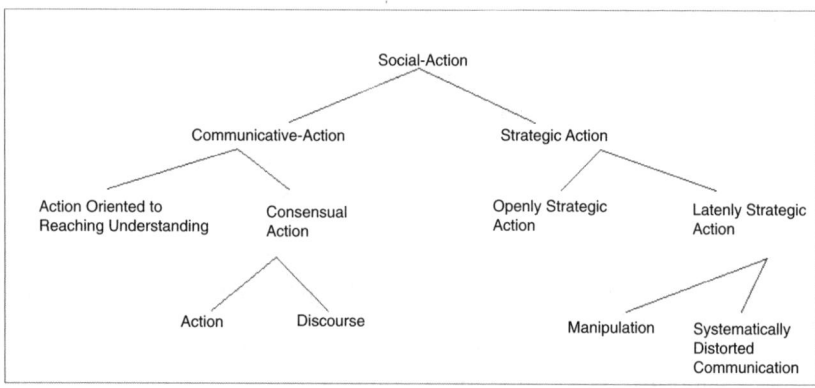

Figure 12.5 Two Logics of Social Action

non-distorted form of communication. This provides a communication model that enables members to conduct the unbiased communicative-rational formation of commonly agreed intentions. It is a model of non-alienated communicative forms of interaction. Management, in sharp contrast, is highly dependent on formal hierarchical structures and power relations enshrined in Weber's (1924 & 1947) idea of the institution of the *office*. This places severe restrictions not only on the production process but also on communication. Such communication restrictions are however a vital part of management. According to Taylor, workers are to be reduced to resemble a *trained intelligent gorilla...unable to understand the real science of doing this class of work*. Crucial to the success of Taylor's factory system is the prevention of knowledge that could be gained through communication.[454] Production, the division of labour, and instrumental communication require action that is solely oriented towards success. This is the clearest expression of efficiency and instrumental rationality. Today, more sophisticated and systematic restrictions are placed on communication.

In conclusion, the two logics of collective and communicative action at work can only develop once humans have gone through the labour process that converts them into workers. While the process by which the worker is reified and becomes a commodity – so long as he does not consciously offer resistance to it – dehumanises him and cripples and atrophies his 'soul', it remains true that precisely his human nature is not changed into a commodity.[455] Unlike management and HRM, labour is able to set up structures for communicative action and ideal speech that do not operate under profit demands supplied by the market place.[456] Labour is less likely to subscribe to instrumental rationality, hierarchy and system integration.[457] On a somewhat simplified level, the arguments above can be summed up as follows:[458]

Table 12.5 shows how the two different types of communication – instrumental communication versus communicative and regulated commun-

Table 12.5 Two Logics of Communicative and Strategic Action

Type of Communicative Action	Strategic Communication	Conversation and Normative Regulated Communication
Character of speech	Imperatives	Communicative & regulative
Function of speech	Influencing one's opposite	Representation of states of affairs Establishment of interpersonal relations
Speech relations	Top-down relation	Ideal speech situation
Orientations	Oriented towards pre-determined goal and success	Orienting to reaching understanding and emancipation
Action	Strategic action	Communicative action
Basic attitudes	Objectifying	Objectifying & norm-conformative
Rules	Technical	Moral, norms, consensual
Rule violation	The intervention fails	Sanction, reward, punishment
Validity claims	Effectiveness	Truth & rightness
World relations	Objective world	Objective and social world
Communication at company level	Company based communication under instrumental rationality based on market demands under top-down hierarchies	Worker oriented ideal speech communication under communicative rationality based on collective interest and understanding
Gestalt	△	○

ication – differ at several levels. As expressed at the final level – the level of *Gestalt* – one form of communication is hierarchical while the other rejects the top-down approach to communication.[459] One sets specific goals, has an instrumental orientation and seeks effectiveness and success. The other is oriented towards truth, rightness, and sees emancipation and change in a social world as central. Fundamentally, strategic communication seeks the achievement of pre-set goals under means-ends aspects, while normative-regulated communication tries to achieve common understanding for social action.

While labour is potentially more autonomous of system demands such as hierarchy and domination which enables communication to be structured towards truth and rightness, management, in contrast, is bound to instrumental rationality. This dictates a fundamentally different form of communication that is directed towards effectiveness and success. The investigation into the two logics of collective and communicative action has resulted in two different modes of communication. Both sides will find it hard to reconcile these differences. Management is unwilling to establish truthful forms of communication while labour has to fight against system imperatives that colonise their domain. The establishment of *communicative action* directed towards common understanding, communicative agreement, and consequently, social action is different for labour and management. How these two groups can nevertheless develop ideal speech situations and communicative action is discussed in the following chapters.

13
Communicative Action V: Communicative Ethics at Work

The final section on communicative action is a guide on how to use ideal speech situations to convert communicative action into social action. The previous chapters have outlined current relationships at work, communicative distortions, and ideal speech in conjunction with the two logics of communication. This part focuses on providing a useful and workable framework for communication. As previously shown, communication under conditions of current managerial hierarchies supported by managerialism is largely limited to instrumental communication and therefore suffers from severe communicative restrictions that have to be maintained as they preserve managerial hierarchies and management's legitimacy.

Communicative distortions are utilised by management as deliberate and intentionally created conceptual ideas in support of goal oriented instrumental rationality.[460] The idea of domination free discourse on the objectives of work using ideal speech can only be found in *communicative rationality* leading to communicative understanding.[461] This identifies communication and rationality as essential parts of the work discourse. Today's usage of terms such as *rationality* and *communication* has changed since the days of *Enlightenment* when philosophy and science sought to understand the world surrounding us through *rational* means rather than religion.[462] Today, the use of rationality is no longer seen as a fundamental critique on religion but has become an instrument for domination. While originally anti-ideological, instrumental rationality and instrumental communication have become ideologies used to support and legitimise hierarchies and domination. This has not only restructured the public domain but also the work domain. At work, these two terms have predominantly developed into instrumentalism as a characteristic of a purposive-rational system directed towards the management of work. At the other end of the scale a form of communication is found that establishes a communicative rationality of work where understanding also creates a communicatively established normative system.

This distinction can be traced back to Marx.[463] He separated the term '*work*' located in the world of political economy from the term '*symbolic interaction*' positioned in communication. While this separation can be translated into management and communication, the communicative domain not only links management to labour but is also a domain in its own right. The concept of the communication domain links communicative rationality to communicative action and the conditions of ideal speech which allow individuals to communicate without system integrative interference of instrumental rationality. In this model, communication is neither pre-structured nor oriented towards goals that are pre-set under conditions of instrumental management.

In order to protect communication from these system interferences, Habermas sets *communicative action as a switching station for the energies of social solidarity*.[464] This is a fundamental shift in perspective providing for a paradigm change from sole rational purposiveness to social interaction. This shift promises to illuminate the very process of communicatively established mutual understanding. It supersedes simple understanding by going beyond many well-known means such as managerial instructions, provision of information, communicative commands, etc. Instead it enhances communication from communicative understanding towards communicative action where communication is no longer just a form of expression but an action that is intimately linked to social action. Rationality is no longer enshrined in managerial instrumentality that carries strong connotations of pre-set goals and means-ends rationality[465] but in a communal and communicative existence. This communicatively established understanding of rationality is radically different from instrumental rationality and directed towards social change. Its basis is any action that seeks to alter existing forms of production and reproduction. It seeks the conversion and subversion of socially constructed and hierarchically shaped institutions. Communicative rationality is able to show that present socially constructed institutions do not exist as neutral or natural entities but as a manifestation of the power relations that constructed them. Communicative action allows the participants in ideal speech situations to uncover the hidden power relations implicit in these current institutions. Understanding power and power relations enable the uncloaking of institutional structures and makes visible the power that is enshrined in all institutions and organisations. As power relations are inherently political, almost always asymmetrical and never neutral, communicative action cannot be directed towards the preservation of these institutions. The design of communicative action allows communicative participants to enter into a situation where issues of *substantive* severity can be discussed and decisions can be made towards sustaining or converting power relations. Communicative action is, finally, also directed towards the organisational form of communication itself. Only this allows a critical reflection of communicative power structures and with it the detection and abolition of hidden and visible power relations inside communicative action and ideal speech situations. It enables communicative participants to guard against such domineering power relations that tend to encroach in versions of distorted speech and instrumental communication and seek the colonisation of ideal speech situations in order to preserve the current powers of hierarchical communication.

The hierarchically constructed power relations are mediated through two steering media: money and power. These media that guide modern societies have become visible in the all inclusive relationship between the *private* and *public* domains as well as between the *work* and the representative *democratic-administrative* domain. Today, the system integrative force of money and power is manifested in the daily lives of societal members and increasingly infiltrates all areas of human existence. The money and power code, powerfully transmitted through mass media, contaminates the administrative, the managerial, the work, and the economic domain.[466] Each of these domains operates with several sub-sets of minor exchange relationships which are mediated through the same money and power code. This is shown in Figure 13.1.

Figure 13.1 shows the exchange relationship between the *private* and the *public* domain on the one side and the administrative and work domains on the other. In the work domain, labour is mediated by a managerial power structure which is further mediated through monetary income from employment. The structural determinants of the employment domain force labour into a position where the money and power code has increasingly unlimited access. The process of exposing labour to this code has been labelled as de-regulation, neoliberalism, flexibility and the like.[467] Labour's private-work domain interchange is regulated through system demands of the managerial and economic system that creates goods and services to satisfy the economic demands that were created by the private domain. The *administrative-state* and *public-democratic* domain interchange is governed through the money and power code.[4687] This is a two-way interchange as taxes support the upkeep of the administrative-state domain while decisions on taxes are governed through a public-democratic domain that is largely disconnected from public will formation. The disconnection is achieved through a mass mediated process between the individual and the functional apparatus of state and administration that receives legitimacy through routinely and largely ritualistically organised forms of representative democracy.[469] This is further regulated through the power medium of mass loyalty that the public extends to the administrative system.

Figure 13.1 The Steering Media between the Four Main Domains

The administrative system, in return, provides two power media that steer public domains – organisational accomplishments and political decisions. Instrumental communicative structures continuously support the two steering media of power and money (Figure 13.1) and as a result, social pathologies have become highly visible. Space for symmetric speech and communicative action has been eroded as societal steering moved from communication to the money and power code. Neither the private/work nor the public/administrative interchanges are governed by communicative action. Seen as an interchange between the private and economic-managerial domain, the world of work is governed by labour's ability to provide its labour power and the money-medium as a result from the income labour receives from employment.

While income from employment as a money-medium serves privatised reproduction in the private domain, the interchange of labour power only occurs in the public domain. Work is conducted via an exchange that demands the existence of a *public* labour market administered through state interventions, officially sanctioned monetary exchanges, and power relations organised publicly.[470] Therefore, work can only be seen in a private/public dichotomy. It represents private consumption and publicly administered labour market participation at the same time. The centrality of work to these exchange mechanisms can be shown as follows:

Figure 13.2 depicts the centrality of labour at work and its links to the four domains of private-public and employment-administration. In today's society the exchanges between the four domains and labour operate through the money and power code. Labour engages in an exchange between public domain and administrative system as a contributor to taxes and through mass loyalty to the administrative system while it receives organisational accomplishments and political decisions from the administrative system and therefore engages in a private⇌employment and public⇌administrative interchange. The money and power steering media also increasingly govern employment.

When money and power started to colonise the domains of society, the domain of employment became part of a managerial replacement process that pushed the steering media of money and power in and communicative action out. During the process of this replacement non-hierarchical forms

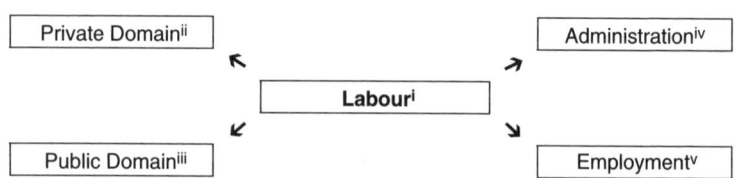

Figure 13.2 The Central Position of Work inside the Four Main Domains

of communication became severely damaged. Ideal speech directed towards mutual understanding and truth lost influence while instrumental forms of communication supportive of the code became powerful. This ended or at least severely restricted all forms of unhindered and non-distorted communication. Management's ability to direct instrumental communication at work as well as the ideology of managerialism itself increasingly exercise their colonising powers. At the same time, labour's ability to resist these attempts decreases. Labour can assist the process of combating colonising attempts and maintaining their forms of communication by utilising communicative action and ideal speech and, by doing so, create communicative situations that allow the uncovering of domineering structures.

As labour occupies a central position in present societies (Figure 13.2^{i}), it can establish links to other domains. These links provide important exchange mechanisms between the private (ii) and the public domain (iii) as well as the administrative (iv) and the employment domain (v). Based on this central location and its significance to production and reproduction, the work domain is somewhat unique to society as only this central position provides labour with important linkages to other domains. Communicative action that is designed to lead to positive social change can therefore only result from the labour domain. The private domain (13.2^{ii}) is structurally governed by money and power enshrined in mass-consumption.[471] The public domain (13.2^{iii}) is ruled by mass mediation through corporate media while relatively large state machineries linked to highly ritualised forms of representative democracy are governing the state-administrative system (13.2^{iv}). These domains feature powerful system integrative mechanisms. The employment domain, even though governed by management's instrumental rationality, is the only domain in which the two logics of collective and, above all, communicative action become visible. The domains of labour (production and reproduction) and employment (labour market and work environment) are, more than any other domain, able to show the divergence of specific interests assigned to labour and management.

While system integrative elements have more or less ended undistorted communication in the private, public and administrative domains (13.2$^{\text{ii,iii,iv}}$), the employment and work domain remains different. While in the previous three domains labour has been reduced to a consumer (13.2^{ii}), a listener of mass media (13.2^{iii}) or an administrative or democratic object of power (13.2^{iv}), it remains labour in the employment domain (13.2^{v}).[472] System integrative forces in the private, public and administrative domains have constructed labour as mere observers and reduced them to *objects of power* in an overwhelmingly managerially guided process. This process of objectification applies particularly to the employment domain (13.2^{v}). Despite these tendencies and because of the centrality of the employment domain and the centrality of labour to present society, labour in the employment domain is still better equipped to distinguish their own interests from the managerial

Table 13.1 System Integration and Outcomes

(a) Domain	(b) System Integrative Forces	(c) Outcomes against Labour
(i) Private	Consumption, affirmation, affluence	Labour = object of standardised consumption
(ii) Public	Corporate mass mediated reality	Labour = object of ideological apparatus
(iii) Administrative	Representative democracy & state	Labour = object of ritualised democracy
(iv) Employment	Management, managerialism, HRM[473]	Labour = object of managerial power

interests. The system integrative forces set against labour are shown in the following table. These forces are manifested in the four basic domains (Figure 13.2^{i-v}). Table 13.1 also shows the outcomes of these system integrative forces as visible in present societies.

Table 13.1 shows that labour is encircled by system integrative forces in every single domain. In the private domain (i), labour is reduced to a consuming entity while the public domain treats labour as a mere object of corporate mass media and reduces it to receive dis-information through an ideologically guided apparatus (ii). In the administrative domain, labour finds itself exposed to two system integrative forces. Firstly, it becomes an object of a ritualised representative democracy that is guided through the same corporate mass media that establishes consumerism.[474] Secondly, labour also becomes an object of state power through state regulation and the remaining elements of the welfare state. In the employment domain, labour is turned into an object of managerial power as soon as it converts from any other domain into the domain of work.[475] However, unlike in the previous domains (i–iii), system integrative forces have been less able to cloak the reality of work. Labour can still experience the realities of the employment domain (iv) more immediately than in any other domain. In this domain – in which the process of converting *humans* into *resources* is located – the reality of work is also much less mediated through corporate mass media. Above all, the work domain is much less able to atomise workers. While labour can be atomised into an individual consumer (i), a TV-watcher (ii), or an individual voter (iii), the individual worker (iv) is much harder to establish. Work in the 21st century remains a collective task. Conflicts of interest are also more visible in the work domain (iv) than in any other domain.[476] First and foremost, only the domain of employment can provide a communicative forum to establish ideal speech and communicative action directed towards social action as system integrative forces are less able to colonise communication.

The underlying idea behind communicative action is the ability to provide a favourable environment for the conduct of forms of communication that are directed towards *ideal* communication[477] where human actors are able to uncover the managerial set of instrumental rationalities and become the highest judges of their own interests. Truth and societal realities are not to be found in technical means, managerial ideologies, administrative bureaucracy, or processes that are conducted under instrumental rationality.[478] They are directed towards Kant's idea of *what is* and even more so to his concept of *what ought to be*[479]. This necessarily carries connotations of speculative and utopian ideas; however, these are elementary as a defence against the colonisation of communication that seeks to arrest communication inside a one-dimensional TINA framework.[480] Marcuse (1968:143) noted this by emphasising *when truth cannot be realised within the established social order, it always appears to the latter as mere utopia*. The truth-hindering element of techno-scientific managerialism has to be separated from communicatively and ethically established forms of mutual understanding.[481] The key to unlock the human ability of self-conscious and self-reflexive understanding lies in ideal speech's quest for truth. In this undistorted form of communication free discussions based on good will, argumentation, and ethical dialogue replace means-ends discussions in instrumental-rational, goal directed fashion. Ideal speech as undistorted communication provides a forum for reflective forms of communicatively established rationality. Here, power plays, social status, ideology, myths, manipulations, rhetoric, ruling by technical expertise, apprehension, lack of self-confidence, misinterpretation, hierarchies, etc. are replaced with equal access to dialogue in an attempt to bring out the best arguments.

Ideal speech relies on the validity claims of comprehensibility, sincerity, truthfulness, legitimacy, and honesty and means equal access and equal opportunities to issues, claims and counter claims directed towards the establishment of mutual understanding in order to achieve a form of communicatively established closeness to the truth of *what is* – the true state of work affairs – and *what ought to be* – the true state of what work affairs should be like.[482] Such an *internally* – socially and communicatively established among participants inside a communicative group as opposed to atomistic, individually, and externally or managerially guided – and *normatively* secured consensus – based on social and ethical norms – builds the foundation of a communicatively grounded consensus based on truthful and open discussion and relying on critical reflections. The element of communicatively established truthful states of affairs is crucial in order to overcome all forms of communication that are confined to means-ends instrumental rationalities as directed under conditions of managerialism. An analysis of truthful states of affairs cannot be accomplished inside the confinements of speech that is guided by instrumental rationality. Four elements are necessary to find truth communicatively and overcome all forms of communicative distortions. These elements act as supportive conditions that have to be met.

Table 13.2 Four Elements of the Communicative Consensus Theory of Truth

No.	Elements that have to be met by ALL participants
i)	Only complete statements have to be made by a participant in such workplace groups, not single sentences. These have to be exposed towards *'true/false'* responses of other members;
ii)	The truth of a statement or statements are measured on constructive speech acts so that statements are deemed true as directed towards consensus when assertions made are also communicatively accepted as justified;
iii)	A statement or statements are only accepted as truthful and justified when they are built on critical-rational consensus of *all* participants;
iv)	Any critical-rational consensus on truth has to be established argumentatively under conditions of ideal speech and communicative action.

Table 13.2 shows that communicative action and ideal speech put a high premium on truth. Communicatively established objective truth can only be reached when *all* criteria (Table 13.2^{i-iv}) have been met. Unlike many other theories, this *communicative theory of truth* is based on reaching a common agreement on the nature of truth and what can be accepted as truth. Truth as prescribed by this theory can never be set once and for all. The core element of this theory is that truth is communicatively established and therefore can change as social circumstances adjust as well.[483] Unlike natural, mathematical, and physical truths, a communicatively established truth is always a temporary social truth. Furthermore, the way such a truth is established depends on stringent conditions (Table 13.2^{i-iv}) that include domination free forms of communication. In the *communicative theory of truth* no outsider and no domineering insider – leader, boss, chair, etc. – can influence, order, or dictate truth. Once participants in such a dialogue have overcome societal forms of domination, ideologies, and communicative distortions – mostly engineered from managerialism (ideology) and from management (domination) – then members of this communicatively established speech community can move towards truth.

Under conditions of the two logics of communicative action this means foremost a fight against distortions such as the all-embracing *we* used by management where it assumes the role of a spokesperson for labour. Distortions allow management to articulate viewpoints thus turning labour into objects of managerial processes subjected to management's forms of communication under instrumental-rational conditions. Managerial consensus is not established but secured through truth-alien forces such as hierarchies, authoritarianism, and leadership.[484] Any managerially dictated but fake consensus always faces insecurities and because of that it seeks security by appealing to labour for legitimacy. In doing this, management relies on labour's agreement to the pre-organised managerial dialogue. However, truthful forms of legitimacy can only be established communicatively, not normatively through managerial norms as they violate virtually all provisions set out in Table 13.2$^{\text{i-iv}}$. Under managerial leadership, labour is coerced into false affirmation (13.2^{i}); consensus is not communicatively established as just (13.2^{ii}) but formed through instrumental rationality and means-ends dictates (13.2^{iii}); and finally, conditions of ideal speech and communicative action cannot be met by management (13.2^{iv}) as management relies on normative consensus where norms are set by management.

In many cases such normatively established forms of legitimacy are established by the pre-structuring of discourses and offering labour participation in them. Under conditions of managerial system integration, labour should participate in all levels of decision making processes of the company in which they work. This is portrayed as employee empowerment, employee involvement, or co-decision making and the like. In the idealistic *new workplace* that has repeatedly been claimed to be *new, workplace democracy* is widely advocated as a theoretical-practical exploration of organisational democracy where labour can participate in the private for-profit sector.[485] Workplace democracy is seen as a system of governance that values the ideals of democracy, self-reflection, collective development, and individual opportunities thus reflecting elements of the human relations school. In today's political democracy as inside the world of work, these ideas of democracy transfer the instruments of system integration into the workplace by managerial structuration of communication processes wherever necessary to achieve system integration.[486] The instrumental goal of such offerings to labour is twofold. It opens participation under strict guidelines of a managerially pre-designed discourse in equally pre-designed forums of communication while at the same time closes opportunities for labour to work towards communicative action under conditions of ideal speech and therefore prevents a discourse that opens possibilities for positive social change. Managerial offerings towards participation in managerial and decision making processes are issued under conditions of instrumental action that predominantly serve system integrative goals.

To avoid such system integrative forms of communication, often hidden in the guise of managerially guided participation in joint-committees and the like, labour needs to set up domains that are separate from those already infiltrated by the colonisation of distorted communication based on instrumental rationality as well as by the distortions provided through corporate mass media and managerialism. Only such an autonomous domain, independent from management, is able to preserve authentic individuality and reject managerialism's drive towards one-dimensionality so that forms of communicative action can be established independent from management and managerialism. This domain should be designed to include a number of elements as opposed to managerialism's one-dimensionality.[487]

The core of labour's self-preservation lies in the construction of a communicative domain that is independent from management as outlined in

Table 13.3 Core Elements for an Autonomous & Communicative Domain

	Labour's Autonomous & Communicative Domain	One-dimensional & Managerial Domain
i)	Labour's ability to think and act autonomously and critically that is directed towards emancipation;	Managerial domination of thought, communication, and behaviour;
ii)	Free from all forms of managerial domination;	Servitude to managerial control and conditioning;
iii)	Freedom of self-determination, critical-rational choice, dissent, and refusal;	Conformity, affirmation, false needs & false need hierarchies, managerial conscious;
iv)	Creative communication and self-activity directed towards social growth and development;	Mimesis: apparatus, mechanical, Panopticon, and the reproduction of conformist behaviour;
v)	Reflective & critical awareness of labour's needs not trapped in *what is* but directed to *what ought to be*;	Uncritical and affirmative acceptance of managerial needs as universal needs;
vi)	Sense of labour's power and selfhood;	Sense of managerial power;
vii)	Labour's power and independent and self-conscious will formation;	Managerially induced acceptance of powerlessness & conditioned behaviour;
viii)	Labour's ability of communicative action and social action.	Management's ability of instrumental communication & profit-directed means-ends action.

Table 13.3. In contrast to the infiltrative powers of managerial behaviour enshrined in hierarchies and authoritarian communication structures, labour's domain needs to be constructed on principles based on communication and action that is autonomous of management and managerialism (13.3[i]). It can only function as a truly communicative domain when it is isolated against managerial forms of control and conditioning and when system integration is replaced with a form of social integration that allows members of the domain to integrate socially rather than systematically through a managerial system (13.3[ii]).[488] The new domain needs to include the freedom of self-determination independent from a domain in which humans are managerially determined as functions – human resources, human material, objects of power – inside a confined system of alienation (13.3[iii]).[489]

Individual creativity is almost by definition excluded from a domain that is organised mechanically and directed towards one-dimensional so-called organisational goals [=profit]. If creativity is not avoided, it is at least re-directed away from humans and towards the same one-dimensional organisational goals. In the labour domain, however, creativity is directed towards the human goals of social and individual advancement (13.3[iv]). This demands that human creativity, interests, and needs not be trapped in Kant's *what is* but are directed towards what *ought to be*. They should also not be directed towards a false hierarchy of managerial needs often declared to be universal when in reality they are partial (13.3^v). The sense of an all-encompassing managerial power has to be overcome and replaced with a sense of labour's selfhood and self-awareness so that communication inside the labour domain can move from being labour *in* itself towards labour *for* itself (13.3^{vi}). Communicatively established self-consciousness and independent will formation in the labour domain can overcome one of managerialism's core ideologies, the feeling of powerlessness and helplessness (13.3^{vii}). Finally, only an independent or autonomous domain that excludes management and its ideology of managerialism is able to establish communicative action so that ideal speech acts are no longer guided by instrumental communication based on managerial means-ends dogmas (13.3^{viii}). In sum, labour's communicative ability can only flourish if a communicative forum is constructed that is independent from management as communicative forms inside the managerial domain are contaminated by instrumental rationality that redirects communication away from human communication and towards managerial communication.

The ethics of communicative action in the labour domain

As much as management is linked to instrumental rationality that serves goal achieving purposes, labour – free from such constraints – is able to direct communicative action under conditions of ideal speech towards positive social change. In doing so, labour can claim to use forms of discourse that are ethically superior to managerial forms of discussions which operate *restrictive* rather than *elaborative*. Labour can convincingly demonstrate that its elaborative forms of communication can overcome *restrictive codes* of managerially guided communication that has been narrowed to allowing only *simple sentences, limited and inexplicit means of referring to things, lack of abstraction and lack of self-reference* (Chilton 1983:36). Using communicative action allows labour to demonstrate that it can reach higher moral levels than managerialism's confinement inside the restrictive code.[490] This code of managerial communication only provides an institutional framework for the unethical enforcement of rules as these rules have not been established via common agreement inside the framework of communicative action. Restrictive codes and non-communicatively established rules that govern communication at work are deeply enshrined in a managerial framework designed to limit communicative abilities and prevent any move towards communication that overcomes management's *restrictive code* by cementing managerial rules that govern forms of communication. This not only locks communication inside the *restrictive code* but also restricts any moves to use elaborative codes directed towards communicative action.

Almost by definition, managerial communication must reduce communication to an understanding of *how*, restricting labour's understanding of *why*. Under such restrictions, labour's communicative participation is managerially pre-designed to understand the world of work as a managerial world. Labour is guided to internalise this in order to prevent the development of their potentials for communicative and social action. Therefore labour's ethically based ability for communicative action needs to be separated from managerial means-ends versions of non-ethical communication.[491] Once ethical discourse is constructed separate from the colonising effects of management, communicative action can occur under a specific set of formulations. These are enshrined in the demands issued by ideal speech. Only if these demands are fulfilled, ideal speech situations can become operative.

The idea of communicative action has never set parameters on how to establish ideal speech. There are no conditions in a cookbook like fashion and there is definitely no *one best way* as many managerial books are suggesting. By not issuing a simplistic solution for simplistic problems written by simplistic writers, the concept of communicative action avoids many falsehoods of managerial consultants – *We have the answer to your problems* – management training courses, MBA-programmes and the like.[492] There are also no *easy-guides* for management-labour relations. Despite their promises, all of these guides have continuously failed to deliver.[493] Illusionary promises are to be avoided simply because there is no defined set of specific natural rules that solve complex and, above all, human made problems in the world of work.

Defined sets of parameters favouring a particular institutional form over another should be excluded in the same way as any statements that contain connotations to paternalism, such as *we know what is good for your business!* While communicative action under conditions of ideal speech cannot be tailored and packaged in a ready-to-be-picked-up way, some universal parameters can assist the process that discusses and introduces communicatively created rules for discourse establishment. In sharp contrast to strategic managerial communication under conditions of instrumental rationality, communicative action does not seek to pre-determine any outcomes between human actors.[494] There is a distinct absence of pre-set goals, communicative KPIs, pre-designed achievements, agendas to be completed, etc. In these discourses each participant has equal rights of access to the discourse over how to establish forms of ethical speech situations. General assistance towards the establishment of non-hierarchical discourse forums can however be provided as communicative action is not a form of total *laissez-faire* approach.

The ethics of communicative action lies in ethical parameters that support a form of communication that allows participants to engage in non-hierarchical and domination-free dialogues. This assists labour, more than management, in their quest to establish ideal speech. The concept of applying the principles of universal and ethical communication to work leads to a practical-ethical discourse. Unlike management's instrumental communication that emphasises on *practical* communication, labour's communicative action focuses on *ethical* communication. In the managerial version of communication a dichotomy between *practical* versus *ethical* communication is constructed that is in some cases even artificially manufactured as a dilemma between both. In sharp contrast, labour's communicative action will always assign the only ethically possible premise – that of communicative ethics – over practicality. Communication on a higher ethical level than the one provided by management's instrumental communication has to subsume all forms of communication under ethical consideration.[495] Ethical communication cannot be asphyxiated in means-ends structures, in instrumental rationality, in *what is* rather than *what ought to be*, in falsehoods such as *getting on with the job*, etc. Any form of ethical communication has to break the unethical confinements of *means* and must elevate communication to the level of *ends*. It rejects ideas such as management is *getting things done through people* in which people are reduced to a *means*. In a Kantian world of human ethics people can never be reduced to *means*; they are always considered as *ends*. Herein lies the difference in the unethical approach of Human Resource Management that views humans almost exclusively as material, as resources, and as means to achieve organisational goals. Similar to Kantian human ethics, ethical communication treats communication not as a *means* – to achieve organisational goals, profits and the like – but as an *end* in itself. This establishes communication as a fundamentally ethical issue that regulates the way in which humans relate to each other.

Under managerialism the terms ethics, business ethics, morality, and even *corporate social responsibility* have only been introduced to eclipse the social and economical asymmetries operative at work as they provide enough ideological and communicative distortions to eliminate all truly ethical claims from the domain of work. The intrinsic meaning of ethical communication, however, is designed to highlight communicative distortions and uncover hidden base issues of a managerial system that is economically and humanly unethical and that results in unethical communication based on authoritarian, non-democratic and asymmetrical power. This comes at no surprise, as management is the sole actor who guides a system representing the dominant economic interest in present society. Above the economic base structure – managed by management – a political, legal, and ideological structure guided by managerialism is erected. This superstructure has been assigned with the task to deny all forms of ethical communication while at the same time it eclipses many unethical issues created by the system with the pretence of being ethical. The unethical existence of managerialism deeply influences the management of labour at work and vice versa. In much the same way managerialism guides communication at work that is also not subsumed under the demands of ethics but designed to prevent any form of communication that could assist a process in which human consciousness could be shaped through a critical-ethical analysis of human's social existence. The managerially restructured process of distorted communication eclipses all accesses to contradictions and unethically steered elements of the system and prevents a movement in which human consciousness is determined by their objective existence in the world of work. Instead every effort – conditioned reward systems, communicative distortions, etc. – is made to prevent such self-enlightening and ethical forms of communication.

This system prevents morality and ethics to be seen as independent from the imperatives of the managerial system and autonomous of forms of communication that come with this system in the world of work. Both morality and ethical communication are inextricably linked to the management mode of corporate life as well as to the ideological apparatus established and guided through managerialism above the level of corporate existence. The interplay of ethics between managerially guided *base* and *superstructure* can be linked to the way economic affairs are distributed and guided. The ethics of the ruling class are the ruling ethics in every epoch; the class – slave-, land- and eventually business-owners – that is ruling the *material* forces of society is at the same time its ruling *ethical* force. The managerial and business-owner class that has the means of *material* production [corporations] at its disposal, consequently also controls the means of *mental, ideological,* and *communicative* production and re-production [corporate mass media], so that the ethics of those who lack the means of ideological and communicative production and re-production are on the whole subjected to it. The ruling ethics are nothing more than the ethical expressions of the dominant material relations grasped as ethics. The relations that make the one class the ruling one always represent the perpetrated *ethics* of this dominance.[496]

In society, ruling ethics that guide mass-communication are designed for an illusionary community with an equally illusionary general interest to re-direct human desire for an ethically structured communicative domain towards a corporate mass media domain that provides steering ethics for all members of society. In the world of work, the ruling ethics guide managerially induced instrumental communication – designed for all organisational members with the general interest to re-direct labour's desire for ethically structured communication – towards the managerially guided domain of instrumental communication that issues corporate ethics for all members of the world of work. In both domains those who represent the ruling ethics also define ethical communication. The pretended ethics is designed to give individuals misguided beliefs and values that are established on the basis of instrumental communication in the world of work and on the basis of distorted communication through corporate mass media. Without any grounding in ethical communication, the values, morals and ethics in both domains – work and re-productive domain – are established normatively through asymmetrical and unethical power structures. These are not the ethics of human society and human work arrangements but represent a form of distorted ethics.

Even though the ethics of both present domains are normatively, not communicatively grounded, the domains are covered by ethical considerations, foremost by Kant's *categorical imperative*.[497] The value of Kant's idea lies in the basics of ethics that has guided the behaviour between humans ever since human society was established. Throughout human history, tribal leaders, kings, priests, churches and the like have developed ethical codes of conduct. In contrast to these codes, communicative ethics seeks to establish a code of behaviour that is no longer based on philosophy, politics, economic determinants, etc. but on communicative means, i.e. communicative action so that moral agents – humans – are free to establish a moral code for themselves. This moves ethics from being established *for* humans to being developed *by* humans. It advances everyday communication at work to ethical levels as dialogues are conducted under conditions of communicative action. The philosophical idea of ethics becomes the idea of social action enshrined in communicative action. It is no longer enough to accept a given ethics developed by someone somewhere; from now on, ethics of society and work can only be developed through participation in communicative action and mutual agreement that is achieved under the strict conditions of ideal speech.

Ethics based on communicative action has moved beyond the *egocentric* viewpoint of traditional philosophy and those who have tried to develop ethics *for* others.[498] In this way, ethics is no longer justified by philosophical arguments (Singer 1994) but developed out of a communicative process.[499] This process is philosophically closer to Hegelian dialectics, operative as thesis→anti-thesis→synthesis and to Karl Marx who sought to supersede (aufheben) philosophy by realising it in communicative action (Habermas). The combined ideas of Hegel, Marx, and Habermas end the traditional division of labour between ethical philosophy and humans.[500] Under the ethical conditions of communicative action not only the division of labour between philosophy and everyday life but also between philosophy and science (managerial or otherwise) becomes untenable. This means that Kant's idea of *everything in modernity must be exposed to critique* becomes an imperative for ethical dialogue. Philosophy, science, work experiences and critical reasoning merge inside the ethical requirement of communicative action. Reason freed from constrains of instrumentality and directed towards its truthful critical-emancipatory potentials can no longer be split into modern science, positive regulation, and ethics and traditional isolations between science, morality, and art can no longer prevail in the same way as the compartmentalisation of work into issues such as management, labour studies, organisational theory, and the like. As much as nothing can be excluded from the communicative power of ethical debates, nothing can be excluded from critical-emancipatory examination.

Reaching understanding on these ethical and practical issues demands a fundamental change of the way in which people in the world of work communicate. Long-held cultural traditions and cemented power structures have to be overcome across the whole spectrum of communication at work.

Every agreement has to be reached communicatively on the grounds of ethical and critical-emancipatory reasoning.[501] One of the first conditions that have to be met is the requirement to establish a social – not only a communicative – relationship between participants of communicative action. Such speakers do not only express their own beliefs but also simultaneously seek the affirmation of *all* other participants in the process. Inside this framework, speech acts serve three functions: a) they critically and ethically reproduce societal traditions, b) they create social – not system – integration among discourse participants,[502] and c) they establish new – ethically grounded – interpretive frameworks and new interpretations of work.[503] Commonly established understanding is not only reached by observation and listening but through active participation in the form of a speech *act*, i.e. through communicative *action*.[504] Such ethical communication is about *what to do* and as such always includes an element of what *ought to be,* transcending the objective reality of work affairs – *what is* – through communicative action.

Forms of communication under communicative action have to be conducted under the ethical demand of the better argument where the *force* of the better argument is no *longer a force* but directed towards achieving social and communicative affirmation among participants.[505] Statements are issued in a truthful, sincere, non-deceptive, and non-manipulative way with the intention of a *yes/no* response directed towards common agreement. Without the ability of participants to engage in *yes/no* responses freely and unhindered by any power structures, consent and mutual agreement remain partial and incomplete. The idea is that *only those* [ethical] *norms can claim to be valid that meet (or could meet) with the approval of all affected in their capacity as participants in ethical discourse.*[506] Communicatively established rules – such as *the approval of all affected* – are not mere conventions or customary habits; they are an absolute inescapable presupposition for communicative action. Only those moral norms, common agreements, and plans for social action can be deemed ethically valid that have met the consent of all participants. To achieve this, the morally judging subjects in such discourse must be able to put themselves in the position of all those who would be affected by the proposed action plan. Habermas (1990:198) emphasised such a *discourse can also be viewed as a communicative process simultaneously exhorting 'all' participants to ideal role taking.* This role-taking ability has to be extended to a general assumption that goes well beyond the perceptions of the immediate participants in communicative action. In that way, ethical communication provides a somewhat built-in procedure that ensures participants' awareness of ethics and this somewhat universal-ethical demand necessarily always encompasses an element of Kantian *what ought to be.*

14
Practical Conclusions

A universal and practical discourse forum

The following section will discuss the five key elements of universal and practical discourse in greater detail, starting with rules that can govern participation on communicative action. The second part issues general ideas about communicative rationality while the third section deals with communicatively established rules for such discourse forums. The final two parts discuss feelings and attitudes as well as time and places for the establishment of ideal speech situations followed by an outline of possibilities to draft workable discourse forums. These will provide a real and hands-on solution to establish communicative action at work.

i) Participation

Participants should not be prevented from participating in the discourse and their statements should not be hindered.[507] However, there are limits to the size of a discourse forum. If too many participants are included in a forum, discussions can become unworkable as individuals are unable to fully participate. A discourse forum should not become an undifferentiated crowd of people as this might have a destructive influence on the discourse. Those who seek to participate in a discourse based on ideal speech should have valid reasons to do so and be able to justify these. They should provide a sincere, genuine, and authentic interest in the discourse forum. However participation is not an end in itself. Discourse pragmatics demands that those with a justifiable interest in taking part in a discourse should not be prevented to participate and no one should assume a position based on privileges or power structures.

ii) Communicative rationality

While discourse forums can be established at work, they need to exclude any colonisation via system imperatives that hinder ideal speech. In such forums, communicative rationality should be applied when making statements during a discourse.[508] These statements should subscribe to the demands issued by ideal speech. Participants in discourses at work should try to come to an understanding about appropriate speech acts that serve discussions directed towards communicative understanding. Communication should also be based on a requirement that focuses on ethical relevancy which means that communicative action can only be established when dialogues are based on an ethical awareness that needs to be linked to Kohlberg's (1981 & 1984) ideas of moral development.

iii) Communicatively established rules for a discourse forum

Commonly achieved understanding can only be reached in an open and fair exchange of ideas. Rules and procedures for such a discussion should subscribe to the pragmatics of argumentation.[509] Communicatively established rules on ideal speech need to have moral substance. All participants can raise problematic statements as long as they can support them and these statements are linked to the discourse. Overall, rules supporting ideal speech at or about work should be comprehensible and understood by all members of a discourse group. It is relevant for work-participants that they constitute a discourse forum through their own participation. Once discourse participants have communicatively reached an understanding and established the rules, these should be applied consistently. At the same time, participants need to be able to change rules if a demand to do so has been issued. This is the same demand that guides all forms of ideal speech. Changes on rules can only occur when *all* participants have reached an understanding on the change.

iv) Feelings and attitudes

Any participant in a discourse forum can – at any time – issue new claims into the discourse, much in the same way as they can introduce the expression about their own views, attitudes, desires, wishes, needs, etc. Not only should they be able to express their own opinion but also interpret that of others. On valid grounds, these views, attitudes, etc. can be opposed or supported. By issuing their views and attitudes, participants can enter into a discourse. Their views need to stand up to previously issued arguments by other participants but if they do not, participants must be asked to explain their arguments further. Speech participation must reflect on an inviolability of discourse contributors. All issued statements during the course of a discourse should be viewed with respect and treated in a non-judgmental way.

v) Time and places

Limitations of time, space, place, and resources should be eliminated as much as possible in order to establish a discourse. Today's world of work is closer than ever linked to time sequences, time management, and time constraints. However, work related discourse under conditions of ideal speech can occur at work as well as off work. An off-work discourse is a more likely scenario as it is more likely to be free of system imperatives that have potentials for colonisation that hinder ideal speech.

Drafting a workable discourse forum

At a much more tangible level, the five demands issued above can be converted into more workable elements by creating some basic principles for ideal speech. The drafting of such principles that support discourse can be divided into nine sub-sections (1–9).

Table 14.1 shows the seven principles as an overview that will be outlined in detail. They are not a once-and-for-all set recipe to be followed in order to establish ideal speech situations but a general guide for participants on communicative action.

1) Forum layouts

The ideal layout (Table 14.1[a]) for discussion forums suggests an assembling of representative and competent participants in specific forums in order to enhance the quality of discourse. This coming together should be guided by a common interest in the quality of the discourse which should, however, not suffer from a random inclusion of any or too many participants. The quality demand also translates into the exclusion of all power plays, hidden or otherwise. A forum can be designed to work on problems of practical-ethical judgement and normative-substantive discussions. There is also an option to set up different discourse forums to work on the same or similar problems in order to compare outcomes once each discourse forum has reached common understanding. The same applies to discourse forums that are split into smaller groups to work on different or similar problems. Each of these organisational forms of discourse forums should be subject to communicatively reached understanding. This is the guiding principle for all discourse forums or sub-units. A group of participants in such forums or sub-forums may decide to consult with outside experts when necessary. This

Table 14.1 Seven Basic Principles for Ideal Speech

No.	Basic Principles for Ideal Speech
i)	forum work layouts,
ii)	moderators and speakers,
iii)	different skills and levels of knowledge,
iv)	contract zones,
v)	speech rules,
vi)	methods of ideal speech, and
vii)	principle vs. case orientation & the danger of group thinking

may only happen after an agreement on such experts inside the discourse forum has been reached.

2) Moderators and speakers

A capable, competent and responsible speaker or moderator can be chosen as an independent voice (Table 14.1[b]). This serves the establishment of a somewhat more *neutral* or *impartial* person in the discourse forum. Since such a person should not assume a decisive position of power over other participants, the key is to find a person that supports communicative action directed towards understanding. The moderator or speaker should not be a leader or move into a leadership position as ideal speech demands horizontal, not vertical level discussions. The introduction of any kind of hierarchy is to be avoided. Therefore, such a person should be prevented from moving into a position of negotiator, expert, ruler, judge, etc. In sharp contrast to a new leader, a moderator should oversee communicatively established rules of the discourse forum, foster open discourse and not seek personal preferences. In some instances, this person can even assume the role of a *devil's advocate* in order to stimulate the discourse forum.

3) Different skills and levels of knowledge

Whenever one participant is treated differently from another, the reason for this must be explained and communicatively established agreement on such un-equal treatment sought (Table 14.1[c]). Reasons for different treatment of participants can include un-equal experiences or backgrounds which can lead to asymmetric power relations in a discourse forum. This has to be avoided and the fundamental principle of equal participation must be enforced. Despite disparities and differences in levels of knowledge and skills among participants any utilisation of special interests should be limited and can only occur inside communicatively established rules. On the other hand, a person or interest group inside a discourse forum should not be excluded because of their different skills or knowledge.

4) Contract zones & vetoes

One option is the introduction of a *contract zone* as a set of decisions that are supported by all participants (Table 14.1[d]). Contract zones can be established when an agreement cannot be made communicatively. They enable a discourse forum to go forward in the case of non-agreeable situations. Any discourse can lead to non-conclusive outcomes. In such cases, *contract zones* provide a preliminary outcome that can, at a later stage, be re-examined by a subsequent discourse forum. Such subsequent discourse forums or *contract zones* can be vital for the communicative process but only if participants have reached an agreement about the introduction and use of the contract zones. This is the case when non-conclusive outcomes occur due to a veto. A *right of veto* can function as a *trump* in any discourse forum. The strongest advantage of a *right to veto* can be found in the power to protect minority voices. Here, it is able to block a majority decision via the right of the minority. It forces discourse to focus on finding common agreement that is communicatively established and denies the majority to over-rule the minority. On the negative side, a *right to veto* can block a discourse forum and hinder its workability by effectively preventing positive outcomes. In some cases, it can lend enormous and even unreasonable power to a rather insignificant viewpoint issued by a participant or a relatively small group of participants. However, a *right to veto* provision can also lead to a rational discourse as everyone is aware of such relatively strong powers that carry possibilities of disabling or delaying common agreement. As such, the right to veto should be used carefully as it can point in the opposite direction of a communicatively established agreement. Finally, it only serves a purpose when a communicatively established understanding has failed and communicative action could not be established. More than anything, a *right of veto* provision is an indicator for a discourse forum that has already left behind ideal speech and communicative action and is moving closer to social action.[510]

5) Speech rules

In discourse forums and during the formulation of arguments, participants should not contradict themselves (Table 14.1[e]). In the same way, each participant should only communicate about those issues that carry connotations to their personal interests, seriousness and beliefs that morally support the argument. All participants who aim to apply a predicate X to an object *1* must also be prepared to apply X to every other object that contains similar elements as expressed in *1* in all relevant occasions. Finally, different participants should not articulate the same expression with different meaning as a definite link between expression and meaning must be coherently presented.

6) Methods of ideal speech

A participant of a discourse forum who attacks the statement of another participant or an already established norm or code of conduct that is not subject to the discourse must explain the reason for doing so (Table 14.1[f]). Only when such an attack is supported through communicatively established agreement, it can become part of a discourse. Otherwise, the attack has to be withdrawn. Whenever a participant is issuing a new argument or statement, s/he is only requested to produce further arguments on the subject matter if counter-arguments have been issued by other participants.

7) Principles vs case orientation & the danger of group thinking

Finally, there are issues related to the participants and their interests (Table 14.1[g]). Participants have to apply certain options and criteria to discuss issues objectively. These basic rules can assist the establishment of discourse

Table 14.2 Basic Rules Assisting the Structuring of Discourse

Level	Forms
(i) People	Separate the people from the problem.
(ii) Interests	Focus on interests, not on positions.
(iii) Options	Invent options for mutual gain.
(iv) Criteria	Insist on using objective criteria.

forums (Table 14.2).[511] They are related to the participants of such forums (Table 14.2^i) as well as to their interests (Table 14.2^{ii}) and opinions (Table 14.2^{iii}) and finally to the application of objective criteria during discourses (Table 14.2^{iv}).

Table 14.2$^{(i–iv)}$ shows the four basic rules for discussion in discourse forums that are important in assisting the establishment of conditions supportive of ideal speech. The first rule suggests that communicative action can be established when participants focus on issues rather than on people. Ideal speech situations are designed to follow a set of communicative rationalities that are enhanced when discourses focus on the issues at hand. Secondly, while the overall interest of an ideal speech situation is directed towards achieving communicatively established understanding, ideal speech is not achieved by *winning* or *losing* an argument. Discourse is never about *having* an opinion as it lives from argumentative exchanges rather than from a view that turns an argument or claim into something that is *owned* by someone. Arguments are, therefore, not seen as a position or an object that can be lost. Ideal speech is about finding common understanding through interest mediation.

Thirdly, options for mutual gains should be established as they are able to enhance discourse. Within ideal speech situations there are several mutual gains to be made along the way to establish common understanding. These should be utilised to the fullest extent. Finally, there should also be a focus on using objective criteria. The idea is not the denial of subjectivity but a reduction of bias and irrational preferences. All of this, however, might still not be enough to prevent one of the greatest dangers of such forums, commonly known as *group thinking*.

Group thinking is a version of group dynamics commonly regarded as having negative connotations.[512] It can develop inside isolated groups that are established as close forums (Janis 1982). Such groups operate as social groups in which highly pathological social behaviour determines wrong outcomes of discussions. *Group thinking* is a social, psychological and pathological, not a linguistic phenomenon. Because of its dangerous and largely negative effects, participants of communicative action need to be guarded against it. Janis (1982) has established several useful rules that support discourse forums governed by ideal speech and are able to reduce or avoid *group thinking*. Each participant should critically assess a discourse forum's course of action. In an open and fair forum, a climate of open criticism should be as much encouraged as the ability to accept such criticism. One of the best guards against *group thinking* is mutually acceptable critique – Kant's dictum *in modernity everything has to be exposed to criticism* and Hegel's idea of dialectic. Under dialectical thinking, a discourse issue has to be presented as *thesis* or *theme* but also needs to be exposed to a *counter-theme*. This is what Hegel saw as anti-thesis. Together with Kant's *what is* and *what ought to be*, they result in Hegel's synthesis. Participants in discourses as much as discourse moderators need to assess discourse claims in the light of this.

In addition, discussion moderators should be impartial and refrain from stating personal preferences. Separate working groups might be set up to discuss separate questions utilising the option to bring in divergent view points. Sub-groups might also be established in such cases and external and internal experts and counter-experts can be invited into these groups. They can play *the devil's advocate*. This is particularly useful as it breaks the negative cycle of internal group dynamics that can lead to *group thinking*. The external voices can be used as strong support for discourse. Finally, extra time allocation might solve conflicting issues that demand the construction of alternative meanings.

8) Forms of agreements: full, working, mini, and quasi

Full agreement can be reached once discourse participants are in mutual understanding about an issue and have reached a commonly established platform for consensual agreement. However, there might be cases when full agreement is not possible. As a measure to build provisional or preliminary consensus the introduction of *working agreements* may be considered. Such an agreement is seen as a somewhat under-theorised and under-justified agreement as common understanding is not at its centre. It is, however, supported by arguments reflecting communicative and normative qualities and values.

The lower level of *mutual acceptance* can provide a foundation for a working agreement. In this case, the strength of ideal speech is somewhat weakened as the level of support moves downward from mutual *understanding* to mere *acceptance* while the likelihood of reaching agreement improves. In other words, the level of reaching agreement moves upward even though such a working agreement has a lower level of support compared to a full agreement. *Mini*-consensus is reached when discourse participants come to an intermediate conclusion through the exclusion of disagreements. This form of dialogue emphasises on positives directed towards agreeable issues. This is not to say that conflicting issues are avoided; rather the opposite is the case. Conflicting issues need to be part of any discourse as they are very important in moving it forward. Similarly, a *quasi*-agreement can be reached when discourse participants are not able to reach mutual understanding but are aware of the reasons why. Such an agreement on the cause of disagreements can then be used as a foundation for further discussions to

Table 14.3 Five Levels of Discursive Agreements

Level of Agreement	Type of Agreement	Description of Agreement
1	Communicative Action	Established understanding that converts into social action
2	Consensual Agreement	Consensual understanding on direction of social action
3	Working Agreement	Preliminary understanding demanding further discourse
4	Mini – Consensus	Exclusion of disagreements and focus on agreeable issues
5	Quasi – Consensus	Consensus on reason for disagreements, demands discourse

reach a full agreement by overcoming previous disagreements. These different levels of agreement can be shown in an upward scale.

Table 14.3 shows an upward scale of discursive tools that can be applied to move towards a level of mutual understanding that translates into social action.[513] Stage three to five are only interim levels of consensual agreements that demand further discourse. Level one and two provide a borderline between communicatively established consensus that reaches an agreement on the direction of social action and social action itself (14.3^1).

While discourses at level three to five carry strong connotations of ideal speech, those at level two and one switch from communication to communicatively established action. Table 14.3 is not to be seen as a model with stages that have to be passed in order to reach level one. It needs to be understood as an indicator that discourses can occur at different levels with the ultimate goal of a communicative understanding that fulfils the demands of ideal speech (14.3^1). Nor does it indicate that passing one level takes discourse participants automatically into the next stage, or that participants might skip one or several levels. There may be situations where discourse participants enter a discourse at level two and proceed to level one. In other cases they might only reach one of the preliminary levels of discourse. Participants however need to communicate further to reach level one and overcome all existing internal conflicts. During all stages listed in Table 14.3 conflicts among participants can arise even though they should decrease as discourse moves upwards towards level one. At level one, communicative action is not conflict oriented but conducted in a way to achieve communicative understanding.

9) Conflict resolutions

Conflicts among participants can occur in many forms of group discussions and discourses. Disagreements are standard occurrences and often have two possible sources. Firstly, one or several participants may indicate interpretive differences that appear unsolvable or secondly, discourse participants have different preferences over the outcome of a discourse. This can be the case when different interests meet. In management-labour relations differing interests are inherent in almost every communicative relationship between both. This often leads to asymmetrical communication based on hierarchy, domination, and power which are forms of instrumental communication rather than communicative action. There are structural determinants that hinder attempts by discourse participants to move towards an ideal speech situation. When compared to other communicative settings, they are more likely to lead to disagreements. It is by far easier to achieve communicative action and ideal speech when the labour and management domains are separated as this avoids many of the colonisation attempts and reduces communicative distortions. Only when the labour domain is established independent of the managerial domain, it can remain free from colonisation and communicative distortions.

Discourse-participants in the labour domain often spend considerable time on discussions to interpret reality. This is necessary as different discourse participants interpret reality in different ways despite having similar interests. This affects discourse participants in the management domain to a much lower degree as they are supported by the prevailing ideology of managerialism. Because of ideological colonisation, reality in the labour domain is often distorted while management experiences managerial ideology as supportive.

Serious conflicts are more likely to arise when participants from both domains leave their respective domains and meet in the exchange domain of management-labour forums. Here, conflict resolution is much harder as underlying differences in interest play a larger role. Within the labour or management domain discourse participants are by far more able to reach similar understanding as disagreements can more easily be overcome through rational consensus formation.

In the labour domain, there is a higher need to discuss *how* labour should act and what kind of means should be used to establish communicative action directed towards social goals. Once such goals are agreed upon, discourse participants can discuss how communicative action translates into social action. At this stage clarification of *means* can be reached through *pragmatic discourse* that focuses on rather *mechanical* issues without neglecting ethical issues.[514] The reflection on ethical issues in accordance with Kohlberg (1981 & 1984) is essential. Ethical discourse is always in demand, especially when disagreements over collective goals are discussed, and needs to be linked to the discourse participants' values. A classical form of pragmatic discourse can be found in instrumental wage bargaining between labour and management.[515] Here, labour seeks to reach the best possible outcome achievable under conditions often not set by labour and therefore pragmatic discourse is enhanced through *ethical-political discourse* in a process that seeks hermeneutical understandings on meanings and interpretations. In contrast to members of the management domain, members of the labour domain must always seek to combine or mediate between several viewpoints. This demands that any discussion includes elements of *ethical-pragmatic discourse* and is also linked to a discussion reflective of an *ethical-political discourse*. Practical, ethical, and realistic solutions cannot be separated from agreements on meanings, interpretations, and the means of achieving social goals. Disconnecting *pragmatic* from *ethical-political* discourses will not lead to conflict resolution inside the labour domain and cannot move a discourse towards communicative action.

Much in the same way as *pragmatic* and *ethical-political* discourses need to be linked, consideration of moral issues – *moral discourse* – cannot be excluded from labour's discourses either. Unlike management, labour's discourse demands a linkage between all three forms of discourse. They are of utmost relevance in order to establish communicative action. Labour's discussions under *moral discourse*s are geared towards reaching understanding under conditions that include ethical provisions. This allows the interests of all discourse participants to play an equal role in the establishment of communicative action for positive social change. While conflict resolution in the management domain can focus on pragmatic issues without taking ethical-political discourse into account, labour does not *add* value because moral and ethical values are inherent in any discourse. They are never a simple *add-on* like the values attached to instrumental discussions in the managerial domain. Non-ethical discourse in the labour domain is impossible as there is no pretence of *value neutrality* and much in the same way, there cannot be a process of *adding* values to a discourse. In the labour domain, all discourses have to be ethical discourses. They can move towards a pragmatic, an ethical-political or a moral discourse but can never neglect either one of these three forms of discourse. Conflict resolution in labour's domain is fundamentally different from conflict resolution in the management domain. Management can – and often does – move outside the pragmatic, ethical-political, and moral discourse triangle.

There are however exceptions to these rules, as even a perfect application of all rules and discourse aids does not necessarily prevent a communicative failure for labour. Firstly, there is the issue of *bounded rationality*. The labour domain is set in sharp contrast to the neo-liberal and economic rationalist view. It does not operate under the false equation of perfect access to information leading to perfect decisions. Instead, participants in the labour domain are aware that:

- neither a socially constructed society
- nor a socially constructed company
- nor a socially constructed workplace

offer perfect access to all available information. Therefore, an economic-rational view based on instrumental rationality is structurally impossible.

When ideal speech participants reach common understanding about the structural impossibilities of managerial communication, serious doubts about perfection of managerial solutions can be raised. This common understanding has particularly serious consequences. Today management and managerialism tend to follow the ideology of economic *'ir'*rationalism. This belief system denotes a worldview that seeks perfect models. In the mind of the so-called *rationalists*, these are perfect models but imperfect realities. In sharp contrast to the ideological trappings of managerialism, labour is much freer in admitting imperfections and incomplete solutions that are the result of a socially constructed world based on a less demanding ideological content of their views. Consequently, bounded rationality aspects can more openly deal with these imperfections.[516] Labour is able to overcome *bounded rationality* by gaining a realistic and critical view of information access where information is examined for possible ideological contents and deformities of economic irrationalism. Labour can identify the shortcomings of irrational assumptions on pathological models. One of the most prevalent models is the following equation:

---

perfect information access → perfect discourses → perfect solutions

---

Figure 14.1 Perfect Information and Perfect Solutions

Labour's awareness of *bounded rationality* enables them to critically analyse discourse by examining their own abilities. Without such self-reflective analysis all discourses are somewhat limited. Often the impediments are linked to imperfect access to the totality of available information. Being aware of these limitations does not weaken labour's ability but strengthens it as *bounded rationality* concerns enter labour's discourse. Awareness of these fallacies enables labour – often more than management – to see the imperfections in reality and instrumental rationality.

As much as standard social science and traditional communication science seek to deliver unfaultable recommendations, they can fail.[517] Similarly, the rationality of discourse in the labour domain should not be taken as an absolute certainty. The aim of these recommendations and communicative aids is to assist labour in discourses geared towards positive social change using methods of communicative action. In many discussions inside the labour domain, the use of communicative action methods can still create dilemmas and these are often unsolvable.[518] One such example is the conflict between time-consuming communications to reach consensus versus demands for action. As discourses are often linked to considerable time constraints, discourse participants will be exposed to some form of unjust restrictions.

Table 14.4 lists some of the most severe restrictions often experienced during communicative action when conducted under conditions of ideal speech. As much as it is regrettable, some participants (i) have to be excluded from

Table 14.4 Elements Restricting Discourse

No.	Forms of Discourse Restrictions
i)	some voices will have to be excluded from discourses,
ii)	some discussions might be distorted even under conditions of ideal speech and communicative action,
iii)	even discourses under conditions of ideal speech might bring about unfair and unwarranted outcomes,
iv)	even discourses under conditions of ideal speech might still include unjust and unfair processes,
v)	even good discursive procedures and discourse participants that subscribe to ideal speech might consider their own discourse outcomes as bad but in such cases, these discourse participants can decide themselves whether such outcomes are valid or not,
vi)	as of yet, there is no procedure in place that automatically guarantees the correct results, and finally
vii)	a communicative process that is able to produce better common understanding geared towards positive social change than the concept of ideal speech under conditions of communicative action is not in sight.

discourse arrangements geared towards ideal speech. For example, participants interested in means-ends, instrumentalism, and instrumental communication may have to be excluded to fight colonisation attempts from other domains. Some forms of communication including communicative results might still carry elements of distortions (ii) even though some participants have already been excluded. In general, participants need to be aware of such system integrative attempts that seek to colonise ideal speech.[519] If successful, these attempts can convert communicative action into instrumental communication thus in many cases marking the end of an ideal speech situation.

As communication under conditions of ideal speech progresses, unfair, domineering, and unwarranted argumentations may still occur (iii). During the course of such discussions, participants need to intervene whenever they detect elements contradictory to the demands of ideal speech and exclude them as there is no guarantee for success in ideal speech situations (v). Even if conducted within all guidelines as outlined above, communicative action linked to ideal speech does not automatically guarantee successful achievements. The basic idea behind *ideal speech* is that it only sets parameters for discourse. It never determines the outcome and is not to be understood as assured. There is no inescapable or inevitable logic built into communication that necessarily or routinely will lead to certain outcomes. However, in sharp contrast to other forms of communication it is able to direct participants towards achieving a common and, above all, communicatively established understanding. From there, participants can convert communicative action into social action geared towards positive change (vii) at the workplace.

In sharp contrast to managerial institutions, workers and their communicative forums are able to establish conditions of ideal speech as demanded by Habermas.[520] In symmetrical ideal speech settings that are free from domination by market forces or management intervention, all participants have an equal chance to employ constructive, regulative, and representative speech acts free from distorted communication. Goals have to be established communicatively using the concept of ideal speech and all participants have an effective equality of chances to take part in the dialogue. Conditions for ideal speech situations are not linguistic but social in character. Workers can determine social and material conditions in a way that enables ideal speech situations to materialise.

To achieve conditions of ideal speech for a discussion on future actions, workers have to meet the following three vital conditions. Most significantly, they need to ensure that participants are able to determine the settings for communication. This is done through the involvement of participants in pre-communication planning and helps to set up communication under the demands of ideal speech. System integrative demands that seek to pre-determine discussions towards pre-set outcomes have to be avoided and all features of external and internal domination must be excluded.

Internal constraints are found in the unconscious reflection of hierarchies and other forms of domination prevalent in industrial settings. *External* constraints from managerial purposive or instrumental rationality – such as a managerial SWOT analysis aiming to identify actual and potential strengths, weaknesses, opportunities, and threats[521] – can also infiltrate or colonise ideal speech situations, confining communication to managerial techniques. This has to be avoided as it constructs boundaries of communication by hindering ideal speech. Such instruments pre-determine communication not only by shaping it but also by including some ideas and excluding others.

Lastly, general symmetric conditions have to be established so that the force of the better argument can flourish – in other words, conditions that seek to enhance a cooperative search for the truth.[522] Workers need to be able to raise problematic validity claims. At the same time participants need to be *relieved of the pressure of action and experience* (Habermas 1997). Discussions under conditions of ideal speech are not quick fixes or fast solutions. The goal remains to establish communicative agreement for social action. While communicative constraints have to be abolished, participants need to issue claims that must be defended by reason. This alone defines whether an argument rightfully stands or not. The final test of a claim lies in the virtue of convincing validity. Eventually all claims have to be either redeemed or rejected. This is the intrinsic property of all arguments that can be tested by other participants at any time in order to seek understanding among workers, lead to communicative consensus, and finally to social action.

Seeking consensus and social action can be seen as interrelated practices that move communicative action towards social action. Both also need to avoid communicative distortions and the colonisation of communication through pathologies and manipulations. Communicatively established understandings have to be within moral and ethical judgements that cannot be disassociated from social conventions and historical colorations of life. This is most clearly expressed in Kohlberg's (1981 & 1984) seven stages of moral development. Elevating moral standards in this way avoids pathologies and the colonisation of communication. Participants need to focus their attention towards ideal speech practices directed towards a revitalisation of possibilities for social action. Such discourses can uncover expressions that have so far been buried alive. Traditions of liberation and emancipation that have historically relied on potentials of resistance need to be reactivated and participants need to withdraw from instrumental communication and turn their intentions towards progressive forms of communication that are not neutral. They *move towards specific ends and all these ends are defined by the possibilities of ameliorating the human condition.*[523] Discourses and communication among labour as one social actor at work – away from a managerial or a hidden transcript – might however have to occur *off-stage* and beyond direct management surveillance to turn relations of *domination* into relations of *resistance*. Both domination and resistance have a dialectical closeness. The thesis of *domination* must incur the anti-thesis of *resistance* leading to the synthesis of positive social change. Social actors *at work* – through the assumption of a role as low-profile work- or study-groups – can create a dissident sub-culture beyond official power structures, freeing up communicative space in which undistorted communication is possible. Such a practice can be expressed as follows:

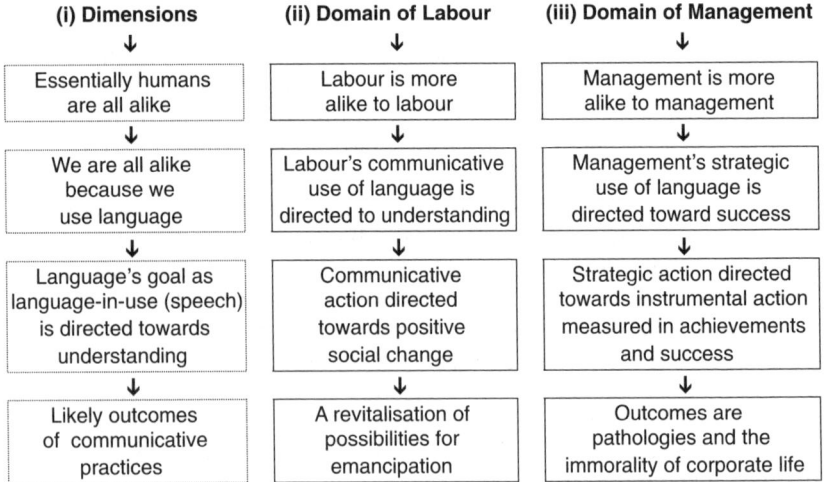

Figure 14.2 Four Inter-Related Dimensions of Ideal Speech Practice

The first column of Figure 14.2 shows the link between different levels of human action and communication (i) including the expected outcomes of different practices. These are applied to two domains: labour (ii) and management (iii). As both are more likely to be communicative inside their respective domains, communication carries connotations of these domains and the use of language is more likely to be similar within each of their respective domains.[524] Speech as language-in-use also relates differently inside each domain. In the labour domain, speech conducted as ideal speech is directed towards social change while under conditions of goal-achieving instrumental action it is directed towards measurable success. At the point of outcomes, ideal speech inherently manifests itself with potentials for emancipation from domination whereas instrumental forms of speech lead to fundamentally different outcomes to be seen in pathologies and the immorality of corporate life as goal-achieving strategies are not communicatively established. At workplace level, one of the clearest indicators of these pathologies is the fact that management is in constant need to readjust labour to the pathologies of corporate life. To eclipse these managerial pathologies, management has invented a raft of distortions that are used in relatively large sections of managerial communication. Any dissent is labelled *organisational misbehaviour*. In sharp contrast to managerial communication, communicative action and ideal speech act as some sort of *switching stations*. They create social and communicative energies and convert or redirect them towards social solidarity and positive social change.[525]

To conclude, the two logics of collective and communicative action have been able to uncover the fact that management's instrumental rationality is unable to establish conditions for ideal speech situations. On the other hand, workers' option to move beyond pre-structured communication is wide open. Communicative rationality and the establishment of ideal speech truly opens-up avenues for communicative action. Communicative forums for workers have to be established in a domination free environment that allows interactions through discourse organised by different groups of workers. Forms of such extended communication have to meet conditions for ideal speech and the search to reach understanding about social action must be common to all actors. However, the concept of consensus as a basic demand for workers' discussions on collective action is central to their formulation of future strategies. Once communicative consensus on social action is achieved, communicative action can be converted into social action that is directed towards positive social change.

Notes

1. Orwell's Nineteen Eighty-Four (1949).
2. See: Descartes (1628); Locke (1689a & 1689b); Kant (1781); Hegel (1807 & 1821); Marx (1846a&b, 1848 & 1890); Comte (1853); Lukacs (1923, 1971, 2000); Horkheimer (1937 & 1947); Popper (1965); Habermas (1985), Feyerabend (1981 & 1987); Rorty (1979 & 1982); Ingram (1991).
3. This has been expressed by Horkheimer's *Traditional and Critical Theory* (1937); Weber's *Science as a vocation* (1948); Popper's *The Logic of Scientific Discovery* (1965); and Fuller's *Kuhn vs. Popper: The Struggle of the Soul of Science* (2003).
4. Ever since Adam Smith (1759 & 1776), Hegel (1807 & 1821), Marx (1848), Taylor (1911), Weber (1924 & 1947), Marglin (1974) and others, the *division of labour* into labour and capital and later management has been well-known. Writers affirmative to managerialism – *The Servants of Power* (Baritz, 1960) – often pretend and present the world of work one-dimensionally as if it could only be seen from one – the managerial – point of view. This is done in spite of an all too often presented claim to be *value neutral*, *objective*, and *purely* scientific. Quite often management writers who are part of a hegemonic meaning structure do no more than testify that their writings are everything but *objective* and *scientific*. They rather represent – consciously or unconsciously – what has been defined as ideology, *knowledge in the service of power*. In this specific case, it is managerial knowledge in the service of management and managerialism to cement an asymmetrical power relationship that defined the division of labour ever since its analytical power highlighted a domineering power relationship between those who *are managed* and those *who manage*.
5. To teach managerial or business communication – a field known as *organisational communication* as if it were disconnected from human society and behaviour – is to pass on the same conceptual confusion to students that pretends that human communication and managerial communication are two separate things. Even more problematic is the contradiction between so-called *management philosophy* and the almost total absence of any philosophy in managerialism in the truthful philosophical sense of the word. This is prevalent in almost all books on management and managerial textbooks (Perlmutter 1997 & Harding 2003).
6. In this context, human communication is often portrayed as subjective, chitchat gossipy, unproductive, wasteful, unnecessary, and inefficient, while business communication receives positive attributes such as effective, clear, precise, efficient, competent, necessary, and needed.
7. While Hegel and Marx have used the division between labour and capital to highlight *A Critique of the Political Economy* – so the sub-title of *Das Kapital* (1890) – they have always used these categories inside a dialectical framework (Hegel 1807 & 1821, Marx 1846b & 1848) in order to link both as *thesis*, *antithesis*, and *synthesis*, rather than to separate them as is commonly done in affirmative-positivist academia. Today, even the term *political* has been artificially separated from the term *economy* even though both cannot be

understood disconnected from each other. But this, so it appears, is exactly the idea of the separation.

8 Textbooks and general books on communication often fall in three basic categories: a) *dominant or hegemonic readings*, where the audience accepts and resigns to what is inscribed in the coding and the structure of the text; b) *negotiated reading*, where the audience accepts parts of the message of the text while resisting other parts; and finally, c) *oppositional or counter-hegemonic reading*, where the audience rejects the message because its own values clash with those inscribed in the coding and in the structure of the text. In a publication-reader exchange driven by the market, publishers and writers seek to enhance (a) because of saleability and reduce (b) and (c).

9 See Kellner's *Boundaries and Borderlines: Reflections on Jean Baudrillard and Critical Theory*, http://www.uta.edu/huma/illuminatinos/kell2.htm.

10 Many scientists belong to a rather strange group of people who believe that no one in their immediate vicinity understands them but there is this some other academic in some office 10,000 miles away who really does.

11 A quite common statement about managerial communication is that *management is the process of getting things done through people, and without effective communication the process is much more complicated and often fails in its objectives – no one knows what anyone else is supposed to be doing*. Getting things done is no more than a codeword for all those activities that make profit. *'Things'* usually denotes managerial orders while *'through people'* means no more than using people (means). As long as they are needed they are *'the most important asset of our business'*; once they are no longer required, they are downsized – yet another codeword for fired. Secondly, management can be thankful, in fact, we all can be thankful, because without *'managerial communication no one would know what one is supposed to do'*. *'Supposed to do'* is the codeword for carrying out managerial orders. Finally, such statements also reflect the total absence of ethics or communicative ethics – something rather bothersome to business communication and often relocated in the far corners of today's textbooks, if mentioned at all. Finally, *'getting things done through people'* reduces people to means rather than treating them as ends. The foremost philosopher of modernity, Kant (1781), emphasised that ethics rests on the premise that ethical treatment of people means to treat people as *ends* and never as *means*. Given Kantian ethics, management can never be ethical because – at a normative and an empirical level – management has to treat people as a *means* (through people) and never as *ends* (the appreciation of humans as such without domination, alienation, etc). The contradiction between ethics (human=end) and non-ethical management (human=means) constitutes the most basic and most severe unsolvable dilemma between ethics and management, including the human *resource* or human *material* (*Menschenmaterial*) side of management, Human Resource Management.

12 *Management studies* have commonly been labelled *management science* to give the perception of being *scientific* while avoiding the unwanted term *social* of *social* science. People should not get the impression that management has anything to do with being *social*, thus avoiding any connotation that managerialism seeks to subordinate society into its service. Secondly, the term management science represents no more than a contradiction in terms; especially when related to the positivist idea of natural science, management is anything but scientific. Not much managerial knowledge is proven knowledge (Chalmers 1994) but a reduction of relative unscientific processes to

simple ideas, buzzwords, codewords, fashions (Abrahamson 1996), models, and ideologies (cf. Taylor's ox, gorilla, workers should be stupid, etc. 1911). Thirdly, the term *management science* also avoids another problem of the discipline, the almost pathological lack of theory expressed in the total absence of *-ology or -sophy*. There is no manag*ology* or manag*sophy* because there is no '*science of ...*', just a few key terms and MBA-jargons often expressed as '*10-steps to...*', '*the One-Minute-MBA*', etc.

13 Unlike in the real world of real philosophy, managerialism has reduced philosophy to managerial issues. In the managerial sense, 2000 years of philosophy are reduced to a functional *that's how it is done around here*. Even the so-called *scientific management was, to a large extent, a philosophy of management, and efficiency* [where] *piece-rate compensation* (was) *the most visible manifestation of that philosophy* (Jex 2002:10). In the realm of managerialism, philosophy has been de-philosophised and tortured to something like *the idea behind...XYZ...is*. It reflects almost nothing of what philosophy set out to achieve, see: Descartes (1628); Hegel (1821); Einstein (1949); Chomsky (1967 & 1968); McNeill & Feldman (1998).

14 Many have highlighted these irrationalities during the last 150 years between Marx (1848) and Harford's *The Undercover Economist* (2006).

15 The unsolvable contradiction of managerialism being value-*adding* to advanced capitalism and at the same time *value neutral* is a difficult but largely successfully managed act that managerialism has learnt to perform to perfection. While issuing the ideology of *value neutrality* to m*anagerialism*, disciplines that truly add value to human existence such as fine arts, dance, philosophy, performing arts, sociology, cultural studies, history, etc. are increasingly made to suffer in market-driven and efficiency-gaining universities that have been forced under the torturous dictate of managerialism designed as a one-dimensional system that levels KPIs (key performance indicators), achievable student attributes, degree-saleability, and labour-market conformity well above many academic disciplines.

16 There used to be a long forgotten time, when Enlightenment thinkers such as *Humboldt* and the French *encyclopaedists* had ideas about the semblance of the universal knowledge of humanity inside an organisational form called university. In this, the mature, enlightened, and *mündige* (self-reflective, mature & moral-ethical) *citoyen* (enlightened citizen) of a civil society experienced education as a humanist endeavour, educating, character forming, and enlightening. Today, education has been successfully reduced to a conditioned exercise under task-performing learning-reward exchanges constructed as assessed achievements-for-degrees operations. This sort of conditioned training is guided through instrumental conditioning (reinforcements) in order to modify human behaviour towards system integration.

17 In that way, books in the genre of management are exposed to the same market-forces as management itself and they even gain reputation by their saleability. A managerial bestseller is the best as the market brings out the best. The idea of *fast-food must be good because millions eat it every day* applies to management books as well. In fact, in the managerially conditioned mind, *everything(!)* is measured in only one way: in the one-dimensional idea of saleability. Everything else is discarded as the case of America's Smithsonian institute shows: On October 16th 2004, the *Washington Post* reported that *the Smithsonian Institution is dismantling Smithsonian Books, a widely respected publishing division of the museum and research complex that dates back 150 years...*

The cutback follows the failure of an effort that started in 2002 to make *Smithsonian Books profitable*. Their books must be bad – they did not sell. In the world of management books saleability is driven to pathological levels, a book that is a not or just a marginal seller is discarded, a book published by *University of… Press* is regarded as second class because it does not necessarily have to be exposed to market forces, while books by purely commercial publishers are regarded highly because they survive the market. It is saleability, not content that matters and when content matters then it is only content the market approves of. In such a market-driven world, Einstein's eight-page theory of relativity would have never seen the light of the day because it did not sell.

18   The imitation of magazines like *Cosmopolitan, Playboy, Business Weekly*, and the *Harvard Business Review* is driven to extreme levels as many textbooks for management testify (Perlmutter 1997 & Harding 2003). They include carefully worded enticing text-boxes (not extensive texts in order to adhere to the conditioned 30-seconds TV-advertising conditioned attention span of the consumer), short stories, invented anecdotes, common stereotypes, highly selective pictures, manipulated photographs, short summaries, neatly arranged graphs, etc., all of which are arranged to increase saleability, not science. Ever since Galileo and later Darwin, science had been controversial but in sharp contrast, today's textbooks are uncontroversial because controversies might damage saleability.

19   The *value free* and value-adding characteristics of management and managerialism are further expressed in strategic *value*-adding chains, *value* analysis, *value* chain management, *value* commitment, *value* conflicts, *value* engineering, and cultural *values* so that *organisational values* can be communicated (O'Hair et al. 2005:27).

20   In popular management literature, contradictions are portrayed as unwanted and even unwarranted or system alien because management is linguistically portrayed as an extension of real science. This is framed in input-output terms disallowing contradictions. However, as the real world of management and work contains contradictions, they are explained away or portrayed as negative, controversial, debatable, and doubtful because any admittance of Hegelian contradictions in the world of management would damage the carefully constructed ideology of linearity and *scientification* of management and managerialism.

21   However, even in the world of management, managerialism, organisational communication, general communication, and the world of work, there are a few notable exceptions: Alvesson (1996); Hyman (1979, 1987, 1989); Offe (1976, 1984, 1985, 1988); Deetz (1992, 2001); Forester (1985 & 1989); Postone (1993); Mumby (1988, 1997, 2000, 2001); Ackermann & Heinzerling (2004); Ackroyd & Thompson (1999); Thompson (2004); Feenberg (1988, 2002, 2004); Barker (1993, 1999 & 2005) and a few others.

22   See: Baritz's *The Servants of Power* (1960); cf. Marx (1846b); Mannheim (1929); Horkheimer (1937 & 1947); Horkheimer & Adorno (1947); Adorno & Horkheimer (1944); Dahl (1957); Althusser (1965); Marcuse (1966); Gouldner (1976); Anthony (1977); Zizek (1989); Thompson (1990); Eagleton (1994); Mumby (1997); Chomsky (2002); Cooke (2006).

23   In a vast array of literature on communication and the world of work or even management and managerialism, the issue of philosophy is largely absent and ethics is – if not totally banned into a distant corner of today's standard

textbook – dealt with shortly and in many cases without any reference to ethical philosophy. In some particularly obscene cases, business ethics is, for example, reduced to employees taking pens from the workplace, answer private e-mails at work, or copying personal documents. In other cases, two millenniums of philosophy on human ethics is reduced to CSR: corporate social responsibility. While CSR is neither ethical nor philosophical or particular social, it keeps up – at least linguistically – the appearance that ethics is covered and that is all that is required. Once the appearance of being ethical is established behind the managerial reference to the invented acronym of CSR, the issue of ethics suffers a RIP-treatment (*rest in peace*) while the real world of practise and pragmatics moves on, largely unbothered by bothersome ethics.

24 In many cases the university education that too many managers receive is no longer connected to philosophy and science; it has been reduced to vocational training expressed in functional curricular demands and in distant-learning, modular, short-term, KPI-driven and core attributes to achieve a Bachelor or Master of Management and Business. In some cases, successful apprentices advance to PhD level without ever being concerned what the 'P' in PhD actually stands for.

25 The maximisation of profits is the sole and one-dimensional goal of management even though some might still believe, for example, that large multinational hamburger chains seek to provide a healthy, delicious cuisine as well as a fine dining opportunity for the cultural betterment of humanity. Others may see industrial *fast-food* manufactured by large corporations as a highly destructive enterprise that sells pre-historic *cave-food* (fat and sugar) while being environmentally devastating. It sacrifices human health (obesity, etc.) on the altar of profits, so they claim. The driving forces are profits, not ethical concerns for rainforests, human health, inhumane working conditions, etc.

26 In many cases the core demand towards theory of being able to create predictive values is stripped in favour of, for example, seven-steps and a few boxes that have to be worked through or simply applied. Overall, this mechanistic approach seeks to apply engineering methods (manipulation of nature) into human settings (manipulation of humans) without much consciousness or critical reflection. The difference between what Horkheimer (1937) called traditional (natural science = human science) and critical theory (natural science ≠ human science & natural tools) is ideologically cloaked to make nature and humans equal. See also: Adorno & Horkheimer (1944) & Feyerabend (1981:176ff).

27 Managerialism operates as a strict anti-historical subject because it needs to avoid that the consumers of their ideological products realise that there are *particular stages of development in production, commerce and consumption and* [that management is no more than] *a corresponding social constitution* [stabilising] *a corresponding organisation,* [economic] *order and* [social] *classes* (Karl Marx in a letter to P. V. Annenkov in the year 1846a). Otherwise the non-objective science and highly ideological character of managerialism would be exposed. Managerialism could only appear at a specific time in the history of human production and re-production, fulfilling a specific ideological task that managerialism itself wants to avoid to be put into any historical context. As a consequence, managerialism falls into the Hegelian *Zeitgeist* trap.

28 It is understandable that substantial advances in humanity and human understanding – and this despite business libraries full of business, managerial, and empirical literature – *have not* and *cannot* come from these publications considering that even the history of science demonstrates beyond doubt

29 that the revolutionary and significant advances of social and natural science did not derive from empiricism, but from new and often controversial theories.

29 Watson (2003:32) noted *under a general heading of, say, Leadership, we see columns and dot points. One column is headed Strategies and the other Results. Under Leadership we get windy summaries of ambitions.*

30 Books on management have fallen thick as snowflakes in Siberia (Lanham 2006:32; Barry et al. 2001).

31 The linguistic cloaking of profits as organisational goals simplifies meaning and disposes of the need for critical reasoning. Hegelian dialectics [thesis, anti-thesis, & synthesis) that provides a comprehensive method for understanding the world is reduced to logic: $1^{(management)} + 1^{(organisation)} = 2^{(organisational\ goals)}$. It constructs a simple reality for the simple mind. On the other hand, what is relevant is not what is said but what is not said. Such linear arguments do reflect more on what Poole has termed *Unspeak* (2006).

32 Behind the word *value* resides profit for those *who manage* and wage-dependency, job insecurity, etc. for those *who are managed*. Offe and Wiesenthal's seminal article (1980) has shown the asymmetrical relationship between both.

33 One way to set up such an interpretive framework is to portray management as being without beginning and ending, as something eternal and inherent to society. The Harvard Business Review editor Margretta (2002:4) achieves this, for example, in the following way: *society has always had managers...owners and overseers. In the same way, we've always had doctors...* The fact that management is a rather recent phenomenon that was created by capital to manage for it (Marglin 1974) and later developed into managerialism to operate *for* itself and *inserting* itself factually and ideologically between labour and capital is hidden behind the HBR-editor's *always had* theme. A fact that is simply wrong. Similarly, not all societies ever had *overseers* and definitely not *owners*. The ideology of managerialism, as expressed by the HBR-editor, seeks to create a natural acceptance of hierarchy, and domination by people over people. The final ideological moment arrives with the equalisation of *mangers* with *doctors*. We always had both of them, we are told, even though *doctors* – as part of modern scientific medicine – are also a more recent development because they only appeared with the rise of modernity and science. The fact alone that one needs to equalise oneself [managers] with such a vital function of society indicates a strong ideological need for legitimacy, to be seen as socially useful and needed, something almost self-evident for doctors but – and this is the crucial difference – not for managers. Finally, doctors – and this is also in harsh difference to managers – actually *do* something while managers *do* not. As Margretta (2002:196) herself states, managers 'create performance *through* others'. Doctors, unlike managers, do not do things *'through'* others. They simply *do* it by themselves. In many respects the equalisation of *manager=doctor* shows not only severe structural shortcomings but also highlights several ideological needs of management, managerialism, and its entourage of affirmative writers.

34 The arrival of managerialism at universities is, for example, expressed in the fact that writing an academic book is rewarded with five points on my KPI (key performance indicator). What counts is measurable *outcome* expressed in an ISBN plus a few minor indicators to show a book is academic. What is not measured is *content*. Watson (2003:29) illustrates this in the following way: *James and J. S. Mill wrote books that changed the course of history while working for*

the East Indian Company, a multinational. Today they wouldn't. Today they would be attending countless meetings, seminars and conferences to update their knowledge of work-related subjects, all of them conducted in the mind-maiming language of *managerialism*. Today, the world of James and J. S. Mill has ended even in the previously non-managerial world of universities. Nowadays, the language of managerialism (KPIs, etc.) has been enshrined in individual *Workload Agreements*. These are neither *agreements* nor *individual* because everyone has to measure up to the *same* KPIs. This is a pre-set management tool to manage academics –delegated downwards & reported upwards [↓↑] – not agreed upon [⇆]. Hence, the term *agreement* is no more than a reflection on Orwell's *Newspeak* in his novel *Nineteen-Eighty-Four*. It measures *'countless meetings'* (Watson 2003:29) against research measured in pure output (KPI=6p/3yrs) on a scale that has become more and more geared towards Watsonian *meetings* rather than intellectual endeavour. The managerial KPI structure for academics is set against books with *content* but in favour of a fast production of academic literature measured by *numbers*. The enshrined *short-termism* with an average shelf-life of two to five years for books and annual KPIs of one article ($1^{academic\text{-}article}=1.5^{KPI}$) supports the managerial tool of university workloads and the managerially driven output of academic books. Only sophisticated tricks, invented numbers, etc. (Burawoy 1979 & 1985) or what an *Enron*-boss once called *creative accounting* can bypass managerial KPIs and allow academic engagement that seeks to come close to *James and J. S. Mill*. For the most part of academic life, managerialism has successfully excluded this from universities, just as Watson has outlined (2003:29 & 32).

35   The universality of managerialism is expressed in countless publications on almost all eventualities of human society ranging from *managing your personal finances, managing your children, managing your car loan, managing your sex life*, to *managing your marriage*, etc. (Parker 2002).

36   What is demanded here is that *we all think like managers* (Margretta 2002:7). Unfortunately, there are not only managers but the system of management also demands that there are those *who are managed*. Therefore, almost by definition *we* [most of us] cannot and should not think like managers, even though managerialism tells us to do so. Secondly, if all people thought like managers, all social relations between humans would be exposed to managerialism. Once we start managing our sex-life, we most likely have lost it. Similarly, once you manage you husband, wife, girl- or boyfriend, child, brother or sister, you are moving towards very doubtful relationships that view people as a managerial *means*, not as an *end* (Kant 1781). In short, a world in which *we all think like managers* would not be worth living in (Singer 1994).

37   Managerialism has produced shelves with books that send the message *do as we tell you or face annihilation!*, usually with codewords such as *best practise, competitive advantage, strategic advantage*, etc. Unnoticed remains the fact that even after decades of sales, there is still not one solution to success, otherwise everybody would follow the same route to excellence. Above all, all people would be successful, something that is, given heaps of company collapses and insolvencies, obviously not the case despite large numbers of managerial self-help books. It appears as if managers using these handy tips, consultants, business schools, successful models, etc. operate more on belief-systems than on empirical facts because eventually all markets create more losers than winners (Smith 1759) and this despite the claim of using objective science to *guarantee success!*

38   According to Margretta (2002:4), *society has always had managers*. Even at the point when *homo erectus* became *homo faber*, the tool-making animal. According to the HBR-editor, the first things that those early humans created were not communally shared tools, food, hunt, etc., but the manager! Later when private property and landholding became the economic dominant form of existence organised in tribes, and later families, again managers managed it. And slave-drivers were actually not slaves but managers. Similarly, the feudal lord wasn't God-given and supported by the Church. He [and it was most definitely a he!] was no more than a feudal manager. How could human society ever have developed without managers? On a more serious note, however, the TINA idea, or better ideology, of the historical illusion of an ever-existent manager seeks to cement two things: the acceptance of managerialism and the top-down, hierarchical order of an authoritarian regime that guides humans for the better part of every ordinary working day.

39   Margretta's (2002:3) *'up close'* is designed to carry the connotation of *...and personal...* so that all persons are aware of the power that management and managerialism have over their personal lives. Management and managerialism can hold their – sometimes even invisible – hands over us at any time during the 8hrs-day. It has been known, however, that these *hands* have not only become visible but have also become very touchy when managerial power comes into *'play'!* The HBR-editor's words about *'up close'* might indicate on how *'close'* these hands can be! In short, if we perform well (always to management's expectations), management also has the power – in accordance with rules set by management – to reward those who show compliance to KPIs (key performance indicators) with *performance related pay* (PRP). In that way, management has also positioned itself in a location that allows them to perform the ability of Skinnerian *reinforcement* (reward) and *punishment* (dismissal).

40   Margretta (2002:6) does, like many others, portray the myth of self-organising teams that are only to be found in managerial literature because in the managerial world of work, they – almost by definition – are never self-organising but managerially organised inside a managerial framework. Even inside the textbook pages of a somewhat hallucinonatory world of affirmative management-writers, these self-organising teams are not self-organised but organised by none other than management. Statements such as *take the place of managerial hierarchies* have always been simply an expression of pure managerial ideology as teams have never taken the place of hierarchy. There are simply no companies that operate on communally organised teams with equal rights, responsibilities, and ownership. And in almost all cases, teamwork mirrors managerial domination in the form of managerially appointed team leaders. Statements such as *self-organising work teams will take the place of managerial hierarchies* are not just wishful thinking but part of a well crafted managerial ideology. These are deliberate and largely successful attempts to cloak the reality of domination inside the world of work.

41   Taylor's (1911) *scientific management was, to a large extent, a philosophy of management, and efficiency and piece-rate compensation* [as] *the most visible manifestations of that philosophy* (Jex 2002:10). In all too many management textbooks, communicative attempts are made to link management to philosophy even though the word *philosophy* is not used to enlighten readers on questions such as *how should we live, what is the meaning of life, what is good,*

what is ethical, or Kant's *what ought to be*. The ideological use of the term philosophy is to pretend that management is inherently good and somehow linked to a higher form of thinking. In reality, both cases are to be answered in the negative. *Piece-rate and efficiency* are neither philosophical but managerial questions and neither are connected to truly philosophical questions (Descartes 1628; Rousseau 1750 & 1755; Kant 1781; Hegel 1807 & 1821; Marx 1846b & 1890; Wittgenstein 1921; Lukacs 1923; Volosinov 1929; Adorno 1944; Einstein 1949; Marcuse 1966, 1968, 1969; Chomsky 1968; Habermas 1968, 1975, 1985; Searle 1969; Singer 1975, 1993, 2000; Gadamer 1976; Rorty 1979 to name a few).

42 Cf. Jex 2002:10.

43 See: Hegel (1807 & 1821); (Marx 1848 & 1890); Horkheimer & Adorno (1947); Jay's *The Dialectical Imagination* (1974); Gouldner (1976); Habermas's *The Analytic Theory of Science and Dialectic* (1976a); Buck-Moss (1977); Jameson (1990); Bhaskar's *Dialectic – Pulse of Freedom* (1993), Lukacs' *A Defence of History and Class Consciousness – Tailism and the Dialectics* (2000).

44 Like many ordinary dictionaries, standard management literature often seeks to present standard definitions. In negating ideas such as *symbolic interaction*, they seek to pretend as if there were 'a' singular – or even 'the' – meaning of something created in a socially constructed world. All these attempts to create narrowly defined meanings called definitions miss two things. Firstly, words to not have meanings; people have meanings for words. In other words, meanings are created by common agreement between people and not by what is written by one – in this case a management book – and accepted by another as singular truth. Secondly, any singular meaning or definition pretends a singular perspective from which a (or *the*) definition has been created (Morgan 1986 & 1993). A one-dimensional perspective leads to a one-dimensional view, something strongly encouraged by managerialism but not feasible in the reality of a socially constructed environment that creates the meaning of a sign between communicating subjects as an *in flux* movement and not as a fixed term.

45 The philosophical idea of *a priori* knowledge is – less among philosophers than among social scientist – hotly debated. On the one side, there are those who believe a scientist needs to, and in fact can, switch off all subjectivity and engagement with the social world that surrounds him. In a sometimes mistaken idea about what constitutes *bias* and what constitutes *objectivity*, the proponents of this view seek to assume that a scientist is someone going through a door into science leaving – once the door is shut – all social existence, values, and subjectivity outside. It assumes a *pure reason* idea that has not only been successfully challenged by Kant's *Critique of Pure Reason* (1781) – but also an idea in which the physical nature is viewed mechanistically – like Copernican mechanical movements – so that science can only be understood through logic and rationality (Descartes' *Cartesian* idea of 1628; Comte, 1853; Popper 1965 & 1999; cf. Fuller 2003). On the other side there are those who believe that such an assumption is not sustainable. They believe – perhaps beginning with Kant's *Critique of Pure Reason* (1781) – that humans are not neatly separate-able into *objective* and *subjective* because they can neither be separated nor can either one be switched of at will (cf. Freud's *it, ego & super-ego*). The only way of dealing with the objective-subjective dilemma is not to see it as a dilemma but as an inseparable dialectical relationship. In the subject-object dialectic, a scientist is not seen as someone

who can switch off subjectivity when going through a door but subjectivity is enhanced to moral consciousness (Kant 1781; Hegel 1807 & 1821; Horkheimer 1937 & 1947; Adorno 1976; Kohlberg 1971, 1981 & 1984).

46   See Adorno's *Negative Dialectics* (1973).

47   Wood (2004:43) emphasised that *the best theory is the simplest one that is capable of describing, explaining, understanding, and instigating social change*. It is also geared towards the idea of the *practical relevance* of any critical theory.

48   Some have argued that the reason why humans, compared to animals, have extremely large brains when compared to body size is because humans, unlike animals, are constantly forced to construct meaning when they relate to each other. When we see someone, the first thing we do is the so-called *male-female distinction* and then we examine each others' faces as facial expressions can sometimes tell more than human words. But it is the ability to communicative verbally, to speak – something animals do not have – that creates humans as well as the ability to construct complex, reflective, and self-reflective forms of communication based on *syntax* (grammatical rules) and *semantics* (meaning structures).

49   See: Skinner (1948, 1953, 1971 & 1974) and Arnold (2005) but also: Chomsky (1971) & Anderson (1990).

50   Hegelian *Zeitgeist* can even mean that those who are unaware of their own history are bound to repeat it and this is one of the core elements of managerially distorted communication. Those who are unaware of the historical consequences of such a viewpoint are made to repeat what *has been* done and still *is* done over and over again. For example, the pathologies of advanced capitalism ranging from slave labour, child labour, industrial accidents, job insecurity, atypical work, downsizing, bullying, and mobbing, to poverty, and starvation.

51   A simple case to understand the difference between *conditioned association* and *symbolic association* can be made, for example, by viewing smoking and advertising. What the tobacco industry is seeking is not a conscious reflection about smoking (*symbolic association*) so that the victim makes a rational choice about it by associating one symbol – smoking – with another one – that of cancer. What is sought is the opposite. The victim should be conditioned to make only *conditioned associations*. To achieve this, the advertising industry, marketing psychologists and neuro-physicists are constantly inventing new conditioning structures that enforce associations of smoking to associations to, let's say, coolness, sophistication, and the like. This link needs to be established as *conditioned association* over and over again by the advertising industry; hence we hardly see an advertisement only once. The overall Pavlovian idea is the *conditioned association* of smokingösophisticationöhigh social status. The rationality of *symbolic association* that scientifically links smoking with cancer has to be pushed aside in favour of an emotional link established through *conditioned associations*.

52   See: Buck-Moss (1977); Adorno (1973); Held (1997:200ff.)

53   The literature on management *has much less to say of and for those who are managed* (Marsden & Townley 1996:660).

54   There is hardly any discourse or dialogue about the *truth* of a commercial good – only its saleability. There is no philosophical *truth* in a Hamburger or Big-Whopper, but a lot of saleability. Similarly, *ethical* considerations – if present in managerial texts at all – take a backseat position. In short, there is less *ethics* in a Hamburger or Big-Whopper than saleability.

55 The dictum that a truthful assessment of the state of affairs in the world of work can only be established communicatively – by using communicative action – and not normatively, excludes all claims to superior knowledge by any leader, elected trade union official, party boss, social scientists, etc. There is no superior book or form of pre-conceived knowledge, only knowledge that is established communicatively under the conditions of ideal speech (Habermas 1990).
56 See: *The rise of Science* in Bertrand Russell's *A History of Western Philosophy* (1945); Horkheimer (1937 & 1947) & Benhabib *et al.* (1993); Honneth's *Max Horkheimer and the Sociological Deficit of Critical Theory* (1993); Birnbaum (1971); Feyerabend (1981 & 1987); Apel (1980); Feenberg (2004).
57 Loosely adopted from Mumby (2001:594).
58 The point of having powers that structure meaning is to enable management to represent reality. It also imposes intentionality on workers who are otherwise not inclined to accept such intentionality. To do this, management creates language in a way that supports this goal. The intentional imposition of such meaning structures determines both: a) a formal structure of language shaping the *syntax*; and b) the meaning content shaping the *semantics* of language. Chomsky (1966:42) noted that *the syntax of a language* [has] *two systems of rules: a base system that generates deep structure and a transformational system that maps these into surface structures*.
59 On the issue of interpretation, Searle (1996:134) emphasises that *I am reluctant to use the word 'interpretation' because it suggests something that is definitely false. The use of this word suggests that there is an act of interpreting whatever we understand something or perceive something, and of course, I don't want to say that. I want to say we normally just see an object or understand a sentence, without any act of interpreting. I might want to reserve the work 'interpretation' for cases where we actually perform a conscious and deliberate act of interpreting.*
60 Means-ends schemes put thinking and acting into a highly mechanical relationship. On thinking in such a purely mechanical way, Chomsky (1966:26) once noted that *if a man acts in a purely mechanical way, we may admire what he does, but we despise what he is.*
61 Gadamer (1976:3) emphasised that *language is the fundamental mode of operation of our being-in-the-world and the all-embracing form of the constitution of the world* and that *the appearance of the concept of 'language' presupposes consciousness of language* (1976:62); see also: (Passer & Smith 2007:274ff.).
62 Goodrich (1920); see also: Dunlop (1958); Thompson (1963); Fox (1966, 1973, 1974); Ramsay (1977 & 1980); Kochan, Katz & McKersie (1986); Storey (1992); Littler (1993); Edwards (2003 & 2006); Stewart (2005); Peetz (2006); Adams (2007).
63 Chomsky (1966:59) noted that *the universal condition that prescribes the form of any human language is grammaire générale.*
64 Searle (2002:17) noted, *something is a symbol only if it is used, treated or regarded as a symbol. Something is a symbol only relative to some observer, user or agent who assigns a symbolic interpretation to it.* Searle (1996:75) continued that *symbols do not create cats and dogs and evening stars; they create only the possibility of referring to cats, dogs, and the evening star in a publicly accessible way.*
65 Searle (1996:66) noted there are *the three essential features of linguistic symbols: they symbolise something beyond themselves, they do so by convention, and they are public.*

66 According to Searle (1969:16), *all linguistic communication involves linguistic acts. The unit of linguistic communication is not, as has generally been supposed, the symbol, word or sentence, or even the token of the symbol, word or sentence, but rather the production or issuance of the symbol or word or sentence in the performance of the speech act.*

67 Adopted from Hartley & Bruckmann (2002).

68 The meaning of words always depends on the concrete circumstances into which they are spoken. There is no single definition of a word that covers all the uses we give it in ordinary discourse.

69 See Austin (1962:1 & 109) & Graham's J. L. *Austin – A Critique of Ordinary Language Philosophy* (1977).

70 Quote taken from Radford (2005:172).

71 Czech philosopher Edmund Husserl (1990) distinguishes between *signs* and *expression*. He sees a *sign* as something that stands for something else such as smoke being a sign of fire, hence a sign indicates or points to something else. The link between signs and expression are not self-evident, they are human constructions. Such connections have to be created by a person indicating a pre-existence of knowledge before it is linked to a sign.

72 See Foster (1985) & Therborn (1973).

73 Husserl (1990:269) defined the link between meaning and sign as *to mean is not a particular way of being as in the sense of indicating something.*

74 *It was all done by repetition – not merely of the same words, but by the repetition of bits of meaning implied by words which were physically different: strong, firm, hold; our, together; action, future, new birth; freedom-n-justice, freedomocracies* (Chilton 1983:35).

75 Members of a domain create *collective intentionality* as they share intentional states such as beliefs, desires, and intentions. *In my view all these efforts to reduce collective intentionality to individual intentionality fail. Collective intentionality is a biological primitive phenomenon that cannot be reduced to or eliminated in favour of something else* (Searle 1996:23,24).

76 According to Gadamer (1976:60), *human language takes place in signs that are not rigid, as animals' expressive signs are, but remain variable, not only in the sense that there are different languages, but also in the sense that within the same language the same expression can designate different things and different expressions of the same thing.*

77 According to Searle (1969:16), *speaking a language is engaging in a rule-governed form of behaviour.*

78 Schramm's initial idea of decoding/encoding has been applied by Mohan *et al.* (2004:17) to the world of work resulting in a neutralisation appearing only as 'A' and 'B' in today's managerial textbooks.

79 Thompson (1990:21) argues that *we are seeking to understand and explain a range of phenomena that are, in some way and to some extent, already understood by the individuals who are part of the social-historical world; we are seeking, in short, to re-interpret a pre-interpreted domain.*

80 Most likely the statement *different things mean different things to different people* is no more than a rhetorical device to highlight two things, (a) we have different meanings and implied in it (b) we need to find a common meaning.

81 *Deep structures* can be distinguished from *surface structures*. The former is the underlying abstract structure that determines its semantic interpretation; the latter, the superficial organisation of unit which determines the phonetic interpretation and which relates to the physical form of the actual utterance, to its perceived or

intended form (Chomsky 1966:33). The deep structure that expresses the meaning is common to all languages. The transformational rules that convert deep to surface structures may differ from language to language (Chomsky 1966:35). These transformational rules also differ between the language used by workers and the use of managerial language as the latter has to carry more ideological baggage and has to transfer issues that belong to the domain of critical rationality into the domain of instrumental rationality. For example, critical rationality, truth, and ethics are daily sacrificed on the altar of organisational goals [profit] or *value-adding* goals [value-adding is an interesting term for managerialism that seeks to be seen as *value free*!]. These maxims set strong parameters highly conflictive of ethics (Kohlberg 1971, 1981, 1984; Singer: 1993, 1994, 2000). There is no truth and next to no ethics in most commercial goods, only saleability and profits – otherwise sweatshops, child labour, slave-labour, etc. (see ILO, ICFTU, www.sweatshoplabor.com, UNICEF, etc.).

82 In that respect, one can argue that humans are meaning creators and sign users. We are meaning and sign making animals. The creation of signs, their use and the understanding of their meaning are elementary aspects of human society.

83 According to Searle (1969:4) *Linguistic philosophy is primarily the name of a method; the philosophy of language is the name of a subject. Linguistics attempts to describe the actual structure – phonological, syntactical, and semantic – of natural languages.*

84 *Primary socialisation is the first socialisation an individual undergoes in childhood, through which he becomes a member of society. Secondary socialisation is any subsequent process that inducts an already socialised individual into new sectors of the objective world of his society* (Berger & Luckmann 1966:150; cf. Birnbaum 1969; White 1969; Segal 1970).

85 *In this case, we are dealing with a stereotyped linguistic formula that does not really give the reasons for why we hold something to be true, but rather reject the need for further proof* (Gadamer 1976:69).

86 According to Soviet philosopher Volosinov (1929:103), meaning *is like an electric spark that occurs when two different terminals are hooked together. Those who ignore [that] and attempt to define the meaning of a word...want in effect turn on the light bulb after having switched off the current.*

87 Edwards et al. (2006:130–131) have expressed a similar two-domain dichotomy when discussing labour's concerns in figure 1 and capital concerns in figure 2.

88 HRM seeks to replace the original meaning of *strike* – the improvement of wages and working conditions – with new meanings. These meanings are designed to carry negative connotations. Today strike is linked to a *loss* of working days, to damaging competitiveness, and to an outdated version of resentment.

89 The linguistic of the term *'company'* originates in the Latin/Italian terms 'con' for sharing (*com*-pany) and the term *'pane'* (Italian for bread: com-*pany*). Originally, companies were bread-sharing mercenaries or hired killers (cf. Klikauer 2007:102ff.)

90 See Fromm's *Man is not a Thing* (1957).

91 The common meaning of *connotation* is to be something that is implied in a word, additional to a literal or primary meaning.

92 See: Berger & Luckmann (1967); Barry & Elmes (1997).

93 See: Marcuse (1966:12); Fromm (1955 & 1957); Blumberg (1990).

94 At certain periods of time, not so much in recent history, common myths have been engineered. This also affects present situations. For example, *McCarthyism* in the USA in the 1950s reached almost obscene levels. Similar events occurred in England and other western countries and also reached those of the anti-communist bloc. More recent examples include an utmost precise replication of the communist myth when transferred to terrorism. In many cases, this occurs without much editing. It also negates the problem that terrorism is a method, not a political ideology. *The War on Terrorism* – which we are told to fight – is in reality a war on a method, just like pancake making or any other method. It is not like fighting against anarchy because it represents a political idea, the idea of life without state and rules created from above and followed by those below.

95 The protection of particular interests communicated through symbols was seen as an important idea for nation building. This was once a progressive idea that served to get rid of the aristocracy. Today the bourgeoisie has merged with nation and state and excluded almost all elements that the bourgeoisies decided had no relevance. Any values linked to a historical past of a once important process of bourgeois emancipation were excluded. This included key issues such as the end of religious and feudal domination, Enlightenment, critical thinking, and emancipation. They were deemed a dangerous cross-fertilisation and excluded in order to avoid contamination of today's managerial value system, which is geared towards system stability (Offe & Wiesenthal 1980).

96 A popular myth of such a middle class is manifested in statements where the ordinary in the advanced world becomes the guiding image for all countries as expressed in the words *everyone has a mobile phone today*. Hidden behind this myth remains the fact that roughly 50% of the world population will hardly ever make a single telephone call as many live on less then $2 per day.

97 While popular TV soap operas cover the reproductive domain in great length and detail, the productive domain is almost totally absent from TV programming. Even more absent is the link between both. On the rare occasions when the productive domain is portrayed, this is done in a highly distorted fashion.

98 *There is nothing commonsensical, for example, about the fact that light can behave both as a wave and as particle. Common sense told us that the earth was flat* (Poole 2006:59).

99 See: Marcuse (1966:193); cf. Fromm's *Marx's contribution to the knowledge of man* (1968).

100 According to Harding (2003:13), *management textbooks are cultural products (cultural studies) which inculcate generations of students into the body of knowledge known as 'management'. They serve to legitimise a body of knowledge (Foucault) and to organise a language (Derrida) which constructs the subject position (Butler) of management*. Reading – and writing – such management books can be a dangerous activity as it establishes a writing-reading-thinking link. *It can only mean that writing and thinking are, if not the same thing, quite inseparable. If you write like porridge you will think like it, and the other way around. And if you have to read porridge all the time you may well begin to speak it, even in extremis: so when your child is killed you may tell the press, as one man did this year, that you can only pray to 'God that you will have closure'* (Watson 2003:171).

101 *The explosive historical dimension of meaning is silenced* (Marcuse 1966:202).

102 Quoted from Marcuse (1966:101); See also Feyerabend (1981 & 1987); Apel (1980).

103 *Remembrance of the past may give rise to dangerous insights, and the established society seems to be apprehensive of the subversive contents of memory* (Marcuse 1966:101), hence there is only a microscopically small number of Hollywood movies about the 8-hour-day, strikes that secured health benefits, pay rises, better working conditions, ending of child labour, etc.

104 While morality is not a functional necessity under current conditions of production and reproduction, in an amoral society, however, morality can become a political weapon (cf. Kohlberg 1981 & 1984). An amoral society can be summed up in the words of Marcuse (1969:18), amoral *is not the picture of a naked woman who exposes her pubic hair but that of a fully clad general who exposes his medals rewarded in a work of aggression.*

105 At a second level, terms such as organisations also eclipse the very origins of the term that later rose to prominence in organisational studies, organisational behaviour, and organisational theory. The supposedly neutral term *organisation* dates back to mechanical engineering. It entered managerial language via an ideology that sought to make a socially constructed world of work engineer-able. It did so by hiding *power* and *domination* behind an engineering ideology.

106 Loyalty is often considered to be a *One-Way Street*, see also: the *Death of Corporate Loyalty*.

107 For origins and developed frameworks on system see Luhmann (1995). The core of system theory lies in the search for order and regularity and ultimately increased control by advantaged groups over others. It develops hypotheses that posit a direct or indirect casual link between variables suggesting that many variables exist in mutual or circular casual relations and such links are seen as time dependent. The core element of system theory can be found in the assumption that social systems are like technical or mechanical systems. An increase in a quantity of one variable leads to an increase in an expected outcome. Any decrease in such quantity will lead to a lesser outcome. System changes are seen as quantitative and incremental. Consequently, humans are integrated into a system as just one more factor that makes up the social apparatus based on a one-dimensionality that dismisses critical reasoning as system-alien. Instead and most dangerously even something like *Critical Management Studies* (CMS) has become no more than a little playing field for critical academics while at the same time it has successfully been integrated into the prevailing paradigm of managerialism. Today, it has become a function of system conformity and affirmation. For example, CMS is used to reduce system theory as a system open to critique to provide proof of its liberal credentials. *It serves to coordinate ideas and goals with those exacted by the prevailing system, to enclose them in the system, and to repel those which are irreconcilable with the system* (Marcuse 1966:16).

108 Quoted from Hendry & Seidel (2002:3), see also Luhmann (1995).

109 The existence of a Rolls-Royce as status symbol needs a specific condition. *The status exists only if people believe it exists, and the reasons function only if people accept them as reasons* (Searle 1996:69).

110 In the case of *working hard* those who manage define what hard work is and who is supposed to work hard while those who are managed are supposed to accept it.

111 The heroic military leader was able to cause the death of thousands of troops. All too often this increased *his* (usually a man!) standing. Similarly, the business community regards modern business and management leaders who

cause the dismissal of hundreds of workers as high achievers. To achieve that, they need to convince their society and the management community of their heroic achievements. These followers need to perceive things through a managerial frame that is called story or message (Barry & Elmes 1997).

112 At the same time Barry & Elmes' article on *Strategy Retold* (*Academy of Management Review*, vol. 22, no. 2) cloaks its advice for managers in the language of post-modernism to make it appear trendy and acceptable for an academic management journal. Behind the screen of post-modernism, the article gives relatively clear instructions to management on how to formulate a business strategy in story telling terms (cf. Holman & Thorpe 2002).

113 See: Lockwood (1964 & 1996); Mouzelis (1974).

114 Distortion or to distort goes back to its Latin origins meaning *distorquere* with connotations to *torquere* = to twist.

115 *In speaking their own language, people also speak the language of their masters, benefactors, advertisers. Thus they do not only express themselves, their own knowledge, feelings, and aspirations, but also something other than themselves. Describing 'by themselves' the political situation, either in their home town or in the international scene, they (and 'they' includes us, the intellectuals who know it and criticise it) describe what 'their' media of mass communication tell them – and this merges with what they really think and see and feel* (Marcuse 1966:198).

116 Ideology can be seen as *meaning in the service of power* (Thompson 1990:7). One of the core achievements of managerial myths is their capability to harmonise. This enables the framing of facts – that are managerially constructed – as reality. Managerial realities do not even have to confirm each other as these myths cover social and economical contradictions and establish a faked harmony between different managerial realities and the ideologies that blankets them.

117 The limits of language and its ability to represent and reproduce a state of affairs also constitute the limits of a comprehension of the world. Anything that cannot be represented through the use of language is located beyond our ability of expression as it is transferred into the realm of meaninglessness.

118 Foster (1985:39) has emphasised that a *sign is a construct between socially organised persons in the process of interaction. Therefore, the forms of sign are conditioned above all by the social organisation of the participants involved and also by the immediate condition of their interaction...ideology may not be divorced from the material reality of the sign. Nor must the sign be divorced from the concrete forms of social intercourse.*

119 Apel challenges the view that language is a system, *language is not formalisable into a system and as such it is too amorphous and heterogeneous to serve as a foundation of anything. Furthermore, such foundations, were they to be had, are unnecessary and even hazardous ballast* (Mendieta 2002:157).

120 Most important are Wittgenstein's *Tractatus Logico-Philosophicus* (1921), *Philosophical Investigations* (1953), and *The Blue and Brown Books: Preliminary Studies for the Philosophical Investigations* (1958). Trained as an engineer, so-called *early* Wittgenstein drew on mathematical logic to explain language. The *late* Wittgenstein was concerned with a critique of language. He emphasised that *the limits of my language mean the limits of my world* and *what we cannot speak about we must pass over in silence.*

121 The idea of language as a game greatly supports the idea of systems and game theory. In Harford's (2006:161) chapter on *Game theory for dummies*, he writes *all games need some simplifying assumptions before they can be modelled; if*

theories use the wrong assumptions, then they will produce perfect solutions to the wrong problems...Game theory expresses the way people would act as the solution to a mathematical equation. It is the *game theory = mathematical = scientific* equation that explains game theory's popularity today. It also explains the great popularity of Wittgenstein's *language as a game*. It supports ideas such as *it is really all a game, sometimes you win, sometimes you lose*. It pretends language use is circular and there is no real winner. It takes out all asymmetrical distribution of access in shaping language. It pretends we are all volunteers in playing a game, which is not the case. However, his *game* idea introduced two important notions into our understanding of language: a) no language is private and b) meaning is not a matter of propositional logic, meaning is in language use.

122 See Radford (2005:170). On playing and playing along, Adorno (1944:55) noted, *those who do not play along, and that's as much to say, those who do not swim bodily in the stream of human beings, become afraid of missing the bus...*

123 Orwell's *Nineteen Eighty-Four* (1949:312) states *the purpose of Newspeak was not only to provide a medium of expression for the world-view and mental habits proper to the devotees of [HRM], but to make all other [non-HRM] modes of thought impossible*. This was done partly by the invention of new words [such as HRM, Strategic HRM, Business Process Reengineering, TQM, etc.], but chiefly by eliminating undesirable words [such as class conflict, class war, labour-capital conflict, industrial relations, labour unions, strike, etc.], and by stripping words of managerially unwanted meanings. As far as possible, all secondary or critical meanings have been altered or removed. The term *human* in Human Resource Management is stripped of any connotation that could remind one of humanity and human treatment at work. What is left is a resource – the resource of human material.

124 The end result of such dangerous development has been described in George Orwell's *Nineteen Eighty-Four* (1949:37), if such HRM textbooks *could thrust its hand into the past and say of this or that even, it never happened – that, surely, was more terrifying than mere torture or death...and if all others accept the lie which [such books] imposed – if all records told the same tale – then the lie passed into history and became truth. Who controls the past...controls the future: who controls the present controls the past...reality control.*

125 The HRM language of performance management is nothing more than the continuation of primary socialisation in the world of work (secondary socialisation) by other means (Cole 1988; cf. White 1969; Segal 1970). Once successfully conditioned to Pavlov's dog-like action + reward system, a child like a worker will carry on unconsciously. This has been summed up by Orwell (1949:309) as *now be good, and I'll buy you a toy*. At a more sophisticated level, this has been labelled *performance management*, a term deeply enshrined in the world of HRM.

126 Marx' Kapital: *Sie wissen das nicht, aber sie tun es – they do not know it, but they are doing it* (Zizek 1989:28).

127 According to Lafargue (1883:8) class dominance could occur *because the working class, with its simple good faith, has allowed itself to be thus indoctrinated*. With the rise of corporate mass-communication, a class based access to mediated reality triumphed.

128 To see subordination as natural goes back to Aristotle who *defended the practice of slavery by asserting that some human beings were slaves by nature* (Poole 2006:73). Today *natural subordination* takes a different form. According to

Marcuse (1966:132), society is still organised in such a way that procuring the necessities of life constitutes the full-time and life-long occupation of specific social classes, which are *therefore* [H.M.] unfree and prevented from a human existence. In this sense, the classical proposition according to which truth is incompatible with enslavement by socially necessary labour is still valid. The classical concept implies the proposition that freedom of thought and speech must remain a class privilege as long as this enslavement prevails. The thoughts and speeches of thinking and speaking subjects largely depend on the performance of a superimposed function. It depends on fulfilling the requirements of this function and on those who control these requirements. The dividing line between the pre-technological and the technological project rather is in the manner in which the subordination to the necessities of life – *to earning a living* [H.M.] – is organised and, in the new modes of freedom and un-freedom, truth and falsehood that correspond to this organisation.

129   As Gadamer (1976:39) stated, *all the knowledge won by science enters the societal consciousness through school and education, using modern information media, though maybe sometimes after a great – too great – delay. In any case, this is the way what new socio-linguistic realities are articulated.*

130   See also Baudrillard's *The Mirror of Production* (1975), *Seduction* (1979), and *The Illusion of the End* (1994).

131   See: Lockwood (1964); Mouzelis (1974); Morrow (1994: 221–222); Lockwood (1996).

132   The sign PRP stands for *Performance Related Pay*, a system best summed up by Elliott (2006:28) as, *over the past 25 years sales and profits for FTSE 100 companies have risen by about 3% a year – broadly in line with the growth rate of the economy – but salaries in boardrooms have gone up by 25% a year.*

133   See Adorno & Horkheimer (1944); Gay (1997); Alvesson (2002).

134   See Townley's excellent work on *Reframing Human Resource Management: Power, Ethics and the Subject at Work* (1994) and Cairnes, G. *et al.* (2003) on *Organizational Space/Time: From Imperfect Panoptical to Heterotopian Understanding.*

135   Most modern textbooks on management and HRM are not even written as an active engagement with a subject as they tend not to present a critical reflection by an author. Many textbook-writers lack authority and authenticity as they purely parrot what has been said elsewhere. All too often writers who *compile* such textbooks do not even write them. These so-called '*textbook authors*' neither author nor authorise a text. Their main task is to convert the already written ideas of other authors into a textbook format. The writing of a textbook writer is in fact pre-written. The mind of the textbook writer is already '*written*' before the writing process starts. By parroting or mirroring or simply copying or reproducing what an original author wrote, the textbook writer becomes a mere instrument of the original author.

136   In the modern Newspeak of HRM, even conflict is no longer conflict. It is now a misunderstanding or a misinterpretation of HR policies. All of this is done to eliminate conflict as well as any conflicting thought (*Crimestop*) and eventually to eliminate any conceptualisation of labour itself.

137   See: Barry's *Company: A Novel* (2006).

138   *The first principle of marketing, according to some schools, is to 'turn needs into wants'. Marketing asserts, first, the right to choice and, second, the right to manipulate you by any means short of extortion and blackmail into believing that there is no choice but to buy a particular product* (Watson 2003:63).

139 Therborn (1977:4) has emphasised that *democracy is one of the key words of contemporary ideological discourse, despite – or perhaps because of – the fact that so little serious research has been devoted to it.* While this applied in 1977, when he wrote it, it equally applies today, as there is very little to almost no research on democratic management. Equal to democratic management, industrial democracy or workplace democracy has been successfully erased from today's research and popular management literature.

140 Inside modern textbooks, a *tabloid-isation* can be observed. This is a process that turns academic books into tabloid newspaper reading moving ethics into a distant corner. Once confined inside a secure corner of a tabloid-text, ethics can be shown as removed and aloof from the real business world. In other cases, ethics is reduced to being part of a collection of sound-bytes that *make up(!)* the modern textbook.

141 Watson (2003:54) has reproduced one of the most eloquent examples of managerial language: *building an online platform for integrated customer centric service delivery.*

142 Managerial capitalism produces strong irrationalities that are covered up by rational means-ends or cost-benefit theories. For example, *researchers have compared the price of phone calls made while driving with the 'price' of deadly risks. Since risk is not, like cell phones and calling planes, directly bought and sold in the marketplace, economists have tried to place it where it is sold indirectly…economists have estimated that groups of workers doing dangerous jobs are paid, on average, a total of about US$5–6 million more, per work-related death. By comparing the price of cell phone use with this 'price' of risky work, economists have concluded that banning cell phone use in cars makes no economic sense* (Ackermann & Heinzerling 2004:2).

143 While management claims to represent science and technology and everything else represents myths and is anti-modern, it nevertheless produces managerial myths – obviously never to be labelled as such – to support and legitimise its very existence. While in pre-modern times myths were an expression of primitive and immature thought and the process of civilisation has invalidated them, management has *returned rational thought to mythological status* (Marcuse 1966:193).

144 On the issue of *free choice*, Adorno (1944:37) noted, *free choice has been liquidated as the result of the objective processes of the market society. It has entirely become a function of paid propaganda-bureaus and is measured in terms of the investment being wagered by the name-bearer or interest-group behind it.*

145 Watson (2003:35) notes *corporate leaders sometimes have good reason to twist their language into knots and obscure the meaning of it, but more often it is simply habit. They have forgotten the other way of speaking: the one in which you try to say what you mean.*

146 Searle's (1996:47) observation is particularly helpful at this point, *obviously, for most institutions we simply grow up in a culture where we take the institution for granted…in the very evolution of the institution the participants need not be consciously aware of the form of the collective intentionality by which they are imposing functions on objects.* In other words, the inherited working culture coupled with modern mass mediated managerialism makes us accept institutions such as management as we simply grow up with it. We are kept unaware of the collective intentionality of managerialism as much as possible so that it can impose its functions on us turning us from subjects into objects of power (Bauman 1989).

147 Theories of ideology seek to explain the way in which humans create and hold certain ideas. They not only shape their world but also their social relationships to others. Once the guiding force of feudal relations was transformed by modernity, ideology became more important (cf. Mannheim 1929). Adorno defines ideology a *objective necessary and yet false consciousness. He means by this false or distorted consciousness that is necessary for reasons relating to the maintenance of the modern capitalist socio-economic system* (Cooke 2006:4; cf. Feyerabend 1981 & 1987; Bell 1960 & 1973).

148 Destutt de Tracy's *four-volume Éléments d'Idéologie, published between 1803 and 1815, examined the faculties of thinking, feeling, memory and judgement, and the characteristics of habit, movement and the will, among other things* (Thompson 1990:30). *Napoleon's use of the term 'ideology' conveyed a negative sense by suggesting that the ideas concerned were both erroneous and impractical, both misleading and divorced from the practical realities of political life* (Thompson 1990:55).

149 If one takes Karl Mannheim's (1929) dictum of ideology as a *general* formulation (a) and as a *special* formulation (b) and views both as being in a dialectical relationship, then general formulations can be seen as general experience of ideology in the social domain, while a more specific formulation of ideology occurs in the more special domain of work. Unlike general formulations of ideology, specific formulations of ideology appear in the domain of work. They are applied to work while general formulations may in some cases be supportive. However, not all general formulations can be transferred into the domain of work and visa versa (cf. McNeill & Feldman (1998:222).

150 Louis Althusser (1965) saw ideology as a repressive apparatus operational in two domains: a) the repressive state apparatus and b) a repressive private apparatus constituted by churches, political parties, and mass media. Undoubtedly, managerial ideologies would fall into Althusser's private domain, even though they would not be unsupported by the ideological state apparatus.

151 Contrary to this early view, Thompson (1990:9) has argued *the concept of ideology in terms of interplay of meaning and power* [isn't just] *pure illusion, as an inverted or distorted image of what is 'real'...as a camera obscura*. This represents the world by means of an image turned upside down.

152 Quoted from Eagleton (1994:8). On the power of the ruling class, Orwell (1949:224) commented that *if one is to rule, and to continue ruling, one must be able to dislocate the sense of reality. For the secret of rulership is to combine a belief in one's own infallibility with the power to learn from past mistakes.*

153 According to Austin (1962:3), *it has come to be seen that many specially perplexing works embedded in apparently descriptive statements do not serve to indicate some specially odd additional feature in the reality reported, but to indicate (not to report) the circumstances in which the statement is made or reservations to which it is subject or the way in which it is to be taken and the like. These possibilities cannot be overlooked.* To overlook them means the exposure to what has been termed *descriptive* fallacy. See also: Graham (1977).

154 According to Searle (1969:132), the *naturalistic fallacy...is the* fallacy of supposing that it is logically impossible for a set of statements of the kind usually called descriptive to entail a statement of the kind usually called evaluative.

155 On socialisation Offe (1976:21) noted that *primary and secondary socialisation form a style of life and work the origin of which is no longer apparent in the social-philosophical and ideological model of the achieving society: the ideology infiltrates the level of behaviour and there solidifies into a scheme which is immune from all criticism* (cf. Cole 1988; cf. White 1969; Segal 1970).

156 For most people, the relations of power and domination which affect them most directly are those characteristic of the social context within which they live out their everyday lives: the workplace (Thompson 1990:9).
157 In the *Critique of Cynical Reason*, Peter Sloterdijk puts forward the thesis that ideology's dominant mode of functioning is cynical, which renders impossible – or, more precisely, vain – the classic critical-ideological procedure. The cynical subject is quite aware of the distance between the ideological mask and the social reality but nonetheless still insists on the mask. The formula, as proposed by Sloterdijk, would then be: *they know very well what they are doing, but still, they are doing it…one knows the falsehood very well, one is well aware of a particular interest hidden behind an ideological universality, but still one does not renounce it* (Zizek 1989:29).
158 The idea of taking things as they are in a *what is* fashion carries connotations of *Naïve Realism* (Russell 1973:13, cf. 1945).
159 See: Adorno's *Late Capitalism or Industrial Society* (1968).
160 According to Anthony (1977:24) *management education is truly ideology in the sense that it aims to influence behaviour by inculcating beliefs and expectations…an ideological explanation of this element in managerial education also explains the astonishing absence of controversy.* The one-dimensionality of management ideology or managerial education is underwritten not only by a total absence of controversy but also by a reduction of internal conflict to simple arguments that in general do not oppose but complement each other.
161 On mass consumption, Adorno (1944:45) noted, *every program must be sat through to the end, every 'best seller' must be read, every film must be seen during its first release in the movie theater. The abundance of what is consumed without choice becomes calamitous. It makes it impossible to find one's way, and just as one looks for a guide [Führer: literally 'leader' or 'guide', but a pun on Hitler's official title] in a monstrous department store, so too does the population, penned in by attractions, wait for a leader of their own.* Marcuse (1966:25) added, *the creation of repressive needs has long since become part of socially necessary labour – necessary in the sense that without it, the established mode of production could not be sustained.*
162 Naturally, TV's business programmes hardly tell us everything, but television is – next to normal advertisements – one of the principle media to proliferate managerialism. In addition, it is, of course, the glossiest medium for marketing as well (cf. Davis & Silk 1978).
163 On the public media, Adorno (1944:43) noted, *newspapers daily and naively trumpet [the news]…but mean absolutely nothing and could be replaced on demand tomorrow by exactly the opposite ones, the ears of those who follow the party line display musical acuity, as soon as there is the slightest hint of disrespect for slogans divested of theory…[business news] meshes seamlessly with hurrah-optimism.*
164 *A Critique of the Political Economy* is the subtitle of Marx' book *Das Kapital*.
165 Modern mass media work with *double-distortion*. Progressive policies are *negatively distorted* to appear negative or even dangerous for society. On the other hand, conservative policies are *positively distorted* to appear positive for society. Increasingly, this occurs under the heading *reform*. The term *reform* originated in a period of *reformation* designed to reform, i.e. move on towards betterment, of the church. Today's distortion of *reform* converts an originally positive term into a winding back of social regulation. It is not *reform* or *conservative*, i.e. to conserve or maintaining the *status quo*, but a reactionary policy. Today's policies of *reforms* are not forward moving or progressive

reforms. Instead, they wind back social achievements. These *reforms* do not even conserve things. They are deeply reactionary. They seek an earlier status that has long been surpassed.
166 Of course, there are the accessional pictures of the dying poor in some remote countries but the link that their death has a connection to our rampant overconsumption is never established. We can free our conscious with a little donation here and there. We do not need to understand *'why'* this is all happening and what could be done to stop the senseless death of millions. Finally, we can drown our conscious in paternalism and determinism. *That is just the way it is* or *it has always been like that*. There is a multitude of ideologies in today's toolboxes ready to be used to ease our conscience and to make us forget the social pathologies that the present system creates.
167 An *'end of ideology' is…an ideology all in itself: what it recommends is that we forget about moral justifications altogether and simply concentrate on enjoying ourselves* (Eagleton 1994:18).
168 See Baudrillard (1994).
169 *So mindless is some of this talk, we observe, that one of the great paradoxes of competition goes unnoticed: The end or objective of competition is the end or termination of competition* (Cheney & Carroll 1997:619).
170 Ideologies have the assigned task to legitimise social and economic statuses while repressing alternatives at the same time. They also seek to – at least as a surface structure – consolidate the existing contradictions of the present social and economic conditions. They also shield the system against people's exiting options – the non-part-taking in consumption – while also providing interpretive schemes for system integration elements (Offe 1976:13).
171 George Orwell (1949:223) saw the problem of contradictions solved thought the engineering of what he termed *'Doublethink'. Doublethink means the power of holding two contradictory beliefs in one's mind simultaneously, and accepting both of them. To tell deliberate lies while genuinely believing in them, to forget any fact that has become inconvenient, and then, when it becomes necessary again, to draw it back from oblivion for just so long as it is needed, to deny the existence of objective reality and all the while to take account of the reality which one denies – all this is indispensably necessary.*
172 Thompson (1990:20) has argued that *if mass communication has become a major medium for the operation of ideology in modern societies, it is because it has become a major medium for the production and transmission of symbolic forms, and because the symbolic forms thereby produced are capable of circulating on an unprecedented scale, reaching millions of individuals who may share little in common other than their capacity to receive mass mediated messages.*
173 See Adorno's chapter *96 on Janus' palace* (1944:58–59).
174 Any *interpretation of ideology necessarily involves a social-historical analysis of structured relations of power* (Thompson 1990:25).
175 The role of Max Weber for the German bourgeoisie has been extensively discussed in: Therborn (1973:53ff).
176 *In the overdeveloped countries, an ever-larger part of the population becomes one huge captive audience – captured not by a totalitarian regime but by the liberties of the citizens whose media of amusement and elevation compel the other to partake of their sounds, sights, and smells* (Marcuse 1966:249).
177 See: Baudrillard (1979).
178 To make such workers fit into managerial structures the so-called FIFO ideology is of great assistance. It says: *Fit in or f… off!*

179 An illustrative example has been provided by Hodge & Kress (1979:17–29) using a UK newspaper editorial in the *Guardian: A Necessary Measure*. It analyses the language applied to frame an industrial conflict.
180 For details on Antonio Gramsci see: Gamble, Marsh & Tant (1999).
181 Quoted from: McGee (1980:14) & Eagleton (1994:13). In the words of George Orwell (1949:205), *all rulers in all ages have tried to impose a false view of the world upon their followers*.
182 Interpellation is a parliamentarian term. In a parliament it describes an interruption of the order of the day by demanding an explanation from the minister concerned (Concise Oxford Dictionary).
183 This has been discussed by, among many others, Bosquet (1980) and Ramsay (1980).
184 It does not come as a surprise that not only relationships at work are socially constructed but also the way in which people communicate at work (Mohan et al. 2004:19).
185 See Gay (1996:59) & (1997).
186 An interesting example of *how* the mass media structure words, dialogues and meanings in a hegemonic way has been given by Marcuse (1969:78) on the *Vietnam War*. Today, one can replace the word *Vietnam* with any given Middle-Eastern country. Similarly, the word *communist* can, of course, be replaced with *terrorist*. *The linguistic pattern constantly repeats itself: In Vietnam, 'typical criminal communist violence' is perpetrated against American 'strategic operations'; the communists have the impertinence to 'launch a sneak attack' (presumably they are supposed to announce it beforehand and to deploy in the open); they are 'evading a death trap' (presumably they should have stayed in). The Viet Cong attack American barracks 'in the dead of night' and kill American boys (presumably, Americans only attack in broad daylight, don't disturb the sleep of the enemy, and don't kill Vietnamese boys).*
187 See also: Burawoy (1979), Herman (2002).
188 See Herman (2002), see also: Herman & Chomsky (1988); Herman & McChesney (1997).
189 In the world of work, the analytically weak idea of *'culture'* carries a wide range of connotations, among them those of business culture, company culture, corporate culture, work culture, etc. Many of them also carry ideas on individual conduct at work, risk tolerance, direction, integration, management conduct, control, reward systems, conflict tolerance, and communicative patterns. See also Adorno & Horkheimer (1944) & Gay (1997).
190 Statt (1994:187) emphasised that *play gradually gives way to work…socialisation is crucial for the world of work…the rewards for achievement and the punishments for non-achievement* [have been part of the school and the work regime]*…and these lessons are learned within a highly structured context of values, meanings and feelings associated with working.* Socialisation for the world of work begins at school in the earliest years of a child's education (Statt 1994:189; cf. White 1969; Segal 1970; Cole 1988).
191 Once communicative behaviour can be shaped in this way, social behaviour at work can be shaped as well because *organisations* [codeword for profit making companies] *want to prevent employees from engaging in behaviours that stand in the way of organisational success* [codeword for profit] (Jex 2002:239).
192 On this, Adorno (1944:79) noted, *the principle of commerce contributes to the continuation of what is utterly anti-democratic, of economic injustice, of human degradation.*

193 Habermas (2006:6) has described this process as: *the democratic practice of voting constitutes a collective enterprise and requires of the participants that they proceed on the assumption that every vote 'counts'.*

194 For the most part, ideology operates below consciousness by constructing a-historical subjects to be fully functional and operative in present society.

195 Democracy has been linked to the public or consumption domains as well. There is a *pseudo-democratic justification of income disparities through the theory of market populism, which identifies individual spending with universal suffrage. This theory claims that the popular will builds the financial muscle of big business: millions of consumers 'vote' for Wal-Mart every time they shop there. Any intelligentsia linked to a state bureaucracy and aspiring to impose its egalitarian utopia is one step from a dictatorship* (Le Monde Diplomatique, Engl. edition, June 2006:14–15). By linking mass guided consumption to democracy in this way, a hegemonic ideology is hardened against any critical suggestion by portraying it as a dictatorship. By doing so it covers the real dictatorship. In this way, the theory of consumerist democracy becomes a perfect example of Orwellian ideas (cf. Fromm's chapter on *Freedom & Democracy*, 1942).

196 On common sense, Adorno (1944:31) noted, *precisely those who wish to make no concession to the stupidity of common sense must guard themselves against stylistically draping together thoughts, which are themselves to be convicted of banality.*

197 The doctrine of declaring their construction of reality as natural is part of the doctrine described by George Orwell in his novel *Nineteen Eighty-Four, in the past the need for a hierarchical form of society has been the doctrine specifically of the High.*

198 See also Habermas (2006:1).

199 See Stadon (2001:7) who describes that Pavlov (1849–1936) *ran a large institute in the Military Medical Academy in St. Petersburg from 1895 for many years.* In short, conditioning and *behaviourism's* origins lie in military studies, perhaps because the *death-delivering* and *death-incurring* tasks of soldiers needed more conditioning than others. It appears the transition from *behaviourism* in the Russian military to managerialism in everyday life has been, at least partly, been successful.

200 One can be certain that the time spent by a customer in a supermarket is exactly measured. In the same way it is measured where such a customer goes, how long a customer spends searching for a particular product, and above all how long the same customer is willing to wait at the check out (cf. Adorno's 1944:82–83 & 88 contribution to *Customer Service*).

201 See Adorno & Horkheimer (1944:24). On obedience, disobedience and authority, see also: Engels (1874), Adorno et al. (1964), Etzioni (1959), Sennett (1980), Fromm (1981).

202 Ever since the French Revolution, the term citizen [French *citeain* or *citoyen*] has been seen in opposition to *bourgeois*. The urban city based class of *bourgeois* expressed a commercial class while the *citoyen* expressed freedom, liberty, and democracy. Since then, citizenship is closely linked to democracy. Habermas (1997a:127) has described this as: *the citizens themselves became those who deliberate and, acting as a constitutional assembly, decided how they must fashion the rights that give the discourse principle legal shape as a principle of democracy.* Introducing a special issue of the *Canadian Relations Industrielles/ Industrial Relations Journal* (2006:620), Coutu and Murray have discussed this in: *Towards Citizenship at Work? – An Introduction* (2006:617–630). They begin their introduction with a historical overview followed by an outline of what is

to come in the special issue of the journal. Any critical examination of industrial citizenship is not undertaken. While full of historical details, any discussion of whether industrial democracy can lead to workers' emancipation is avoided. Similarly, whether or not democracy is merely a device to guarantee worker's loyalty in a pre-set managerial framework of system is not discussed either (cf. Canfora 2006).

203 The idea that consuming adds value to humans is linked to the idea of *commodity fetishism*. Commodity fetishism is an inauthentic state of social relations arising with capitalist market relations entering social relations. It transforms social relations into market relations based on the centrality of property and property relations. People within capitalist societies find their material life organised through the medium of commodity, trading their labour-power (as exchange commodity) for money (another exchange commodity). Human life is reduced to an exchange function. The idea of *commodity fetishism* is *not* linked to Sigmund Freud's idea of sexual fetishism.

204 Good examples that show the ideological use of history to put management and HRM in a certain light are: Kaufman's *The Origins & Evolution of the Field of Industrial Relations in the United States* (1993) & Kaufman et al. *Industrial Relations to Human Resources and Beyond – The Evolving Process of Employee Relations Management* (2003).

205 See also: Kaufman (1993 & 2002); Kerr, Dunlop, Harbison & Myers (1960) & McCarthy (2000).

206 Life of working people often took place in *Labor Camps* as shown in the movie *Grapes of Wrath* with the actor Henry Fonda.

207 One of the most striking examples of the failure of the managerially pushed ideas in such organisations has been the case of the US company Enron (Gladwell 2002; cf. Kaufman et al. 2003:7).

208 All too often standard HRM textbooks do not start with the historical beginnings because they seek to negate, neglect, or hide the sometimes rather brutal past of managing people at work. To hide the dark historical past (Engels 1892, Thompson 1963) of domesticating workers, HRM textbooks often start with companies to work for, HRM recognises the importance of people, theoretical perspectives of HRM (as if there was one!), conceptual – not historical – foundations of HRM, what does a HR department do, skills for HR professionals, competitive challenges, etc. etc. – all in an effort to avoid the painful past.

209 In this version of history, objectivity, neutrality and value free-ness are hidden behind endless historical numbers (usually dates and years) to give the perception of 'this is what happened'. The social construction of company history and of texts that portray this history remains cloaked behind often sheer overwhelming numbers, dates, figure, graphs, time tables, etc.

210 Even though written from a post-modern perspective, Barry and Elmes' *Strategy Retold* (1997) provides insightful ideas on how literary elements are used to portray companies and corporations in a managerially favourable light.

211 It appears as if Albert Einstein's *education is what remains after one has forgotten everything he learned in school* remains valid.

212 One can almost be assured that if Orwell's statement on: *who controls the past controls the future: who controls the present controls the past* is correct, then our period might be constructed by future generations as a time when globalisation brought wealth to all. At the same time, the insanity of capitalist rationality results in mass starvation, hunger, and poverty. In future history books,

this will be safely reduced to a few isolated sections. How this has been done is described in Hobsbawn's work (2004) & Pilger's (2006) *Freedom Next Time*.
213 The lovely Mr Darcy in Jane Austin's novels is such a fine character while child labour and worker's abuse (including the frequent rape of female workers), all prevalent in the 19th century, remains unseen in today's TV programs and the mass produced and equally mass consumed literature.
214 In the case of Jex (2002:240) this has been made explicit and conscious: *one underlying assumption which is so basic that we rarely question it, is that an organisation has the right to influence the behaviour of its employees*. In other words, with the purchase of labour, individuals foreclose their ability to behave in any other way as determined by an employer/manager. Furthermore, the influencing or straightforward manipulating of human behaviour in the interest of profit is the *right* of those who buy YOU (body, mind, and spirit).
215 In Orwellian terms, textbook writing for managerialism is often no more than *to hire the services of professional 'language manipulators' to supplement [their] own linguistic domination* so that their *views* can be hidden behind *inter-views* in order *to maintain a balanced view (that is an uncritical view)* (Chilton 1983:33–34).
216 An illustrative example has been provided by Hodge & Kress (1979:17–29). It uses an editorial in the *Guardian on A Necessary Measure* about industrial conflict over coal. An editorial approach is often introduced to managerial communications. In printed company announcements such highly edited communication reflects certain messages that are beneficial to management. Messages are distorted in an effort to adhere to management's instrumental interests. Consequently, managerial textbooks advocate editorial training for managers (Himstreet & Baty 1961: 28).
217 Quoted from Hoggart (2004:14).
218 *The philosopher Pascal, who argues that human beings do not kneel down to pray because they believe in God but rather they believe in God because they kneel down to pray. In Pascal's view, religious thoughts and beliefs are shaped by (immersion in) religious practice, and Althusser believes this extends to all aspects of ideology. Unlike religious, modern ideology correctly represents imaginary relations to real conditions rather than straightforwardly misrepresenting real relationships* (Crossley 2005:152 &154).
219 *Discourse* defines a *dissertation* of *treatise* on an *academic subject* or a *lecture* or *sermon* (The Concise Oxford Dictionary, 9th Edition). At work, none of the above takes place even though academics tend to apply what they do in their work to the world of work in general. However this is not the case. In the world of work communication is structured as a hierarchical top-down affair with reporting upwards and directing downwards. In sharp contrast academic discourses are fundamentally different; they are horizontal, not vertical.
220 See Gay (1996:59 & 1997).
221 One way of limiting people's ability to understand is to limit the range of words they can use. *Don't you see that the whole aim of Newspeak is to narrow the range of thoughts?* George Orwell once wrote.
222 Stabilising interests are not only supported by affirmative ideology but also by depoliticising human society in the form of consumerism, entertainment and even *info*tainment that *co*ntain and *co*ntaine*ri*se thinking. *Modern mass communication has created centripetal attention structures that bottle celebrity, and celebrities, for sale. They create machine-made frames. They also create a winner-take-all*

society [in which] attention engineering is replacing product engineering as the centre stage (Lanham 2006:11 &18).

223 Over the past 50 years the greatest change has been the ideology of consumer choice that directs all questions of taste and fashion. Mediated for most people through television, it established the illusion of *choice* – something previously only experienced by the upper class – in the minds of the affluent workers. Today restricted life-choices [school, college, work & consume, retirement, death] are compensated with an endless variety of choices between only cosmetically different cars and tooth brushes. Life-choices have vanished as consumer-choices have exploded.

224 The achievements made in the mass-communicative domain with restructured and corporatised consumers have been re-created in the world of work: the masterpiece psychology has been destroyed in favour of mass-manufactured sameness; mass-production has replaced skilled handwork; mass-audiences of airheads with a completely ornamental life have replaced connoisseurship; trendiness has ousted timelessness; and senseless repetition has replaced rarity (Gare 2006).

225 Definitions are acts of name assignments. They give names to things and this can be a dangerous act especially when the names for things are incorrect or deliberately created to achieve specific ends. When this is done, speech often does not sound reasonable or things are not done properly. When things are not done properly, the structure of society is harmed (Poole 2006:1).

226 Those who frame the true purpose of corporate existence as culture, consciously or unconsciously eclipse the true and underlying fact of profit making. When corporate purposes are made to appear as culture, the system receives a stabilising legitimacy.

227 See: Linstead *et al.* (2004:93–122), cf. Alvesson (2002).

228 Unspeak has been invented – actually by no one other than Shakespeare – but it has been brought to attention recently by Poole (2006). In contrast Orwell's Newspeak commutates an entirely new language while Hoggart's *Adspeak* (2004:193) describes the colonisation of everyday language by advertising slogans, terms, mottos, phrases, etc. See also Hoggart's *Everyday Language and Everyday Life* (2003).

229 Resistance is, however, not only defined as uncultured; the rhetoric capitalism supported via corporate mass media has sought to dampen any attempts by workers to engage in resistance. This has been rhetorically supported by well-ingrained phrases such as *that's not the end of the world, time heals all wounds, you can't win them all, every cloud has a silver lining, good health is better than wealth*, etc. (Hoggart 2003:34–37).

230 On the leadership continuum between autocratic/dictatorial and democratic management, it creates the illusion of allowing workers some sort of autonomy over their own decision making processes.

231 Once the disconnection of work and democracy has been achieved, the world of work moves a step closer to Orwell's prediction made in the novel *Nineteen Eighty-Four* (1949:207): *cut off from contact with the outer world, and with the past, man* [like workers] *in interstellar space, who has no way of knowing which direction is up and which is down. The rulers...are absolute, as the Pharaohs or the Caesars could not be.*

232 For the most part, ideology operates below consciousness as an unconscious form by constructing a-historical subjects to be fully functional and operative in present society.

233 If the key to the classic liberal idea of *a free* society is the need for *free* speech, then our present society is relatively unfree. At present access to communicative media that transmit free speech are relatively restricted in the hands of corporate media. Therefore, one can safely assume that we live in a society where the corporate mass media has access to free speech but not the ordinary member of society. We live in a *corporate-only free speech society*. See Chomsky's *Free Speech in a Democracy* (1985) & Herman & Chomsky's *Manufacturing Consent – The Political Economy of the Mass Media* (1988). See also: Fowler's *Language in the News* (1991).

234 Interestingly, standard textbooks like Mohan *et al.* (2004:363) barely mention rhetoric while Krizan *et al.* (2005) does not mention it at all and for O'Hair *et al.* (2005:440) rhetoric is only mentioned on the back page as a passing reference to an antic period (similarly to Eunson 2005:379 & Blundel 2004:106).

235 See the early use of rhetoric as outlined by Kennedy (1993 & 1994); rhetoric has also included the idea of *ethos, pathos, and logos*.

236 At its most extreme and apocalyptic level, rhetoric still exists in George Orwell's *Nineteen Eighty-Four* (1949:49), *Big Brother's familiar style: a style at once military and pedantic, and, because of a trick of asking questions and then promptly answering them...easy to imitate.*

237 Rhetorical or alternative-avoiding tools used as an ideology – knowledge in the service of power – are: metaphor (short analogies) in the form of *orientational metaphors* (up/down, on/off, etc.), ontological metaphors (the mother of all systems), or structural metaphors (time is money); metonymy (Hollywood is a metonym of glamour); Irony (using words and images to convey the opposite of what they literally mean); paradox (an extreme form of irony); cliché (first and foremost or at this point in time); allusion (an indirect or implicit reference to a well-known place, person, event or text); definition (sets boundaries between terms); analogy (a form of an example where a story is described together with the thing exemplified in order to make it clearer); simile (a weak metaphor signalled through 'as' or 'like'); overstatement or understatement; oxymoron (a contradictory term); alliteration (a phonetic form where words begin with the same sound); and allegory (when fictional narratives support abstract ideas).

238 On the other end of the scale, the extreme opposite case of life in poverty has been rhetorically supported by a language of acceptance (Hoggart 2003:23–34). When the extreme forms of poverty disappeared for roughly 2/3 of the population in advanced capitalist counties, the rhetoric also moved towards countries where extreme poverty is the main condition of human existence. With it moved the rhetoric of *they are poor because they are corrupt, they have too many children, etc.* even though advanced countries have roughly 200 people per square kilometre, Asia has 100 and Africa has 50!

239 This follows Poole (2006). To *Unspeak* something means to disallow conflicting meanings. It constructs them one-dimensionally. When something is labelled as *balanced*, no one seeks to present an un-balanced view. When something is labelled as *extreme*, no one seeks to express such a point any further.

240 When management declares issues as not to be spoken of, then this carries connotations of the religious taboo of medieval times as outlined by Durkheim's *Elementary Forms of Religious Life* (1912). In that way managerialism uses the rhetoric tools of religion to silence unwarranted issues, a technique that has produced system stabilising results for more than 2000 years.

241 In the words of Watson (2003:52), *they are ritual words. It is as if, like someone with schizophrenia or depression, they are not quite of the real world. They have forgotten the language the rest of us speak.*

242 In advanced societies, the limiting of life-choices and communicative choices are compensated with free market choices where freedom lies solely in the freedom of choice. In this way the well-conditioned consumer can exercise freedom within the set parameters of the free market. Inside it, the consumer is happy to have a choice even though it means choice reductions in vital areas of human life. Limiting communicative choices at work [one-dimensionally structured forms of communication] and in the consumption domain largely through a linear mass-communication system that allocates power to a *sender* [corporate mass media] and passive affirmation to a receiver [consumer] goes hand in hand with choice enhancing consumerism. Choices over things have led to a diminishing choice of communication. Orwellian Newspeak that seeks to reduce vocabularies is – in post *Nineteen Eighty-Four* societies – complemented with a choice over things. The choice to think is replaced with the choice to have things. Epictetus was correct in saying *it is not things but what we think about things that trouble humankind.* Ritualistic and communicative choice-reducing mechanisms have limited our thinking about things and so the untroubled mind can indulge itself in mindless consumption slaughtering human thinking on the altar of things.

243 HRM and its subdivision HRD (development) *is concerned with influencing, some might say shaping human behaviour* (Stewart 2007:63), other might say manipulate and condition human behaviour.

244 Long before one reaches a business school, ordinary schools have already had their opportunities in domesticating individuals. Albert (2006:96) has described this as *eighty per cent of us are presently taught in schools to endure boredom and take orders, because that's what capitalism needs from workers. Another eighteen per cent are made ambitious, as well as callous to the condition of those below, and ignorant about their own callousness. At the very top, two per cent are made cruel and greedy. Of course it isn't perfectly cut and dried, as portrayed, but this is the overall, average picture.*

245 Apart from establishing managerial status through rituals, *some status indicators need to be explicitly linguistic, that is, they need not be action words. The most obvious examples are wedding rings and uniforms* (Searle 1996:120). While uniforms indicate these non-linguistic statuses for the military, it is the pin-striped suit, the business lounge, the business class, the business lunch, etc. for managers.

246 Workers are faced with an increased number of sophisticated persuaders. This process is: discard or adopt old habits > adapt > reinforce > add the new. This process reinforces those older attitudes which suit the new world's new purpose; secondly, it discourages those which do not suit; thirdly, it encourages new and more suitable styles – suitable to its own ends (Hoggart 2004:5).

247 In Orwellian (1949:172) terms, *the terrible thing that* [management] *had done was to persuade you that mere impulses, mere feelings, were of no account, while at the same time robbing you of all powers over the material world.*

248 Nature with singing birds, frogs, forests, trees, etc. or the *nature of management* – as an often used term by management and managerial textbooks – should always appear as a *natural* form of existence and not as a socially constructed form as it allows management to be natural and naturally have meetings. The internet business database EBSCO listed (2006) 65,000 articles that discussed

the nature of... while the American *Academy of Management Review* alone listed 492 articles with *the nature of...* in it.
249 There are, however, a few isolated cases of company boards with *directors* with special representation. Very few even have workers' representatives. This however remains well below the level of participation that could seriously impact on corporate decisions. Despite the rhetoric of co-decision making, involvement, participation, etc., decision making remains firmly in the hands of managers.
250 Such meeting arrangements can be seen as *a sign because a sign is something that stands to somebody for something in some respect or capacity*. Meeting arrangements are powerful signs that signify top-down power relations to *somebody* (workers) in *some* (power) respect (Eco 1977:15). The managerial arrangement of meetings is no more than a sign that *'stands in'* for power relations that define relations between management and workers.
251 Almost by definition, meetings in workplaces are held, run, led, organised, and structured by 'a senior staff member' (Mohan et al. 2004:189). Behind the term senior staff member resides no more than the hierarchical top-down structure. In addition, the term staff member is used to eclipse the fact that those who chair are all too often managers, i.e. set apart from normal 'staff members', however, the term 'staff member' is designed to hide this by giving the appearance s/he is just another staff member drawing on a pretended equality where none exists.
252 Adopted from: Tuckman (1965), Stiff & Mongeau (2003:314).
253 In this concept, leaders are assumed to be almost natural even though they are created and sustained in a social process. Leaders – may it be management or political leaders – are a socially constructed reality. Leaders are at their best (sic!) when fighting a market share war (management) or a real war (politics). The sub-leader of the most heinous leader (Führer) in human history, Hermann Goering, put his finger on it in 1946, not long before he committed suicide. Gustav Gilbert, an intelligence officer, interviewed him in his jail cell in Nuremberg during the war crimes trials. The transcripts of these interviews were published in 1947 in Gilbert's *Nuremberg Diary*. Gilbert said to Goering that in a democracy the people have some say through their elected representatives and that in the US only Congress can declare war. Goering's recorded reply was: 'That is all well and good, but voice or no voice, the people can always be brought to the bidding of the leaders. That is easy. All you have to do is tell them they are being attacked and denounce the pacifists for lack of patriotism and exposing the country to danger. It works the same way in any country'. Old Hermann certainly knew a thing or two.
254 A useful tool in the hands of management is a managerial *Communication Manual*. It ensures control over *what* has been discussed in meetings, which issues leave meetings and which do not. It regulates the way reports are written, and for *what* purpose. In this way, even after a meeting, results can be written up or even be re-written so that they adhere to a managerially constructed company policy, i.e. management ideology.
255 Blundel (2004:103) provides a good example on how standard textbooks construct the issue of persuasion: *Sometimes we are seeking to persuade others. For example, a manager needs a volunteer to work over the weekend in order to complete a project, or a trade union negotiator calls for improvements in working conditions*. The above basically translates into the following: *sometimes* means: as we all do from time to time! The *'we'* essentially means: *we all* use persuasion and

not only managers do so. Managers do what everyone does. *Others* mean: they are just *others*, not workers. Hence management-worker power relations are eliminated. His example, however, mentions a manager and a volunteer. The *worker* is not mentioned. Above all, being a *volunteer* is a positive term. Of course, no manager would ever use *more* than simple persuasion to get a worker to do weekend work! *Over the weekend* hides the fact that this was time we used to spend with our family! *To finish a project* means: to increase company profits, naturally! *Trade union...* means: see! They do the same, they persuade others too; they are just the same. Gone are the hierarchical command structures of management and the labour market structures of capitalism. The structural force of capitalism that turns us into workers is reduced to a *voluntary* exercise and joining a trade union, which is actually a voluntary act, is levelled to so-called voluntary weekend work. In sum, the act of persuasion has started with textbooks like this.

256 Quoted from Smith (1982:326). While this 1957 version of persuasion is today regarded as unethical, contemporary advertising uses the insertion of the word *'sex'* and sexual images such as erogenous zones that are airbrushed into advertisements for all sorts of products, including items such as tooth brushes, Ritz crackers or cars [what is the link between naked women and a car, one might innocently ask]. While the use of sexual images is not always highly visible, they play on the sub-conscious mind because they create a sexual stimulus that helps selling.

257 Persuasion has been seen as *a symbolic activity whose purpose is to effect the internalisation or voluntary acceptance of new cognitive states or patterns of overt behaviour through the exchange of messages* (Smith 1982:7; cf. Stiff & Mongeau 2003:12; Gass & Seiter 1999).

258 As Gadamer (1976:11) once put it, *effective propaganda must always try to influence initially the judgement of the person addressed and to restrict his possibilities of judgement"*. It is based on the subtle power that resides in its behind-the-scene power to influence decisions and define reality. The master of effective propaganda was the German Nazi Herman Goering who was interviewed by Gustav Gilbert (*Nuremberg Diary*, 1947) before he committed suicide in his cell in Nuremberg. Gilbert said to him that in a democracy the people have some say through their elected representatives and that in the US only Congress can declare war. Goering's recorded reply was: *That is all well and good, but voices or no voices, the people can always be brought to the bidding of the leaders. That is easy. All you need to do is tell them they are being attacked and denounce the pacifists for lack of patriotism and exposing the country to danger. It works the same way in any country.* Today's non-Nazi version of propaganda has been discussed in Herman & Chomsky's *Manufacturing Consent* (1988:2). It is not the Nazi state anymore – in fact, no state at all – but corporate media that creates and disseminates propaganda. Their *propaganda model* includes *(1) the size, concentrated ownership, owner wealth, and profit orientation of the dominant mass media firms; (2) advertising as the primary income source of the mass media; (3) the reliance of the media on information provided by government, business and 'experts' funded and approved by these primary sources and agents of power; (4) flak as a means of disciplining the media; and (5) 'anti-communism'* [or anti-unionism or today's anti-terrorism] *as a national religion and control mechanism (on no. 4, see: http://www.thirdworldtraveler.com/Herman%20Manufac_Consent_Prop_Model.html & http://www.chomsky.info/onchomsky/20031209.htm).*

259 O'Keefe (2006:331) writes that *accurate diagnosis of the bases of resistance is fundamentally important to effective persuasion*. In other words, persuasion management starts with diagnosing those workers' attitudes that could provide an element of resistance towards the restructuring or manipulation of workers' minds. Such a diagnosis, according to O'Keefe (2006:331) is of absolute significance. Therefore, management often puts a heightened emphasis on attitude surveys because they can detect such resistance so that management can adjust their strategy and tactics to target workers' ability to resist.

260 While Orwell (1949:200) saw *what is concerned here is not the morale of the masses, whose attitude is unimportant as long as they are kept steadily at work*, today's managerialism depicts an active interest in the attitudes of workers.

261 Persuasion operates like Orwell's version of the *bi-directional Telescreen* where *objects of power* are requested to actively participate in their own domestication and thought-exposure to a domineering authority.

262 Adorno (1944:55) noted that *nothing is being done to humanity from the outside only: dumbness is the objective Spirit [Geist]*.

263 It appears as if perception is one of the key issues for managerialism and even management gurus – this term refers to the lack of theory and because theory is generally regarded as dangerous and something that does not contribute value to the bottom-line – have encompassed perception as a core value of managerialism. It forms the so-called 4Ps = *perception, persistence, people, and persuasion*. In the first place, appearance or *Keeping up the Appearance* [a BBC-show] is of vital importance and part of the self-preservation ideology of managerialism. Persistence indicates that if you hammer a point long enough it will be accepted as truth. This is the core method of any propaganda. People are next on the list because managerialism needs to get people to do what they want them to do. To achieve this 'people' [i.e. workers or those to be managed] need to be persuaded, not convinced. Persuasion operates on the level of *conditioned association* rather than *symbolic association* as convincing would demand. In fact persuasive techniques only exist because they are targeted towards *conditioned association*. Otherwise they would not be required.

264 The destruction of any alternative has been expressed in Orwell's *Nineteen Eighty-Four* (1949:312) as *the purpose of Newspeak was not only to provide a medium of expression for the world-view and mental habits proper to the devotees of [management], but to make all other modes of thought impossible*.

265 Sometimes, they are hidden in the way as described by Jex (2002:6) when organisational or industrial psychology is portrayed as being within the general field of psychology. *The scientist-practitioner model has become so important that it serves as the underlying philosophy for most graduate training*. Here the science-practice relationship is simply depicted as ⇆, where industrial psychology is *to apply what they have learned in 'real world' settings. However, many in academic also use their research skills to help organisations solve a variety of practical problems*. The divisional character of work – split into those who manage and those who are managed: management and labour – is hidden behind the term *practitioner* and the ideologically shaped character of converting academically created knowledge – often with industry grants – is depicted as ⇆. Terms such as 'the real world' however indicate at least two things. Firstly, because the real world is real it is a fact that has to be accepted as real – *what is* – excluding all alternatives (TINA) and anything that looks like *what ought to be*. Secondly, what is done in academic settings – as opposed to real settings – is rather unreal hence it has to subsume its existence under the

278 Notes

demands of the *real world* and those are the demands of management, the end-user of manipulative organisational or industrial psychology.

266 See also: Packard's *The Hidden Persuaders* (1959) on the status seekers, explorations of class behaviour in America, and the hidden barriers that affect individuals, communities, and the future.

267 According to Cairns' *Reinforcement* (2006:147–148) it occurs when a stimulus is *matched with an emitted response (an operant action) that increases the likelihood of that action/response being repeated...* with a positive (giving reward such as food, praise, wages, tokens) or negative (taking away such a reward) *reinforcer* strengthens managerially deemed supportive action.

268 In society such opinion altering actions can be linked to what is called *Dog Whistling, the name now given to the trick of tapping the political potential of suppressed prejudice, fear and envy through apparently harmless but carefully 'coded' words, and turning it against the rest of the country. The constant fog of lies and half-lies, filtered truth, information, misinformation, disinformation – spin and counter-spin – is endemic to the information age* (Watson 2003:86).

269 In contrast to surveys on workers' attitudes, management sometimes relies on what is called the *Company Grapevine*. This internal communications network includes every form of private conversations between two workers to the latest anecdotes shared in the cafeteria. It is considered as much a communicative vehicle for management as a company in-house newsletter or employee-management meetings. The outstanding characteristic of the grapevine is its speed while one of the greatest weaknesses is the distortion of messages as they speed through the network. Ninety per cent of companies do not have a policy dealing with the grapevine. Neither do they manage informal communication networks even though company grapevines are good tools. Grapevines enable management to find out what employees think. Often negative information about a company or management is also transmitted.

270 The linguistic invasion of the mind can take on forms such as the conversion of meaning of, for example, *disabled workers* to mean *a leech who cuts off his leg so he can get a free ride from the government* or the word *poor* is converted into *not-so-wealthy* while the rest are the *wealthy* and the *truly wealthy* (Lewis & Moss 1977:54).

271 The idea of persuasion lies in the pretence of choice when one recommendation or recommended action is made to appear the best to reap rewards or gain social approval or gain an improved self-image.

272 Unlike in the grim and nihilistic Orwellian novel *Nineteen Eighty-Four* where the state is the sole institution for mind-control, advanced capitalist societies rely less on both mind-control/brain-washing and the state but more on persuasion and affirmation guided through corporate mass media. With the development of large corporations that took over the ideological apparatus which was left unattended with the demise of church and religion, system integration did not move towards an all-domineering and all-controlling super-state but to the private realm that can, more directly than the state, support capitalism through the creation of affirmative workers [work domain] and consumers [consumption domain]. The all too often claimed public discourse and the public domain are no more than sub-systems of the consumptive domain in which democratic elections are reduced to routines of product-choosing rituals. This is evident in political advertising, political image consultants, and the hiring of commercial marketing companies for political elections.

Notes 279

273 For example, how could you strike against *Pfizer* and stop the production of *Viagra* needed by so many men or against Mercedes-Benz, such a wonderful car, or how could you go on strike against a hospital and leave patients suffering!
274 On the side of managerialism, *the system tends to defend their beliefs by avoiding exposure to counter arguments rather than developing support for the beliefs* (Smith 1982:286). In the world of persuasion and managerial affirmation the reverse is the case because managerialism does not rely on any avoidance of counter arguments. Instead it relies on the development of positive support for the belief through communicatively engineered work regimes and corporate mass media.
275 Today, historical links between social achievements and workers' fights for them are no longer prevalent because corporate mass media has successfully severed the historical link between workers' collective action and social advancements such as holidays, maternity leave, hospitals, public health insurance, unemployment benefits, social welfare, etc. There is – with very few microscopic exceptions – virtually no Hollywood movie about a strike. Similarly, the workplace – where most movie-watchers spend eight hours per day, 50 weeks a year for roughly 40 years – is surprisingly absent from cinema, TV, magazines, most newspapers, etc. An archaeologist digging up our world in 5,000 years viewing our movies, TV and magazines must come to the conclusion that we all lived in mansions, had super-large cars, spend our days in leisure and pleasure largely occupying us with the latest gossip concerning airheads (Gare 2006). Similarly, the image created about our past is filled up with kings, queens, heroic wars, trivial romances, etc. (Zengotita 2005) while those on the receiving end of thousand of years of slavery and feudalism are largely absent, much in the same way as workers in today's corporate mass media.
276 See: Williams (2002).
277 Interestingly, there are numerous attitude surveys done by management to investigate workers' attitudes but none by workers to investigate managers' attitudes. This might be seen as a clear expression of the differences between *those who manage* and *those who are managed*.
278 Statt (1994:185) noted that *the term socialisation is sometimes used as though it describes something that was done to people by people, without their consent or participation*. The ideology of *people to people* is used to eclipse the asymmetrical relationship between those *who socialise* and those who are *socialised*. Secondly, when a child is conditioned virtually from birth onwards to adjust to a rigid time (feeding-) regime, socialisation is very much done without the child's consent and when the same child enters kindergarten and schools it is again exposed to conditioning without their consent. Finally, humans are from the same time frame onwards conditioned and socialised to participate in their own domination as humans are made to grow up inside authoritarian structures (Adorno *et al.* 1964).
279 Unlike Orwell's idea of Newspeak that is the only language in the world whose vocabulary gets smaller every year (Lewis & Moss 1983:50), the idea of language intensity demands from management that more – not less – words are used to create the state of language intensity that assists persuasion.
280 To decimate an enemy in the market place or inside a firm is similar to the antique Roman act of killing every tenth (10=deci) soldier after a lost battle by previous generals (managers) of the Roman army.
281 See: Bolinger (1968:258); see also: Bolinger's *Language – The Loaded Weapon* (1980).
282 See Gadamer (1976:90); cf. Gadamer's *Truth and Method* (1974).

283 Euphemisms are types of semantic changes or shifts as they change the meaning of a word. This is also done through the *extension* of words when a word's meaning is broadened or in the process of *narrowing* a word. Euphemisms are also used to create a new meaning replacing an old (negative or positive) one. This is called amelioration or pejoration. In semantic drifts, the meaning of a word drifts towards an entirely new meaning. Further semantic concepts are the figurative use of words, grammatical*isation* and metonymy.

284 See: Mintzberg (1987a); see also: Mintzberg's *The strategy concept I: Five Ps for strategy, and Strategy concept II: Another look at why organizations need strategies* (1987) & *The Nature of Managerial Work (1973)*.

285 The height of this kind of thinking has been summed up by Margretta (2002:8): making sense of the modern world would mean making sense of management. No more is needed to understand the modern world!

286 See: Maslow (1943); Himstreet & Baty (1961:11).

287 According to Herman & McChesney (1997:37) the ideological orientation of corporate media becomes evident *in press reports and their near-hysterical reaction to reports of unexpected employment gains or 'unfavourable' wages settlements (wages go up too much)*.

288 Commonly, five core elements are used when corporate mission statements are created: mission, goals, external analysis, internal analysis, and strategy. These are linked to managerial values – not labour's values – such as business relationships, progress, integrity, people, technology, and environment.

289 It uses authoritarian language adapted to suitable occasions by managers when they seek to impress workers (Bolinger 1968:266).

290 Classical conditioning has been associated with Pavlov (1849–1936, Nobel Prize winner for medicine 1904) who observed his dog's saliva when entering the laboratory. Instrumental conditioning is associated with Skinner (1953). According to Chomsky's critique on Skinner (1971) – *Skinner claims that persuasion is a weak method of control* – Skinner's conditioning is a much more effective method to control the human mind.

291 *There is the old joke according to which two dogs meet in Moscow, one of them very fat and wealthy, the other pathetically emaciated. The latter asks the former: 'How can you find food?' The former 'zoosemiotically' replied: 'That's easy. Every day, at noon, I enter the Pavlov Institute and I begin to salivate: immediately afterwards a conditioned scientist arrives, rings a bell and gives me food'* (Eco 1977:20).

292 According to Chomsky's *Critique on Skinner* (1971), *the tendencies towards centralised authoritarian control ... can easily be detected in modern industrial society*.

293 See Bolinger's (1980) chapters on *Signs & Symbols* and *Power & Deceptions*.

294 The image or idea of humans and humanities for a behaviourist is fundamentally different from that of Freud's psycho-analysis. The former sees humans as an object of power because humans can be tricked into doing something without understanding the process behind it. In the second case, the human is fully informed on what is happening and takes an active part. In the second case, humans remain humans while in the former they are reduced to lab rats (see Lemov's *World as Laboratory – Experiments with Mice, Mazes and Men* (2006)).

295 See: Aubrey & Chilton's *Nineteen Eighty-four in 1984 – Autonomy, Control & Communication* (1983); cf. Aubrey (1983).

296 See: Chomsky's *On Resistance* (1967).

297 As Chomsky (1966:18) once noted *animals live in a world of 'Zustände'* [instincts], *not of 'Gegenstände'* [created tools & things] *in a human sense*. See also Karl-Otto Apel (1980:225ff.).
298 Chomsky (1968) once noted, that *the essential difference between man and animal is exhibited most clearly by human language*.
299 Human survival has not been based on the *Survival of the Fittest* – often wrongly assigned to *Charles Darwin* – but on the Darwinian survival of the adaptable. Only those who can adapt to environmental change can survive. The socially conservatives however have successfully managed to lock the idea of the *Survival of the Fittest* into the minds of the general public – supported by mass media – because relentless competition in a fight of all against all is one of the core foundations of the ideology of the present system. If necessary, even Charles Darwin has to suffer from the deliberate misuse by those in power to create 'knowledge in the service of power' i.e. ideology.
300 The romantic illusion of Robinson Crusoe is no more than a system integrative ideology that seeks to portray the totally sufficient individual, an idea that only ever existed in the minds of conservative novelists but never in *Gemeinschaft* nor in *Gesellschaft*. In any case, survival of Mr Crusoe [a white man] was made easy on the backs of a native savage [justifying and legitimising colonialism, racism, and imperialism] appropriately named *Friday*, a working day!
301 It is pointless to teach apes to speak as they lack the necessary physical apparatus.
302 The most important specialization of the human brain is its capacity for language because syntax and grammar demand very demanding calculations.
303 Typically, art and culture could only develop after human groups were able to create surplus value so that daily routines in food gathering and hunting did no longer completely take up every day of existence. Only after humans had reached the developmental stage where they produced more than they needed to survive, time could be allocated in non-immediate survival needs.
304 Translation of Marx' work taken from Thompson (2004:94).
305 See Habermas (1979 & 1997 & 1997a); cf. Bronner (1994: 283–320).
306 This relationship extends into communication because man has no innate *langue* – man does not speak by nature (Chomsky 1966:15) because speech acts are social acts and as such they have to be learned by humans. They do not come naturally. There is no natural language as there is no natural ability to speak.
307 Morality is seen in accordance with Kohlberg's (1971, 1981, 1984) morality model of: 1. the punishment and obedience orientation (Fromm 1981), 2. the instrumental relativist orientation, 3. the interpersonal concordance or 'good boy-nice girl' orientation, 4. the law and order orientation, 5. the social-contract legalistic orientation, 6. the human-ethical principle orientation, 7. the universalistic principle orientation beyond humanism, extending to plants and animals.
308 Habermas (1997), Alvesson & Sköldberg (2000:119), Habermas (2001:vii), Levy, Alvesson & Willmott (2003).
309 Speech and actions are intricately linked because they co-determine each other. The meaning of speech acts depends largely on the types of actions they are likely to produce.
310 Originally developed by Deetz (2001:17), this table has been altered significantly to reflect the (b-c) link. Only speech acts that take place in (b) can lead to (c).

311 This has changed the role of the engineer in post-industrial systems because engineers no longer engineer engines; they engineer brands.
312 In his text on *The Right to be Lazy*, Paul Lafargue (1883) writes *capitalist ethics, a pitiful parody on Christian ethics, strikes with its anathema the flesh of the labourer; its ideal is to reduce the producer to the smallest number of needs, to suppress his joys and his passions and to condemn him to play the part of a machine turning out work without respite and without thanks.*
313 According to Searle (1969:17), *a theory of language is part of a theory of action, simply because speaking is a rule-governed form of behaviour.*
314 According to Gadamer (1976:45,55,101), understanding is not a mere reproduction of knowledge. It is neither merely an act of repeating the same thing. In the final analysis, all understanding is self-understanding. We cannot understand without *wanting* to understand or allowing something to be said.
315 Reflective thinking, so Adorno (1944) relates to the Hegelian concept of consciousness. Adorno (1944:16) wrote *in Hegel, self-consciousness was the truth of self-certainty, according to the words of the Phenomenology [of Spirit], the native realm of truth.*
316 Adapted from Searle (1979 & 2002).
317 *No matter how one defines truth and objectivity, they remain in relation to the human agents of theory and practice, and to their ability to comprehend and change their world* (Marcuse 1966:170).
318 See: Habermas (1997a). Mutual understanding is not transposing oneself into another person but to understand what a person says is to come to a mutual understanding or agreement about a subject matter.
319 According to Searle (1996:151) *actual human efforts to get true representation of reality are influenced by all sorts of factors – cultural, economic, psychological, and so on. Complete epistemic objectivity is difficult, sometimes impossible, because actual investigations are always from a point of view, motivated by all sorts of personal factors, and within a certain cultural and historical context.*
320 Quoted from Radford's (2005:169) excellent work on the *Philosophy of Communication*.
321 One can argue that care must be exercised in using the ability to speak as evidence for the inadequacy of mechanistic explanations. The users of speech acts have to use them with *care* because meaning can not be constructed mechanistically so that it falls on communication and speech acts to take *care* of the responsibility to make oneself understood and communicate something that can not only be understood by others but also can find agreement.
322 According to Loise Althusser and Slovenian social-philosopher Slavoj Zizek the danger of ideology lies in the *ideology=false consciousness* equation because *The Sublime Object of Ideology* (1989) establishes a highly distorted image of reality. Ideology, however has moved on from *they do not know it but they are doing it* to *they know it but they do it anyway*. While in pre-mass media the first statement holds truth, the creation of an all-encompassing corporate mass media apparatus gave capital/managerialism the confidence to move to the latter. For Zizek the pathologies of the current system can only be overcome in a *rapid re-politicisation of the economy* (Zizek) – something that can be achieved through ideal communicative action.
323 Although the following quote (see Figure 9.1) is ordinary, it is still a useful example. The following case has been selected at random from a recent textbook. This particular example has been taken from Eisenberg & Goodall's *Organizational Communication – Balancing Creativity and Constraint* (2001). It is

not relevant that it has been taken from this particular textbook. The main point is that almost all textbooks include such statements or very similar ones. It is not important to prove that this particular textbook includes this particular sentence but what the underlying ideology is that sentences like this portray (cf. Barratt 2003).

324 Metaphors like this are used to guide the textbook reader into the safe harbour of acceptance and affirmation to the managerial system. Essentially, managerial textbooks can be divided into three categories: a) *dominant or hegemonic reading*, where the audience accepts the meaning that is inscribed in the coding and in the structure of the text; b) *negotiated reading*, where the audience accepts parts of the message of the text while resisting other parts; and finally, *oppositional or counter-hegemony reading*, where the audience rejects the message because their own values clash with those inscribed in the coding and in the structure of the text. The logic of the ideology of the *market place of ideas* dictates the kind of reading that is best sellable. Therefore the most likely textbook appears to be category a) because future managers should not reject parts of what is written for them and they definitely should not be exposed to *oppositional or counter-hegemony reading* when system integration is demanded by the market place as well as by managerialism.

325 See Friedrich Nietzsche's *The Will to Power* (1886).

326 On organisational communication Deetz (2001:4–6) emphasises W*hat is organisational communication?* is misleading. A more interesting question is *What do we see or what are we able to do if we think of organisational communication in one way versus another. Unlike a definition, the attempt here is not to get it right, but to understand our choices.* However, it can be understood as: a) a speciality in a department, b) a phenomenon that exists in organisations as the logic of textbooks that discuss organisational communication, or c) *communication as distinct mode of describing and explaining organisations.* In Deetz's (2001:6) definition, organisational communication in organisations takes place among *organisational members*. Profit oriented corporations become neutral-sounding *organisations* and controlled, hierarchically ordered and managerially structured communication becomes *organisational communication*. Above all, those who are exploited in this process are now *organisational members* (sic!) They are made to appear as if they were members of a local health spa! They join voluntarily and gain nice benefits from doing so. The harsh world of paid employment forced upon many by a profit oriented system is communicatively neutralised via the conversion of wage labour into *membership* that carries connotations of voluntarism and pleasurable benefits.

327 Power is a non-egalitarian but continuous practice inside – not external to – relationships, as it is not conducted by the top but through the relationship between top and down. Power always meets resistance.

328 Originally, *rhetoric* as applied in Athenian societies meant persuasion and influence while *rhetor* was the usual Greek term for politician. *Rhetoric has not always been a dirty word, the opposite of sincerity, truth, and good intentions'* (Lanham 2006:19). It could be applied in different social forums and was intended as a dialectical instrument that supported the quest for truth. It was not seen as an opposition to truth. Under Roman domination, *rhetoric* moved to today's use as an effective form of a communicating authority directed towards personal gains, political control, and power.

329 Monk (1997:21–41) has expressed this as *Management by Meetings*.

330 Self-censorship means that an actor does not put forward a claim or a statement out of fear. Such fear relates to a position taken that could be rejected by domineering groups and result in negative consequences.
331 This is, of course, not always the case as management seeks to exclude decision making from unwarranted infiltration by democracy. To achieve this, decision making is communicatively framed as technical [logics, mathematical formulas, etc.] or strategically forcing those on the receiving end into narrowly framed forms of thinking such as SWOT (strengths, weaknesses, opportunities, and threats), cf. Chandler's *Strategy and Structure (1962)*, Miles & Snow (1978); Porter (1980), Ohmae (1983), Hyman's *Strategy or Structure* (1987); Whittington (1993), Billsberry (1996), Howard's *Strategy*, (2003), Spulber (2004), Bigler & Norris (2004).
332 The fact that the profit motive also determines the conditions of communication has been noted in the domain of democracy as well. In public as in democratic life, the steering realm of democracy – parliament – has been removed – at least partially – from the influence of the profit motive. Therefore, democracy in most western countries is located in a discourse domain somewhat relocated from the underlying functions of capitalism. This allows the pretence of democratic representation untouched by the profit driven forces of capitalism. It may be possible to pretend the separation of democracy and the market system in the public domain. At work, however, this pretence is impossible to maintain. Otto Bauer's work on *The Crisis of Democracy* (1936) already testified to that. He wrote, ... *majorities had to capitulate before manoeuvres on the stock market and resign, despite their parliamentary majorities, handing power to the parties and the men whom the stock market trusted.* Furthermore, in *Observations of an Unpolitical Man* (1918) Thomas Mann wrote, *the capitalist class has succeeded in transforming even democracy's institutions into instruments of its own class domination* (all quotes from Canfora 2006:114 & 116–117).
333 See: Weber (1922, 1924, 1947, 1948) & Marcuse (1964b); see also: Ramsay (1977), Barker (1993).
334 In the words of social-philosopher Zizek, *a King is only King because his subjects loyally think and act like he is King* (Sharpe 2006). In other words, managerialism is only managerialism because *objects of power* loyally think and act like managerialism is king.
335 On lies, Adorno (1944:7) wrote: *lies are told only when someone wants others to know they aren't important, that the former does not need the latter, and does not care what they think. Today the lie, once a liberal means of communication, has become one of the techniques of brazenness, with whose help every single person spreads the iciness, in whose shelter they thrive.*
336 In sociological, behaviourist, and philosophical terms there is a difference between *reflective* and *reflexive* thinking/responses that even sociologically trained scholars quite often tend to misunderstand. While the former indicates a conscious process of critical thought and deliberation directed towards a Kantian and Hegelian understanding of thinking, the latter denotes simple – often unconscious or even conditioned – reflexes in a behaviourist sense (Pavlov, Watson & Skinner). The difference can also be seen as *conditioned* association (reflexive) versus *symbolic* association (a type of thought that links/associates abstract symbols).
337 See: Saussure (1906–13); Habermas (2001).
338 To ethics, so Adorno (1944:35), belongs the term *anti-ethics*. On this he noted: *Anti-ethics, by rejecting what is unethical in ethics as repression, simultaneously*

makes the latter's innermost concern its own: that every form of violence ought to vanish, along with every restriction... the implicit sense of the ethics of the rulers, that whoever wants to live has to grab what they can... Essentially, all forms of ethics [Moral] are formed on the model of what is unethical [Unmoral], and to this day reproduce the latter at every stage. Slave-ethics [Sklavenmoral] is in fact bad: it is still only master-ethics [Herrenmoral] (Adorno 1944:75). See also: Singer (1994).

339 One possible definition of *moral* could be to see it as conforming to accepted standards of general conduct. It is the capability of moral actions that sees humans as moral agents. *Ethics* can be seen as the science of morals in human conduct. Moral philosophy seeks to understand moral principles and rules of conduct.

340 One of the foremost thinkers has been Marx, even though he did not directly deal with ethical issues. However, his material conception of history (as a development of the earlier Hegel) explains all ideas – including moral and ethical ideas – as the product of a particular economic stage that society has reached. Therefore, feudal societies will regard *loyalty* and *obedience* to one's lord as the chief virtue. A capitalist economy, on the other hand, requires a mobile labour force and an expanding market, so that *freedom*, especially the freedom to sell one's labour, is the key ethical concept.

341 Obviously, ethics have been in existence long before society converted from feudalism to modernity. Ethics started before feudalism when humans tried to develop a code of conduct about how to live together. This still ongoing process started when humans became humans. At that time, ethics was concerned with reflections on the best way to live. Early moral thinkers found that no group is able to stay together and survive if its members make frequent attacks on each other. In a *war of all against all* (Hobbes' *Leviathan*, 1651) human life would have ceased to exist. What guarantees human life is cooperation, collective existence, and ethical conduct. *We have evolved not to be ruthless proto-capitalists, but to enter into mutually beneficial forms of cooperation* (http://cogweb.ucla.edu.debate/SingerPM.html). The first Greek philosopher, Plato, advocated that one should act justly to be at one with oneself as justice leads to a happy life and injustice to an unhappy life. Following that, *Stoicism* saw ethical life to be founded in the universality of reason, rejecting ethical relativism. The complete opposite was advocated in feudal Europe, when Niccolo Machiavelli (1513) wrote *it is necessary for the prince, who wishes to maintain himself, to lead how not to be good, and to use this knowledge and not use it, according to the necessities of the case*. Not surprisingly he – rather than Plato or Stoicism – is preferred in managerial literature today. With *David Hume* (1711–76) feudalism's dark past came to an end and ethics moved towards the discussion of *what is* and *what ought to be*, between *facts* and *values*.

342 With *Jean-Jacques Rousseau* (1712–78) ideas such as the general will represent the rational foundation of ethics in society started to exist. Following that, Kant's (1724–1804) *categorical imperative* rationally defines ethics, disregarding individual feelings or wants. Kant's idea can be expressed as *to act that you treat humanity in your own person and in the person of everyone else always at the same time as an end and never as a means*. Hegel's (1770–1831) ethics is determined by the recognition that human *nature* (!) is not fixed but human ethics develop in the society in which one lives. Marx (1818–83) who is more known as a scientist than a moralist, advocated that *ideas of the ruling class in every epoch are the ruling ideas* and as long as society is divided into classes,

morality would serve the interests of the ruling class. More than most other writings, business ethics as expressed in any standard management textbook testifies to that (cf. deGeorge 2006; Ferrell 2007).

343 On *greediness* Adorno (1944:9) wrote, *the greedy of today regard nothing as too expensive for themselves, but everything as too expensive for others. They think in equivalencies, and their entire private life stands under the law of giving less than they get back, but always just enough to get back something.*

344 The three remaining sins are: a) pleasure without conscience, b) religion without sacrifice, and c) politics without principles.

345 The first pathology (wealth without work) allows some to accumulate tremendous wealth without doing any work while others just live off the work of others. This can be seen in the rich and poor divide measured in the Gini-Index. That knowledge is without character (b) is most prevalent in the scientific and rational destruction of animals, humans, and the environment (Singer & Watson 2006). Thirdly, the invention of corporate social responsibility and business ethics including a raft of books testifies that commerce and business operates without morality and ethics (c). This can also be seen in preventable industrial *accidents,* animal *testing* (sic!), rainforest *harvesting* (sic!), etc. Finally, the disconnection of science and moral values – labelled as neutral science, objective science or sound science etc. – disconnects science from humanity and moral consciousness (cf. Koselleck 1988; Wheeler 2005:122, McWilliams *et al.* 2006).

346 See Kohlberg (1971, 1981, 1984) & Habermas' *Moral Consciousness and Communicative Action* (1990:116ff.).

347 For a good and critical adaptation to managerialism see Linstead *et al.* (2004: 260–264).

348 The fear of punishment appears to be deeply enshrined in Christian value systems. In an article on *US Evangelists are Twisting the Bible,* Giles Fraser (2006:16) wrote *he that spareth this rod hateth his son: but he that loveth him chasteneth him betimes (Proverb 12:24)...Somehow, after eight of 10 licks, the poison is transformed into gushing love and contentment.* See also Passer & Smith (2007:627–631).

349 Apart from the very occasional mentioning in mass media, child labour has, for the most part, been made to disappear from the standard headlines because corporations in advanced countries have been able hide the use of child labour through spatial elements (outsourcing to non-OECD countries) and corporate elements (subsidiaries, franchises, and loosely knitted network companies, etc.). In that way, the issue of child labour has moved into the background for most people in advanced countries while the majority of people remain unbothered by corporate mass media. The appearance of a problem that no longer exists prevails.

350 See: ILO (2002), http://www.unicef.org/protection/index_childlabour.html, http://www.hrw.org/children/labor.htm.

351 See Kafka's *In the Penal Colony* (1919), cf. Feldman (1998). On this, Adorno (1944:74) emphasised that *Bettelheim's observation on the identification of the victims with the executioners of the Nazi camps contains a judgement on the higher seeding-grounds of culture, the English 'public school' [original in English], the German officer academy. The absurdity perpetuates itself: domination reproduces itself all the way through the dominated* (cf. Neumann 1933).

352 Smith (1982:58) noted that in the mechanical Skinner model *people were regarded as reactive victims of environmental causal forces with no freedom of*

choice or capacity for self-direction. See also: Katz & Kahn (1966:334); Mackintosh (1983); Newmeyer (1986); Anderson (1990 & 1992); Carlson & Buskist (1997); Stadon (2001); Austin & Wilson (2001); Ludwig (2001); Jex (2002:243); Baum (2005); Marin & Pear (2007).

353 See Chomsky (1959, 1971) and D'Agostino's *Chomsky's System of Ideas* (1986); cf. F. D'Agostino's *'Chomsky's System of Ideas'* in: *Philosophical Quarterly* vol. 37. pp. 477–81 (1987).

354 People who were raised in an authoritarian home under strict, harsh, inconsistent, and emotionally repressive parental regimes are left with a weak ego and low self-esteem – the ideal human material to be converted from humans into human resources because they totally depend on pleasing (positive reinforcement) and obeying to parents and later managers to gain approval.

355 Quoted from (Chomsky 1971:33); cf. Apel (1980:180ff.).

356 See: Reich (1946); Arendt (1951, 1958 & 1994); Bauman (1989).

357 Concurrent with turning humans into objects of power goes with the fostering of mechanisms that disallow these objects of power ever to realise what they are made into. Adorno (1944:22) has commented on this. He wrote, *part of the mechanism of domination is that one is forbidden to recognize the suffering which that domination produces, and there is a straight line connecting the evangelical lecture on the joy of life to the construction of slaughter-houses for human beings so far off in Poland, that everyone in one's own ethnic group can convince themselves they don't hear the screams of pain.*

358 Next to this simplified company structure, individuals are made to feel promoted through the allocation of status symbols, fancy titles, etc. to create an imaginary rather than a real promotion.

359 Katz & Kahn (1966:352) emphasised that *most people don't get promoted at all. Most production workers remain production workers, and most typists remain typists.*

360 See: Marcuse (1966); Foucault (1995); Leslie's *Walter Benjamin – Overpowering Conformism* (2000).

361 Classic to this is a quote by no other than Milton Freedman. Delaney (2005:2004) writes, *Friedman, in his classical book Capitalism and Freedom, noted that 'there is one and only one social responsibility of business – to use its resources and engage in activities designed to increase its profits…'*.

362 Chomsky (1994:9) has provided a good example of deals that are governed purely by self-interest. He wrote, *146 countries that ratified the International convention on the rights of children, but one had not: the US. That's a standard pattern of international conventions on human rights. However, just of fairness, it's only proper to add that…conservatism is catholic in its anti-child, anti-family spirit, so the World Health Organisation (WHO) voted to condemn the Nestle Corporation for aggressively marketing their infant formula which kills plenty of children. The vote was 118 to 1. I'll leave you to guess the one. However, this is quite minor compared with what the WHO calls the 'silent genocide' that's killing millions of children every year as a result of the free market policies for the poor and the refusal of the rich to give any aid. Again, the US has one of the worst and most miserly records among the rich societies.* While written in 1994, it appears that not much progress has been made since then.

363 If one seeks to position Human Resource Management inside Kohlberg's stages of moral development, then HRM can safely be located at level three (3) as it complies with management's wishes and is instrumental rather than ethical. This *rules out a truly Kantian ethical position*, notes HRM writer Legge (2005:39; cf. 1995). Even though Legge stays away from positioning HRM

288 *Notes*

inside Kohlberg's model, she nevertheless discusses HRM's utilitarianism as *a major justification of capitalis*, providing there is such a thing as an ethical justification of capitalism. Having gone through several arguments, Legge eventually fails to make a claim for the ethics of HRM. Her work – like many others – also fails to develop a comprehensive framework for such a discussion. The saddening fact remains that one of the best textbooks on HRM deals with ethics on barely two pages. Finally and despite all the references to Kant, the book fails on Kant's *what is* and even more so on Kant's *what ought to be*.

364 For a comprehensive discussion of the political economy of trust, see Korczynski (2000).

365 The 'we...' ideology of HRM is put into three perspectives by Stewart (2007:73): *knowledge = cognitive domain = we think; values = affective domain = we feel; skills = action domain = we do*.

366 In managerially guided books this conversion portrayed as *organisational socialisation represents the processes by which an individual makes the transition from 'outsider' to 'organisational member'* (Jex 2002:62). There are individuals – not workers – who work in – not profit making companies– but organisations and they are not *made to* but make it themselves. And naturally, they have been *outsiders* [outsider=negative; insider=positive; and who wants to be an outsider if one can be an insider] but now they can be organisational members and who would not want to be a member in an organisation like a sports club, tennis hall, football team, etc. The conversion of humans into a profit maximising human resources/material makes it possible that *new members can learn the culture of an organisation* (Jex 2002:62). It pretends that it is not a deeply psychological process that relies heavily on behaviourist theories that converts truly individuals into conforming objects of (managerial) power directed towards profits but one is given the opportunity *to learn a culture*. The conversion process is made to appear as opportunity-giving (to learn) while system integration into a one-dimensional managerial process of *productive behaviour* (Jex 2002:87) is pretended to be *culture*, i.e. arts, music, opera, movies, paintings, sculptures, etc. even though work regimes are very different from what culture used to mean and often in the non-commercial – non culture-industry sense (Adorno 1944; Alvesson 2002).

367 Most interestingly, the voice in advertising is almost always a male voice because the male voice sounds more authoritative and therefore establishes an authority over a target audience and entices them into buying.

368 See: DeVitis (1974) as well as Bowles & Gintis' *Schooling in Capitalist America: Educational Reform and the Contradictions of Economic Life* (1976; cf. 1981 & 2001).

369 A good example of labour-management relations at stage four is DeCeri & Kramer's (2005:629) chapter on *Fundamental Rights of Employees*. Further examples can be found in almost any textbook on management or HRM. It is not surprising that most books, and especially most textbooks, on management and HRM hardly locate ethics above the ethical development stage of three or four. (cf. Scott 2005:173ff. & Laffer 2005:274–276).

370 Managerial rules, much in the same way as Human Resource Management policies, operate implicitly or formal and explicitly or informal. In the first case, rules are stated publicly (codified HR policies) while the latter are non-codified (dress codes, etc.), cf. Knowles (1955).

371 In system theory, rules are established as neutral elements that establish system equilibriums and by doing so, they simultaneously establish the man-

agerial *status quo*, i.e. they cement – theoretically and practically – the power relationship between management and labour. Hence, system theory is a most welcome tool in the hands of – conscious and un-conscious management writers and affirmative researchers because it establishes domination redirecting and confining emancipatory energies towards the self-balancing of the system.

372 See Budd & Scoville's (2005:5) table 1 that includes *fairness and justice*. Bowie's chapter on *Kantian Ethical Thought* (2005:61ff.) in the same volume is appropriately labelled so. It dares not to enter into ethics beyond the 18th century. It leaves Hegel, Marx, and more present discussions out (Bauman (1989), Parker (1998), Singer (2000 & 2005), Nussbaum (2004), Sunstein & Nussbaum (2004), Gleason *et al.* (2005)).

373 See: Windsor's *Corporate Social Responsibility: Three Key Approaches* (2006).

374 A good example for the *marginalisation* of ethics in current management literature is Durand & Calori (2006). Sameness, Otherness? *Enriching Organizational Change Theories with Philosophical Considerations* on the Same and the Other. It shows that the philosophy of ethics is reduced to *considerations* and allowed only to impact at the edges of managerialism when it *enriches* organisational change. See also McWilliams's (2006:1) ...*strategic implications*, indicating that ethics – now reduced to *social responsibility*, i.e. just '*a*' responsibility – can add value to strategy via *strategic implications* (cf. Jones 2003; Parker 1998 & 2003; Clegg *et al.* 2006).

375 *Participative* or *deliberative* democracy can be seen as the opposite of *representative* democracy found in most so-called democratic societies today. The idea behind this version of democracy is not to *give* your vote so that some representatives can use and abuse it but to structure democracy in a more direct way (Eriksen & Weigard (2003:112); cf. Lösch (2005); (Gastil & Levine 2006)).

376 See: Gimmler (2001), Kalyvas (2001), Oquendo (2002), Gilabert (2005).

377 See: Lewis & Moss (1977:50).

378 One of the most prominent voices in advancing animal rights has been the philosopher Peter Singer's *Animal Liberation* (1975), *Practical Ethics* (1993), *Writings on an Ethical Life* (2000). See Singer (2005), and Singer & Mason (2006).

379 Bauman (1989); cf. Marsden & Townley (1996).

380 A logic statement consists of subject and predicate. Both need to be subjected to proof or disproof.

381 See Habermas (1979), *Communication and the Evolution of Society*.

382 *Naturally, agents are capable of lying, just as they are capable of having false beliefs. The point is that lying and error are intelligible only against a background of veracity and veridicality* (Heath 2003:22).

383 According to Gadamer (1976:83), *the great value of semantic analysis rests in no small part in the fact that it breaks through the appearance of self-sameness that an isolated word-sign has about it. Ultimately, it seems a semantic ideal emerges, which stipulates that in a given context only one expression and no other is the right one. Semantics is a doctrine of signs, in particular, of linguistic signs. Signs, however, are a means to an end* (1976:87).

384 *In the established vocabulary, violence is a term which one does not apply to the action of the police, the National Guard, the Marshals, the Marines, the bombers. The bad words are a priori reserved for the enemy, and their meaning is defined and validated by the actions of the enemy regardless of their motivation and goal* (Marcuse 1969:75). Marcuse's contemporary, Adorno (1944:5), commented

on this *by adapting to the weaknesses of the oppressed, one confirms in such weaknesses the prerequisite of domination, and develops in oneself the measure of barbarity, thickheadedness and capacity to inflict violence required to exercise domination.* Furthermore, he (1944:65) emphasised that, *Violence, on which civilization is based, means the persecution of all by all, and those with persecution manias miss the boat solely, by displacing what is brought by the whole onto their neighbors, in the helpless attempt to make incommensurability commensurable.*

385   On the managerial ability to manipulate, Adorno (1944:22) noted *the decomposition of human beings into capabilities is a projection of the division of labour on its presumed subjects, inseparable from the interest in deploying them with ulterior motives, above all in order to be able to manipulate them.*

386   See: Olson (1971); Offe & Wiesenthal (1980); Mook (1987); Roy & Parker-Gwen (1999).

387   In contrast even to Marcuse's *One-Dimensional Man* (1966) that portrays instrumental or technical rationality as having *liquidated all transcendent and oppositional forces* carrying strong connotations towards *a pessimistic critique of contemporary culture* that has been *detached from political and economic analysis* (Thompson 1981:76), Offe & Wiesenthal (1980) re-open Marcuse's pessimistic scenario by applying the dialectics of thesis and anti-thesis to work processes. Their conclusion is a Hegelian one in which the synthesis of both leads to the advancement of human society directed towards autonomy, emancipation, and domination-free forms of communication.

388   In sharp contrast to the socio-economic realities of the labour market, *recent political and economic orthodoxies treat markets as self-evident, permanent and incontestable, in the natural or organic view of capitalism* [as an] *inevitable, colonising, all-powerful and all-conquering system, even a supernatural force that is unstoppable. The result of such imagery is that 'there is no alternative' but to obey the logic of this all-powerful force* (Williams 2005:21).

389   The shaping of individual interest over collective interest has recently been shown in Stewart's *Individualism and Collectivism in the Sociology of the Collective Worker* (2005).

390   Karlson's *The Ontology of Work* (2004) provides a good discussion of work even though it remains somewhat trapped in the idea to find 'a' definition of work, not realising that a definition can only be found as an agreement between sender and receiver about a commonly accepted agreement on *'what is'*. It is a lively, active and socially created process with no physical law, only an ever-moving social process that needs to enshrine Hegelian dialectic that has to be applied when seeking hermeneutical approaches towards the issue of work. Finally, symptomatic for the ontological idea is that it restricts thinking to *'what is there'* in an attempt to create *The Order of Things* (Foucault 1994) seen from four perspectives: realism, empiricism, positivism, and post-modernism. Neither one reaches beyond the classical ontological statement, *every knowledge base, knowledge system, or knowledge-level agent is committed to some conceptualisation, explicit or implicit.* The real problem with ontology does not lie in the truth content of this statement but that has moved into the centre of epistemology restricting it in large sections to the analytical-empirical approach (Habermas 1987).

391   One of the prime tasks of such organisations has been described by Adorno (1944:19) – *the almost insoluble task consists of refusing to allow oneself to be rendered dumb, either by the power of others or by one's own powerlessness.*

392 See: Adams' *The Employee Free Choice Act: A Sceptical View and Alternatives* (2007).
393 Brenkert (1983:36) noted that *labour-power is not simply a burst of energy. It must be (self-) controlled, directed, and expressed in certain ways.*
394 *A thousand influences constantly press a working man down into a passive role* (Chilton 1983:41) that enforces system integration.
395 See: Engels (1892); Tucker (1978); Thompson (1963).
396 It remains an interesting fact to note that among the sheer endless amount of books and even more so textbooks – often not really written but compiled – every year on the issue of organisational behaviour (OB) there are virtually none on organisational misbehaviour with the most notable exception of Ackroyd & Thompson (1999). One might even be attempted to argue that if workers show organisational behaviour – or system integration – why are there so many books published about it? Maybe the annual publication of a raft of OB books shows again that the two logics of collective action at work – system integration vs. resistance – has not yet fully resulted in the complete system integration or affirmative mindset of workers – something that is, given Hegelian dialectic, never possible because managerially directed work (thesis) will always meet workers' resistance (anti-thesis) to create a synthesis.
397 Quoted from: Ackroyd & Thompson (1999:148–149).
398 Trapped in the control mindset of Labour Process Theory, Ackroyd & Thompson (1999:149) stop short of making the transition from control to affirmation. The real issue is not self-control but affirmation because the battle over *winning the hearts and minds* (148) of workers has already left the control and self-control realm. The issue of the 21st century is system integration and affirmation to the present system of production. The socialised (Bowles & Gintis 1976, 1981, 2001; Cole 1988), mass media guided (Chomsky 2002; cf. Sitton 2003:75), HRM-incorporated (Townley 1994; Cheney & Carroll 1997) and psychologically workplace conditioned (Arnold 2005: 291) workers find themselves in a one-dimensional mindset that is not controlling but creating affirmation. In sum, as long as labour process theory remains stuck in the control-theory mindset it will not be able to move its analytical power to the pressing issues of system integration and methods used to create affirmation to the system. In the modern workplace where layers of supervision and disciplinary power disappear together with the protective power of trade unions (Goodrich's *The Frontier of Control*, 1920), the off-work system integrative forces can no longer be isolated and narrow examinations of work as solely workplace based – neglecting the increasing importance of Basis-Überbau structures – as they are no longer able to deliver an analysis that reflects on the realities of powerful system integrative ideologies communicated to workers in the work as well as the off-work domain.
399 See Arnold (2005:292; cf. Carlson & Buskist 1997:128–142).
400 To cover up the asymmetry of pathologies and risk that are unequally allocated to the domain of those who are employed, the sociological illusion of the so-called 'risk-society' (Hyman 2006:216) has been created. It sees to portray that risks are equally distributed in society and class divisions vanish in the face of environmental disasters such as Chernobyl. Even though this might be true to a limited extent – as some people can fly to Florida for weeks when an atomic accident and radioactive fallout covers Europe while others have to carry on working – most risks in today's society are unequally distributed and after two decades of neo-liberalism most of the costs of the

pathological system have been shifted towards working people. Since 30 years tax systems in most advanced countries have shifted the tax burden onto workers while relieving the rich and capitalism from their duty to cover the effects of their system. Today, most of the costs and life risks created by the system have to be covered class-internally after decades of 'broadening the tax-base' public service cuts and tax-concessions to the rich. More than ever before in post-war advanced capitalism, today's risks are asymmetrically distributed. There is no *Risk Society* but a shifting of risks onto working people while simultaneously seeking to eclipse this shift under the illusion of a Risk Society. It argues that risks have been part of human existence (Hyman 2006:216) even though the slave might have faced different risks from the slave-owner and the feudal peasants faced different risks compared to the lord! Even Hyman's example of Bhopal (2006:217) should have made one aware that risks have been unequally distributed between those who died in India and the CEO retiring comfortably on his New England Estate in the USA only to be flashed out by Greenpeace recently. It appears that in the *Risk Society* some face the poison gas risk in Bhopal while others face the retirement risk on their estate.

401   Once humans have been converted into human resources as a means, not an end (Kant), the managerial process of *getting things done through people* where the term *'through'* represents the means – not ends – orientation of the managerial process, the following occurs as a system operative: *instead of producing use values directly in relation to their needs, people – whether as capitalists, or as workers whose labour has been bought and subsumed by capitalists – produce goods and services that can be sold in the market* (Sitton 2003:22; Williams 2005:16).

402   Given that *language provides finite means but infinite possibilities of expression constrained only by rules of concept formulation and sentence formation* (Chomsky 1966:29), these infinite possibilities of expressions increase with groups size and therefore groups engaging in ideal speech are forced to find a way of balancing this process.

403   The one-dimensionality of present society has been summed up by Adorno (1944:24) as *between the pleasure of emptiness and the lie of plenitude, the ruling condition of the spirit [des Geistes: mind] permits no third option.*

404   Any alternative lifestyle or alternative forms of human existence are portrayed as extremely negative by the mass media. This is applied to everything between Copenhagen's Christiania and Australia's Nimbin. Historic forms of alternative forms of living (Spain 1936, etc.) are shown to be unsuccessful because capitalist and counterrevolutionary forces have been able to annihilate them using massacres, torture, killings, etc. (George Orwell's *Homage to Catalonia*). See also Canfora's (2006:106 & 120ff.) discussion on the *Paris Commune* that was put down with the shooting of 30,000 people and the arrest of another 40,000 exposing them to the harshest form of imprisonment. Canfora (2006:121) summed it up as *class genocide*. Overall the annihilation of all alternatives serves an important purpose. It mentally confines humans into the mindset of an endless treadmill of being a consumer-worker-consumer-worker-consumer, etc. Humans are designed to take part in a never ending rat race without enabling those who win the race to be able to realise that even when they – in the end – have won the rat race, they are still no more than rats!

405   Sitton (2003:28) has emphasised that since ends are no longer determined in the light of reason, it is also impossible to say that one economic or political system, no matter how cruel and despotic, is less reasonable than another.

406 See: Roy & Parker-Gwen (1999:205).
407 *Orwell's socialism was neither born out of trade union struggle nor the intellectual study of Marxist theory. Encouraged by such personal experiences in his five years in Burma as an officer in the Indian Imperial Police, he had learned to dislike autocratic rule of all types* (Aubrey 1983:13).
408 See: Etzioni (1959), Mintzberg (1973), Storey (1992).
409 See Alonso's *Fordism and the Genesis of the Post-Fordist Society: Assessing the Post-Fordist Paradigm* (2006).
410 This can be understood in Walter Benjamin's words of *it is only for the sake of those without hope that hope is given to us* (Kellner 1991:xxxviii).
411 As the behaviourists Gallistel & Gibbon (2002:1) wrote, *reinforcing stimuli are manipulated*. Expressed less behavioralistically, individuals have to be manipulated – through *reinforcing stimuli* – to show *conditioned responses*, i.e. consumption. Individuals need to be exposed to constant bombardment of marketing and advertising to be manipulated into buying things they do not need with money they often do not have to impress people they often don't even like.
412 The most known words on planet earth are *Coca Cola* not God, Mohammed, Buddha, Bible, Jesus, etc.
413 Most dramatically, in both domains – work and consumption – classical labour process theory (Alonso & Lucio 2006) have undervalued this shift failing to realise that the issue of *control* has been surpassed by conditioned affirmation rendering one of the most important issues for labour process (LP) writers obsolete. While many have carried on regardless, their writings increasingly weren't capable of reflecting realities at work. In short, while LP theorists produced more and more on *control*, reality had moved on towards conditioned system affirmation via Human Resource Management. While LP theorists narrowly examined and sometimes over-examined the workplace, control had almost completely ended in favour of work-system affirmation via HRM techniques linked to the consumptive world. In short, labour does not need to be controlled to consume – it is manipulated to do so – and in the same way it does not need to be controlled to work.
414 In his preface to *'A contribution to the Critique of Political Economy'* (1890), Marx wrote, *the sum total of these relations of production constitutes the economic structure of society, the real foundation, on which rises a legal and political superstructure, and to which correspond definite forms of social consciousness* (Tucker 1978:4).
415 See: Buck-Moss' *Marx Minus the Proletariat: Theory as Praxis, chapter 2,* (1977); Habermas (1988); Herman & Chomsky (1988); D'Agostino (1986); and Galbraith (1958).
416 See: Part Three *The Brain and Language* in: Jones *et al.* (1992:130).
417 Behaviourists' core idea is that they *seek to explain action by influences from outside* (Skinner 1948, 1953, 1971, 1974); see also: Mook (1987:9 & 43–53).
418 The move away from animalistic life towards forms of control and eventually to a conditioned work environment has not enhanced society towards rational foundations. Chomsky (1966:14) noted that *this freedom from instinct and from stimulus control is the basis for what we call 'human reason'*. As long as human behaviour is controlled or conditioned through stimulus control, it cannot be based on rationality. In a Kantian sense, any move towards a rational society has to be directed towards a society where the fundamentals are critical, not instrumental rationality.

419 Herein lies the crucial difference between the *Menschenbild* (anthropological image of humans) of *behaviourism* and Freud's psychoanalytical approach. The former operates with manipulation in a top-down relationship conditioning an *object of power* (humans). In the latter case, an equal relationship between patient and psychologist is essential in which self-reflection and self-analytical processes allow the identification of psychological deficits. This is depicted in the famous Freudian sofa where Freud sits at the top of the sofa outside the vision of the patient so that self-reflection and self-analytical processes are not hindered by visions of a superior doctor dressed in the famous white coat which Freud never but Pavlov always wore.

420 Any modern *HRM* or *Work Psychology* textbook testifies to the behaviourist conditioned link between effort and reward. This link has been almost perfectly outlined in Arnold (2005:291). The perfect example for HRM is PRP: *'performance'* (behaviourist: conditioned response) *'related'* (behaviourist: conditioning via reinforcement) *'pay'* (behaviourist: stimuli). One of the clearest examples in advertising is the *smoking cigarettes=sophistication* link. This link cannot be established via symbolic association [i.e. and intellectual process] because it would render body-damage with the prospect of cancer and death to cognitive analysis. The *smoking=sophistication* link has to be established through *conditioned* association; otherwise it would not work (Gallistel & Gibbon 2002).

421 See Bauman (1989); Sitton (2003:27).

422 Despite Chomsky's (1971) powerful critique on conditioning in *The Case against B. F. Skinner*, methods created by Pavlov (1928) and Skinner (1953) have infiltrated the workplace as a raft of today's textbooks on *The Psychology of Work* testify.

423 As irritating as it might sound but the conditioned response in animal laboratory conditions relates to a pigeon pushing a button while the reward is the appearing food once a lever is pushed. The *behaviourist* idea of conditioning seeks to eliminate cognitive processes by locating them inside human's animalistic past transferring animal behaviour to human behaviour. On the one hand, this sets limits to human conditioning as humans are not animals, while on the other hand, it makes conditioning possible. Otherwise advertising might have a hard time conditioning people into smoking harmful cigarettes, and modern textbooks on psychology and work psychology would no longer carry Pavlov and Skinner. But they do.

424 The problem with *natural rewards* as with so many so-called natural phenomena in the social world has been expressed by Thompson (1981:1) as *the social world consists of speaking and acting subjects who constantly make sense of themselves and others, and whose meaningful and wilful activities cannot be comprehended by the methods of the natural science*. What Thompson is outlining is that the use of the term *natural* has a double effect because it firstly carries ideological connotations of being natural [=real=unchangeable] and secondly it re-locates social issues into a natural world that closes off any attempt to make them understandable because they have been deliberately miss-located into the natural domain. The analytical instruments that make the natural world comprehensible cannot – without incurring significant ideological and methodological distortions – be applied to the social world and vice versa.

425 According to Arnold (2005:285), Premack (1965) *demonstrated by experiment that an event that serves as a reinforcer for some behaviour may not have a reinforcing effect on other, different behaviour*.

426 The issue of job enrichment was not included in Arnold's (2005) list.
427 See: Arnold (2005:289); Cialdini's *Influence – The Psychology of Persuasion* (The Business Library, 1984); and Zanna *et al. The Persistence of Persuasion* (1994).
428 Despite subjectivism and post-modernism's attempts to portray the world as a collage of narratives in which the individual is powerlessly exposed to the prevailing power-knowledge paradigm, labour – upon their daily experience – understand that the world of work is not a mere figment of illusion inside the confines of the post-modern narrative but real existing and objectively analysable, criticisable, and that this process can lead to emancipation from dominant modes of operations. The world of work is fundamentally an objective reality that has – at least in its fundamentality – not changed since the days of Adam Smith and Karl Marx because those who manage and those who are managed still experience the world of work in two fundamental different ways due to their fundamentally different position in the labour process.
429 See: Olson (1971); Offe & Wiesenthal (1980); Roy & Parker-Gwen (1999).
430 Even though traditional management writers have emphasised the idea of rational decision making, rational and calculated decisions, the core idea of instrumental rationality does not always occur, not even in management (Langer 1994; cf. O'Hair *et al.* 2005).
431 This is not to say that labour does not operate in hierarchical forms. It has never been free to totally resist colonising attempts. In many cases, labour's communicative forms have taken on domineering structures – almost any trade union meeting testifies to that. However, and unlike management, these hierarchies are not a structural imperative and are alterable. The unconscious reproduction of such hierarchies testifies to *what is* rather than to *what ought to be*.
432 On solidarity, Adorno (1944:50) once commented, *human beings must rely on free and solidaristic cooperative labour under common responsibility*.
433 For example, workers in a car plant's body shop are no more important than workers from the final assembly. There is no hierarchical level between them. But managers in various parts of such firms often not only feel but are in fact more important than other managers. In each section or productive shop (body shop, final assembly, etc.) there is a hierarchy of managers at work. This ranges from foreman to supervisor, to section bosses, shift coordinators, manufacturing managers, etc.
434 Deetz (1992) has shown this as the suppression of democracy by managerial ideology (corporation) and instrumental rationality (theme) expressed in bureaucratic forms (state). These are not limited to an individual organisation or corporation but are in fact symptomatic of larger corporations and expressed in a managerial system that colonises domains that were previously organised under communicative action. Hence, democracy as an expression of communicative rationality is under threat through corporate managerial and instrumental colonisation.
435 Marcuse (1966) argues that form and value of control become commercialised in such a way that opposition and even reflection are automatically suppressed.
436 See Llewellyn & Harrison (2006).
437 Good examples of domain specific meaning construction are studies on communication inside labour unions revealing distinctive semantic patters of communication (Tompkins 1961 & 1965). He found that top managers and top union leaders shared similar definitions and terminologies. This shows the successful colonisation at the top level.

438 See Habermas (1997a:97) and Hegel (http://iep.utm.edu/h/hegelsoc.htm).
439 Brenkert (1983:61) noted that *language is as old as consciousness, language is practical, real consciousness that exists for other men as well, and only therefore does it also exist for me; language, like consciousness, only arises from the need, the necessity of intercourse with other men.*
440 As Adorno (1944:94) commented, *the individual [Individuum] is universal not merely as the biological substrate, but simultaneously as the form of reflection of the social process, and its consciousness of itself as something existing in itself.*
441 Quoted from Habermas (1997a:27), cf. Bronner (1994:283–320).
442 See Williams (2005:21).
443 Max Weber (1924 & 1947) has shown these in his works.
444 On this Habermas (2006:6) noted, *there is already a massive body of small-group studies which construe political communication as a mechanism for the enhancement of cooperative learning and collective problem-solving.* The idea of communicative action and ideal speech is, of course, not geared towards *cooperative learning and collective problem-solving* but towards emancipation even though this particular body of small-group studies seeks to limit them to problem-solving.
445 There are many examples of this inherent conflict. For example, individual capitalists are cautious to invest in employee training and development because they symbolise no more than a cost to them. On the other hand, the system needs an educated workforce to move from the military-industrial complex to the military-industrial-*education* complex. During the last decades, employers have been able to shift this cost to the state but increasingly it is shifted to employees. Today, employees invest considerable sums of money into highly functional training that in their private lives is of absolutely no use to them. It can only be appropriated by a firm. This training – often wrongly called *education* – has almost no personal *use* value but has *exchange* value as workers can exchange their conditioning against money in the form of wages.
446 Unlike those who manage commercial, business, and managerial affairs, those who are managed do not invest. Investment is a financial term that seeks a financial return. In everyday language this term is often used wrongly as, for example, in *I have invested $10,000 in my new car* or, more obscenely, I have *invested so much in my boyfriend.* In the first case, the car was purchased for consumption not for financial returns. In the second case, the ideology of managerialism has infiltrated private relationships where the unconscious idea of returns has become paramount and (self-)destructive (Adorno 1944; Fromm 1995).
447 Today, the term working class has all but completely disappeared from the public domain since corporate mass media have restructured this domain. Hoggart (2003:2) commented this with *today, when we do not like any longer to speak of 'the working class' and sometimes deny that it still exists, we are uneasy about giving a name to its smaller, but evidently worse-off successor, the underclass.* Apart from the underclass often employed in atypical forms of work, the vast majority of today's working class – now called middle class or aspirational class – is still exposed to sell their labour on the labour market. While their objective class interest *in itself* remains the same, their equally objective class interest *for itself* has been redirected towards consumption.
448 In theoretical terms this provides a structural shift from understanding the social reality of work as collective action (Olson 1971; Offe & Wiesenthal

1980; Roy & Parker-Gwen 1999) to the theory of communicative action (Habermas 1997).

449 While class relations demand from workers to work and participate in the labour market even though this market is radically different from commodity markets as workers – even after two centuries of capitalism – still do not have anything except their labour to sell on this market, in standard managerial text books, the asymmetrical relationship that defines this market is ideologically coded as *organisations must first attract potential employees* (Jex 2002:55). Formulations like this keep the perception alive that there are no economic forces behind workers' need to seek employment but it is just a matter of *attraction*. The neutral sounding word *organisation* is, of course, the codeword for profit-oriented company that negates the historic reality of child labour, sweat shop labour, bonded labour, slave labour, etc. and, above all, inhuman work arrangements found in advanced as well as developing countries.

450 Workers are made to find additional arguments on why wages are individual and not collective and why performance related pay is crucial rather than productivity gains, surplus-values created for shareholders, profits, inflation rates, cost of living, etc. Managerialism and Human Resource Management's task is to guide this self-alienating process into the direction conducive to managerialism.

451 See: Schank's *Goal-Based Scenario* (1994).

452 The symmetrical interest representation in both domains is further complicated in the labour domain through several dilemmas that labour has to come to terms with. Communicative action can lead to either individual or collective involvement. It can lead to economic or political action. Labour can act as producer or consumer. Furthermore, labour is always exposed to opportunism through the pragmatic acceptance of current conditions.

453 *Empiricism, in agreement with common sense, holds that a verbal statement may be confirmed or confuted by an observation, provided it is a statement which is significant and is not one of logic* (Russell 1973:16).

454 The prevention of unwanted and managerially unwarranted knowledge, however, starts *before* humans are converted into human resources and before people are turned into workers. Schools and universities already resemble the lines of the factory model with material procurement [the competitive recruitment of students from kindergarten onwards], resource planning, supply procurement, process planning, quality control [endless auditing by management], resource maintenance, deliveries, and operations – all elements that are familiar to any school or university under managerialism (cf. Fromm, 1957; Alvesson, 1996).

455 See Habermas (1997:368) and Williams' (2005:14) commodification thesis and the possibilities of the non-commodified spheres: a) non-exchanged or substantive work, b) non-monetary goods- and service exchanges, and c) not-for-profit exchanges.

456 See Marglin (1974), Offe & Wiesenthal (1980), Hyman (1987).

457 See Horkheimer (1937), Benhabib *et al.* (1993), and Weber (1947).

458 Based on Offe & Wiesenthal (1980) & Habermas (1997:329, vol.1). The triangle represents top-down communication of one to the many. The circle represents communications under conditions of ideal speech.

459 On psychology, Searle (2002:13) commented, *within the field of consciousness our experiences are characteristically structured in a way that goes beyond the structure of the actual stimulus. This was one of the most profound discoveries*

of the Gestalt psychologists. It is most obvious in the case of vision, but the phenomenon is quite general and extends beyond vision. In other words, we can recognise this ☺ as a face even though it is not a real face just the *Gestalt* (shape) of a face.

460 It is the task of critical theory to unveil the ideological distortions of everyday speech (Thompson 1981:3). Speech conducted inside the world of work is a form of everyday speech, hence the task of critical theory is to disclose communicative distortions used at work. *This critique aims not only to unveil conditions of possibility, but also to unmask illusion and error; its driving force is the dialectic, that 'portentous power of the negative', which discloses the contradictions within each successive mode of experience* (Thompson 1981:72). The idea of managerialism and instrumental rationality seeks to construct the world of work as un-contradictory. It represents the extreme opposite of critical thinking that tries to overcome dominations because managerialism in its one-dimensionality sustains forms of hierarchical and authoritarian structures.

461 See: Habermas (1997), Alvesson & Sköldberg (2000:119), Habermas (2001:vii), Levy, Alvesson & Willmott (1992 & 2003).

462 See: Lukacs' (1923, 1971, 2000).

463 According to Brenkert (1983:6 &10), *Marx did not write a treatise, any pamphlets, or even any essay on ethics and morality* [because at Marx's time they] *represented to him a kind of dream-like acquiescence in the face of the increasing degradation suffered by larger and larger numbers of people in modern society.* Today, these numbers encompass about 4/5 of the world population because of decades of globalisation.

464 Quoted from Habermas (1997a:57); cf. Bronner (1994:283–320).

465 See: Agamben (2000).

466 The *development of television and other forms of electronic media meant* [that the money and power code could become] *more pervasive and persuasive than ever before* (Chilton 1983:36). In short, the mass media have played a significant role in eroding the public sphere by promoting corporate interests as opposed to free debate thus hiding the powerful money and power code behind entertainment, infotainment, and the like. Apart from portraying the world as a world of commercial goods, mass media also served as a powerful tool during the conversion from social control to social affirmation (cf. Sitton 2003:75).

467 In order to break the power and money code, theories of semiotics (Eco 1977:3) have to be applied because unlike other issues related to communication, semiotics deals with theories of codes, signs, and the production and understanding. Unlike grammar and syntax – semiotics is directed towards uncovering the meaning of things. One might also call it a theory of signification.

468 Apart from the infiltration of the state and democratic domain by the money and power code, democracy's *mass-loyalty creating powers* (Sitton 2003:77) have been, at least partially, redirected towards consumer capitalism when the Liberal idea of *I'm spoiled for choice* is re-guided towards consumption and away from democracy in a *de-politicised* but highly commercial world (Hoggart's *Decline of the News*, 2004:53). Choice no longer means political choice but commercial choice and, as a final insult, even politicians become consumer choices in a system that reduces political choice to getting the best deal for oneself, thus exposing politicians to the relentless mechanisms of market capitalism.

469 We live in democratic times, in that hardly a political leader or activist anywhere would claim to be anything other than a democrat (Dryzek 1996:3) even though, or maybe even because of the fact that democracy has been diluted to an affirmative mass-loyalty creating a subsystem of advanced capitalism (Canfora 2006). System stabilising elements are provided by an iron-triangle of (a) self-interested politicians who are sometimes exposed to democratic (largely re-) elections (pretence of mass-participation but factual mass-affirmation), (b) bureaucrats (legal framework for system integration), and c) lobbyists (capital's interest representation). See also Sitton's monetary-bureaucratic complex (2003:xiv).

470 The organisation and the use of labour is not a private affair. It occurs in a highly regulated or deregulated domain that is organised by system demands from capitalism because of a systematic inability of individual capitalist firms (management) to guarantee the system of labour markets. Therefore interchanges between the domains of labour-employment and labour-private (consumption) have to be organised *publicly*, not privately.

471 Some have even run into the danger of thinking that sex is not sellable itself and therefore opposed to consumption even though sex as used in advertising, marketing, and mass-consumption helps selling. Sex, therefore is commercially a rather worthless exercise for capitalism and therefore, *they spat the word 'sex' as though they were ejecting a dirty frog, a nasty experience and against 'proper' nature* (Hoggart 2004:8). It appears that when having sex people cannot shop and vice versa. Sex takes useful energies away from consumption, energies that have been re-directed towards consumption so that shopping (profit) rather than sex (next to no profits) becomes a *fulfilling act*. On this Kellner (1984:245) noted, *advertising promises commodity solutions to problems or associates the product with the 'good life': advertisements for certain shampoos or mouthwashes, for instance, promise popularity and intensified sex appeal; soft drinks promise fun, youth, community; cars promise power and social prestige; worthless tonics promise health and vitality; mass-produced clothing promises individuality and style; and a bevy of products of dubious worth promises solutions to a variety of problems. These expectations and anticipations are, for the most part, 'false promises'; need for products based on these expectations are 'false needs'* (cf. Davis & Silk 1987).

472 Today's consumer society is defined by the fact that *never before have so many people bought so many physical objects, so many varied consumer goods, or expressed their personality so fully through them. Houses get bigger, and one is seldom enough. Cars metamorphose into trucks, and with the Hummer, into tanks* (Lanham 2006:1).

473 For decades now, the ideology of Human Resource Management has pretended to be *new*, to have successfully replaced old personnel management. The marketing cult of the new has infiltrated personnel management as it has managerialism – business process reengineering, business units, KPIs, PRP, TQM, QCs, etc. – because *the cult of the new is the idea of modernity, the New becomes sensational, in its most garnish media sense...Goebbels boasted that at least the* [at that time NEW] *National Socialists were not boring* (Jameson, 1990:191). The same can be said about any NEW *management fashion* (Abrahamson 1996), including HRM. At least it is not boring!

474 Interestingly, when the globally operative McKinsey consulting firm sought to find the single most important driving force behind capitalism it turned out to be *The Consumer*.

475   In this, managerial regimes are inevitably variety reducing systems as the human being to-be-converted into a human resource has to show a pattern of behaviour that is not only predictable and conforms to the work regime but is also useful to management. This is highly relevant because patterned behaviour is necessary for the functioning of work regimes. Work regimes must create compliant behaviour that is rigid enough to adapt to an equally rigid work system.

476   Inside the three core interests that all workers share (wages, working time, and conditions), conflict can arise over managerial values (efficiency & profit) vs. workers' values (human work forms, etc.), policies and directions, goals (profit vs. people), methods (ethical vs. unethical business and work practices). Despite all managerial rhetoric, managerialism cannot be able to totally deny conflict because of the dialectical structure of workplace relations, conflicts and contradictions between management and labour. Apart from Hegelian dialectics that is operative in the domain of work, there is also the fact that conflict is embedded in human relationships. Given management's awareness of this, it has developed two fundamental strategies to deal with conflict. These strategies always include a) assertiveness and b) cooperation. Both are related to the extent to which workers attempt to satisfy their interests. This is the move from collective *communication* to collective *action* or from willingness to *communicate* to the willingness to *act*. Management always seeks to prevent conflict with workers at these three levels: Firstly, it seeks to prevent any communication about different interests to avoid the highlighting of contradictions between management and labour and, if this fails, management seeks to prevent the conversion of communication into action and, if this also fails, finally seeks to prevent social action.

477   An ideal type is formed from characteristics and elements of the given phenomena but it is *not* meant to correspond to all of the characteristics of any one particular case. It is *not* meant to refer to perfect things, moral ideals or statistical averages but rather to stress certain elements common to most cases of the given phenomena. An ideal type is formed by the one-sided accentuation of one or more points of view and by the synthesis of a great many diffuse, discrete, more or less present and occasionally absent concrete individual phenomena, which are arranged according to those one-sidedly emphasised viewpoints into a unified analytical construct. Ideal types always include a dialectical view that encompasses not so much the *what is* but more the *what ought to be*.

478   For Searle (1996:200) *truth, in short, is a matter of accuracy of a certain sort of linguistic representation*.

479   Brenkert (1983:52–53) noted that *without transcendental freedom…no moral law and no accountability are possible…*given freedom from coercion and constraint, morality should be possible. See also Karl-Otto Apel's *From Kant to Peirce: the Semiotical Transformation of Transcendental Logic* (1980:77ff.)

480   See Williams (2005:16).

481   This is not to be mistaken from what is asked from too many in managerial positions: the only thing required from us is lip-service to morality (Hoggart 2004:20), and this *not despite of* a raft of books and textbooks on corporate social responsibility, company ethics, business ethics, etc. but because of these books and the fact that ethics faces a formidable challenge in advanced capitalism and managerialism.

482   See: Russell (1973).

483 See: Gadamer (1974); Hodge & Kress (1979).
484 In most managerial textbooks the true state of undemocratic authoritarianism that guides today's world of work is hidden behind the term *leadership*. In that way, managerial textbooks can avoid the negative connotations by focusing on the positives of leadership. The positives or negatives of a leader are still to be found in its German translation: Führer!
485 Democracy and workplace democracy have the great advantage that they leave the prevailing economic structure untouched – political democracy in the economic sphere and workplace democracy in the managerial sphere – while democracy can only be seen as *a system for processing conflicts without killing one another* (Dryzek 1996). In simple words, the times when strong men assembled on a field and hit one another with sticks until one was left standing (=leader) are over. Today, the stick is replaced with a paper to vote on every three to five years. The rest stays the same because humans have not advanced beyond the basic fundamentals of this system of leader-selection. Finally, despite some minor attempts to introduce democracy into the workplace, it leaves the core of managerial power unchecked. Similarly, the introduction of democracy into the public domain leaves the core institutional settings of advanced capitalism untouched and unchecked. These are *designed to be off-limits to democratic control, such as central banks, intelligence services, military organisations, and transnational economic authorities like the World Trade Organisation and the International Monetary Fund* (Dryzek 1996:6).
486 The idea of democracy at work has only been allowed into the popular mind when it had been necessary as a system stabilising element. The foremost example has been the time in the immediate vicinity of the aftermath of World War I when European workers revolted against the capitalist system partly inspired by the events in Russia in 1917. To give less radical and more social-democratically oriented workers [Menshevik rather than Bolshevik] the illusion of workplace democracy in many European workplaces, democratically elected workers' councils were introduced as they were able to channel conflict into the safe-box of democratic games while leaving property relations untouched. The second time workplace democracy or industrial democracy reappeared in the aftermath of the year 1967 when foremost French and Italian workers joined radical students demanding radical change. By the 1980s these movements where either successfully integrated (JCCs, co-determination, WCs and EWCs) or isolated (Red Brigades, RAF, etc.) and the idea of industrial democracy died down during the 1990s until it no longer played any significant role in the popular press, trade union circles, and academic writings (cf. Canfora 2006). See also Ramsay (1977).
487 Loosely adopted from Kellner (1984:236–237).
488 While Kellner (1984:239) noted that *social controls are no longer internalised through the ingression of society into the mental structure of individuals, but are embodied in the societal apparatus and ideology which requires submission to its rules, dictates and institutions*. However, social control is no longer necessary – neither through *ingression into mental structures* nor through the *embodiment in social apparatuses* because – to an ever increasing extent – control has been replaced through affirmation in a system that conditions the *individual's very gratification* towards mass-affirmative socially conforming behaviour that is administered through consumer capitalism mediated through corporate mass media.
489 See: Lanning's (2001) *Ethics and Self-Mastery: Revolution and the Fully Developed Person in the Work of Georg Lukacs* (cf. Sitton 2003:22).

490 In textbooks on managerial communication it is not uncommon to find that the restrictive code issued by managerialism reduces ethics and ethical communication to statements such as these: *competent people are likely to search for organisations that maintain high ethical standards* (O'Hair et al. 2005:30). Usually, a deeper analysis of ethics and ethical communication is bypassed by references to individual cases such as anecdotes from a few highly unethical corporations or, even better, unethical behaviour by individual CEOs.

491 This is not needed because *Habermas has repeatedly rejected self-management schemes* (Sitton 2003:135), but become management's fundamentals are structured against possibilities of communicative action. If management were to engage in communicative action, it needed to cease to be management because instrumental communication, the means-ends-theorem, anti-democracy, authoritarianism, hierarchical structures and positions based on power that are not communicatively established are all elements that work against meaningful and ethical engagement in communicative action. Management and communicative action are diametrically opposing themes. Finally, the *self* cannot be *managed*, either from the outside or from the inside. The idea of self-management is contradictory.

492 In standard textbooks on business ethics and ethical communication, ethics is – although often sub-titled as *Communication Ethics* – reduced to – in some case six, seven, or in this case eight – steps to be followed. Once accomplished, the impression is given that this is all it takes to act and communicate ethically. In O'Hair et al. (2005:29–30), the ingredients of ethics are: 1. maintain candour; 2. keep messages accurate; 3. avoid deception (the basic idea behind strategy and strategic communication); 4. behave constantly; 5. keep confidence; 6. ensure timeless communication; 7. confront unethical behaviour; and 8. cultivate emphatic listening. The 1 $^1/_2$ pages on ethical communication in O'Hair et al.'s standard textbook on *Strategic communication in Business and the Professions* end together with a hint that competent people search for ethical companies.

493 This is the case despite more than 100 years of training and more than 50 years of management studies.

494 See O'Hair et al.'s *Model of Strategic Communication* (2005:24). On this Habermas (1990:101) commented *action oriented towards success and action oriented towards reaching an understanding are mutually exclusive types of action*.

495 See: Fromm (1955 & 1957); Arendt (1958); Kohlberg (1971, 1981 1984); Brenkert, (1983); Singer (1993, 1994, 2000).

496 Adopted from Brenkert (1983:62).

497 According to Kant's philosophy the idea of the *categorical imperative* has been designed to indicate that one must act only in accordance to those maxims which one can at the same time relate to the validity in terms of their ability to be universal. While in the past this had been established philosophically – Kant – a post-Kantian categorical imperative is formed by a procedure of moral argumentation inside communicative action.

498 Communicative action strongly negates the idea of an individual pathway to truth because a Robinson Crusoe-like existence through which the sceptic demonstrates mutely and impressively that he has dropped out of communicative action is inconceivable, even as thought experiment (Habermas 1990:100). The idea of communicative action can only be realised when subjects *externalise themselves*. No one can maintain an identity by himself. Communicative action also rejects any *monological* approach to ethics.

499 This is not the *Münchhausen* dilemma in which *Münchhausen* pulled himself out of the mud by pulling his head. The idea of communicative ethics is not circular because there are no circular mechanisms for ethics, only a few basic parameters for ideal speech that lead – as one form of many possible forms of dialogue – to ethical debates. The idea of communicative ethics established through communicative action also breaks the spell of Adorno's *negativism* (1944) that is also found in Horkheimer (1947), Horkheimer & Adorno (1947), and in Marcuse (1966 & 1968); cf. Benhabib (1993, especially Habermas' *Remarks on the Development of Horkheimer's Work*, Chapter 3).

500 This sort of *aufheben* includes the end of a division of labour between managerial writers in the field of business ethics and communicative ethics for business and management that has – due to instrumental rationality and instrumental communication – positioned itself in a greater distance to humans – and labour in the world of work – than to philosophers. And this is precisely the reason why management and managerialism *live off* their specially assigned writers of business ethics and not *from* or rather *with* closeness to philosophy.

501 In matter where ethical reasoning is supreme it is the communicatively established understanding rather than force of inner illumination – church, individual philosopher, religious morality, etc. – that is decisive.

502 As such, communicative action cannot be *value neutral* because communicative subjects are still subjects, in fact they move back from being objects of power in the managerial domain to being subjects inside the ethics of communicative action.

503 One of the best methods to establish dialogues that are directed towards communicative ethics can be found in the use of the scale provided by Kohlberg (1971, 1981, 1984); cf. Habermas (1990:128–129).

504 Participants in communicative action must reach understanding about issues in the world of work if they want to carry out social-emancipatory action plans on a consensual basis, on the basis of some jointly defined action situation. In so doing, they presuppose a formal concept of the world of work as the referencing point that provides the means and meanings to analyse the world of work. Speakers inside communicative action need to make reference to the world of work, a socially constructed world that can be socially reconstructed. The operational part of such plans, again, depends on mutual agreement and for that shared visions of *what ought to be* depend upon an agreement of a shared understanding of *what is*.

505 In contrast to instrumental communication under conditions of means-ends rationality that includes *strategic* action seeking to influence, manipulate, persuade, or even coerce others to behave and communicate in a pre-designed way, communicative action is based on social and communicative affirmation that has a *social* rather than a *system*atic binding/bonding effect among participants. This bonding/binding experience is counter-balanced by the competitive element that is part of the dialectic between argument and counter-argument that drives the dialogue towards common agreement. It is at the same time a version of disputation and a cooperative search for truth and common understanding. This is a deeply solidaristic process through the establishment of shared and commonly agreed ethical standards that not only affect the world of work but society in general. In establishing solidarity through communicative action, communication can provide a powerful vehicle to enhance a commonly agreed emphasis directed towards equality,

solidarity, respect, and the common good. Equal rights of participants and an equally shared respect for personal dignity are vital for the ideal speech situation to flourish.

506 Quoted from Habermas (1990:66). Entering into such a form of ethical communication means to re-enter a form of dialogue suppressed by managerialism that lives on instrumental communication.

507 *In general, statements are attempts to describe issues or situations in the world, which exist independent of the statement. The statement will be true or false depending on whether these things really are the way the statement says they are* (Searle 1996:200).

508 Eco (1977:159) noted that *Kant explicitly states in the first Kritik that the activity of our reason consists largely…in the analysis of ideas which we already have with regard to object*. Kant saw that when we communicate or construct statements during a discourse, we reflect on the objective world through ideas that we – at least partially – have already been familiar with. The creation of such ideas, however, has to be done rationally. Only this process can advance discourses (cf. Habermas 1985; Ingram 1991).

509 See Karl-Otto Apel's *Scientism or Transcendental Hermeneutics? On the Question of the Subject of the Interpretation of Signs in the Semiotics of Pragmatism* (1980).

510 Social action must, in many parts, be able to overcome all forms of *a priori* conditioned social control mechanisms that colonises the human mind from early childhood onwards (DeVitis 1974). See also Tracy's *Action-Implicative Discourse Analysis* (1995).

511 See: Fisher and Uri (1981:15).

512 Groupthink is a highly problematic mode of thinking. It occurs when group members intentionally conform to what they perceive to be the consensus of the group. The group tends to find a solution or a common agreement that is, in fact, not based on objective assessments. Groups reach false conclusions and false agreements because of false internal assumptions. Groupthink causes a discourse group to reach false conclusions. It can result in irrational decisions and actions. For a single person, these decisions seem to be wrong but the unhealthy dynamic of a group can let these decisions appear as correct. Groupthink is dysfunctional social group behaviour. In some cases groups can agree to pursue certain goals to which the individual members might not even have agreed. The best known example of group thinking has been the US invasion of the Bay of Pigs in Cuba. This wrong decision is largely attributed to groupthink. It may also be attributed to a hysterical anti-communism displayed by the American government.

513 Neither *thought* nor *communication* can bring about social change unless it is transformed into social action.

514 On this, Chomsky (1966:26) once noted that *if a man acts in a purely mechanical way, we may admire what he does, but we despise what he is* (cf. D'Agostino 1986; Apel 1980:180ff.).

515 See: Postone's *Labor and Instrumental Action* (1993: 179–182).

516 Many conservative models of human behaviour in social sciences assume that humans can be reasonably approximated or described as rational. This is especially the case in system theory, behaviourism, and rational choice theory. Many neo-liberal economics models assume that people are hyper-rational, and would never do anything to violate their preferences. In reality, however, most people are only partly rational as subjective factors of life prevail. They are emotional and sometimes even irrational. Hence many of their actions are

not rational actions. Agents trapped in bounded rationality experience limits in formulating and solving complex problems. The processing, receiving, storing, retrieving, and transmitting of information and meanings is not thoroughly rational.

517 They fail as much as natural or managerial science can fail when products remain unsold, commodities are unwanted, bridges collapse, satellites crash into planets, space rockets explode, computers break down, software deletes or atomic power stations release deadly radioactive gases.

518 A dilemma can be seen as a situation that requires a choice between options that are – or seem – equally unfavourable or mutually exclusive, a problem that seems to defy a satisfactory solution, or as an argument that presents two alternatives, each of which has the same consequence.

519 Managerialism and advanced capitalism do not only have to deal with system integration and the social integration of workers that could – although at present this is rarely the case – mobilise counteractive forces (Kelly 1998); both also have to deal with system problems and system contradictions (Offe 1976:7).

520 See: Habermas (1997), Postone's *Habermas' Critique of Marx* (1993); Fromm's *Marx's Contribution to the Knowledge of Man* (1968); Fromm (1995); Apel (1980:136ff).

521 The SWOT analysis is a managerial tool used for instrumental planning. As a tool it is used to evaluate the strengths, weaknesses, opportunities, and threats of a managerial project or business venture. It is a form of instrumental decision making and confines thinking and communication into four boxes directed towards highly functional forms of communication. In extreme cases, this can be a form of TINA (Williams 2005:16). It pretends a) that there are no alternatives to SWOT, b) it delivers infallible outcomes, c) it is overtly rational and d) it delivers the right decisions at the right time.

522 Even though social philosophers have created the idea of *the survival of the fittest* and the *fight of all against all* to survive – two core ideas that fit capitalism's idea of competition – and corporate mass media have successfully but wrongly assigned it to Charles Darwin, the vast majority of animal life relies on cooperation, not competition. Equally, Darwin's idea has always been the idea of the *survival of those who can adapt* themselves to natural changes. Overall, animals, early humans, and humans in advanced societies rely more on cooperation than on competition to survive even though the present and somewhat human-alien system of economic affairs is at least ideologically based on competition while large parts of our economy are still based on cooperation. Ideologically however, this is supported by the faked supportive ideology assumption that it was Darwin who created the *survival of the fittest*.

523 See Marcuse (1966:18) & Fromm's *On Being Human* (1961) in: Buechler (2006).

524 On the social character of language, Chomsky (1966:26) noted *for Humboldt, a language is not to be regarded as a mass of isolated phenomena – words, sounds, individual speech production, etc. – but rather as an 'organism' in which all parts are interconnected and the role of each element is determined by its relation to the generative process that constitutes the underlying form.* For that reason, language – managerial language or the language developed in the workers' domain (historically it was connected to the *workers milieu* that has been comprehensively defeated by corporate mass media) – can only be established as a social interconnection. It is not an isolated phenomenon and as such the language uses of both domains have influenced each other. What has been seen during the

last 200 years is a gradual replacement of workers' language by the language of managerialism. There is no more talk of workers' cooperatives; today it is all about key performance indicators. Similarly, Thompson (1981:2) commented that *language* [can only be] *viewed as a practical medium through which individuals participate in the world*.

525 Increasingly labour has to overcome managerialism's and corporate mass media guided de-solidarisation. See mechanical and organic solidarity (cf. http://durkheim.itgo.com/solidarity.html).

Bibliography

Abrahamson, E. 1996. Management Fashion, *Academy of Management Review*, vol. 21, no. 1.
Ackermann, F. & Heinzerling, L. 2004. *Priceless – On Knowing the Price of Everything and the Value of Nothing*, London: The New Press.
Ackroyd, S. & Thompson, P. 1999. *Organisational Misbehaviour*, London: Sage.
Adams, R. 2007. The Employee Free Choice Act: A Sceptical View and Alternatives, *Labor Studies Journal*, vol. 31, no. 4.
Adorno, T. W. 1944. *Minima Moralia – Reflections from the Damaged Life*, Dennis Redmond (2005) translation: http://www.efn.org/~dredmond/MinimaMoralia.html
Adorno, T. W. 1968. *Late Capitalism or Industrial Society?* – Opening Address to the 16th German Sociological Congress, http://ww.efn.org/
Adorno, T. W. 1973. *Negative Dialectics*, London: Routledge.
Adorno, T. 1976. Sociology and Empirical Research, in: Adorno, T. *et al.* (eds). *The Positivist Dispute in German Sociology*, London: Heinemann.
Adorno, T. W. & Horkheimer, M. 1944. *The Culture Industry: Enlightenment as Mass Deception*, Transcribed by Andy Blunden 1998; proofed and corrected Feb. 2005, web-download, November 2005.
Adorno, T. W. *et al.* 1964. *The Authoritarian Personality*, New York: John Wiley.
Agamben, G. 2000. *Means without Ends – Notes on Politics*, Minneapolis: University of Minneapolis Press.
Albert, M. 2006. *Realizing Hope – Life Beyond Capitalism*, London: Zed Books.
Alonso, L. 2006. Fordism and the Genesis of the Post-Fordist Society: Assessing the Post-Fordist Paradigm, in: Alonso, L. & Lucio, M. (eds) *Employment Relations in a Changing Society*, Houndsmill: Palgrave.
Alonso, L. & Lucio, M. (eds) 2006. *Employment Relations in a Changing Society*, Houndsmill: Palgrave.
Althusser, L. 1965. *For Marx*, London: New Left Books.
Alvesson, M. 1996. *Communication, Power and Organisation*, New York: deGruyter.
Alvesson, M. & Sköldberg, K. 2000. *Reflexive Methodology – New Vistas for Qualitative Research*, London: Sage.
Alvesson, M. 2002. *Understanding Organisational Culture*, London: Sage.
Alvesson, M. & Willmott, H. 1992. Critical Theory and Management Studies: An Introduction, in: Alvesson, M. & Willmott, H. (eds) *Critical Management Studies*, London: Sage.
Alvesson, M. & Willmott, H. (eds) 2003. *Studying Management Critically*, London: Sage.
Anderson, J. T. 1990. Skinner and Chomsky Thirty Years Later, *Historiographia Linguistica*, vol. XVII, no. 1/2.
Anderson, J. T. 1992. The Behaviorist Turn in Recent Theories on Language, *Behavior and Philosophy*, vol. 20, no. 1.
Anthony, P. D. 1977. *The Ideology of Work*, London: Routledge, excerpt reprinted in Grey, C. & Willmott, H. (eds) 2005. *Critical Management Studies – A Reader*, Oxford: Oxford University Press.
Apel, K.-O. 1980. *Towards a Transformation of Philosophy*, London: Routledge.
Arendt, H. 1951. *The Origins of Totalitarianism*, Orlando: A Harvest/HBJ Book.
Arendt, H. 1958. *The Human Condition*, Chicago: University of Chicago Press.

Arendt, H. 1994. *Eichmann in Jerusalem: A Report on the Banality of Evil*, New York: Penguin.
Arnold, J. 2005. *Work Psychology – Understanding Human Behaviour in the Workplace*, London: Prentice-Hall.
Aubrey, C. 1983. The Making of 1984, in: Aubrey, C. & Chilton, P. (eds) *Nineteen Eighty-Four in 1984 – Autonomy, Control & Communication*, London: Comedia Publishing Group.
Aubrey, C. & Chilton, P. 1983. *Nineteen Eighty-Four in 1984 – Autonomy, Control & Communication*, London: Comedia Publishing Group.
Austin, J. L. 1962. *How to do things with words*, Oxford: Oxford University Press.
Austin, J. & Wilson, K. 2001. Response-Response Relationships in Organisational Behaviour Management, *Journal of Organizational Behavior Management*, vol. 21, no. 4.
Baritz, L. 1960. *The Servants of Power: A History of the Use of Social Science in American Industry*, Middletown: Wesleyan University Press.
Barker, J. R. 1993. Tightening the Iron Cage: Concertive Control in Self-Managing Teams, *Administrative Science Quarterly*, vol. 38, no. 2.
Barker, J. R. 1999. Communication, Organisation, and Performance, *Administrative Science Quarterly*, vol. 44, no. 3.
Barker, J. R. 2005. Tightening the Iron Cage: Concertive Control in Self-Managed Teams, in: Grey, C. & Willmott, H. (eds) *Critical Management Studies – A Reader*, Oxford: Oxford University Press.
Barratt, E. 2003. Foucault, HRM and the Ethos of the Critical Management Scholar, *Journal of Management Studies*, vol. 40, no. 5.
Barry, M. 2006. *Company: A Novel*, New York: Doubleday.
Barry, J. et al. 2001. Between the Ivory Tower and the Academic Assembly Line, *Journal of Management Studies*, vol. 38, no. 1.
Barry, D. & Elmes, M. 1997. Strategy Retold, *Academy of Management Review*, vol. 22, no. 2.
Barthes, R. 1957. *Mythologies*, New York: The Noonday Press.
Barthes, R. 1967. *Elements of Semiology*, London: Cape.
Baudrillard, J. 1975. *The Mirror of Production*, St Louis: Telos Press.
Baudrillard, J. 1979. *Seduction*, Houndsmill: Macmillan.
Baudrillard, J. 1994. *The Illusion of the End*, Stanford: Stanford University Press.
Baudrillard, J. 1998. *The Consumer Society – Myths and Structures*, London: Sage.
Baum, W. 2005. *Understanding Behaviorism – Behavior, Culture, and Evolution*, Oxford: Blackwell.
Bauman, Z. 1989. *Modernity and Holocaust*, Oxford: Blackwell.
Bell, D. 1960. *The End of Ideology*, Glencoe: Free Press.
Bell, D. 1973. *The Coming of the Post-Industrial Society*, Harmondsworth: Penguin.
Benhabib, S. et al. (eds) 1993. *On Max Horkheimer – New Perspectives*, Cambridge: MIT Press.
Berger, P. & Luckmann, T. 1967. *The Social Construction of Reality*, New York: Garden City.
Bhaskar, R. 1993. *Dialectic – The Pulse of Freedom*, London: Verso.
Bigler, W. P. & Norris, M. 2004. *The New Science of Strategic Execution – How Established Firms become Fast, Sleek Wealth Creators*, London: Praeger.
Billsberry, J. 1996. *The Effective Manager*, London: Sage.
Birnbaum, N. 1969. *The Crisis of Industrial Society*, Oxford: Oxford University Press.
Birnbaum, N. 1971. *Toward a Critical Sociology*, Oxford: Oxford University Press.
Blumberg, H. 1990. *Work on Myth*, Cambridge: MIT Press.
Blundel, R. 2004. *Effective Organisational Communication – Perspectives, Principles and Practices*, London: FT Prentice Hall.

Blundel, R. 2004. *Effective Organisational Communication*, London: Prentice Hall.
Bolinger, D. 1968. *Aspects of Language*, New York: Harcourt & Brace.
Bolinger, D. 1980. *Language – The Loaded Weapon*, London: Longman.
Bosquet, M. 1980. The Meaning of Job Enrichment, in: Nichols, T. (ed.) 1980. *Capital and Labour – A Marxist Primer*, London: Fontana Press.
Bowie, N. 2005. Kantian Ethical Thought, in: Budd, S. & Scoville, J. (eds) *The Ethics of Human Resources and Industrial Relations*, Champaign: Labor and Employment Relations Association.
Bowles, S. & Gintis, H. 1976. *Schooling in Capitalist America: Educational Reform and the Contradictions of Economic Life*, New York: Basic Books.
Bowles, S. & Gintis, H. 1981. Contradictions and Reproduction in Educational Theory, in: Barton, L. (ed.) *Schooling, Ideology, and Curriculum*, Sussex: Falmer Press.
Bowles, S. & Gintis, H. 2001. *Schooling in Capitalist America Revisited*, http://www.unix.oit.umass.edu/~bowles
Bowman, J. R. 1982. The Logic of Capitalist Collective Action, *Rationality and Society*, vol. 21, no. 4/5.
Brenkert, G. G. 1983. *Marx's Ethics of Freedom*, London: Routledge.
Brimeyer, T., Easker, A. & Clair, R. 2004. Rhetorical Strategies in Union Organising – A Case of Labor versus Management, *Management Communication Quarterly*, vol. 18, no. 1, pp. 45–75.
Bronner, S. E. 1994. *Of Critical Theory and its Theorists*, Oxford: Blackwell.
Buck-Moss, S. 1977. *The Origins of Negative Dialectics – Theodor W. Adorno, Walter Benjamin, and the Frankfurt Institute*, New York: The Free Press.
Budd, J. & Scoville, J. 2005. Moral Philosophy, Business Ethics, and the Employment Relationship, in: Budd, S. & Scoville, J. (eds) *The Ethics of Human Resources and Industrial Relations*, Champaign: Labor and Employment Relations Association.
Buechler, S. 2006. *Why We Need Fromm Today: Fromm's Work Ethic*, www.erichfromm.de.
Bühler, K. 1934. *Sprachtheorie* [theory of speech], Jena: G. Fischer Press.
Burawoy, M. 1979. *Manufacturing Consent*, Chicago: Chicago University Press.
Burawoy, M. 1985. *The Politics of Production*, London: Verso.
Cairns, G. et al. 2003. Organisational Space/Time: From Imperfect Panoptical to Heterotopian Understanding, *ephemera* (ephemeraweb.org), vol. 3. no. 2.
Cairns, L. 2006. Reinforcement, in: Hargie, O. (ed.) *The Handbook of Communication Skills*, (3rd edition), London: Routledge.
Carlson, N. R. & Buskist, W. 1997. *The Science of Behavior*, London: Allyn and Bacon.
Canfora, L. 2006. *Democracy in Europe – A History of an Ideology*, London: Blackwell.
Chalmers, A. F. 1994. *What is this thing called Science?*, 2nd edition, Milton Keynes: Open University Press.
Chandler, A. 1962. *Strategy and Structure*, Cambridge: MIT Press.
Cheney, G. & Carroll, C. 1997. The Person as Object in Discourses in and around organizations, *Communication Research*, vol. 24, no. 6, pp. 593–630.
Chilton, P. 1983. Newspeak: It's The Real Thing, in: Aubrey, C. & Chilton, P. (eds) *Nineteen Eighty-Four in 1984 – Autonomy, Control & Communication*, London: Comedia Publishing Group.
Chomsky, N. 1959. Review of Skinner's Verbal Behavior, *Language*, vol. 35, no. 1.
Chomsky, N. 1966. *Cartesian Linguistics – A Chapter in the History of Rationalist Thought*, London: Harper & Row.
Chomsky, N. 1967. On Resistance, *The New York Review of Books*, December 7th (internet download).
Chomsky, N. 1968. *Language and Mind*, New York: Harcourt Brace.

Chomsky, N. 1971. The Case against B. F. Skinner, *The New York Review of Books*, December 30th (internet download).
Chomsky, N. 1985, Free Speech in a Democracy, *Daily Camera*, September (internet download).
Chomsky, N. 1994. Democracy and Education, *Mellon Lecture*, Loyola University, Chicago, October 19th, download: www.zmag.org/chomsky/talks/.
Chomsky, N. 2002. *Understanding Power*, New York: Norton.
Cialdini, R. 1984. *Influence – The Psychology of Persuasion*, Melbourne: The Business Library.
Clegg, S. *et al.* 2006. Business Ethics as Practice, *British Journal of Management*, vol. 17, pp. 1–16.
Cole, M. 1988. *Bowles and Gintis Revisited – Correspondence and Contradiction in Educational Theory*, London: Falmer Press.
Comte, A. 1853. *Essential Writings on Positivism*, original translation by Harriet Martineau, 1853, reprint 1975 by New York: Harper.
Cooke, M. 2006. Resurrecting the Rationality of Ideological Critique: Reflections on Laclau on Ideology, *Constellations*, vol. 13, no. 1.
Coutu, M. & Murray, G. 2006. Towards Citizenship at Work? – An Introduction, *Relation Industrielles/Industrial Relations*, vol. 60, no. 4.
Crossley, N. 2005. *Key Concepts in Critical Social Theory*, London: Sage.
D'Agostino, F. 1986. *Chomsky's System of Ideas*, Oxford: Clarendon Press.
D'Agostino's, F. 1987. Chomsky's System of Ideas, *Philosophical Quarterly*, vol. 37, pp. 477–481.
Dahl, R. A. 1957. The Concept of Power, *Behavioural Science*, vol. 2, pp. 210–215.
Davis, H. & Silk, A. 1978. *Behavioral and Management Science in Marketing*, New York: Ronald Press.
DeCeri, H. & Kramer, R. 2005. *Human Resource Management in Australia – Strategy, People, Performance*, Sydney: McGraw-Hill.
Deetz, S. 1992. *Democracy in an Age of Corporate Colonization*, Albany: State University of New York Press.
Deetz, S. 2001. Conceptual Foundations, in: Jablin, F. & Putnam, L. (eds) *The New Handbook of Organisational Communication – Advances in Theory, Research, and Methods*, London: Sage.
DeGeorge, T. 2006. *Business Ethics*, 6th ed., Upper Saddle River: Pearson/Prentice Hall.
Delaney, J. 2005. Ethical Challenges to Labor Relations, in: Budd, S. & Scoville, J. (eds) *The Ethics of Human Resources and Industrial Relations*, Champaign: Labor and Employment Relations Association.
Descartes, R. 1628. Rules for the Direction of our Native Intelligence, in Descartes, R. 1988 edition of *Descartes Selected Philosophical Writings*, Cambridge: Cambridge University Press.
DeVitis, J. L. 1974. Marcuse on Education: Social Critique and Social Control, *Educational Theory*, vol. 24, no. 3.
Dryzek, J. 1996. *Democracy in Capitalist Times – Ideals, Limits, and Struggles*, Oxford: Oxford University Press.
Dunlop, J. 1958. *Industrial Relations Systems*, New York: Holt.
Durand, R. & Calori, R. 2006. Sameness, Otherness? Enriching Organizational Change Theories with Philosophical Considerations on the Same and the Other, *Academy of Management Review*, vol. 31, no. 1.
Durkheim, E. 1912. *The Elementary Forms of Religious Life*, translated by Karen E. Fields (1995), New York: Free Press.
Eagleton, T. 1994. *Ideology*, London: Longman Press.

Eco, U. 1977. *A Theory of Semiotics*, London: Macmillan.
Edwards, P. 2003. The Future of Industrial Relations, in: Ackers, P. & Wilkinson, A. (eds) *Understanding Work and Employment – Industrial Relations in Transition*, Oxford: Oxford University Press.
Edwards, P. 2006. Industrial Relations and Critical Realism: IR's Tacit Contribution, *Warwick Papers in Industrial Relations*, no. 80, March 2006 (download).
Edwards, P., Belanger, J. & Wright, M. 2006. The Bases of Competition in the Workplace: A Theoretical Framework, *British Journal of Industrial Relations*, vol. 44, no. 1, pp. 125–145.
Edwards, R. 1979. *Contested Terrain*, London: Heinemann.
Einstein, A. 1949. *Philosopher-Scientist*, Cambridge: Cambridge University Press, also: www.marxist.prg/refernce/archive/Einstein.
Eisenberg E. & Goodall H. 2001. *Organizational Communication – Balancing Creativity and Constraint*, Bedford: St Martin Press.
Elliott, L. 2006. Takeovers aren't delivering, *Guardian Weekly*, vol. 174, no. 16.
Engels. F. 1874. *Von der Autorität*, Almanacco Repubblicano per l'anno 1984, reprinted in: Marx-Engles Werke, vol. 18, 5th edition, Berlin: Dietz Press.
Engels, F. 1892. *The Condition of the Working Class in Britain in 1844*, London: Allen & Unwin (reprint 1952).
Eriksen, E. & Weigard, J. 2003. *Understanding Habermas – Communicative Action and Deliberate Democracy*, London: Continuum.
Etzioni, A. 1959. Authority Structure and Organisation Effectiveness, *Administrative Science Quarterly*, vol. 4, no. 1.
Eunson, B. 2005. *Communicating in the 21st Century*, Milton: Wiley.
Feenberg, A. 1988. The Bias of Technology, in: Pippin, R. et al. (eds) *Marcuse – Critical Theory and the Promise of Utopia*, London: Macmillan Press.
Feenberg, A. 2002. *Transforming Technology – A Critical Theory Revisited*, Oxford: Oxford University Press.
Feenberg, A. 2004. Heidegger and Marcuse – The Catastrophe and Redemption of Technology, in: Abromeit, J. & Cobb, M. (eds) *Herbert Marcuse – A Critical Reader*, London: Routledge.
Feldman, S. 1998. Playing with the Pieces: Deconstruction and the Loss of Moral Culture, *Journal of Management Studies*, vol. 35, no. 1.
Ferrell, O. 2007. *Business Ethics: Ethical Decision Making and Cases*, 7th Edition, Boston: Houghton.
Feyerabend, P. 1981. *Realism, Rationalism and Scientific Method – Philosophical Papers Volume 1*, Cambridge: Cambridge University Press.
Feyerabend, P. 1987. *Farewell to Reason*, London: Verso.
Fiske, J. 1990. *Introduction to Communication Studies*, London: Routledge.
Fisher, R. & Uri, W. 1981. *Getting to Yes – Negotiating an Agreement without Giving in*, London: Random House.
Forester, J. 1985. Critical Theory and Planning Practice, Forester, J. (ed.) *Critical Theory and Public Life*, Cambridge: MIT Press.
Forester, J. 1989. *Planning in the Face of Power*, Berkeley: University of California Press.
Foster, J. 1985. The Declassing of Language, *New Left Review*, I/150, March–April.
Foucault, M. 1994. *The Order of Things: An Archaeology of the Human Science*, London: Vintage Books.
Foucault, M. 1995. *Discipline and Punish: The Birth of the Prison*, New York: Vintage Books.
Fowler, R. 1991. *Language in the News – Discourse and Ideology in the Press*, London: Routledge.

Fox, A. 1966. Managerial Ideology and Labour Relations, in *British Journal of Industrial Relations*, vol. 4, no. 3, pp. 366–378.
Fox, A. 1973. Industrial Relations: A Social Critique of Pluralist Ideology, pp. 185–233, in: Child, J. (ed.) *Man and Organisation*, London: Allen & Unwin.
Fox, A. 1974. *Beyond Contract*, London: Faber.
Fraser, G. 2006. Suffer, the little children, *The Guardian Weekly*, vol. 174, no. 26, p. 16.
Fromm, E. 1942. *The Fear of Freedom*, London: Routledge.
Fromm, E. 1955. *The Sane Society*, New York: Rinehart Press.
Fromm, E. 1957. Man is not a Thing, *Saturday Review*, vol. 40.
Fromm, E. 1961. On Being Human, in: Buechler, S. 2006. *Why We Need Fromm Today: Fromm's Work Ethic*, www.erich-fromm.de.
Fromm, E. 1968. Marx's Contribution to the Knowledge of Man, *Social Science Information*, vol. 7, no. 7
Fromm, E. 1981. *On Disobedience and other Essays*, New York: Seabury Press.
Fromm, E. 1995. *To have or to be?*, London: Abacus.
Fuller, S. 2003. *Kuhn vs. Popper: The Struggle of the Soul of Science*, Cambridge: Icon Books.
Gadamer, H. G. 1974. *Truth and Method*, Evanston: Northwestern University Press.
Gadamer, H. G. 1976. *Philosophical Hermeneutics*, Berkeley: University of California Press.
Galbraith, J. K. 1958. *The Affluent Society*, Boston: Houghton Mifflin.
Gallistel, C. & Gibbon, J. 2002. *The Symbolic Foundations of Conditioned Behavior*, London: Lawrence Erlbaum Press.
Gamble, A., Marsh, D. & Tant, T. (eds) 1999. *Marxism and Social Science*, London: Macmillan.
Gandhi, M. (1925), Seven Social Sins, quoted from the weekly journal: *Young India*.
Gare, S. 2006. *The Triumph of the Airheads and the Retreat from Commonsense*, Sydney: Media21 Publishing.
Gass, R. & Seiter, J. 1999. *Persuasion, Social Influence, and Compliance Gaining*, Sydney: Allyn and Bacon.
Gastil, J. & Levine, P. (eds) 2006. *The deliberative democracy handbook: strategies for effective civic engagement in the twenty-first century*, Burlington: Ashgate.
Gay du, P. 1996. *Consumption and Identity at Work*, London: Sage.
Gay du, P. (ed.) 1997. *Production of Culture / Culture of Production*, London: Sage.
Gilbert, G. 1947. *Nuremberg Diary*, New York: Farrar & Straus.
Gilabert, P. 2005. The Substantive Dimension of Deliberate Practical Rationality, *Philosophy and Social Criticism*, vol. 31, no. 2.
Gladwell, M. 2002. *The Talent Myth*, www.newyorker.com/printables/fact/0207222fa_fact
Galbraith, J. K. 1958. *The Affluent Society*, Boston: Houghton Mifflin.
Gleason, A. Goldsmith, J. & Nussbaum, M. C. 2005. *On nineteen eighty-four: Orwell and our future*, Princeton: Princeton University Press.
Gimmler, A. 2001. Deliberative Democracy, the Public Sphere and the Internet, *Philosophy and Social Criticism*, vol. 27, no. 4.
Gouldner, A. W. 1976. *The dialectic of ideology and technology: the origins, grammar, and future of ideology*, New York: Seabury Press.
Goodrich, C. L. 1920. *The Frontier of Control*, London: Pluto Press.
Graham, K. 1977. *J. L. Austin – A Critique of Ordinary Language Philosophy*, Hassocks: Harvester Press.
Grant, D. et al. (eds) 2004. *The Sage Handbook of Organisational Discourse*, London: Sage.
Grote, D. 2006. *Discipline without Punishment – The Proven Strategy that turns Problem Employees into Superior Performers*, 2nd ed., New York: American Management Association.

Habermas, J. 1968. *Knowledge and Human Interests*, Boston: Beacon Press, in: McNeill, W. & Feldman, K. (eds) 1998. *Continental Philosophy – An Anthology*, Oxford: Blackwell.
Habermas, J. 1975. Towards a Reconstruction of Historical Materialism, *Theory & Society*, vol. 2, no. 3.
Habermas, J. 1976a. The Analytic Theory of Science and Dialectic, in: Adorno, T. *et al.* (eds) *The Positivist Dispute in German Sociology*, London: Heinemann.
Habermas, J. 1979. *Communication and the Evolution of Society*, Boston: Beacon.
Habermas, J. 1985. *The Philosophical Discourse of Modernity*, Cambridge: Polity Press.
Habermas, J. 1987. *Knowledge and Human Interest*, Cambridge: Polity Press.
Habermas, J. 1988. *Structural Transformation of the Public Sphere*, Cambridge: MIT Press.
Habermas, J. 1990. *Moral Consciousness and Communicative Action*, Cambridge: Polity Press.
Habermas, J. 1997. *The Theory of Communicative Action: Reason and the Rationalisation of Society*, Volume I & II, reprint, Oxford: Polity Press.
Habermas, J. 1997a. *Between Facts and Norms*, Oxford: Polity Press.
Habermas, J. 2001. *On the Pragmatics of Social Interaction – Preliminary Studies in the Theory of Communicative Action*. Cambridge: MIT Press.
Habermas, J. 2006. *Political Communication in Media Society*, Key Note at the 56th Annual Conference of the International Communication Association, Dresden (Germany), June 19th to 23rd, 2006.
Halimi, S. 2006. The populace versus the intellectuals – US: phoney culture wars, *Le Monde Diplomatique* (Engl. Edition), June, pp. 14–15.
Harding, N. 2003. *The Social Construction of Management – Texts and Identities*, London: Routledge.
Harford, T. 2006. *The Undercover Economist*, Oxford: Oxford University Press.
Hartley, P. & Bruckmann, C. 2002. *Business Communication*, London: Routledge.
Heath, J. 2003. *Communicative Action and Rational Choice*, Cambridge: MIT Press.
Hegel, G. 1807. Phenomenology of Spirit, in: McNeill, W. & Feldman, K. (eds) 1998. *Continental Philosophy – An Anthology*, Oxford: Blackwell.
Hegel, G. 1821. The Philosophy of Right, in: McNeill, W. & Feldman, K. (eds) 1998. *Continental Philosophy – An Anthology*, Oxford: Blackwell.
Held, D. 1997. *Introduction to Critical Theory – Horkheimer to Habermas*, Cambridge: Polity Press.
Hendry, J. & Seidel, D. 2002. The structure and significance of strategic episodes: social system theory and the routine practice of strategic change, *Research Paper*, Munich: Ludwig-Maximilian University, memo.
Herman, E. S. & Chomsky, N. 1988. *Manufacturing Consent – The Political Economy of the Mass Media*, New York: Pantheon Books.
Herman, E. S. 2002. *Manufacturing Consent: The Political Economy of the Mass Media*, New York: Pantheon Books.
Herman, E. S. & McChesney, R. W. 1997. *The Global Media – The New Missionaries of Corporate Capitalism*, London: Continuum.
Himstreet, W. & Baty, W. 1961. *Business Communication*, Belmont: Wadsworth Publishing.
Hirschman, A. 1970. *Exit, Voice, and Loyalty: Responses to Decline in Firms, Organizations, and States*, Cambridge: Harvard University Press.
Hobbes, T. 1651. *Leviathan*, Baltimore (1968): Penguin Books.
Hobsbawn, E. 2004. History: a new age of reason – return to asking the big why questions, *Le Monde Diplomatique* (Engl. Edition), December 2004, p. 1 & 11.
Hodge, R. & Kress, G. 1979. *Language as Ideology – Transformations and Truth*, (2nd ed. 1993), London: Routledge.

Hoggart, R. 2003. *Everyday Language and Everyday Life*, London: Transaction Publishers.
Hoggart, R. 2004, *Mass Media in Mass Society – Myth and Reality*, London: Continuum Press.
Holman, D. & Thorpe, R. 2002. *Management and Language*, London: Sage.
Honneth, A. 1993. Max Horkheimer and the Sociological Deficit of Critical Theory, in: Benhabib, S. et al. (eds) *On Max Horkheimer – New Perspectives*, Cambridge: MIT Press.
Horkheimer, M. 1937. Traditional and Critical Theory, in: Horkheimer, M. *Critical Theory – Selected Essays*, translated by O'Connell, M. J. et al., 1972, New York: Herder.
Horkheimer, M. 1947. *The Eclipse of Reason*, New York: Oxford University Press.
Horkheimer, M. & Adorno, T. 1947. *Dialectic of Enlightenment*, London: Verso (1989).
Howard, M. 2003. *Strategy*, Encyclopaedia Britannica, www.search.eb.com.
Husserl, 1990. *Logical Investigations*, (translated: J. N. Findlay), New York: Humanities Press.
Hyman, R. 1979. *Industrial Relations*, London: Macmillan.
Hyman, R. 1987. Strategy or Structure, *Work, Employment & Society*, vol. 1, no. 1.
Hyman, R. 1989. *The Political Economy of Industrial Relations*, London: Macmillan.
Hyman, R. 2006. Flexible Rigidities: A Model for Social Europe?, in: Alonso, L. & Lucio, M. (eds) *Employment Relations in a Changing Society*, Houndsmill: Palgrave.
ILO 2002. *A Future Without Child Labour*, Geneva: International Labour Organization.
Ingram, D. 1991. Habermas on Aesthetics and Rationality: Completing the Project of Enlightenment, *New German Critique*, spring issue, no. 53.
Jameson, F. 1990. *Late Marxism – Adorno, or The Persistence of the Dialectic*, London: Verso Press.
Janis, I. L. 1982. *Groupthink*, Boston: Houghton Mifflin Press.
Jay, M. 1974. *The Dialectical Imagination – A History of the Frankfurt School and the Institute of Social Research 1923–1950*, London: Heinemann.
Jex, S. 2002. *Organisational Psychology – A Science-Practitioner Approach*, New York: Wiley.
Jones, C. 2003. As if Business Ethics Were Possible, 'Within Such Limits'…, *Organization*, vol. 10, no. 2.
Jones, S., Martin, R. & Pilbeam, D. 1992. *The Cambridge Encyclopaedia of Human Evolution*, Cambridge: Cambridge University Press.
Kafka, F. 1919. In the Penal Colony, in: Kafka: *The Complete Stories*, New York (1971): Schocken Books.
Kalyvas, A. 2001. The Politics of Autonomy and the Challenge of Deliberation: Castoriadis contra Habermas, *Thesis Eleven*, no. 64.
Kant, I. 1781. Critique of Pure Reason, in: McNeill, W. & Feldman, K. (eds) 1998. *Continental Philosophy – An Anthology*, Oxford: Blackwell.
Karlson, J. 2004. 'The Ontology of Work – Social Relations and Doing in the Sphere of Necessity', in: Fleetwood, S. & Ackroyd, S. (eds) *Critical Realist Applications in Organisation and Management Studies*, London: Routledge.
Kassing, J. W. 2002. Speaking Up – Identifying Employee's Upward Dissent Strategies, *Management Communication Quarterly*, vol. 16, no. 2, pp. 187–209.
Katz, D. & Kahn, R. 1966. *The Social Psychology of Organizations*, New York: Wiley.
Kaufman, B. 1993. *The Origins & Evolution of the Field of Industrial Relations in the United States*, Ithaca: Cornell University Press.
Kaufman, B. 2002. Reflections on Six Decades in Industrial Relations: An Interview with John Dunlop, *Industrial and Labor Relations Review*, vol. 55, no. 2, pp. 324–348.
Kaufman, B. et al. 2003. *Industrial Relations to Human Resources and Beyond – The Evolving Process of Employee Relations Management*, London: M. E. Shape Press.

Kellner, D. 1984. *Herbert Marcuse and the Crisis of Marxism*, Berkeley: University of California Press.
Kellner, D. 1991. Introduction to the Second Edition, in: Marcuse, H. 1966. *One-Dimensional Man: Studies in the Ideology of Advanced Industrial Societies*, Boston: Beacon Press.
Kelly, J. 1998. *Rethinking Industrial Relations – Mobilisation, Collectivism and Long Waves*, London: Routledge.
Kennedy, G. 1993. *The Art of Persuasion in Greece*, Princeton: Princeton University Press.
Kennedy, G. 1994. *A New History of Classical Rhetoric*, Princeton: Princeton University Press.
Kerr, C. Dunlop, J., Harbison, F. & Myers, C. 1960. Industrialism & Industrial Man, *International Labour Review*, vol. 135, no. 3–4 (reprinted in 1996).
Klikauer, T. 2007. *Communication and Management at Work*, Houndsmill: Palgrave.
Knowles, W. 1955. *Personnel Management*, New York: American Book Co.
Kochan, T., Katz, H. & McKersie, R. 1986. *The Transformation of American Industrial Relations*, New York: Basic Books.
Kohlberg, L. 1971. From is to ought, in: Mischel, T. (ed.) *Cognitive Development and Epistemology*, New York: Academic Press.
Kohlberg, L. 1981 & 1984. *Essays on Moral Development*, (vol. 1 & 2), San Francisco: Harper & Row.
Korczynski, M. 2000. The Political Economy of Trust, *Journal of Management Studies*, vol. 37, no. 1.
Koselleck, R. 1988. *Critique and Crisis – Enlightenment and the Pathologies of Modern Society*, Cambridge: MIT Press.
Krizan, A. C., Merrier, P. & Jones, C. L. 2005. *Business Communication*, 6th Edition, Mason: Thomson South-Western.
Lafargue, P. 1883. *The Right to be Lazy*, written in Saint Pelagie Prison, translated by Charles Kerr and first published by Charles Kerr Cooperative, download: www.marxist.org/archive/lafargue/1883/lazy.
Laffer, G. 2005. The Critical Failure of Workplace Ethics, in: Budd, S. & Scoville, J. (eds) *The Ethics of Human Resources and Industrial Relations*, Champaign: Labor and Employment Relations Association.
Langer, F. 1994. The Illusion of Calculated Decisions, in: Schank, R. & Langer, E. (eds) *Beliefs, Reasoning, and Decision Making*, Hillsdale: Lawrence Erlbaum.
Lanham, R. 2006. *The Economics of Attention*, Chicago: University of Chicago Press.
Lanning, R. 2001. Ethics and Self-Mastery: Revolution and the Fully Developed Person in the Works of Georg Lukacs, *Science and Society*, vol. 65, no. 3.
Legge, K. 1995. *Human Resource Management: Rhetoric and Reality*, London: Macmillan.
Legge, K. 2005. *Human Resource Management: Rhetoric and Reality*, Anniversary Edition, London: Macmillan.
Lemov, R. 2006. *World as Laboratory – Experiments with Mice, Mazes and Men*, New York: Hill and Wang.
Leslie, E. 2000. *Walter Benjamin – Overpowering Conformism*, London: Pluto.
Levy, D. L., Alvesson, M. & Willmott, H. 2003. Critical Approaches to Strategic Management, in: Alvesson, M. & Willmott, H. (eds) *Studying Management Critically*, London: Sage.
Lewis, F. & Moss, P. 1983. The Tyranny of Language, in: Aubrey, C. & Chilton, P. (eds) *Nineteen Eighty-Four in 1984 – Autonomy, Control & Communication*, London: Comedia Publishing Group.
Likert, R. 1961. *New Patterns of Management*, New York: McGraw-Hill.

Likert, R. 1967. *The Human Organization: Its Management and Value*, New York: McGraw-Hill.
Linstead, S., Fullop, L. & Lilley, S. 2004. *Management and Organisation – A Critical Text*, Basingstoke: Palgrave.
Littler, C. R. 1993. Industrial Relations Theory: A Political Economy Perspective, in: Adams, R. & Meltz, N. M. (eds) *Industrial Relations Theory*, London: The Scarecrow Press.
Llewellyn, N. & Harrison, A. 2006. Resisting corporate communications: insights into folk linguistics, *Human Relations*, vol. 59, no. 4.
Locke, J. 1689a. *A Letter Concerning Toleration*, translated by William Popple, http://www.constitution.org/jl/tolerati.htm
Locke, J. 1689b. *An Essay Concerning Human Understanding*, produced by Steve Harris and David Widger, http://www.gutenberg.org/etext/10615
Lockwood, D. 1964. Social Integration and System Integration, in G. K. Zollschau & W. Hirsch (eds) *Explanations in Social Change*, London: Routledge & Kegan Paul.
Lockwood, D. 1996. Civic Integration and Class Formation, *British Journal of Sociology*, vol. 47, no. 3.
Lösch, B. 2005. *Deliberative Politik. Moderne Konzeptionen von Öffentlichkeit, Demokratie und politischer Partizipation*, Münster: Dampfboot-Verlag.
Ludwig, T. 2001. One the Necessity of Structure in an Arbitrary World: Using Concurrent Schedules of Reinforcement to Describe Response Generalisation, *Journal of Organizational Behavior Management*, vol. 21, no. 4.
Luhmann, N. 1995. *Social Systems*, Stanford: Stanford University Press.
Lukacs, G. 1923. *History and Class Consciousness*, London: Merlin (English edition 1971).
Lukacs, G. 1971. Lukacs on his Life and Work, *New Left Review*, I/68, July–August.
Lukacs, G. 2000. *A Defence of History and Class Consciousness – Tailism and the Dialectics*, London: Verso.
Mannheim, K. 1929. *Ideology and Utopia*, reprinted (1936), London: Routledge.
Mackintosh, N. J. 1983. *Conditioning and Associative Learning*, Oxford: Clarendon Press.
Marcuse, H. 1964b. Industrialization and Capitalism in the Work of Max Weber, republished in Negations, 1968.
Marcuse, H. 1966. *One-Dimensional Man: Studies in the Ideology of Advanced Industrial Societies*, Boston: Beacon Press.
Marcuse, H. 1968. *Negations – Essays in Critical Theory*, Boston: Beacon Press.
Marcuse, H. 1969. *An Essay on Liberation*, Boston: Beacon Press.
Marglin, S. 1974. What do bosses do? – The origins and functions of hierarchy in capitalist production, *Review of Radical Political Economy*, vol. 6, no. 2.
Margretta, J. 2002. *What Management Is – How It Works and Why It's Everyone's Business*, New York: The Free Press.
Marris, R. 1966. *The Economic Theory of 'Managerial' Capitalism*, London: Macmillan.
Marsden, D. 1999. *A Theory of Employment Systems – Micro-Foundations of Societal Diversity*, Oxford: Oxford University Press.
Marsden, R. & Townley, B. 1996. The owl of Minerva: reflections on theory and practice, in: Clegg, S., Hardy, C. & Nord, W. R. (eds) *Handbook of Organisation Studies*, London: Sage.
Marin, G. & Pear, J. 2007. *Behavior Modification – What It Is and How To Do It*, Upper Saddle River: Prentice Hall.
Marx, K. 1846a. Letter to P. V. Annenkov on Pierre-Joseph Proudhon's book on The Philosophy of Poverty, 28th December 1846, printed in: Tucker, R. (ed.) 1972. *The Marx-Engels Reader*, 2nd Edition, London: Norton Press.

Marx, K. 1846b. *The German Ideology*, in: McLellan, D. 1985 (ed.) *Karl Marx: Selected Writings*, Oxford: Oxford University Press.
Marx, K. 1848. *The Communist Manifesto*, www.sozialistische-klassiker.org/ME/ME03.html.
Marx, K. 1890. *Das Kapital – Kritik der politischen Ökonomie (Capital – A Critique of Political Economy)*, Hamburg: 4th edited version by F. Engels, reprinted (1986): Berlin: Dietz Press.
Maslow, A. H. 1943. A theory of human motivation, *Psychological Review*, vol. 50, no. 4.
McCarthy, B. 2000. In the beginning were Beatrice and Sidney: five ages of Industrial Relations, paper presented at: 50th BUIRA Conference at Warwick University 7th–9th July 2000.
McCarthy, T. 1978. *The Critical Theory of Jürgen Habermas*, Cambridge: MIT Press.
McGee, M. 1980. The ideograph: A link between rhetoric and ideology, *The Quarterly Journal of Speech*, vol. 66, no. 1: 1–16.
McNeill, W. & Feldman, K. 1998. *Continental Philosophy – An Anthology*, Oxford: Blackwell Press.
McWilliams, et al. 2006. Guest Editor's Introduction – Corporate Social Responsibility: Strategic Implications, *Journal of Management Studies*, vol. 43, no. 1.
Mead, G. H. 1964. Philanthropy from the Point of View of Ethics, in Reck, A. (ed.) *George Herbert Mead – Selected Writings*, Chicago: Chicago University Press.
Mendieta, E. 2002. *The Advances of Transcendental Philosophy – Karl-Otto Apel's Semiotics and Discourse Ethics*, Lanham: Rowan & Littlefield Publishers.
Miles, R. E. & Snow, C. C. 1978. *Organisational Strategy, Structure & Process*, New York: McGraw-Hill.
Mintzberg, H. 1973. *The Nature of Managerial Work*, London: Harper & Row.
Mintzberg, H. 1987. The strategy concept I: Five Ps for strategy, and Strategy concept II: Another look at why organizations need strategies. *California Management Review*, 30(1): 11–32.
Mintzberg, 1987a. Crafting Strategy, *Harvard Business Review*, July–August: 67–81.
Mohan, T. et al. 2004. *Communicating as Professionals*, Melbourne: Thomson.
Monk, R. 1997. *Just Managing*, Sydney: McGraw-Hill.
Mook, D. 1987. *Motivation – The Organisation of Action*, London: Norton.
Morgan, G, 1986. *Images of Organisations*, London: Sage.
Morgan, G. 1993. *Imaginization – The Art of Creative Management*, London: Sage.
Morrow, R. 1994. *Critical Theory and Methodology*, London: Sage.
Mouzelis, N. 1974. Social and System Integration: Some Reflections on a Fundamental Distinction, *British Journal of Sociology*, vol. 25, no. 4.
Mumby, D. 1988. *Communication & Power in Organisations: Discourse, Ideology, and Domination*, Norwood (NJ): Ablex Press.
Mumby, D. 1997. The Problem of Hegemony: Reading Gramsci for Organisational Communication Studies, *Western Journal of Communication*, vol. 61, no. 4: 343–375.
Mumby, D. 2000. Common Ground from the Critical Perspective, in: Corman, S. & Poole, M. (eds) *Perspectives on Organisational Communication*, New York: Guilford Press.
Mumby, D. 2001. Power and Politics, in: Jablin, F. & Putnam, L. (eds) *The New Handbook of Organisational Communication – Advances in Theory, Research, and Methods*, London: Sage.
Nealon, J. & Giroux, S. S. 2003. *The Theory Toolbox – Critical Concepts for Humanities, Arts, and Social Science*, Lanham: Rowan & Littlefield.
Neumann, F. 1933. *Behemoth: The Structure and Practice of National Socialism, 1933–1944*, London: Victor Gollancz.

Newmeyer, F. 1986. Has there been a 'Chomskyan Revolution' in Linguistics, *Language*, vol. 62, no. 1.
Nietzsche, F. 1886. *The Will to Power* (translated by Walter Kaufmann and R. J. Hollingsdale, 1968), New York: Random House.
Nussbaum, M. 2004. *Hiding from Humanity: Disgust, Shame, and the Law*, Princeton: Princeton University Press.
Offe, C. 1976. *Industry and Inequality – The Achievement Principle in Work and Social Status*, London: Edward Arnold.
Offe, C. & Wiesenthal, H. 1980. Two Logics of Collective Action: Theoretical Notes on Social Class and Organisational Form, in: Zeitlin, M. (ed.) *Political Power and Social Theory – A Research Annual*, vol. 1, Greenwich: JAI Press.
Offe, C. 1984. Ungovernability, in: Habermas, J. (ed.) *Observations on the Spiritual Situation of the Age*, Cambridge: Cambridge University Press.
Offe, C. 1985. *Disorganised Capitalism – Contemporary Transformations of Work and Politics*, Oxford: Polity Press.
Offe, C. 1988. Technology and One-Dimensionality: A Version of the Technocracy Thesis? in: Pippin, R. et al. (eds) *Marcuse – Critical Theory and The Promise of Utopia*, London: Macmillan Press.
O'Hair, D. et al. 2005. *Strategic Communication in Business and the Professions*, Boston: Houghton-Mifflin.
Ohmae, K. 1983. *The Mind of the Strategist: Business Planning for Competitive Advantage*, New York: Penguin.
O'Keefe, D. 2006. Persuasion, in: Hargie, O. (ed.) *The Handbook of Communication Skills* (3rd edition), London: Routledge.
Oquendo, A. 2002. Deliberative Democracy in Habermas and Nino, *Oxford Journal of Legal Studies*, vol. 22, no. 2.
Olson, M. 1971. *The Logic of Collective Action*, Cambridge: Harvard University Press.
Orwell, G. 1946. *Politics and the English Language*, http://orwell.ru.library/essays.
Orwell, G. 1949. *Nineteen Eighty-Four*, London: Secker & Warburg.
Packard, V. O. 1959. *The Hidden Persuaders*, New York: McKay.
Parker, M. 1998. Business Ethics and Social Theory: Postmodernizing the Ethical, *British Journal of Management*, vol. 9 (September).
Parker, M. 2002. *Against Management – Organisation in the Age of Managerialism*, Cambridge: Polity Press.
Parker, M. 2003. Introduction: Ethics, Politics, and Organizing, *Organization*, vol. 10, no. 2.
Passer, M. & Smith, R. 2007: *Psychology – The Science of Mind and Behavior*, Boston: McGraw-Hill.
Pavlov, I. P. 1928. *Lectures of Conditioned Reflexes*, New York: International Publishing.
Peetz, D. 2006. *Brave New World of Work Place – How Individual Contracts Are Changing Our Jobs*, Sydney: Allen & Unwin.
Perlmutter, D. D. 1997. Manufacturing Visions of Society and History in Textbooks, *Journal of Communication*, vol. 47, no. 3.
Pilger, J. 2006. *Freedom Next Time*, London: Bantam Press.
Poole, S. 2006. *Unspeak*, London: Little Brown.
Popper, K. 1965. *The Logic of Scientific Discovery*, New York: Harper Press.
Popper, K. 1999. *All Life is Problem Solving* (translated by Camiller, P. from 'Alles Leben ist Problemlösung'), London: Routledge.
Postone, M. 1993. *Time, Labor, and Social Domination – A Reinterpretation of Marx's Critical Theory*, Cambridge: Cambridge University Press.
Porter, M. E. 1980. *Competitive Strategy: Techniques for Analysing Industries and Competitiveness*, New York: The Free Press.

Premack, D. 1965. 'Reinforcement Theory', in: Levine, D. (ed.) *Nebraska Symposium on Motivation*, Lincoln: University of Nebraska Press.
Radford, G. P. 2005. *On The Philosophy of Communication*, Belmont: Wadsworth Publishing.
Ramsay, H. 1977. Cycle of Control: Worker participation in sociological and historical perspective, *Sociology*, vol. 11. pp. 481–506.
Ramsay, H. 1980. Participation: The Pattern and its Significance, in: Nichols, T. (ed.) *Capital and Labour – A Marxist Primer*, London: Fontana Press.
Redeker, J. 1983. *Discipline: Policies and Procedures*, Washington: Bureau of National Affairs.
Reich, W. 1946. *The Mass Psychology of Fascism*, New York (1970): Farrar, Straus & Giroux.
Robertson, R. 2002, *The Cambridge Companion to Thomas Mann*, Cambridge: Cambridge University Press.
Roper, C. 1983. Taming the Universal Machine, in: Aubrey, C. (ed.) *The Making of 1984*, in: Aubrey, C. & Chilton, P. (eds) *Nineteen Eighty-Four in 1984 – Autonomy, Control & Communication*, London: Comedia Publishing Group.
Rorty, R. 1979. *Philosophy and the Mirror of Nature*, Princeton: Princeton University Press.
Rorty, R. 1982. *Consequences of Pragmatism*, Minneapolis: University of Minneapolis Press.
Rousseau, J. J. 1750. *A Discourse on the Moral Effects of the Arts and Science*, Dijon: Academy of Dijon.
Rousseau J. J. 1755. *Discourse on the Origins of Inequality*, http://oll.libertyfund.org & www.libertarian-alliance.org.uk.
Roy, W. G. & Parker-Gwen, R. 1999. How many logics of collective action, *Theory and Society*, vol. 28, pp. 203–237.
Russell, B. 1945. *A History of Western Philosophy*, New York: Simon & Schuster.
Russell, B. 1973. *An Inquiry into Meaning and Truth*, Harmondsworth: Penguin.
Saussure, F. 1906–13. *Courses in General Linguistics* (lecturer series), edited by Editions Payot, Paris, English edition by Bally, C. & Sechehaye, A., 1983, London: Duckworth & Co.
Schank, R. 1994. Goal-Based Scenario, in: Schank, R. & Langer, E. (eds) *Beliefs, Reasoning, and Decision Making*, Hillsdale: Lawrence Erlbaum.
Schramm, W. 1954. *The Process and Effects of Mass Communication*, Urbana: University of Illinois Press.
Scott, E. 2005. The Ethics of HRM, in: Budd, S. & Scoville, J. (eds) *The Ethics of Human Resources and Industrial Relations*, Champaign: Labor and Employment Relations Association.
Searle, J. R. 1969. *Speech Acts – An Essay in the Philosophy of Language*, Cambridge: Cambridge University Press.
Searle, J. R. 1979. *Expression and Meaning: Essays in the Theory of Speech Acts*, Cambridge: Cambridge University Press.
Searle, J. R. 1996. *The Construction of Social Reality*, London: Penguin Press.
Searle, J. R. 2002. *Consciousness and Language*, Cambridge: Cambridge University Press.
Segal, A. 1970. Censorship, Social Control and Socialisation, *British Journal of Sociology*, no. 21, no. 1.
Sennett, R. 1980. *Authority*, London: Secker & Warburg.
Sharpe, M. 2006. *Slavoj Sizek*, Wikipedia internet encyclopaedia.
Singer, P. 1975. *Animal Liberation: A New Ethics for our Treatment of Animals*, New York: Random House.
Singer, P. 1993. *Practical Ethics*, Cambridge: Cambridge University Press.

Singer, P. 1994. *Ethics*, Oxford: Oxford University Press.
Singer, P. 2000. *Writings on an Ethical Life*, New York: Ecco Press.
Singer, P. 2005. Eating Ethically, *Free Inquiry*, vol. 25, no. 4, June–July.
Singer, P. & Mason, J. 2006. *The Way we Eat – Why Our Food Choices Matter*, New York: Rodale Press.
Sitton, J. F. 2003. *Habermas and Contemporary Society*, Houndsmill: Palgrave.
Skinner, B. F. 1948. *Walden Two*, New York: Macmillan.
Skinner, B. F. 1953. *Science and Human Behaviour*, New York: Macmillan.
Skinner, B. F. 1971. *Beyond Freedom and Dignity*, New York: Knopf.
Skinner, B. F. 1974. *About Behaviourism*, London: Cape.
Smith, A. 1759. *The Theory of the Moral Sentiments*, http://www.adamsmith.org/smith/tms/tms-index.htm.
Smith, A. 1776. *The Wealth of Nations – Books I–III*, London: Penguin Books (reprinted 1986).
Smith, J. 1982. *Persuasion and Human Action – A Review and Critique of Social Influence Theories*, Belmont: Wadsworth Publishing.
Spulber, D. 2004. *Management Strategy*, London: McGraw-Hill.
Stadon, J. 2001. *The New Behaviourism*, Philadelphia: Taylor & Francis.
Statt, D. 1994. *Psychology and the World of Work*, London: Macmillan.
Stewart, J. 2007. The Ethics of HRD, in: Rigg, et al. (eds) *Critical Human Resource Development*, London: Prentice Hall.
Stewart, P. 2005. Individualism and Collectivism in the Sociology of the Collective Worker, in: Alonso, L. & Lucio, M. (eds) *Employment Relations in a Changing Society*, Houndsmill: Palgrave.
Stiff, J. B. & Mongeau, P. A. 2003. *Persuasive Communication*, London: Guildford Press.
Storey, J. 1992. *Developments in the Management of Human Resources – An Analytical Review*, Oxford: Blackwell.
Sunstein, C. R. & Nussbaum, M. C. 2004. *Animal Rights: Current Debates and New Directions*, Oxford: Oxford University Press.
Taylor, F. W. 1911. *The Principles of Scientific Management*, New York: Norton Press (reprinted in Handel, M. (ed.) 2003, *The Sociology of Organizations – Classic, Contemporary and Critical Readings*, London: Sage).
Therborn, G. 1973. The Working Class and the Birth of Marxism, *New Left Review*, I/79, May–June.
Therborn, G. 1977. The Rule of Capital and the Rise of Democracy, *New Left Review*, I/103, May–June.
Thompson, E. P. 1963. *The Making of the English Working Class*, London: Victor Gollancz.
Thompson, J. B. 1981. *Critical Hermeneutics – A Study in the Thought of Paul Ricoeur and Jürgen Habermas*, Cambridge: Cambridge University Press.
Thompson, J. B. 1990. *Ideology and Modern Culture – Critical Social Theory in the Era of Mass Communication*, Oxford: Polity Press.
Thompson, P. 2004. Brands, Boundaries and Bandwagons – Critical Reflections on Critical Management Studies, in: Fleedwood, S. & Ackroyd, S. (eds) *Critical Realist Approach in Organisation and Management Studies*, London: Routledge.
Tompkins, P. 1961. *An Analysis of Communication between Headquarters and Selected Units of a National Labour Union*, Purdue University: unpublished manuscript.
Tompkins, P. 1965. General Semantics and Human Relations, *Central States Speech Journal*, no. 16, pp. 285–289.
Townley, B. 1994. *Reframing Human Resource Management: Power, Ethics and the Subject at Work*, Thousand Oaks: Sage.

Tracy, K. 1995. Action-Implicative Discourse Analysis, *Journal of Language and Social Psychology*, vol. 24, no. 1–2.
Tucker, R. 1978. *The Marx-Engels Reader*, second edition, London: W. W. Norton.
Tuckman, B. W. 1965. Developmental Sequences in small groups, *Psychological Bulletin*, no. 63, pp. 537–555.
Volosinov, V. N. 1929. *Marxism and the Philosophy of Language*, Translated by Matejka & Titunik, 1973, Cambridge: Harvard University Press.
Watson, D. 2003. *Death Sentence – The Decay of Public Language*, Sydney: Knopf.
Watzlawick, P., Beavin, J. & Jackson, D. 1967. *Pragmatics of Human Communication: A Study of Interactional Patterns, Pathologies, and Paradoxes*, New York: Norton.
Weber, M. 1904–05. *The Protestant Ethics and the Spirit of Protestantism*, tr. Talcott Parsons, London: Routledge, reprint 1992.
Weber, M. 1922. *Wirtschaft und Gesellschaft*, edited: Marianne Weber (5th Edition as Studienausgabe), Tübingen: JCB Mohr.
Weber, M. 1924. *Economy and Society*, Berkeley: University of California Press (reprint in: Handel, M. (ed.) 2003. *The Sociology of Organizations – Classic, Contemporary and Critical Readings*, London: Sage).
Weber, M. 1947. *The Theory of Social and Economic Organization*, Oxford: Oxford University Press.
Weber, M. 1948. Science as a vocation, in: Gerth, H. & Mill, C. W. (eds) *From Max Weber: Essays on Sociology*, London: Routledge.
Weick, K. E. 1995. *Sensemaking in Organisations*, London: Sage.
Wheeler, H. 2005. Globalisation and Business Ethics in Employment Relations, in: Budd, S. & Scoville, J. (eds) *The Ethics of Human Resources and Industrial Relations*, Champaign: Labor and Employment Relations Association.
White, E. 1969. Intelligence, individual difference and learning: an approach to political socialisation, *British Journal of Sociology*, vol. 20, no. 1.
Whittington, R. 1993. *What is strategy – and does it matter?*, 2nd Edition, London: Routledge.
Williams, C. 2005. *A Commodified World? – Mapping the Limits of Capitalism*, London: Zed Books.
Williams, R. 2002. *Managing Employee Performance – Design and Implementation in Organisations* (Psychology at Work Series), London: Thompson.
Windsor, D. 2006. Corporate Social Responsibility: Three Key Approaches, *Journal of Management Studies*, vol. 43, no. 1.
Wittgenstein, L. 1921. *Tractatus Logico-Philosophicus*, London (1963): Routledge & Kegan.
Wittgenstein, L. 1953. *Philosophical Investigations*, Oxford: Blackwell.
Wittgenstein, L. 1958. *The Blue and Brown Books: Preliminary Studies for the Philosophical Investigations*, Oxford: Blackwell.
Wood, J. 2004. *Communication Theories in Action*, Belmont: Wadsworth Publishing.
Zanna, M. et al. 1994. The Persistence of Persuasion, in: Schank, R. & Langer, E. (eds) *Beliefs, Reasoning, and Decision Making*, Hillsdale: Lawrence Erlbaum.
Zengotita, T. 2005. *Mediated – How the Media Shapes Your World and the Way You Live In It*. New York: Bloomsbury.
Zinn, G. 1973. *The Politics of History*, Boston: Beacon Press.
Zizek, S. 1989. *The Sublime Object of Ideology*, London: Verso Press.
Zuckermann, M. & Driver, R. E. 1985. Telling Lies: Verbal and Nonverbal Correlates of Deception, in: Siegman, A. W. (ed.) *Multichannel Integrations of Nonverbal Behavior*, Hillsdale: Erlbaum Associates.

Index

5+-day-week, 96

a priori, 11, 12, 32–35, 75, 254, 289, 304
academic disciplines, 3, 17, 248
Academy of Management, 52, 275, 307, 308
accommodative-participative discipline, 184, 192
Ackroyd & Thompson, 192, 249, 291
Adam Smith, 14, 160–161, 189–190, 246, 295
administrative-state, 217
administrative-technical language, 58
Adorno, 46, 164, 166–167, 249–250, 254–255, 262–269, 277, 279, 282, 284–290, 292, 295–296, 303, 307, 309, 313–314
advanced capitalism, 3–6, 76–77, 182–184, 189–190, 248, 292, 299–301, 305
advertisingblitz, 132
advisory meeting, 119
aesthetics, 62, 111–112
affirmation, 3, 7, 40, 69, 127, 155, 183, 190–191, 209, 220, 223–224, 230, 260, 274, 278–279, 283, 291, 293, 298–299, 301, 303
affirmative writers, 3, 8–9
agenda, 121–122, 155
agitators, 135
all in one boat, 9, 66, 117, 166, 188
American Machinist, 163
American middle class, 44
anti-historical language, 45
Arnold, 194–196, 255, 291, 294–295, 308, 318
attitude data, 126
Attitude reinforcement, 133
attitude surveys, 126–127, 130–131, 277, 279
attitude-enforcing, 125
attitudes, 118, 124–133, 135–136, 140, 167, 176, 213, 231–232, 274, 277–279
authoritarian identification, 69

authoritarianism, 7, 13, 15, 96, 138, 165, 222, 301–302
Avoidance of awareness, 115
avoidance-persuasion, 129

Barthes, 34, 41–43, 46, 50, 59, 153, 308
battle for market shares, 132
Baudrillard, 61, 247, 263, 267, 308
Bauman, 171–172, 211, 264, 287, 289, 294, 308
behaviour adjustments, 49
behaviour modification, 194, 196
behavioural control, 128, 129
Behaviourism, 139, 320
behaviourist, 56, 191, 193–194, 196, 280, 284, 288, 294
believable statements, 137
benchmarking, 8
Berger & Luckmann, 60, 258
better working conditions, 36, 48, 172, 260
Bhopal, 292
Big Brother, 1, 140, 273
Bill Gates, 53
black & white view, 138
blaming, 103, 135
blue-collar, 183, 200
Blundel, 118, 273, 275, 308–309
Bolinger, 135, 279–280, 309
bosses, 58, 295, 316
bossy privilege, 164
bottom line, 8, 168
bounded rationality, 19, 240–241, 305
Bourgeois, 43
bourgeoisie, 43–44, 46, 259, 267
Bowman, 206, 309
boycotts, 119
brain-washing, 127, 278
bread, 40, 69, 81, 184, 258
briefing, 118, 120
Brimeyer, 186, 309
Bühler, 59, 309
business communication, 2–4, 150, 246, 247

business ethics, 227, 250, 286, 300, 302–303
business leader, 53–54, 86
business lunches, 100
business magazines, 78
business news, 78, 266
business process re-engineering, 130
Business Report, 77–78
business schools, 8, 252

capital, 5, 51, 71, 102, 106, 180–186, 188–189, 201, 205–207, 246, 251, 258, 262, 282, 299
capital and labour, 102, 185
capitalist firms, 4, 299
categorical imperative, 11, 14, 172, 229, 285, 302
cause-and-effect, 147
celebrative-collective discipline, 184, 192
CEO, 62, 87, 103, 164, 292
chairman, 148
chairperson, 13
Charlie Chaplin, 52
Cheney, 49, 267, 291, 309
child exploitation, 163
child labour, 162–163, 255, 258, 260, 271, 286, 297
childhood, 87, 258, 304
Chilton, 225, 257, 271, 280, 291, 298, 308–309, 315, 319
Chomsky, 163, 248–249, 254–256, 258, 268, 273, 276, 280–281, 287, 291–294, 304–305, 307, 309–310, 313
church, 17, 160, 253, 266, 278, 303
Cicero, 112
class interest, 80, 296
class relations, 42–43, 103, 207, 297
classifications, 2, 12, 63–64, 66, 68–71, 117
classless society, 44
clerical structures, 74
Coca-Cola, 124
co-decision making, 65, 119, 223, 275
co-determination, 38, 76
coding, 30, 81, 247, 283
coercion, 124, 127, 300
coercive strategy, 131
cognition, 17

cognitive and rational validity, 20
cognitive participation, 25
cognitive-instrumental, 174
coherence theory, 175
collective images, 44
colleges, 77
colonisation, 11, 16, 42, 44, 46, 63, 91, 145, 148, 185–187, 201–202, 206, 217, 221, 223, 231, 233, 239, 242–244, 272, 295
commodity of labour, 80, 184
common sense, 2, 44, 52, 96, 98–99, 101, 135, 269, 297
communication theory, 14
communication-in-a-situation, 29
communicative choices, 116, 274
communicative freedom, 114
communicative inequalities, 94, 110
communicative theory of truth, 222
company based HRM, 40
company histories, 52, 102
company history, 103, 106, 135
company-to-company, 182
compartmentalisation, 117, 153, 229
computer, 46, 97, 99
conditioned responses, 192, 293
conditioning, 39–40, 94, 97, 118, 138–140, 163, 166, 189, 191–194, 196, 197, 224, 248, 255, 269, 279–280, 294, 296
consultants, 2, 226, 252, 278
consultative meeting, 119
Consultative voice, 118
consumer, 6, 71, 81, 101–102, 184, 189, 201, 219–220, 249, 272, 274, 292, 297, 298–299, 301
consumerism, 190, 197, 220, 271, 274
consumption, 4, 43, 71, 77, 82, 102, 125, 184, 189–194, 197, 218–220, 250, 266, 267, 269, 274, 278, 293, 296, 298–299
contract zones, 233–234
control, 1, 18–20, 22, 42, 44, 48–49, 58, 64–65, 76, 79–80, 91–92, 94–95, 99–100, 105, 109, 111–112, 122, 127, 150–153, 182, 184, 188, 190, 192, 203, 224, 260, 262–263, 268, 275–276, 278, 280, 283, 291, 293, 295, 297–298, 301, 304
conventions, 30, 40, 169, 230, 244, 287

conversion, 6, 39, 52, 61, 79–80, 89, 94, 97, 180, 201, 216, 278, 283, 288, 298, 300
Copernican system, 49
corporate culture, 63, 94, 111, 154, 268
corporate ethics, 228
corporate head quarter, 40
corporate mass media, 43, 60–61, 78, 93, 110, 129, 139, 163, 182, 186, 193, 220, 228, 272–274, 278–279, 286, 296, 301, 305
corporate media, 44, 110, 219, 273, 276, 280
correspondence theory, 175
corruption, 186
cost-benefit, 3, 5, 48, 129, 153, 179–180, 186, 202, 264
counter-arguments, 10, 235
counter-culture, 144
counter-persuasion, 129
crafting strategy, 135
critical reflection, 10, 14, 20, 163, 216
critical-emancipatory, 7, 11, 183, 229, 230
Critique of Pure Reason, 1, 254, 314
cultural affirmative, 112
cultural existence, 94, 111
cultural interest, 62
cultural system, 20
customer centric service, 264
customer satisfaction, 8
Customer Service, 269
cybernetic, 5, 50
Cycles of Communicative Control, 155

day-to-day communication, 200
de-bureaucratising, 94, 111
deception of the enemy, 165
Deceptions, 133, 280
deceptive communication, 133
deceptive methods, 133
Deceptive persuasion, 133
Decision making, 19, 120
decoder-encoder models, 12
decoding, 24, 32, 36, 257
de-controlling, 94, 111
deep structure, 6, 256, 258
definitions, 2, 52, 75, 93, 110, 177, 187, 254, 295
de-historify managerialism, 13
de-historising, 44

de-layering, 94, 111
deliberative democracy, 168, 289, 312
de-linguisitified exchange, 208
democratic ideology, 61
democratic management, 67, 264
democratic rights, 95, 112
democratic-administrative domain, 217
denotation, 42
deon, 172
depoliticised mass media, 44
Descartes, 28, 246, 248, 254, 310
Destutt de Tracy, 74, 265
devil's advocate, 234, 237
dialectical thinking, 2, 237
dialectical viewpoint, 10
Directive speech acts, 147
dirty tricks department, 41
disagreement, 88, 146
disciplinary procedure, 193
discipline and punishment, 192–193
discourse ethics, 14
discourse game, 61
Discourse pragmatics, 231
dis-empowering, 199
disequilibria, 205
dis-information, 220
Disney World, 87
distributive or integrative, 66
divide-and-conquer strategies, 209
division of labour, 3, 60, 87, 134, 143, 153, 191, 229, 246, 290, 303
dog's breakfast, 138
double system integration, 189
downsized, 89–90, 247
downsizing, 72–73, 130, 188, 255
drama, 52, 210
dramaturgical action, 210

Eagleton, 50, 249, 265, 267–268, 310
easy-guides for management, 226
Eclipse of Reason, 2, 314
economic irrationalism, 241
economy, 39, 49, 71, 78, 90, 143, 215, 246, 263, 282, 285, 288, 305
education system, 182
educational consumer, 4
educational domain, 182
Edwards, 182, 256, 258, 311
egocentric viewpoint, 229
eighthour working day, 45
either-or options, 53

empirical statements, 10
employee empowerment, 223
employee involvement, 91, 223
employment, 42, 132, 140, 163, 180–181, 187, 201, 205, 210, 217–219, 220, 280, 283, 297, 299
encoding, 24, 32, 34, 36, 257
engineering ideology, 46–47, 49, 151–152
engineering language, 144
engineering solutions, 46
Enlightenment, 1, 2, 7, 17, 44, 47, 74, 78, 92, 108, 138, 143, 215, 248, 259, 307, 314, 315
enterprise culture, 94, 110–111
entrepreneur, 77, 106
ethical behaviour, 14, 16
ethical code, 15, 168
Ethical communication, 160, 227
ethical communicative action, 16
ethical conduct, 171, 285
ethical connotations, 160
ethical considerations, 14–15, 228, 255
ethical customer, 168
ethical dialogue, 15–16, 221, 229
ethical discourse, 14, 16, 173, 230, 240
ethical exercise, 170
ethical force, 228
ethical forms of communication, 15, 228
ethical judgement, 161
ethical philosophy, 15, 229
ethically constructed communicative action, 15
ethically established forms of mutual understanding, 221
ethically structured communication, 228
ethically structured communicative domain, 228
ethical-political discourse, 239, 240
ethical-pragmatic discourse, 240
ethics and moral conduct, 15
ethics for others, 229
ethnicity, 186, 209
etiquette, 41
evil scientists, 43
executive meetings, 120
exit option, 119
explicative discourse, 173

extra-verbal means, 22, 177
extremist, 113

factory system, 58, 102, 212
facts of life, 75, 93
facts-of-life ideology, 109
fair day's pay, 99
fair day's work, 99
fairytales, 52
familiar words, 137
familiarity, 32, 137
family, 30, 51, 65, 276, 287
fast-food, 248, 250
fear of authoritarian oppressors, 153
feedback, 5, 25–28, 30–31, 49–50, 65, 150–151, 184, 195
female reproduction, 43
females, 43
feudal society, 77
feudalism, 105, 279, 285
feudalist past, 87, 160
fictional people, 137
Fictions, 68
Filtering, 104
Fiske, 42, 43, 60, 311
flattening hierarchies, 9
force of the better argument, 149, 243
Fordism, 190, 293, 307
Fordist world, 189
Forester, 156, 249, 311
Foucault, 2, 259, 287, 290, 308, 311
France, 38
free choice, 71–72, 83, 264
Fritz Lang, 52
Frontier of Control, 22, 291, 312

Gadamer, 20, 26, 28, 58, 59, 144, 148, 254, 256, 257–258, 263, 276, 279, 282, 289, 301, 312
Gallistel & Gibbon, 193, 293
Gandhi, 160–161, 312
Gass and Seiter, 29, 134
gatekeepers, 2–3
Gay, 187, 263, 268, 271, 312
Gemeinschaft and Gesellschaft, 141
gender, 33, 43, 153, 209
general's office, 40
German army, 8
German Ideology, 74, 317
German Nazi-language, 40
Gestalt, 213, 298

getting on with the job, 227
give and take, 165
God, 17, 30, 74, 77, 80, 160, 253, 259, 271, 293
grammatical rules, 12, 255
Gramsci, 91, 268, 317
Great Britain, 38
Greece, 1, 13, 28, 30, 315
Greek mortals, 30
Greek mythology, 30
group thinking, 233, 235–237, 304

Habermas, 26, 61, 120, 142–143, 147, 149, 159, 172–173, 175–178, 198–199, 201, 205, 216, 229, 230, 243, 246, 254, 256, 269, 281–284, 286, 289, 290, 293, 296–298, 302–305, 311, 313–314, 317–318, 320
hammer and sickle, 81
happy ending, 138
Harvard Business Review, 8, 77, 249, 251, 317
Harvard Business Schools, 8
Harvard University, 8, 313, 318, 321
have your say, 155
Heath, 33, 60, 174–175, 178, 289, 313
Hegel, 13, 191, 229, 237, 246, 248, 254, 255, 282, 285, 289, 296, 313
Hegelian, 2, 10, 11, 140, 179, 183, 202, 229, 249–251, 255, 282, 284, 290–291, 300
hegemonic meaning structures, 13, 91–94, 96, 104, 108–109
hegemonic position, 90, 187
hegemonic systems, 84
Hegemonic tools, 91
hegemonies, 13
hermeneutical understanding, 7, 18
hermeneutics, 18, 20, 28, 32
Hermes, 30
hierarchical concept of management, 39
hierarchical functions, 120
hierarchical managerial meetings, 120
hierarchical ordering structures, 13
hierarchical orders, 98
hierarchical relationship, 83, 150, 164
hierarchical system of communicative channels, 154
high-performance organisations, 103
hired killers, 258

Hirschman, 119, 167, 313
historical business leader, 86
historical concepts, 39–40
historical meanings, 13
historical myths, 44
historical philosophy-science, 7
history of capitalism, 105, 189, 197
history of HRM, 104
history of human production, 250
history of industrialism, 58, 106
history of large corporations, 106
history of management, 102–103
history of managerialism, 105
history of work, 141
Hoggart, 207, 271–274, 296, 298–300, 314
Horkheimer, 2, 46, 166–167, 246, 249, 250, 254–256, 263, 268–269, 297, 303, 307–308, 313–314
horse, 39, 40
horse training, 39
HR department, 135, 270
HR manager, 107
HR officers, 193
HR policies, 46, 263, 288
HR policy, 45–46
HR professionals, 270
HR statements, 135
HRM textbooks, 45, 64, 106, 262, 270
human being into a human resource, 9
human ethics, 227, 250, 285
human freedom, 96
human relations school, 223
human relationships, 46, 300
Human Resource Management, 40–41, 58, 64, 80, 191, 193, 247, 263, 287, 288, 293, 297, 299, 310, 315, 320
human resource managers, 119
human rights, 17–18, 169, 287
human welfare, 168
Husserl's phenomenology, 28
hypocrisy, 128
hypothetical attitude, 174
hypothetical belief, 85
hypothetical options, 85

ideal role taking, 230
idea-o-logy, 74
identity of individuals, 86
identity-identification duality, 63

ideological trappings of managerialism, 241
ideology, 74
ideology of managerialism, 3–4, 7–8, 54, 63, 76–78, 103, 112, 154, 219, 225, 239, 251, 277
induced compliance, 127–128
industrial accidents, 103, 255, 286
industrial action, 65, 211
industrial age, 77
industrial conflict, 87, 129, 268
industrial culture, 79
industrial democracy, 9, 270, 301
industrial relations, 17, 38, 262
industrial society, 44
industrial work regimes, 163
industrialisation, 38
industrialised countries, 79
industrialised societies, 79
industrialism, 74, 105
industrialists, 105
Industrial-Mass Media Complex, 183
input-output, 5, 7, 50, 109, 249
instrumental communication, 11–16, 62, 152, 154, 155, 168–171, 199–202, 204, 209, 212, 215, 217, 219, 225–228, 239, 242, 244, 302–304
instrumental conditions of managerialism, 22
instrumental rationality, 7, 13–14, 16, 18, 37, 46–47, 76, 92, 108, 143, 167, 178, 198, 202, 208, 211–216, 221, 225–227, 240–243, 245, 258, 293, 295, 298, 303
Instrumental speech, 144
instrumentality, 7, 14, 208–209, 216, 229
intelligent gorilla, 212
Interactive socio-linguistics, 33
Interpellation, 268
interpersonal relations, 22, 26, 147, 148, 177, 213
investigative meetings, 119
I-We-Them-It principle, 53

Janus-face, 83, 84
joint-committees, 223
just labour exchanges, 80

Kafkaesque, 140–141
Kant, 1, 11, 14, 16, 34, 97, 148, 172, 204, 208, 221, 224, 229, 237, 246–247, 252, 254–255, 285, 288, 292, 300, 302, 304, 314
Katz & Kahn, 166, 287
Kaufman, 102, 105, 270, 314
kind boss, 105
Kohlberg, 14, 16, 161–162, 170–171, 232, 239, 244, 255, 258, 260, 281, 286–288, 302–303, 315

labour history, 45, 102
labour market, 43, 179–180, 185, 189, 209, 218–219, 276, 290, 296–297
labour participation, 223
labour problem, 105
labour process, 37, 51, 182, 184, 205, 212, 291, 293, 295
labourers, 30
laissez-faire approach, 226
language as a game, 57, 261, 262
language expectancy, 133
language intensity, 132, 279
Language tools, 72
language-in-use, 244–245
language-robbery, 42
latently-strategic instrumental action, 211
leadership, 7–8, 72, 76, 222–223, 234, 272, 301
Let your money work, 51
liberal capitalism, 4, 190
life cycle theories, 109
life cycles, 93
Likert Attitude Scale, 130
linguistic distortion, 98
linguistic invention, 5
linguistic reality, 6
linguistically framed, 5
linguistically imprisoned, 58
Linguistics, 33, 258, 309, 318–319
liveworld, 198
living labour, 51, 181–182, 184, 188
Logic of Collective Action, 179, 318
Logics of Communicative Action, 62
losing an argument, 236
loss of income, 129
Luhmann, 49, 260, 316

Machiavellian personality, 134
Machiavellianism, 165

Management by Fear, 164
management science, 4–7, 247–248
management studies, 3, 17, 302
management textbooks, 67, 259
management training, 226
managerial monoculture, 112
managerial staff, 200
managerial talk, 63, 97
Manufacturing Consent, 94, 102, 110, 154, 273, 276, 309, 313
Marcuse, 17, 42, 58, 64, 69, 75, 79, 117, 155, 170, 184, 189, 221, 249, 254, 258–261, 263–264, 266, 267–268, 282, 284, 287, 289–290, 295, 303, 305, 310–311, 315–316, 318
Marglin, 14, 246, 251, 297, 316
Margretta, 8, 14, 251–252, 253, 280, 316
market forces, 42, 94, 104, 111, 243, 249
marketing, 67, 106, 124, 184, 190, 200, 255, 263, 266, 278, 287, 293, 299
Marsden, 200, 255, 289, 316
Marx, 14, 44, 74, 79, 81, 90, 142, 179, 191, 207, 215, 229, 246, 248, 249–250, 254, 259, 262, 266, 281, 285, 289–293, 295, 298, 305, 307, 309, 311–312, 316–318, 321
mass media, 60–62, 78–79, 82, 93, 110, 130, 163, 183–185, 190–191, 209, 217, 219, 223, 265–266, 268, 276, 281–282, 286, 291–292, 298
mass-commodity, 189
mass-culture, 93, 110
MBA, 7, 62, 226, 248
McCarthy, 159, 270, 317
Mead, 159, 161, 317
meal breaks, 139
means-ends actions, 20
means-ends idea, 113
means-ends of instrumental rationality, 7
means-ends relations, 46
mediator, 98
Medieval Age, 184
medieval mercenaries, 39
medieval organisation, 69
medieval philosopher, 28
Menschenmaterial, 40, 89, 247
mental link, 72
mercenaries, 40, 69, 184, 258
message-receivers, 24
message-senders, 24

meta-language, 56, 176
metaphysics, 160
metonymy, 88, 273, 280
Metropolis, 52
Microsoft, Google, or EBay, 9
middle class behaviour, 43
middle-class = happiness myth, 44
militaristic structures, 40
military, 40, 51, 132, 260, 269, 273–274, 296, 301
Mini-consensus, 237
minority voices, 235
mission statements, 138, 280
misunderstandings, 29
Modern science, 78
Modern Times, 52
modernity, 1, 11, 17–18, 28, 47, 79, 143, 145, 160, 229, 237, 247, 251, 265, 285, 299
monasteries, 74
money and power code, 61–62, 217–218, 298
money-medium, 218
monoculture, 111–112
moral codes of behaviour, 14
moral discourse, 240
Moral Sentiment, 160
moral standards, 160, 244
morality, 14, 46, 67, 160–161, 163, 168, 227–229, 260, 281, 286, 298, 300, 303
morality and ethics, 14, 161, 228, 286
moral-practical forms of communication, 175
moral-practical knowledge, 210
motivations, 42, 49, 151
mottos, 88, 272
Mumby, 34, 84, 99, 249, 256, 317
mutual acceptance, 237
mysticism, 160

narratives, 12, 50, 52–53, 62, 103–104, 132, 273, 295
natural rewards, 194, 294
Nature-Transforming Relationship, 143
negative reinforcement, 131, 139, 163, 184, 196
Netscape, 53
neurotic, 43
Newspeak, 12, 65–67, 71, 252, 262–263, 271–272, 274, 277, 279, 309

Nineteen Eighty-Four, 1, 78, 127, 140, 246, 262, 269, 273–274, 278, 308–309, 315, 318–319
non-democratic workplace relations, 96, 112
non-ethical communication, 226
nonhierarchical communication, 27
non-strikers, 140
norm setting processes, 123

objectification, 219
objects of power, 40, 94, 110, 172, 219, 224, 264, 277, 284, 287
OBM, 196, 197
Offe & Wiesenthal, 15, 259, 290, 295–297
office furniture, 97, 120
official roles, duties, and standards, 167
officialdom, 204
OHS, 45
Oldspeak, 12
Olson, 15, 179–180, 290, 295–296, 318
onedimensional belief, 77
onedimensional message, 4
on-the-job, 194
open forums, 152
Order of Things, 2, 63, 70, 136, 290, 311
organisational accomplishments, 218
organisational asymmetries, 182
organisational behaviour, 194, 196, 291
organisational change, 130, 289
organisational charts, 24
organisational citizens, 184
organisational communication, 2, 6, 46, 150, 152, 203, 283
organisational democracy, 223
organisational dilemma, 182
organisational goals, 4, 6–8, 10, 12, 14–15, 55, 84, 132, 135, 149, 171, 224, 227, 251, 258
organisational input, 186
organisational language, 172
organisational meaning, 203
organisational members, 9, 178, 203, 228, 283
organisational misbehaviour, 65, 245, 291
organisational mobility, 165
organisational performance, 196
organisational power, 181
organisational psychologists, 194

organisational psychology, 193, 196
organisational realities, 100, 181, 182
organisational relations, 198
organisational theory, 46–47, 229, 260
organisational values, 249
Orwell, 1, 56, 65–67, 77–78, 82, 87, 105, 114, 127, 140–141, 156, 188, 246, 252, 262, 265, 267–273, 277–279, 292–293, 312–318
outside experts, 233

parole, 56–57
participative democracy, 112
pathological models, 241
pathological practise of management, 3
pathological social behaviour, 236
Pavlov, 100, 138–140, 262, 269, 280, 284, 294, 318
peace, 12, 87, 250
peasants, 30, 105, 292
performance related pay, 40, 58, 65, 71, 130, 253, 297
personal attitudinal judgements, 128
persuader, 124–126, 128, 135–137
petite-bourgeois, 43
philosophical ethics, 67
philosophical idea of ethics, 229
philosophy, 3, 6–7, 17, 26, 143, 215, 229, 246, 248–250, 253–254, 258, 277, 285, 289, 302–303
phrases, 72, 77–78, 82, 84, 102, 127, 166, 188, 272
Picasso, 12
pipeline, 151–152, 160
Poland, 8, 287
Poole, 4–5, 45, 78, 89, 98, 119, 251, 259, 262, 272–273, 317–318
popcorn sales, 124
positive attitude, 128–129
positive reinforcement, 139–140, 196, 287
posteriori, 34, 75
practical reasoning, 93, 109, 172
pragmatic discourse, 239
pragmatic-consensus theory, 175–176
pragmatics, 16, 23, 173, 232, 250
praising, 135
pre-calculated reactions, 137
prescript model of distorted communication, 152
prescriptive, 2, 50, 115, 167

price inflation-wages spiral, 71
private life, 12, 286
profit making maxim, 9
proletariat, 43–44
Protestant Work Ethic, 51
proxies, 121
public compliance, 127
public discourse, 61–62, 278
public sphere, 61, 298
public-democratic domain, 217
punch-in box, 99
punitive-authoritarian discipline, 184, 192

quasi-agreement, 237
quasi-religious form, 77
quorum, 122

race, 186, 292
radio, 8, 24, 44, 77
rational-calculative model, 180
rationalists, 241
rats, 140, 192, 280, 292
re-classification, 64, 65
religion, 143, 160, 215, 273, 276, 278, 286
religious belief-systems, 17
religious past, 79
reporting upwards, 12, 271
reports, 24, 54, 78, 135, 137, 275, 280
representative speech, 159, 243
resistance, 19, 20, 65, 78, 89–90, 97–98, 111, 184, 191, 212, 244, 272, 277, 283, 291
Resistance is futile, 9
resource allocation, 46
restrictive codes, 225
rewarding, 76, 131
rhetorical action, 113
rhetorical and ritualistic tools, 112
rhetorical tools, 13, 113
rhetorical violence, 89
right of veto, 234–235
right to manage, 119
Ritualisation, 114
Ritualistic communication, 114–115
round table, 120
Rousseau, 160–161, 175, 254, 285, 319
rule creating, 41
rule creator, 41, 100
rule receiver, 100

rule-obedience, 167
rules and laws, 170
rules of the game, 61

salaries, 29, 99, 263
satisfactions, 43
Saussure, 38–39, 56, 57–59, 284, 319
schools of thought, 92
Scientific Management, 6, 162, 320
scientific value, 8
scientification, 5, 249
scientific-practise model, 3
scripted behaviours, 163
Searle, 41, 63, 78, 96, 254, 256–258, 260, 264–265, 274, 282, 297, 300, 304, 319
seating arrangements, 13, 120, 121
secrecy, 125, 161
self-controlling, 49, 50
self-directed learning, 65
self-esteem, 132, 287
self-identification, 69
self-measuring, 50
self-supporting, 50, 209
self-system-balancing, 50
self-worthiness, 132
semantic theory, 175
semantics, 12, 255–256
semiotics, 24, 35, 298
sender-receiver model, 12
sense-making, 19, 29, 153, 203, 205
senses, 34
Sequencing, 116
service of power, 6, 12, 74, 246, 261, 273, 281
Seven Deadly Sins of Society, 160
sex, 78, 252, 276, 299
shared meanings, 19, 98, 203
sharing a pie, 66
signifier, 12, 38–40
sign-to-meaning links, 63
since the beginning of time, 89
Singer, 229, 252, 254, 258, 285–286, 289, 302, 319, 320
Skinner, 138–140, 163, 191, 255, 280, 284, 286, 293–294, 307, 309–310, 320
slogans, 72, 115, 117, 137, 266, 272
social science, 6, 17, 43, 143, 241, 247
social utility, 170
social welfare, 45, 279

socialisation, 33, 57, 75, 131–132, 166, 258, 262, 265, 268, 279, 288, 321
socially constructed reality, 32, 42, 66, 96–98, 275
social-normative considerations, 128–129
socio-linguistic realities, 263
socio-linguistics, 56
solidaristic ethics, 144
solidarity, 22, 37, 59, 61, 126, 130, 146, 200, 202, 205, 209, 216, 245, 295, 303–304, 306
soul, 94, 111, 212
Soviet Union, 81
Speech act, 22
speech-less society, 59
Star Trek's Borg, 9
stereotypes, 115, 117, 249
Storming, 122
strike, 35, 39, 42, 59, 65, 128–129, 139–140, 147, 258, 262, 279
structural violence, 177
sub-culture, 244
sub-humans, 152
sub-ordinates, 152
suggestive questioning, 130
superstructure, 183, 227–228, 293
surface structures, 32, 256–258
surveillance, 92, 108, 145, 244
surveys, 126, 128, 130–131, 278
swipe cards, 99–101
SWOT analysis, 243, 305
symbolic knowledge, 193
syntax, 12, 142, 173, 255–256, 281, 298
system survival, 183, 207
system theory, 5, 49–50, 260, 288–289, 304, 313

tabloid papers, 43
target-audience, 125
Taylor, 6–9, 14, 87, 162–163, 212, 246, 248, 253, 320
teams, 9, 253
technical reasoning, 93, 109
techno-belief-systems, 46
technological neutrality, 46
technological rationale, 46
technology, 46, 68–69, 72, 96, 143, 161, 211, 264, 280, 312
techno-rational-domination, 46
techno-scientific language, 67

telos of communication, 33
textbook writers, 117
them-and-us, 66, 68
theoretical discourse, 173
time clock, 99
time is money, 12, 273
time management, 232
time sequence, 194
time-&-motion, 182
time-consuming communications, 241
TINA, 8–9, 53, 186, 197, 203, 221, 253, 277, 305
trade unions, 43, 68, 129, 135, 140, 291
traditional communication, 241
transmission of messages, 24
TV, 8, 44, 61, 77, 78, 106, 138, 249, 259, 266, 271, 279
Two Logics of Collective Action, 15, 318
two logics of communicative action, 15, 63, 210, 222
two-way communication, 25, 26, 150
two-way model of persuasion, 125
two-way process, 25, 125

Überbau, 82
ultra vires powers, 122
unethical behaviour, 67, 302
unethical communication, 227
unethical enforcement of rules, 225
unethical existence, 227
union members, 38
universities, 8, 77, 248, 251–252, 297
Unspeak, 89, 98, 111, 113, 251, 272–273, 318
unspoken, 4, 112
utterances, 37

value free science, 6, 10
vampire without fangs, 69
Volosinov, 37, 254, 258, 321

wage-labour, 45, 201
wages, 29, 36, 38, 42, 45, 70–71, 80–82, 99, 137, 172, 187, 193–194, 205, 258, 278, 280, 296–297, 300
Watson, 8, 69, 168, 251–252, 259, 263–264, 274, 278, 284, 286, 321
Watzlawick, Beavin, Jackson, 27
Wealth of Nations, 160, 320
Weber, 13, 51, 86, 204, 212, 246, 267, 284, 296–297, 316, 321

wedge-politics, 209
Weihenstephan brewery, 9
we-issues, 66
win-lose situations, 66
win-lose strategies, 165
Wittgenstein, 57, 254, 261–262, 321
women's natural place, 43
workers' meetings, 119
workers' self-control, 94
workers' spokespersons, 130
working agreements, 237
working group, 123
workplace democracy, 223, 264, 301
workplace relations, 103, 182, 300

Zeitgeist, 13, 250, 255
Zengotita, 44, 186, 279, 321
Zinn, 106, 321
Zuckermann and Drivers, 135